J.K. LASSER PRO™

ESTATE AND BUSINESS SUCCESSION PLANNING

The *J.K. Lasser Pro* Series

J.K. Lasser Pro Expert Financial Planning: Investment Strategies from Industry Leaders Robert Arffa

J.K. Lasser Pro Estate and Business Succession Planning: A Legal Guide to Wealth Transfer Russell J. Fishkind, Esq., and Robert C. Kautz, Esq.

J.K. Lasser Pro Preparing for the Retirement Boom Thomas Grady

J.K. Lasser Pro Wealth Building: Investment Strategies for Retirement and Estate Planning David R. Reiser and Robert L. DiColo with Hugh M. Ryan and Andrea R. Reiser

J.K. Lasser Pro Fee-Only Financial Planning: How to Make It Work for You John E. Sestina

The *Wiley Financial Advisor* Series

Tax-Deferred Investing: Wealth Building and Wealth Transfer Strategies Cory Grant and Andrew Westhem

Getting Clients, Keeping Clients Dan Richards

Managing Family Trusts: Taking Control of Inherited Wealth Robert A. Rikoon with Larry Waschka

Advising the 60+ Investor: Tax and Financial Planning Strategies Darlene Smith, Dale Pulliam, and Holland Tolles

Tax Smart Investing: Maximizing Your Client's Profits Andrew D. Westhem and Stewart J. Weissman

J.K. LASSER PRO™

ESTATE AND BUSINESS SUCCESSION PLANNING

A Legal Guide to Wealth Transfer

Second Edition

Russell J. Fishkind, Esq.
Robert C. Kautz, Esq.

John Wiley & Sons, Inc.

Published by John Wiley & Sons, Inc., New York.
Published simultaneously in Canada.

This publication is designed to provide accurate and authoritative information in regard to the subject matter covered. It is sold with the understanding that the publisher is not engaged in rendering legal, accounting, or other professional services. If legal advice or other expert assistance is required, the services of a competent professional person should be sought.

ISBN 0-471-21448-5

10   9   8   7   6   5   4   3   2   1

Contents

Acknowledgments

After nearly three and one-half years of writing this book there are a number of people we would like to thank.

First, we want to thank Linda Hanley, who without a doubt is one of the most efficient and professional legal secretaries that we have ever had the pleasure of working with. Not only has she typed thousands of pages and hundreds of edits over a three-and-a-half-year period, she has done so at all times with a smile and has shown exuberance during the process. We would also like to thank Jeanne Tyrell, also one of the most efficient and professional secretaries we have had the pleasure to work with, for her assisting in the production of this manuscript, as well as for keeping the office running during the time we needed to complete the book.

Timothy Dengler and Helen Lee, our associates, not only have provided us with substantive insight, but have also helped keep our offices efficient and flowing throughout the course of writing the book. We could not have done it without them, so we thank them as well.

Debra Englander and the good folks at John Wiley & Sons have exhibited from the outset an enormous amount of confidence in this book as well as provided opinions, edits, and input that were invaluable in its creation. Accordingly, we thank them for their contributions and look forward to working with them in the years to come.

As all lawyers know, law firms expect their lawyers to dedicate their time to helping clients and making sure that their hours are spent fruitfully. Yet our partners at Wilentz, Goldman & Spitzer provided us with the encouragement necessary to write this book despite the time we needed out of the office to bring it to completion. At all times they provided us with all of the resources of the firm and continued to support us every step of the way. Without their enthusiasm for this project, it could not have been completed.

Digesting the new Tax Act and writing the second edition could not have been done in a vacuum. Accordingly, we created an advisory board of our friends and colleagues to review chapters and provide their comments. Their insights, ideas, and opinions were invaluable. We therefore wish to thank H. Edward Wilkin III, Clark Ferry, Les Streitfeld, George Reilly, Jennifer Immel, Stephen L. DiLorenzo, Erik H. Rudolph, Greg Butler, Ralph Wright, Walter C. Kautz, William McDevitt, Sefie Silverstein, Stuart T. Cox Jr., Elizabeth C. Dell, and Deborah Perry—for offering their time and services to review parts of the book and help us continue to fine-tune each chapter until we thought the book was ready for circulation. We look forward to working with them for many years in the future and acknowledge with appreciation their time and effort.

When my wife Lori and I married 16 years ago, we had nothing except love, hope, and lots of dreams. Now, 16 years later, we have three beautiful children, Josh, Larry, and Shaina, and still have love, hope, and lots of dreams. You are my partner, friend, and love of my life. Thank you for being a terrific wife and mother.

To Mom, Dad, and my mother-in-law, Brenda Zodkoy, thank you for all your support and encouragement. Collectively, you have provided me with the insight and love required to realize my dreams. While my father-in-law, Mel Zodkoy, died in 1995, he lives inside me on a daily basis.

Russell J. Fishkind

At the other home front, words cannot express my love and appreciation for my wonderful wife, Nancy, and my gratitude for her unwavering confidence in Russell and me, and what we sought to accomplish in writing this book. It was through her encouragement that I was able to undertake this project and through her continual support that I was able to bring it to fruition. I consider myself the luckiest man in the world to have such a beautiful wife and three such wonderful children. It is in this light that I dedicate this book to my wife, Nancy, and my three children, Madeleine, Ryan, and Jeffrey.

I would also like to thank my parents, Barbara and Walter Kautz, as well as my mother-in-law, Helen Mintz, for their unwavering love and support throughout this process. I only wish that my father-in-law, Walter Mintz, was alive today to share in this experience.

Robert C. Kautz

Introduction

The Economic Growth and Tax Relief Reconciliation Act of 2001 (the "Tax Act") was the largest tax cut in the United States since the 1981 tax cuts when President Reagan also sought to stimulate the economy. The bill convincingly passed the House of Representatives, and after much debate in a divided Senate passed there as well; it was signed and introduced into law by President Bush on June 7, 2001.

Causing over 440 Internal Revenue Code changes, this $1.35 trillion tax cut will be phased in over a 10-year period, with the biggest cuts to take effect in the latter 7 to 10 years. However, this new Tax Act may be remembered by tax historians not as one of the largest tax cuts this country has ever seen, but more likely as one that never quite materialized.

This book thoroughly examines the estate and gift tax ramifications of the new Tax Act and helps one to create an estate and/or business succession plan in light of tax reform. Despite the fact that the new Tax Act calls for an ultimate repeal of the estate tax, virtually all accountants, financial planners, tax attorneys, insurance professionals, and bankers agree that the likelihood of an actual repeal of the estate tax is remote.

There are at least five compelling reasons that this conclusion is so universally shared by professionals.

Decreasing Surplus + Increasing Spending = Deficit Spending

A $236 billion budget surplus sounded like quite a cushion when the new Tax Act was passed. But the cushion began to erode when the economy weakened, unemployment went up (and those who remained employed generally earned less), and investors realized little if any gains in their portfolios. Add to the equation declining corporate profits and the phasing in of the lower tax rates, and the result doesn't surprise anyone: The federal surplus is, or is about to become, a federal deficit.

While the surplus shrinks, the need for increased spending soars. Although there is bipartisan support that the war against terrorism and ensuring national security is the country's highest priority, the unanticipated but necessary spending combined with decreasing tax revenues will most assuredly result in deficit spending. Deficit spending is rearing its ugly head again, and a movement for tax increases (or at least stabilization) will ultimately follow in the years to come. Eliminating the estate tax, a several-hundred-billion-dollar tax break to the wealthiest 2% in the country, sits out there like an oversized piñata, and the stick-wielding Congress won't be blindfolded.

Need for Predictable Revenue Sources

The United States Treasury relies on predictable sources of revenue to balance the budget. Estate tax revenues are not only reliable, but are projected to skyrocket as the baby boomer generation grays. However, the new Tax Act includes a repeal of the estate tax in 2010 (albeit for one year); instead, the Treasury will be forced to rely on capital gains tax revenues, a historically unreliable source. It is simply impossible to predict today whether the stock market in 2010 will provide investors with capital gains, and, moreover, whether investors will sell those investments and pay taxes on those gains.

As deficit spending becomes a reality, reliable sources of revenue will become a priority and unpredictable capital gains taxes will not foot the bill. If investors do realize gains, tracking the basis of mutual funds, stock splits, and closely held businesses will become an audit nightmare.

Sunset Provisions

The carryover basis system is not only unmanageable, it has only a one-year life span. To ensure compliance with the Congressional Budget Act of 1974, none of the provisions of the new Tax Act will apply after December 31, 2010. What this means is that absent an affirmative legislative act, including a supermajority vote of the Senate, approval by the House of Representatives, and the then president's approval, all changes promulgated in the Act disappear or sunset on January 1, 2011.

Quite a hurdle, and since we don't know who our president will be, the makeup of Congress at that time, or what the economic climate will be, you certainly can't rely on such a legislative act. But without this legislative act, the current estate and gift tax system, with all of its warts, reappears. Thus, the repeal of the estate tax and implementation of the carryover basis system will be a transient one-year shift until the estate and gift tax system, for better or worse, once again becomes law. Even the ostrich knows when not to stick its head in the sand.

State Estate Revenue Losses

While it's true the estate and gift tax system generates substantial federal revenues for the U.S. Treasury, the states also rely heavily on state estate tax revenues. However, under the new Tax Act, state estate tax revenues will be reduced by 25% beginning in year 2002 and will continue to decrease until the states' estate tax revenues end in year 2005. Reports indicate that the revenues generated by the states from state inheritance taxes range between 2% and 3% of total state revenues. Potential lost revenue to the states could be in the billions of dollars. Lost revenue must be made up somewhere, leading to increased property taxes, sales tax, income taxes, or perhaps a revised state estate tax. As senators and representatives begin to lose revenue in their home states and federal reserves dwindle, the groundswell to reverse or otherwise change the new Tax Act will pick up steam.

Future Elections

Just as President Bush made tax cuts a centerpiece of his election campaign, so too will future presidential candidates, senators, and members of Congress. In fact, between now and when the law is due to sunset, there will be two presidential elections and five congressional elections. In light of the uncertainty built into the current Tax Act, there's no doubt that further reform will become the centerpiece of future elections, especially as we get closer and closer to repeal and then sunset.

These five factors taken together virtually guarantee that the new Tax Act will have to be reassessed and ultimately reformed. Thus, relying on estate tax repeal is a formula for estate planning disaster. Unfortunately, the allure of estate tax repeal feeds one's natural propensity to procrastinate, whereas the current state of the law requires just the opposite. Now more than ever, it is imperative for people to plan their estates in a flexible, commonsense, and proactive manner.

All too often individuals spend a lifetime accumulating and preserving wealth but never plan for transferring the wealth to their loved ones. Perhaps the intensive fact gathering necessary to begin the estate planning process and the challenge of assembling a team of advisers to implement the plan seem like daunting tasks. Yet the planning process can also be enlightening, emotional, provocative, and enormously satisfying. Once it is accomplished, there is often a sigh of relief knowing that the estate or business succession plan has been completed and the financial futures of your loved ones made secure.

The purpose of this book is not to try to replace all of the books and articles that have been written on estate and business succession planning, but rather to attempt to demystify the process in order to help you understand all the elements that go into creating a comprehensive estate or business succession plan.

While we hope that you will have the opportunity to read the book in its entirety, it is designed to allow you to read the specific chapters that pertain to your individual needs. Each chapter addresses a particular estate or business succession tool and includes interesting examples, news accounts, or hypothetical examples to help illustrate how these tools can be utilized. As you will note in reading these chapters, we made the decision not to encumber the reader with excessive citations and references to authorities, but rather to present complex areas of the law in the most straightforward and practical manner possible.

But one thing is for sure. Laws change and life is dynamic, and consequently advice that you receive, books that you read, and plans that you put in place must be reviewed and updated to reflect our ever-changing legal environment. Remaining static—relying on estate tax repeal or allowing procrastination to take precedence over proactive planning—is not a prudent course. As John Lennon once said: "Life is what happens while you're making other plans."

This book was intended to provide you with a comprehensive summary of the wealth transference process, enabling you to become an active participant in creating your own estate or business succession plan. We hope that we have accomplished this goal and you will find our book both enlightening and rewarding.

J.K. LASSER PRO™

ESTATE AND BUSINESS SUCCESSION PLANNING

The Heart of the Estate Plan

Redefining Priorities

Consider the case of Les Tupass. Les began his working career at the age of 22, working eight hours a day, five days a week, and will continue to work until he is at least 65. As a result, Les will spend at least 90,000 hours of his life generating income. However, simply satisfying the debt service on a mortgage, paying the bills, and putting his children through college is not enough for Les. He wants to amass funds during this phase of his life so that when he and his wife, Hope, reach their golden years, they will have created enough wealth to retire comfortably and enjoy the remainder of their lives together.

Assuming that Les is successful, when he and Hope reach the age of retirement a change in their economic strategy will occur. Their priorities will now shift from wealth accumulation to wealth preservation. Assets that were amassed during their wealth accumulation years must now be protected and put to work to secure their comfortable retirement. During the wealth preservation period, Les's priorities will be to look over their stocks and bonds and determine whether the level of risk in their investment portfolio should be modified; analyze their beneficiary designations for individual retirement accounts (IRAs), 401(k)s, pension plans, and profit-sharing plans; review insurance policies and insurance needs; and perhaps even sell their principal residence of 40 years and move to a new community—all to accomplish one goal: to provide security during their retirement years.

During this period, Les will spend at least 10 hours a week working on wealth preservation to ensure that he and Hope are financially secure until the end of their days. Thus, if we assume that Les lives until the age of 85 he will have spent 10,000 hours during this period working on preserving the wealth that he and Hope have accumulated during the first four decades of their lives together.

Thus, it is neither unreasonable nor unrealistic to expect that Les and Hope will spend a minimum of 100,000 hours during the wealth accumulation and wealth preservation periods working on making and keeping sufficient funds to take care of the financial needs of their family and to provide for a comfortable retirement during their golden years.

Too often, the effort stops there. Les and Hope have overlooked an integral part of the process—wealth transference. The failure to incorporate wealth transference into the wealth accumulation and wealth preservation disciplines can result in federal and state inheritance taxes reducing their accumulated wealth by more than half. In essence, Les and Hope will have inadequately provided for their loved ones, creating onerous estate tax liabilities as well as causing unnecessary delays and costs that can lead to family squabbles—or worse, litigation.

The irony is that in proportion to the wealth accumulation and wealth preservation phases—which, as illustrated, can easily soak up 100,000 hours of one's lifetime—the estate planning and business succession planning process, comprising the essentials of wealth transference, requires only a fraction of that time. In fact, if the Tupasses had dedicated only one-tenth of 1% of all the hours they had spent on wealth accumulation and wealth preservation on wealth transference, they could have provided not only for themselves, but also for their loved ones for generations to come. Like most people in their situation, Les and Hope would have been happy to have spent the time developing an estate and business succession plan if they had only known what an estate and business succession plan can do to preserve wealth for their heirs.

Perhaps the reason why the process of estate and business succession planning is so frequently overlooked is that most people are not aware of their options and are too busy accumulating wealth and preserving wealth to take the time to plan for transferring their wealth. What we hope to do in this book is to provide a guide for those individuals who are interested in finding out how they, with a minimum of effort, can accomplish this goal.

What Is Estate Planning?

Estate planning is the process by which you review and assess your asset base, assess the needs of your loved ones, and, with the assistance of a qualified estate planner, implement a plan for the purpose of passing on wealth. The goal of the estate plan is to pass wealth to your loved ones in a manner that encourages harmony, personal growth, and independence in the most tax-efficient manner. The estate plan should be tailored to the unique needs of your family and should be carried out by capable fiduciaries. The documents reflecting your wishes generally consist of a last will and testament or revocable trust, power of attorney, advance directive for health care, and—if appropriate—trusts, created either during your lifetime or through your will at death.

What Is Business Succession Planning?

Those of you who own an interest in a closely held business should strive to implement a business succession plan. A properly drafted business succession plan fosters both leadership and the orderly transfer of control of a family business from one generation to the next. It also minimizes the estate and gift tax consequences which can cripple the ongoing success of the business during the transfer period.

Once the need for a business succession plan has been assessed, it can be condensed into a buy-sell agreement that provides for the transfer of the business upon certain events such as death, disability, or retirement, or it can be structured into a planned giving program. A planned giving program incorporates the use of sophisticated estate planning techniques in order to leverage gifts to the next generation in the most tax-efficient manner.

Fact Gathering

Every individual's life is unique. Therefore, every individual's estate and/or business succession plan must be tailored to his or her individual needs. Once an individual has recognized the need for an estate and/or business succession plan and has preliminarily identified his or her goals, the next step, and one of the most important, is the fact-gathering process. The estate and business succession plan can be effective only if the planner understands and appreciates the family structure, the needs of the heirs, and the goals that the individual hopes to accomplish.

During the fact-gathering process, it is important to develop a rapport with the estate planner so that you can be comfortable discussing all aspects of your life, which at times can be painful and emotional. Opening up to your planner is crucial. Family conflicts, power struggles, and jealousies, if any, need to be discussed early on with the hope that the plan will not exacerbate these issues but rather address them in a way that can help promote family harmony.

Additionally, during the fact-gathering process, the planner must fully understand your wealth base, the needs of your spouse and children, and your relationship with extended family members. Often overlooked during the fact-gathering process is how the relationship with your extended family members can assist you in determining who will serve as your ultimate fiduciaries of the plan. The difference between an estate that is administered efficiently and one that is administered inefficiently may come down to the single issue of who was chosen as the executor, trustee, or guardian.

Recognizing that life is dynamic, this fact-gathering process is one that should be ongoing in nature. Should the facts and circumstances change, as they always do, it is incumbent upon you to contact your advisers so that the plan can be appropriately amended.

Designing and Implementing the Plan

Having identified the need for an estate and business succession plan and having gathered all of the relevant facts, it is time for the estate planner to contribute his or her expertise and design a plan that fits your needs and circumstances. The estate and gift tax rules and the estate and business succession structures being discussed by the planner are at times complicated. However, it is critical that you understand your own plan and feel comfortable asking the planner to explain every aspect of the plan. Therefore, communication with the planner is key.

Once you understand and appreciate the plan, it then must be implemented. Implementation is a comprehensive project that requires not only the execution of the estate planning and/or business succession documents, but also the coordination of all aspects of the plan. Coordination includes integrating beneficiary designations with both the retirement plan and the estate plan, opening trust accounts for trusts created during your lifetime, issuing Crummey letters, moving life insurance into irrevocable trusts, retitling assets properly, following through with the designed gifting program, filing gift tax returns, valuing business assets as required by a buy-sell agreement, updating corporate books and stock ledgers, and educating the successor management team as to their anticipated role in the process. While this list is by no means exhaustive, it is intended to demonstrate just how encompassing the implementation stage is. Therefore, it is imperative that you assemble a team of advisers, each of whom plays his or her own role in implementing the estate and/or business succession plan.

Once the plan has been implemented, maintaining the plan on an annual basis is crucial. One way to help assure the plan is properly maintained is to obtain a planning summary letter to be reviewed annually. It is most helpful when this planning summary letter includes the issues to be addressed on an ongoing basis and highlights the need to maintain the plan as well as to adapt it to one's ever-changing needs and circumstances.

The Team of Advisers

Frequently, individuals seek out a life insurance agent to buy life insurance, an accountant to prepare tax returns, a lawyer to prepare wills, a financial planner to help create wealth, and a banker for individual and corporate banking needs. The problem is that while individual advisers may have been retained, in many circumstances there is a failure of communication between the respective disciplines regarding the implementation of effective estate and business succession planning. In order to best ensure that your estate and business succession plan is properly implemented, you must have all of your advisers working together, acknowledging and appreciating each other's roles, and assuming a certain degree of responsibility to assure the successful implementation of the plan.

In this regard, the insurance agent must assess the changing life insurance needs for you and your family, advise you as to the existing insurance portfolio's performance, make sure that the insurance policy or policies are properly titled, and be certain that the life insurance, either already in place or to be purchased, is the right product for your needs. The accountant must assist in all phases of the planning process, prepare all relevant tax returns, and deal with all financial, tax, and valuation issues. The financial planner must ensure that the assets are properly allocated and the accounts properly titled. In addition, the financial planner must work closely with the accountant to determine which assets are best suited for gifting purposes (taking into consideration all tax issues).

The estate planning attorney must structure the plan, prepare the necessary documents, and coordinate all the other professional advisers to ensure that the plan is put in place. In addition, the attorney must review the documents on a periodic basis to ensure that they conform with any change in circumstances (including changes in the law, as well as changes in the individual's particular situation). Finally, your relationship with your banker will prove helpful in determining whether a corporate fiduciary appointment is appropriate. The banker may also assist in reviewing ownership of assets under management and the status of funding and borrowing needs.

It is this coordination of experts as a team that will create the optimal result when planning your estate. Ideally, the professionals should meet, gather the facts, agree on the implementation of the estate and/or business succession plan, divide responsibilities, and see the plan through to fruition and periodic review.

Capturing the Heart of the Plan

Every person has his or her own concerns and heartaches, as well as goals and aspirations. It is the human elements of love and fear, as well as hope and joy, that shape the estate plan. Thus, when Les and Hope Tupass, working with their team of advisers, come to recognize that wealth transference is as important as wealth accumulation and wealth preservation, then Les Tupass will have more to pass and Hope will spring eternal.

Your Last Will and Testament

Your last will and testament will have a major impact on the lives of your surviving loved ones. As a cornerstone of your estate plan, your last will and testament will help guide the distribution of the wealth that took you a lifetime to accumulate. For a document of such monumental importance, it is interesting to consider how little time most people spend preparing their wills and keeping them up-to-date.

All too often when reviewing a decedent's last will and testament, the heirs can only shake their heads in disbelief when advised that their spouse or parent's last will and testament was 30 years old, and did not, in any way, shape, or form, reflect their wishes. Too often bereaved family members are taken aback when reviewing the two-page will executed years previous. After blowing off the dust and unfolding the yellowed, frayed onionskin pages, the heirs' bereavement turns to frustration (which many times turns to animosity) when the lawyer tells the children that the last will and testament did not contain exemption equivalent trusts, resulting in unnecessary estate taxes. After coming to grips with this conclusion, the children learn that under their parents' wills, assets are to be distributed equally among the children.

However, what if the parents' assets consisted solely of a house valued at $500,000 and an IRA valued at $2 million? The children at first believe that together they will share the assets as well as the unnecessary tax burden. You can understand their horror when advised that the parents had named their youngest daughter as beneficiary of the IRA in 1984, at the time when the IRA's value was nominal. Now the $2.5 million estate is distributable 80% to the youngest daughter and 20% to all of the children.

Suddenly, the room is quiet. As the estate planner continues to read the will, it is determined that the parents had named their lifelong friend as the executor of the will. Years ago, the lifelong friend had died, but the will had not been updated to reflect this event. As a result, there is now no executor named in the will, unnecessary estate taxes must be paid, the distribution of the total asset base is inequitable, and the children, once harmonious in nature, have each retained their own lawyer to try to resolve the estate's inequity. But they have all come to the same conclusion: The estate plan was a disaster and may adversely affect their relationship for the rest of their lives.

In this type of situation, there is a natural tendency to ask, "Well, what did the will say?" in an effort to determine how the parents wanted their assets to be distributed. In fact, the will many times governs only a small portion of a decedent's assets. More specifically, assets such as life insurance, individual retirement accounts, 401(k) plans, pension plans, and real estate or other such assets owned jointly or which utilize beneficiary designations are assets that pass by operation of law, not by will.

Perhaps the will would have reflected the decedent's intentions had all of the decedent's assets been distributable through the last will and testament, but too often asset titling is not integrated at the time the will is executed. Thus, the decedent's last will and testament may not reflect his or her real intentions, and worse, may cause confusion, ill will, and unnecessary taxes. Such results occur when a last will and testament is (1) not kept current, (2) not coordinated with the decedent's asset base, (3) not tax sensitive, and/or (4) not reviewed by the decedent's team of advisers.

This chapter is dedicated to helping you understand the factors that should be reviewed in determining when your last will and testament should be drawn up, when it should be updated, as well as the proper role of a last will and testament in the orderly distribution of your wealth to your loved ones, and the analysis and fact-gathering process that is required before drawing up your last will and testament.

Twenty Factors to Consider in Preparing a Last Will and Testament

As in so many other aspects of life where fact gathering, preparation, and analysis are the key to success, so too are such factors the key to drafting a last will and testament that accurately reflects actual intent of the testator (the person who signs the will).

A review of the following questions may help you focus on the issues that need to be addressed before drafting your last will and testament. Consider the following:

1. Who are your primary beneficiaries, and, if they were to predecease you, who would be your secondary beneficiaries?

2. Should trusts be created under your will for either estate tax purposes or protective measures?

3. Has a detailed asset analysis been prepared that shows the ownership of each asset, how it is titled, and what is its rate of growth?

4. Has an estate tax liability analysis been projected for you?

5. If you are married, have either you or your spouse been married before?

6. Are there children from other marriages or relationships?

7. Are there any obligations owed pursuant to a divorce decree to children or spouses from previous marriages?

8. Have you given enough consideration to the nominations of fiduciaries—namely executors, trustees, and guardians?

9. Would you like to provide bequests for friends, employees, or grandchildren?

10. Do any of your intended beneficiaries have any special needs?

11. Is there any personal property, such as jewelry, furniture, fixtures, or other such heirlooms, that should be incorporated into the planning process?

12. Have your beneficiary designations been integrated with your estate plan?

13. Is the disposition of a family-owned business part of your last will and testament?

14. Are both spouses U.S. citizens?

15. Are there assets in another state that may require ancillary estate administration which could be avoided through use of a revocable trust?

16. Do any health issues currently exist?

17. Have you provided for the charities whose causes are near and dear to you?

18. Have you determined which beneficiaries should pay the estate taxes?

19. Should any of your family members be specifically cut out of the will?

20. Do you have any specific burial arrangements that should be included in the will?

By no means is this list exhaustive. It is intended only to illustrate how complex and diverse the factors are that must be considered before putting pen to paper. Utilization of Figure 2.1, the last will and testament fact sheet, is the best way to begin the estate planning process. This fact sheet will help organize your thoughts and provide the estate planner with the necessary data to begin the initial phase of the estate planning process. Only after completing the fact sheet does the actual analysis of such facts begin.

The next step should be to assemble your team of advisers so that they can all work together.

Assembling the Team

The estate plans that generally are most effective and best represent the intentions of the testator are those that have been assembled with the help of the person's accountant, life insurance professional, banker, lawyer, and financial planner. Incorporating these professionals into the estate planning process may cause only a minimal increase in the cost of the plan, yet it will ensure that the estate plan accurately reflects the true intentions of the testator. You benefit from their involvement in preparing and reviewing the last will and testament and other estate planning documents. Their involvement is also critical in coordinating beneficiary designations for assets that pass outside of your will—such as IRAs, 401(k) plans, life insurance, investment management accounts, and so on—and integrating such assets with the dispositive provisions of your last will and testament.

All too often individuals do not understand their last will and testament. The documents may be long, filled with legalese, and, at times, confusing. It is the job of the estate planning team to make sure that you fully understand the dispositive provisions, tax provisions, fiduciary nominations, and overall effect of the will. Only then can it be deemed the cornerstone of your estate plan, and only when you fully understand all your estate planning documents will you know when they need to be modified as circumstances warrant.

FIGURE 2.1 Last Will and Testament Fact Sheet	

Section 1   Personal Information

Date: _____

About you:

Name: _____   SS#:_____-_____-_____

Home Address:

_____

_____

Home Phone: _____   Work Phone: _____

Date of Birth: _____

Employer:

_____

Occupation:

_____

Employer's Address:

_____

U.S. Citizen? _____ Yes _____ No

Marital Status: Single   Married   Divorced   Widowed   Remarried

Please list your children, if any, and their birth dates:

_____

_____

About your spouse:

Name: _____   SS#:_____-_____-_____

Home Address:

_____

Home Phone: _____   Work Phone: _____

Date of Birth:_____

Employer:

_____

Employer's Address:

_____

U.S. Citizen? _____ Yes _____ No

(Continued)

FIGURE 2.1 *Continued*

Section 2 General Information

Circle Yes or No for each question.

a.   Yes   No   Do you have a will or trust now?

b.   Yes   No   Are you expecting to receive property or money from:

Inheritance _____   Gift _____   Judgment _____   Other _____

c.   Yes   No   Do you have any living children?

If so, how many? _____

d.   Yes   No   Do you have any deceased children?

If so, how many? _____

e.   Yes   No   Are all your children legally yours (e.g., adopted, stepchild)?

f.   Yes   No   Do you have any children under 18?

If so, how many? _____

g.   Yes   No   Do you have any children who require special care?

h.   Yes   No   Do you have any grandchildren?

If so, how many? _____

i.   Yes   No   Do you have any brothers or sisters still living?

If so, how many? _____

j.   Yes   No   Does your spouse have any brothers or sisters still living?

If so, how many? _____

k.   Yes   No   Do you have any children from a relationship other than with your current spouse?

l.   Yes   No   Do you want to specifically disinherit anyone?

If so, who? _____

m.   Yes   No   Do you have long-term health-care coverage?

FIGURE 2.1 *Continued*

Section 3 Current Estate Value

Circle Yes or No for each question.

1.   Yes   No   Do you own a home or any other real estate?
Property Address   Title Holder   Value   Mortgage   Equity

_____

2.   Yes   No   Do you own any other titled property such as a car
                          or boat?
Description of Property   Title Holder   Value   Loan   Equity

_____

_____

3.   Yes   No   Do you have any checking accounts?
Name of Bank   Title Holder   Balance

_____

_____

4.   Yes   No   Do you have any savings accounts and/or CDs?
Name of Bank   Title Holder   Approximate Value

_____

_____

_____

5.   Yes   No   Do you have any stocks, bonds, or mutual funds?
# of Shares   Name of Security   Title Holder   Approximate Value

_____

_____

6.   Yes   No   Do you have any profit-sharing plans, IRAs, or pen-
                          sion plans?
Description   Titled in Whose Name   Value

_____

_____

(Continued)

FIGURE 2.1 *Continued*

7.   Yes   No   Do you have any life insurance policies?
Name of Company   Policy Owner   1st Beneficiary   2nd Beneficiary   Value

_____

_____

_____

8.   Yes   No   Do you have any other items of particular value
such as coin collections, antiques, jewelry,
heirlooms, and so on?
Description   Value

_____

9.   Yes   No   Do you own an interest in a business?

If so, do you have a shareholder agreement?_____

Names of other partners or shareholders: _____

_____

Estimated value of your share of the business $_____

10.   Approximate value of all your remaining personal property not listed
above (clothes, furniture, etc.):

$_____

11.   Yes   No   Do you have any debts other than your mortgage
and loans listed above (i.e., credit cards, personal
loans, etc.)?

If so, please list them below.

Whom Do You Owe?   Amount Owed

_____

_____

12.   Total value of everything you and your spouse own (add items 1–10):

$_____

13.   Total amount you and your spouse owe: $_____

14.   Subtract line 13 from line 12.
Total Net Estate $_____

FIGURE 2.1 *Continued*

Section 4 Appointments

The following questions ask who you would like to serve as executor, trustee, and guardian if necessary.

Executor

An executor is the person or corporation named in your will to administer the settlement of your estate. This appointment involves significant responsibility and therefore is compensated as provided by the laws of the state where your estate is administered.

Please fill in who you would like to serve as executor:

1._____

_____

_____

If this person/bank predeceases you or fails to qualify, who would you like to serve as executor in default?

2._____

_____

_____

If this person/bank also predeceases you or fails to qualify, who would you like to serve as executor in default?

3._____

_____

_____

Trustee

The trustee is the person/bank who would manage the assets held in trust when and if necessary. This appointment also involves significant responsibility and therefore is compensated by the laws of the state where the trust is held or by separate agreement.

Please fill in who you would like to serve as trustee:

1._____

_____

_____

(Continued)

FIGURE 2.1 *Continued*

If this person/bank predeceases you or fails to qualify, who would you like to serve as trustee in default?

2._____

_____

_____

If this person/bank also predeceases you or fails to qualify, who would you like to serve as trustee in default?

3._____

_____

_____

Guardian

The guardian is the person who would raise your minor children in the event your spouse predeceases you.

Please fill in who you would like to serve as guardian:

1._____

_____

_____

If this person predeceases you or fails to qualify, who would you like to serve as guardian in default?

2._____

_____

_____

If this person also predeceases you or fails to qualify, who would you like to serve as guardian in default?

3._____

_____

_____

Section 5 Dispositive Provisions

Gifts

Do you want to make a gift to a charity, foundation, religious group, or fraternal organization? If so, please list the organization and the dollar amount:

Organization   Amount

FIGURE 2.1 *Continued*

Do you want to give any personal items such as a wedding ring or watch to a family member or other individual?

Name of Person   Description of Gift

_____

_____

_____

_____

_____

Remainder of Estate
Who do you want to receive the remainder of your estate?

Name of Person (relationship to you)   Percentage

_____

_____

_____

Section 6 Living Will
A living will is a directive to your family and doctors to withhold artificial life-support equipment or heroic measures if your medical condition is irreversible.

Are you considering executing a living will? Who would you appoint as your agent to follow your directive?

_____ or

_____

Section 7 Power of Attorney
Executing a power of attorney authorizes a person you select to carry on with your financial affairs in the event you become unable to do so yourself.

Who do you want to appoint to be your attorney-in-fact?

_____ or

_____

Change in Circumstances

Having executed your last will and testament as part of the estate plan, you should have a sense of comfort and security that this important task of wealth transference has been appropriately addressed. However, circumstances may arise in the future which require that you review and possibly amend your last will and testament as part of your overall estate plan.

The death of or the souring of a relationship with a spouse, executor, trustee, or guardian is enough to require a new will. Similarly, the death or termination of a relationship with one appointed to be the health-care agent in the living will or the attorney-in-fact in a power of attorney requires that documents be rewritten and new agents appointed.

A substantial increase in wealth will generally dictate that the estate planner review the assets of the estate to determine whether further tax planning is required. Inheritance, personal injury awards, changes in employment, or, better yet, winning the lottery (it happens!) may cause a significant change in your asset base.

Another factor to be considered is the age of the testator. While a will prepared for a 40-year-old may be appropriate for that particular period in the person's life, at a minimum the estate plan should be reviewed when such individual reaches retirement age. Beneficiary options of qualified pension and retirement plans may require integration with the will, or perhaps bequests for grandchildren should be considered. Retirement is a significant economical and emotional event that is cause for an estate plan review.

The death of a spouse may also prompt a review of a previously executed estate plan. Although a will executed simultaneously between a husband and wife may be satisfactory for the surviving spouse, there are several issues that should be reviewed after one spouse dies. Tax planning, fiduciary nominations, distribution of assets, bequests to loved ones, and integrating beneficiary designations of IRAs and qualified plans are pivotal estate planning issues that should be reviewed upon a spouse's demise. Additionally, the estate of the deceased spouse must be administered, and the team of advisers may have suggestions during the administration that will affect the surviving spouse's estate plan.

Marriage, remarriage, divorce, and separation are all critical reasons for updating your estate plan. Such a change will no doubt affect one's net worth and will require that the dispositive provisions, as well as the fiduciary nominations, of the will be changed. Perhaps a prenuptial or divorce decree will be signed. Either document will dramatically affect one's estate. Other changes in one's life such as an illness or the illness of a spouse, moving to another state, the birth of a child, or simply a change in one's intent all necessitate the review of a person's will and overall estate plan.

Finally, in light of the ever-changing tax laws, a will should be reviewed periodically by an attorney, accountant, or financial planner to determine possible tax planning opportunities. The Economic Growth and Tax Relief Reconciliation Act of 2001 brought sweeping changes, necessitating the need to review almost every pre-2001 estate plan. Who knows what Congress will do next?

Creating the Structure of Your Last Will and Testament

When drafting one's last will and testament, there are a number of clauses that are generally consistent among estate planners. The following list is intended only as a summary of some of the clauses most often included in one's will.

1. *Debt and taxes.* Typically a last will and testament will include a paragraph that provides that debts incurred by the decedent or the estate involving funeral expenses and medical bills will be paid first before distributing assets to the beneficiaries of the estate. Secondly, the will may provide a formula as to how estate taxes will be allocated among the beneficiaries. In this regard, the question arises whether estate taxes should be borne equally among the persons receiving the rest of the estate or whether the estate taxes should be allocated among all of the individual beneficiaries having an interest in the estate, including family, grandchildren, and friends receiving specific bequests.

2. *Personal property.* Generally, a last will and testament will also include a paragraph that addresses the disposition of personal property, such as jewelry, clothing, furniture, fixtures, artwork, photo albums, and so on. Some states will allow for the utilization of a personal property memorandum pursuant to which individuals may make a list of tangible personal property and who gets what after they are gone. This memorandum is a separate document outside the confines of a will that may be incorporated by reference into a will. This memorandum may be amended as time passes and need not be executed in the presence of either witnesses or an attorney. (See Figure 2.2 on pages 33 and 34.)

Some states, however, do not allow for the use of a personal property memorandum, so that the will must specifically address the distribution of personal property. For example, some may choose to number each item and have each child pick a number out of a hat and hope for a fair and equitable distribution. Some wills allow the executor to direct the distribution of personal property, but in the event a child is an executor and also a beneficiary, the child may be viewed as biased. The distribution of personal property may help create one's legacy, and, accordingly, is not an area that should be overlooked.

3. *Bequests.* A will may provide that a fixed sum or a fixed percentage of an estate be distributed to children, grandchildren, nieces, nephews, friends, employees, or relatives. As noted, however, it is important to determine whether these types of bequests are subject to reduction by estate taxes or whether these distributions are treated as net distributions not subject to reduction by estate taxes.

4. *Exemption equivalent trusts.* An exemption equivalent trust or disclaimer trust may be created under your last will and testament by directing that the executors carve out the then applicable exemption and further directing how the trust is to be administered during the trust term (see Chapter 5).

5. *Marital deduction.* If an individual dies but is survived by a spouse, the assets may either be distributed outright to the surviving spouse, held in a marital deduction trust or qualified terminable interest property trust, or distributed to a qualified domestic trust or an estate trust deferring estate taxes until the second spouse's demise (see Chapter 6).

6. *Testamentary trusts.* Upon the termination of a marital trust, the assets may then pass in further trust to children, grandchildren, other loved ones, or charitable causes near and dear to one's heart. More specifically, age-terminating trusts for minors, generation-skipping transfer (GST) tax trusts for grandchildren, a special needs trust for a mentally or physically challenged child, a charitable trust, or a spendthrift trust for the fiscally irresponsible are frequently included under the terms of one's will. Such trusts are called testamentary trusts as opposed to trusts created during one's lifetime, which are called inter vivos trusts (see Chapters 8 and 9).

7. *Fiduciary powers clause.* A fiduciary powers clause lists all of the powers that the fiduciaries are provided in order to effectively administer the estate. Typically, the following powers are included:

- To retain and hold any property for any period, without regard to the effect the retention may have upon diversification of investments.

- To sell, exchange, grant options on, transfer, or otherwise dispose of any property.

- To invest and reinvest in common or preferred stocks, bonds, securities, mortgages, investment trusts, common trust funds, mutual funds, evidences of rights or interests, and other property, real or personal, domestic or foreign.

- To render liquid the estate or any trust in whole or in part and to hold cash or readily marketable securities.

- To manage, maintain, repair, alter, improve, insure, partition, subdivide, lease for any term, mortgage, encumber, grant security interests in, or otherwise purchase, dispose of, or deal with any real or personal property.

- To abandon any property deemed worthless, and to abstain from the payment of taxes, assessments, repairs, maintenance, or other upkeep for that property.

- To form one or more corporations, partnerships, or joint ventures, and to transfer assets of the estate or trust to any new or existing corporation, partnership, or venture, in exchange for an interest; and to retain such interest as an investment.

- To enter into, modify, or terminate agreements with any person regarding voting rights, management, operation, retention, or disposition of interests in corporations, partnerships, joint ventures, associations, or other businesses of the estate or trust.

- To vote in person or by general or limited proxy any shares of stock or other securities; to exercise or dispose of any options, subscription or conversion rights, or other privileges or rights of any other nature; and to deposit securities or other property or become a party to any agreement or plan.

- To pay, collect, adjust, compromise, settle, or refer to arbitration any claim in favor of or against the estate or trust, and to institute, prosecute, or defend such legal proceedings.

- To foreclose mortgages and bid for property under foreclosure or take title by conveyance in lieu of foreclosure; to modify, renew, or extend any note, bond, mortgage, or security agreement; to release obligors or guarantors or refrain from instituting suits or actions for deficiencies; and to expend any sums or use any property for the protection of any property or interest in a property.

- To borrow money or assets for any purpose, without personal liability, from any person, and to secure repayment by mortgage or pledge of any property.

- To lend assets to any person, including a beneficiary, the estate of a deceased beneficiary, or an estate or trust in which a beneficiary has an interest, on any terms and conditions, with or without security, for any purpose that may or will benefit the estate, any trust, or any beneficiary.

- To exercise any right of election or other rights that from time to time may be available under the Internal Revenue Code or any other tax law.

- To employ, pay the compensation of, and delegate discretionary powers to accountants, attorneys, experts, investment counselors, agents, and other persons or firms providing services or advice.

- To pay any and all costs, charges, fees, taxes, interest, penalties, or other expenses of the administration of the estate, in installments with interest if desired, and to charge these costs against the income or principal of the estate or trust.

- To hold property in one's name or the name of a nominee or nominees, or in unregistered or in bearer form; to deposit property with a custodian or depository; and to remove property from the state and keep property in other jurisdictions, without bond, surety, or other security.

- To pay any legacy or distribute, divide, or partition property in cash or in kind, and to allot any property, including undivided interests, to any trust, fund, or share; and to merge any trusts that have substantially identical terms and beneficiaries and hold them as a single trust.

- To act or refrain from acting in all respects as if financially uninvolved, regardless of any connection with or investment in any business or any conflict of interest between any fiduciary and the estate or trust.

- To do all acts and execute and deliver all instruments to carry out any of the foregoing powers.

8. *Nomination of fiduciaries.* Perhaps one of the most important clauses in a will is the appointment of fiduciaries:

- Generally, a will nominates the executors and/or coexecutors as well as successor executors in the event one or all of the executors should fail to serve.

- If a trust is created in the will, the will must nominate a trustee and/or cotrustees, as well as successor trustees.

- The will must also nominate a guardian as well as successor guardians if there are minor children.

9. *Common disaster clause.* A will should specify to whom the assets are distributable in the event that both the testator and the intended beneficiary die simultaneously. This is important to note because it may change the disposition of assets and result in estate tax implications. More specifically, if a husband has assets of $2 million and the wife has no assets, the will should direct that the husband will be deemed to have died first. By so doing, the executor retains the ability to protect the exemption equivalent amount of both spouses.

10. *Perpetuities provision.* The rule against perpetuities was intended to prevent assets from remaining in trust in perpetuity. Depending on the estate and whether the rule of perpetuities remains in effect in the state in which the decedent resided at the time of death, a will should address whether a testamentary trust should be protected by the rule against perpetuities. That is, if a trust does violate the rule of perpetuities, the rest of the will should remain valid and only that portion that violates the rule against perpetuities be deemed invalid.

11. *Minors or incompetents.* To the extent that assets are distributable to a minor or incompetent, the will should address what the age of majority is and how money should be expended on behalf of a minor or incompetent.

Executing the Will

Once the fact-gathering and analysis process has been completed and the initial drafts of the will have been reviewed and approved by the estate planning team as a whole, the actual signing of the will is a critical factor in assuring the estate's smooth administration, particularly for estate plans that are "unnatural" (i.e., a will that distributes assets other than 100% to spouse and then equally to surviving children outright). In order for a will to be admitted to probate with ease, the following requirements must be met:

1. The testator or testatrix must be of legal age.

2. The testator cannot be under any undue duress. Inasmuch as numerous will contests are filed every year asserting that there was outside pressure that swayed the testator into distributing assets in a way contrary to his or her real intent, it is important that the witnesses to the last will and testament have spent a sufficient amount of time with the testator to observe that he or she was not under undue duress at the time of the will signing. In this regard, it may also be helpful for the estate planning attorney to sufficiently address in the body of the will the issues that make the will unnatural, so that an objecting party's claim will be refuted by the will itself.

3. The witnesses must also attest to the fact that the testator had mental testamentary capacity at the time the will was executed. Testamentary capacity means that the testator who is signing the will knows the object of his or her bounty (i.e., that he or she knows the terms of the will and who will receive the assets under the terms of the will). It should be noted that many times an individual with questionable mental capacity, but who possesses substantial assets may be referred to as "eccentric," whereas such an individual with few assets is often called just plain "nuts." In either event, if in a fleeting moment of clarity

the testator understands the terms of his will and executes the will in the presence of witnesses, and then resumes the eccentric or even incompetent milieu, testamentary capacity can be established and the last will and testament will be valid.

4. A will should be written. In order for a will to be offered for probate and admitted without litigation or delays by the Surrogate's Court, a will should be typed, signed by the testator or testatrix in the presence of at least two disinterested adult witnesses, and notarized.

5. Many states allow for a self-proving affidavit to be attached to the will in order to dispense with the need for the witnesses to appear in the Surrogate's Court when offering the will for probate. In this manner, the will should contain a statement attesting that it is the testator's last will and testament, that it was executed at such place and time, and that the testator signed the will in the presence of witnesses who are verifying that the testator was an adult (over age 18 or 21), of sound mind, and not under undue duress.

Will contests are unfortunately extremely expensive for all concerned, cause a tremendous amount of anxiety and stress in the lives of everyone involved, and many times result in irreparable harm to family ties. However, wills that have been properly prepared, reviewed by the estate planning team, signed in the presence of witnesses, and properly notarized help minimize the chances of a will being contested. This helps to ensure that the wealth accumulated during one's life will be properly distributed to the testator's loved ones as per his or her intentions. On the other hand, failure to properly draft or execute a last will and testament will significantly increase the chances of litigation, thus increasing administration costs, taxes, delay, and family strife.

Choosing Fiduciaries

Choosing the fiduciaries of your last will and testament may be one of the most critical factors in assuring an estate's smooth administration. Generally, the fiduciaries of your estate include the executors, trustees, and guardians of any minor children. However, many people do not understand the difference between executors and trustees, nor are they familiar with the factors that should be considered in choosing coexecutors and cotrustees.

For some people, there is a reluctance to consider naming a corporate fiduciary, such as a bank or trust company, as executor or trustee. However, once the benefits of including a skilled banking or trust company administrator as a cofiduciary have been thoroughly considered, the inclusion of such an institutional fiduciary many times solves a number of open issues regarding who will manage the affairs of the estate once the testator is gone.

Guardian

Naming a guardian is perhaps one of the most difficult decisions an individual or couple can make. Most people are terrified by the prospect of someone else raising their children. However, in preparing a will that involves minor children, you must name guardians and backup guardians in the event the first-tier guardians are unable to serve. Coordinating your guardians with your executor and trustees perhaps makes the task of choosing your guardians less daunting. In choosing your fiduciaries you therefore must incorporate a mix that integrates relationships and skill sets so that all of the people involved can work effectively and efficiently together.

A guardian is an individual named in a will and appointed by the court to care for a minor or incompetent person. Guardians take personal care of their wards with regard to such matters as education, medical care, religious instruction, housing, and, most importantly, providing love and affection. Thus, choosing the right guardian to care for your children after one or both parents die is many times the single most important decision involved in the making of a will involving minor children. When choosing a guardian, pick someone who is compassionate and hopefully already has a warm relationship with your children, usually a relative or close friend. You should also take into consideration the guardian's spouse, religion, financial ability, the number of children the guardian already is raising, as well as his or her overall stability, morality, and values.

Although there are few restrictions in who can be named as a guardian, you can make the acceptance of guardianship conditional on age, income, and marital status. For example, you can stipulate that your sister will become the guardian of your children only if she is married and under the age of 55 at the time of your death. It is a good idea to name only one person rather than a couple as guardian of the minors, and be sure to name several alternates in case the first choice either predeceases you, fails to meet any conditions, or otherwise is unable or unwilling to serve as guardian. If married, be sure to coordinate with your spouse so that your wills name the same persons as guardians, in the same order of succession, and with the same conditions.

It should be the responsibility of the testator to provide for the financial well-being of minor children, not the responsibility of the guardians. However, being a guardian can pose a significant emotional burden. Consequently, it is most important that you discuss beforehand with the intended guardian whether he or she is willing to accept the appointment. While most people feel honored by the request, some may decline the responsibility. If the proposed guardian fears that his or her income is insufficient to raise additional children, you can assure the proposed guardian that sufficient assets will be available to take care of them, or that a life insurance policy or other type of financial vehicle will be established and managed by a trustee for the children's benefit.

Because children cannot own property, a trustee of the property must manage it for them. The usual practice is to establish a testamentary trust (a trust created in your will) or an inter vivos trust (a trust created during your lifetime) to provide for your children's fiscal needs and to coordinate with the guardian in determining the minor's needs and expenses.

By choosing a different person to serve as guardian than as trustee, a system of checks and balances is created, as well as one of complementary expertise. The guardian who raises the children will not have access to the principal of the children's trust without the trustee's consent. Likewise, the trustee's investments and actions can be closely monitored by the guardian, whose financial ability to raise the children rests with the trust.

Choose executors and trustees who can maintain a positive, constructive relationship with the guardian. Potentially tenuous personal relationships may be cause to appoint a bank or trust company to act as cotrustee to coordinate and converse with the guardian.

You should continually review the relationship with your chosen guardian. Should the relationship sour, you should prepare a new will, or at least a codicil to the existing will, containing a nomination for a different guardian. If one fails to prepare a will and name a guardian, a court will be forced to choose one upon death. Such an appointment may often be contested through litigation, which ultimately divides a family and often leaves the children severed from other family members.

Like the positions of executor and trustee, the position of guardian is also a paid one. However, the fee is nominal, and a guardianship is not considered to be a for-profit enterprise.

Executors and How to Choose Them

Executors are individuals or institutions nominated in a will and appointed by a court to settle the estate of the testator (i.e., to "execute" the provisions of the will). These persons or entities have the responsibility of collecting, managing, and ultimately distributing the estate's assets, paying its debts and taxes, administering the requisite record keeping, and ultimately distributing estate assets in accordance with the will. Being an executor can entail extensive work. Be sure to name successors in case a chosen executor is unable or unwilling to perform the duties. Some states require that executors live in the same state as the testator, while some require they post a bond if they live in another state.

You may choose an executor or coexecutor from a class consisting of your spouse, child or children, accountant, lawyer, trust company, trust family member, or adviser. Requisite skills should include logic, being comfortable with tax forms and working with professionals, good organization and communication skills, a desire to be fair, and a commitment to follow the testator's directions.

A spouse might be chosen, but in certain situations this may not be appropriate. For example, if you have children by a first marriage, appointing your second spouse as executor frequently creates suspicion, skepticism, and, too often, estate litigation.

If both spouses are older and a concern exists that the surviving spouse may not have the energy, mental capacity, or desire to fully complete the duties of being an executor, alternatives should be considered. Appointing an only child who is qualified to serve as executor is often appropriate, but if you have other children, appointing only one of them as executor can cause a family rift.

In situations involving second marriages, complicated or high-net-worth estates, or wills that leave assets unequally, it may be advisable to nominate a corporate executor such as a bank or trust company. The designation of a corporate executor will usually prevent children from alienating each other over disputes regarding how the estate is being administered. While a testator may have reservations about naming a corporate executor, such a designation may keep the peace and harmony in the surviving family structure. A corporate executor provides professional, unbiased expertise, with individuals trained to efficiently administer an estate. While a corporate executor cannot make a poorly drafted will easy to administer, a corporate executor can administer a well-drafted will efficiently and effectively.

The following poem bemoans the fate of an individual who acts as the executor for a friend or relative:

THE EXECUTOR

I had a friend who died and he
On earth so loved and trusted me
That ere he quit this earthly shore
He made me his executor.
He tasked me through my natural life
To guard the interests of his wife
To see that everything was done
Both for his daughter and his son.
I have his money to invest
And though I try my level best
To do what wisely, I'm advised
My judgment oft is criticized.

His widow once so calm and meek
Comes, hot with rage, three times a week
And rails at me, because I must
To keep my oath appear unjust.
His children hate the sight of me
Although their friend I've tried to be
And every relative declares
I interfere with his affairs.
Now when I die I'll never ask
A friend to carry such a task.
I'll spare him all such anguish sore
And leave a hired executor.

—*Today and Tomorrow*, Edgar A. Guest
(Chicago: Reilly & Lee Company, 1942)

Some are concerned that a bank or trust company lacks compassion and interest in the family's affairs. To address this concern, a testator can also name an individual executor to act as coexecutor with the corporate executor. This coexecutor arrangement between a family member and a corporate coexecutor can provide a checks-and-balances system that stabilizes the administration of the estate. The corporate coexecutor administers the will and recommends procedures that, combined with the individual executor's knowledge of the family dynamics, creates a potentially optimal estate administration.

An executor is entitled to be compensated for his or her services in administering the decedent's estate. Most states set the compensation an executor may receive. Typically, compensation is based on a percentage (2% to 5%) of the gross estate. On a $3 million estate, New Jersey would compensate the executors as follows:

5% of the first $200,000	$10,000
3.5% on assets between $200,000 and $1,000,000	28,000
2% over $1,000,000	40,000
Total	$78,000

New York would compensate the executors as follows:

5% on first $100,000	$ 5,000
4% on assets in excess of $100,000 and up to $200,000	4,000
3% on assets in excess of $200,000 and up to $700,000	15,000
2.5% on assets in excess of $700,000 and up to $4,000,000	57,500
Total	$81,500

Executor's fees are considered an administration expense and are paid prior to any debts or distributions under the will (except for reasonable funeral expenses). If your executor is also a beneficiary, note that the executor's fee may be significant and the other siblings may feel it is unjust or unwarranted. Balance this concern against the quantity of work, risk, and liability, and they may realize upon further reflection that the fee is well deserved.

Trustees

A trustee is an individual, a trust company, or a bank that holds the legal title to property for the benefit of others. Like an executorship, a trusteeship is a paid position. Many states have adopted statutes entitling trustees to "reasonable compensation," which is usually 1% of the value of the trust (depending on the value of the assets) every year paid quarterly.

A trustee is generally responsible for (1) the asset management of the trust funds, (2) issuing transaction statements monthly or quarterly, (3) determining requests for discretionary invasions, (4) remitting income as mandated by the trust, (5) rendering accountings when the trust terminates or intermediate accountings during the trust term, and (6) filing tax returns for the trust. In order to ensure that these responsibilities are competently performed throughout the term of the trust, it may be prudent to consider appointing a corporate trustee or cotrustee. It is difficult, if not impossible, to assemble a team of advisers to assure the same tasks at less cost without sacrificing quality.

Testamentary Age-Terminating Trusts for Minor Children

In almost all situations involving minor children, parents should create a testamentary trust (i.e., a trust created under a will) for the benefit of the children. An age-terminating trust is one that is created for the benefit of minor children and provides, for example, that upon the minor attaining age 25, one-third of the trust is distributable; upon attaining age 30, one-half of the remaining balance in the trust is distributable; and upon attaining age 35, the balance is distributable. However, an age-terminating trust also provides the trustees with the discretion to invade principal for the minor's benefit at any time during the trust's duration. By so providing, the trustees are not locked into a rigid system requiring the beneficiary to wait until a fixed age to receive money.

You may choose any ages and fractions for the trust that you deem appropriate, but the reason that choosing ages 25, 30, and 35 may be appropriate is that many times at age 25 a child has either graduated from college or is several years into his or her career and has, to some degree, started to settle down. The distribution of funds at that age may be a good time to buy a car, a small house or condominium, and so on, and may help stabilize a young adult's future.

At age 30, a child may have completed graduate school or be several years into a career or business, and be either considering marriage or already married; again, the settling down process and stabilizing process is starting to take shape—or at least you hope so. Accordingly, a distribution of funds at age 30 may be appropriate.

At age 35, a child may then be several years into marriage and have a child or children, perhaps even a large mortgage. It is at this age that issues such as retirement planning and funding of their own children's education start to become a priority. Accordingly, the final distribution at age 35 may be helpful. These ages represent only benchmarks for consideration. You may change the ages and fractions as appropriate to your children's specific needs.

Perhaps the most important decision to make when creating an age-terminating trust is who the trustee or trustees of the trust will be. The age-terminating trust generally allows a beneficiary to ask the trustee to invade the trust principal for health, education, maintenance, and support. It is up to the trustee to determine whether the discretionary invasion request is, in fact, in the beneficiary's best interest. For that reason, sometimes it is helpful to name not only an individual trustee but also a corporate trustee.

To the extent that the beneficiary is requesting a discretionary invasion for purposes that the individual trustee may not deem prudent, he or she is not saddled with the responsibility of telling the beneficiary no, which could certainly put their personal relationship at risk. The corporate fiduciary can be the heavy, leaving the individual trustee to commiserate with the child and maybe find a less expensive solution to a particular financial problem.

It is this balancing of the fiduciaries, the checking of the coexecutors and cotrustees, and the thoughtful consideration of successor fiduciaries that can mean the difference between an estate riddled with litigation, confusion, and cost and one that perpetuates the testator's intent and benefits the loved ones left behind. The distinction between the two scenarios clearly reflects the degree of planning that went into the drafting of the estate plan.

Bequests to Friends and Grandchildren

An individual's primary beneficiaries tend to be his or her spouse and children. Often overlooked are friends, employees, grandchildren, and godchildren. Creating bequests in the will for special people who have affected your life helps perpetuate that fondness.

The most common ways to create a bequest in a will are to provide either a small percentage of the estate or a fixed dollar amount to pass to such persons.

For example, (1) I leave 1% of my net estate, after taxes and expenses, to each of the following five people, or (2) I leave the fixed sum of $10,000 for each of the following beneficiaries who may survive me.

Generally, a fixed bequest is easier to administer for the executor in that it does not require mathematical computations to determine the amount of the gift. However, you must be sure that a fixed dollar amount does not become outdated due to either inflation or the reduction in your estate (thus negatively impacting the residuary beneficiaries, i.e., your children).

Bequests may be earmarked for certain causes, such as for educational expenses, for a down payment on a home, or for creating a business. It is often helpful when creating a bequest for grandchildren to name custodians and/or trustees of the funds.

Be sure to include language that in the event the intended beneficiary of a bequest predeceases the testator, the bequest lapses and either is distributed pro rata among the other beneficiaries receiving the bequest or is distributed to the "residuary" (i.e., the remainder of the estate).

Passing of Real Estate

Real estate can generally be held in five ways: (1) individually in one's own name (or in the name of one's spouse), (2) as tenants by the entirety, (3) as joint tenants with rights of survivorship, (4) as tenants in common, or (5) in the name of a legal entity, such as a corporation, partnership, or limited liability company.

If a husband and wife own real estate, or real property, in the absence of any titling to the contrary, such real estate is generally held in the name of the couple as "tenants by the entirety." This means that upon the first spouse's death, the real property passes to the surviving spouse by operation of law, rather than pursuant to the decedent's will. Regardless of what the decedent's will says about the property, it passes automatically to the surviving spouse.

The title "joint tenancy with rights of survivorship" is basically the same thing for people other than married couples owning real estate together. Upon the death of one holder, the asset automatically passes to the surviving holder. Again, regardless of what the decedent's will says, holding the property as joint tenants with rights of survivorship automatically triggers the passing of the property to the surviving holder. Because the real property never goes into the decedent's estate, it never passes through probate (although the decedent's interest is includable in his or her estate for estate tax purposes).

A will can govern the disposition of real property when it is held in the form of "tenants in common" or solely in one's own name. As such, upon the death of one of the "tenants" (owners) his or her interest passes directly to the decedent's estate to be disposed of in accordance with his or her directions in the will, rather than passing by law to the surviving holders.

When real estate is owned by an entity such as a corporation, partnership, or limited liability company, the property's disposition generally is controlled by the agreement entered into between the owners of the entity, if one exists.

Understanding the way real estate is titled and how such titling affects a property's disposition upon the death of the title holder is essential in integrating real estate into a will and an estate plan.

Personal Property Memorandum

When children receive cash from their parent's estate, it is either spent, sometimes rather quickly, or invested and accumulated in their own estate. But in either event, cash generally does not hold sentimental value. It doesn't warm the heart, nor does it perpetuate anything that the decedent stood for. Conversely, personal property, such as an engagement ring, artwork, photo albums, or even an old set of golf clubs, may perpetuate one's legacy.

Too often, wills completely fail to address the disposition of personal property. In fact, it may be the very distribution of this type of personal property that perpetuates the legacy of the decedent and should therefore not be overlooked. Care and thought should go into the disposition of personal property in one's estate. "Personalties" include, but are not limited to, clothing, jewelry, electronic equipment, diplomas, collections, heirlooms, paintings, cars, boats, and furniture. Although you can dispose of such personalties in your will by directing the executor to distribute them equally to the residuary beneficiaries, such vagueness often opens the door to hostility and squabbling.

However, because of the frequency with which personalties change status, it may not be prudent to distribute the assets in a will unless the will is frequently updated. Accordingly, many states provide for a "personal property memorandum" that can be amended without the formality involved in changing a will. A personal property memorandum is a separate document that is incorporated into the will by a reference contained in the will, as shown in Figure 2.2.

The personal property memorandum allows the testator to specify who gets what personalties upon his or her death. This document should clearly identify each item by serial number, photographic identification, and/or detailed description. Each should be listed along with the name of the person to whom it should be distributed, including both a first choice and a second choice. In order for it to be legally binding, the personal property memorandum should be

---

FIGURE 2.2 Memorandum as to the
Disposition of Tangible Personal Property of John Smith

Memorandum as to the disposition of the tangible personal of property of

JOHN SMITH, pursuant to his Last Will and Testament dated _____.

Pursuant to ARTICLE SECOND of the aforementioned Last Will and Tes-

tament, I request that items of tangible personal property be disposed of im-

mediately, on receipt of such property, out of my probate estate as follows:

Item Description	First Beneficiary	Second Beneficiary

(Continued)

FIGURE **2.2** *Continued*

_____

_____

_____

_____

_____

_____

_____

_____

_____

_____

_____

I intend that this memorandum shall have no significance apart from its effect on the disposition of my personal property after my death, and I expressly reserve the right to revoke or alter the memorandum at any time prior to my death. I do not intend by this memorandum to create any rights, whether by anticipation or otherwise, in any of the persons mentioned herein.

Dated: _____ Signed: _____

a written document executed in accordance with the laws of the state in which you reside.

Creating a personal property memorandum should never be taken lightly. It has been the experience of many that the most cherished items passing through an estate are personalties such as heirlooms, photo albums, a father's watch, a mother's engagement ring, and so on. These items are treasured and ultimately pass down through the generations. A personal property memorandum is a true legacy-creating technique. Only some states allow for the use of a personal property memorandum; therefore, the advice of counsel is critical.

In the alternative, if you are comfortable with your executors deciding how your personal effects will be divided, you can leave this power to your executors in your will rather than creating a personal property memorandum.

Disinheriting a Spouse and/or Family Members

Consider Mr. and Mrs. Cifer and their two children, Angelica Cifer and Lou Cifer. It seems almost from Lou's birth he was a difficult child. As he matured, little problems turned into big problems. People used to say he "had the devil in him." From theft to drugs and back again, Lou proved clearly irresponsible, deviant, and not worthy of inheriting the substantial fortune ($3 million) that the Cifers had accumulated. Accordingly, when they drafted their wills, they bequeathed one dollar to Lou and the balance to Angelica.

Upon the second spouse's demise, Lou was notified he had inherited only $1.00. He immediately hired an attorney (on contingency) and contested the will. Angelica, not a fighter by nature, grew tired of the intense litigation, legal fees, and anxiety caused by her brother and his lawyer. As a result she settled and split the estate 60%/40%. Lou went through his share of the estate in less than a year.

This result could have been avoided had the Cifers included both an *in terrorem* clause, also known as a no contest clause, and specific language that expressed their reasoning for Lou's meager interest in their combined estates. Lou's $1 left him with nothing to lose and everything to gain by contesting the will. Had the Cifers provided a fixed bequest, such as $50,000, together with an *in terrorem* clause, Lou probably would not have sued. An *in terrorem* clause is intended to strike fear in the hearts of those considering challenging a will. Generally, such a clause provides that in the event an heir challenges a will, he or she automatically loses the intended bequest. Lou's lawyer probably would not have taken the case on contingency, because the $50,000 bequest would have been automatically nullified by a challenge to the will.

Including a bequest to the person against whom the clause *in terrorem* is directed and combining the clause with the reasoning for it almost certainly will chill the waters of a will contest. However, *in terrorem* clauses are not 100% safe from attack, and they are not legal in all states, the reason being that people should not be dissuaded from using the courts in order to establish the legality of a document. Contests most often arise from the disinheritance of children or simply from treating them unequally. This is often due as much to hurt feelings as it is to greed; children just cannot believe that their parents intended to treat them unfairly (while at the same time failing to remember how they treated their parents when they were alive).

For this reason it is usually best, even if it is difficult, to explain your testamentary plans to family and advisers during your lifetime. You can also provide explanations for a bequest, or lack thereof, in the will itself. Whenever you make a choice that could be interpreted as insulting or unfair, you should attempt to explain your decision in explicit language set forth in the will.

There exists a major limitation on who you can disinherit in your will without potential ramifications. In general, before you attempt to disinherit your spouse, you must consider his or her "right of election." A spouse is generally entitled to one-third of the estate unless an agreement has been executed by both spouses, with adequate disclosure and advice of counsel, altering a spouse's right of election. This right of election allows the surviving spouse to opt out of the inheritance as provided in the deceased spouse's will if the surviving spouse would receive less than one-third of the augmented estate under the terms of the will. Generally, however, assets that passed during the marriage count toward the determination of this one-third elective share. Additionally, many states provide that the surviving spouse's asset base also counts toward the one-third elective share.

The use of a prenuptial agreement before marriage may be appropriate since a statutory spousal share can be given up by such an agreement. A prenuptial agreement is generally thought of as a document that protects the wealthier spouse's assets in the event of a divorce. However, the spouses may waive their elective share of rights in each other's estates as well in a prenuptial agreement.

Children from Prior Marriages

It is not unusual for individuals to have been married, divorced, and remarried (sometimes, again and again). Therefore, it is also not unusual for a married couple to have children from a previous marriage (or marriages). Perhaps one of the more difficult estate planning decisions is trying to determine if, when, and how much each class of children should inherit through a will, balanced against the needs of the surviving spouse.

The following factors should be considered:

- Ages of each class of children.

- Financial needs of each class of children.

- Relationship between each class of children.

- Relationships between the new spouse and the children from a previous marriage or marriages.

- Financial needs of the surviving spouse.

- Age of the new spouse.

- Obligations pursuant to a divorce decree.

- Statutory rights of election issues.

- Estate tax implications of transferring assets to children at the time of the first spouse's death (thus potentially subjecting the assets to estate taxes at such time).

- Deferring estate taxes until the second spouse's demise, but at the same time making already grown children wait until a possibly younger spouse's demise in order to inherit their share.

Sometimes the creation of a qualified terminable interest property (QTIP) trust created under the first spouse's will is a solution. This trust, more fully explored in Chapter 6, may provide income to a surviving spouse and, upon that spouse's demise, to the children. However, such an arrangement may create a strained relationship between the surviving spouse and the children of a prior marriage who may wish their stepparent well, but not necessarily longevity.

In other words, should children from the first marriage have to wait until a second spouse's demise to receive their inheritance (particularly if their stepparent is, shall we say, more youthful than their mom or dad)? One way to resolve the dilemma is to designate children from the first marriage as the beneficiaries of an irrevocable life insurance trust so that they do not have to wait until the second spouse dies to inherit as they would if a QTIP trust had been created under their parent's will (see Chapter 6). In this way, the children from the first marriage would receive their inheritance free of estate tax upon their parent's demise, but may not share in assets distributable through the will, leaving such amounts to the children from the current marriage upon the surviving parent's demise.

The estate planning team must also review the divorce decree. Frequently, divorce decrees require that insurance be held for the benefit of minor children. Such an edict must be incorporated into the estate plan. It can also be satisfied through the use of a life insurance trust in order to avoid estate taxes (see Chapter 7). Coordination with a matrimonial attorney is strongly recommended in order to ensure that the trust satisfies the divorce decree.

Who Will Take Care of Your Pets?

"Don't forget *Snowy*." Should a certain fund be set aside for the care of your pet? Naming a caretaker for a pet together with a fixed bequest for food, grooming, and veterinary costs is often overlooked. At a minimum, you should ask the individual you have named as guardian whether that person wants to assume this responsibility.

Grooming, feeding, and veterinary costs can be substantial over the life of a pet. Accordingly, a small bequest for the caretaker is appropriate. Typically, the amount devised would seem not to warrant the utilization of a trust. However, without a trust such a bequest would not guarantee that the funds will be used as intended.

Funeral and Burial Arrangements

Although including burial provisions in a will might seem to be a good idea, one may be well advised to create a separate letter with funeral and burial instructions. This is important because the will may not be read until after the decedent has been buried or cremated. Failure to properly express your intentions leaves the decision as to burial plot and funeral arrangements up to your executor. Buying a plot deed in advance can also take a large burden off bereaved family members.

Letter to One's Executor

In an effort to make your executor's role easier and avoid utter chaos, a letter to your executor may be advisable. The letter should state the location of your will; the names of your lawyer, accountant, insurance professional, banker, and financial planner; and the location of your safe-deposit box and a key. Additionally, the letter should include an inventory of assets and debts, a list of insurance policies, and funeral or burial requests. Make sure the letter is handy—that is, don't put it in the safe-deposit box.

CHAPTER

3

Power of Attorney

During the course of a marriage couples often accumulate assets such as a house titled jointly; retirement plans such as 401(k)s, IRAs, or pension plans; life insurance policies; and investment accounts in their own individual names. The spouses, as one economic unit, may make fiscal decisions together. Transactions such as the sale of a home, the changing of beneficiaries on a life insurance policy, or decisions regarding qualified plan distributions may require either spouse, or often both, to sign the appropriate documents in order to finalize the transaction. If you're a widow or widower, single or divorced, you may be the only authorized signator. Only you can effect changes.

But what happens in the event you are unable to sign your name due to mental or physical incapacity? Short of having a power of attorney, the other spouse or trusted family member does not have the authority to sign such legally binding documents unilaterally on your behalf. Rather, the well spouse or family members must petition the court to declare you mentally or physically incapacitated. Generally the court will appoint a guardian *ad litem*, who is an attorney chosen by the court to investigate the merits of the claim. More specifically, the court must make the determination of whether you are in fact legally incapacitated. The guardian *ad litem* will review your asset base, your medical reports, and the petitioner's motives and ultimately will report his or her findings to the court. This process may take anywhere from four to eight weeks to complete, and legal fees must be paid to both the guardian *ad litem* and the attorney representing the petitioner who brought the action to the court. Only then can the court enter an order authorizing the well spouse or trusted family member to act as agent for the incapacitated spouse under court supervision.

As if the trauma of caring for and enduring the emotional stress of seeing a loved one in an incapacitated state isn't enough, the necessity of having to go through an incompetency hearing is often humbling, expensive, and time-consuming. This proceeding may be avoided completely if you execute either a durable or a springing durable power of attorney prior to incapacity. Properly drafted, a power of attorney may be one of the most important estate planning documents that you can execute.

A power of attorney is a legal contract in which an individual (called the "principal") grants another person (called the "agent") the power to act as such person's "attorney-in-fact." Both principal and agent must be of legal age and sound mind at the time the power of attorney is signed. Generally the power of attorney lists the powers that the principal grants to the agent. The agent certainly does not have to be an attorney, but should be someone whom the principal trusts to handle his or her financial affairs. The principal may create a checks-and-balances system, where appropriate, by naming coagents to prevent potential abuses.

Subject to a few state law limitations, you can include almost any provision you wish in your power of attorney. It should be noted, however, that you cannot delegate the power to make or revoke your last will and testament pursuant to a power of attorney. By executing a power of attorney you may grant the following 24 powers to your attorney-in-fact:

1. To conduct banking transactions.

2. To sign checks, drafts, and other instruments or otherwise make withdrawals from any checking or savings account and to endorse checks payable to the principal and receive the proceeds in cash.

3. To borrow money from the principal's account on whatever terms and conditions may be deemed advisable, including the right to borrow money on any insurance policies issued on the principal's life for any purpose.

4. To make secured or unsecured loans in such amounts, on such terms, with or without interest, and to such firms, corporations, and persons as shall be appropriate.

5. To have access to and control over the contents of any safe-deposit box, to rent safe-deposit boxes, to close them out, and to execute and deliver receipts for safe-deposit boxes.

6. To invest in any stock, shares, bonds (including U.S. Treasury bonds referred to as "flower bonds"), securities, or other property, real or personal, and to vary such investments as the agent in his or her sole discretion may deem best.

7. To purchase, sell, repair, alter, manage, and dispose of personal property at private sale or public sale of any kind, and to sign, seal, execute, and deliver assignments and bills of sale.

8. To purchase or otherwise acquire any interest in or possession of real property; to accept all deeds for such property; and to manage, repair, or improve any real property in which the principal has or may have an interest.

9. To lease, sublease, sell, or mortgage any real property owned by the principal, including a residence.

10. To vote at meetings of shareholders or other meetings of any corporation or company in which the principal may have an interest and to execute any proxies or other instruments in connection with the company.

11. To continue the operation of any business belonging to the principal, or to sell, liquidate, or incorporate any business or business interest, at such time and on such terms as the agent may deem advisable and in the principal's best interest.

12. To ask, demand, sue for, and receive all sums of money, debts, goods, and things of whatever nature or description that are now or will become owing or belonging to the principal.

13. To commence, prosecute, discontinue, or defend all actions or other legal proceedings pertaining to the principal or to settle, compromise, or submit to arbitration any debt, demand, or other right or matter due the principal.

14. To join with the principal's spouse or estate in filing income or gift tax returns for any years for which the principal had not filed such returns and to consent to any gifts made by the principal's spouse as being made one-half by the principal for gift tax purposes, even though such action may subject the principal's estate to additional tax liabilities.

15. To employ lawyers, investment counsel, accountants, physicians, and other persons to render services for the principal and to pay the usual and reasonable fees and compensation of such persons for their services.

16. To make gifts in such amounts as the agent deems proper.

17. To make additions to an existing trust for the principal's benefit, to create a trust for the principal's benefit, and to withdraw and receive the income or corpus of a trust for the principal's benefit.

18. To disclaim any interest in property, to renounce or resign from fiduciary positions, and to exercise any power of appointment that the principal may have.

19. To authorize admission to a medical, nursing, residential, or similar facility and to enter into agreements for the principal's care.

20. To claim an elective share of the estate of the principal's deceased spouse should the spouse die during the principal's lifetime.

21. To procure, alter, extend, or cancel insurance against any and all risks affecting property and persons, and against liability, damage, or claims of any sort.

22. To execute, deliver, and acknowledge deeds, agreements, mortgages, bills, bonds, notes, receipts, and satisfactions of mortgages, judgments, rents, and other debts.

23. To make and substitute a successor agent or agents in the event the named agent cannot assume the obligation.

24. To do, perform, and cause to be done and performed all such acts, deeds, and matters in connection with the principal's property and estate as the agent in his or her sole discretion shall deem reasonable, necessary, desirable, and proper.

If your agent is authorized to act for you in all matters, he or she has what is called a general power of attorney. If your agent has authority to conduct only specified activities, he or she has a special or limited power of attorney. Limiting, or placing conditions upon, the powers of your agent can protect against abuses but also may restrict your agent's ability to deal with unforeseen circumstances.

Before executing a power of attorney, you should be aware of the differences among a durable power of attorney, a springing power of attorney, and a limited power of attorney.

Durable Power of Attorney

A durable power of attorney takes effect as of the date of its execution and continues in effect until death, unless previously revoked. In order for a power of attorney to remain effective after the principal's incapacitation, the document must contain specific language to this effect or the power of attorney will terminate upon the principal's incapacitation. For example, a durable power of attorney should state: "This power of attorney shall not be affected by subsequent disability or incapacity of the principal or lapse of time."

Because a durable power of attorney with the proper language is effective upon its execution and remains effective after the principal's incapacitation, it is not necessary to prove that the principal is unable to handle financial affairs or is otherwise incapacitated as a condition precedent to relying on the power of attorney. At the same time, however, when conveying such broad powers it is important that you designate an agent or agents whom you can trust.

A durable power of attorney is most frequently utilized by spouses who have complete trust and faith in each other's abilities to look after their well-being in times of need. The agent is not saddled with the burden of proving the spouse's incapacity before relying on the powers granted in the durable power of attorney document as is required by a springing durable power of attorney.

Although by law, banks and brokerage firms must honor a properly executed power of attorney, many institutions request individuals to execute their in-house form of power of attorney. The power of attorney provided by the institution is valid only as to that institution and therefore does not replace the need to have a power of attorney for all other assets. Be sure that the agent named on the in-house power of attorney is the same one named in your own power of attorney.

Springing Durable Power of Attorney

Also known simply as a "springing power of attorney," this legal document takes effect when a specified event occurs, generally mental or physical incapacitation or disappearance. Rather than taking effect immediately, it "springs" into effect only upon the specified event. This type of power of attorney should contain the following language: "This power of attorney shall become effective upon the disability or incapacity of the principal."

Many individuals are comfortable with this form of power of attorney because they need an attorney-in-fact only when they are incapacitated, and do not want to grant anyone such broad authority over their affairs before then. The power granted in a springing power of attorney is suspended upon recovery from incapacitation. Thus, the powers spring up upon incapacitation and retract upon recuperation.

There is at least one drawback to the springing power of attorney. Primarily, it may be difficult to determine when the specified event (i.e., incapacitation) has occurred. This can be a source of controversy. Hence, your power of attorney should contain a clear definition of "incapacitation" or "disability," as well as procedures for objectively determining its onset—for example, upon written certification by one or more doctors who have examined you. Incapacitation may be defined in the document as: being unable to manage one's property and affairs effectively for reasons such as mental illness or deficiency, physical illness or disability, advanced age, chronic use of drugs, chronic intoxication, confinement, detention by a foreign power, or disappearance.

Another concern with a springing power of attorney is that there may be some delay between the time the principal becomes incapacitated and the time the attorney-in-fact can act on the principal's behalf. This delay, however, will be minor compared to the time delay related to court proceedings to appoint a guardian *ad litem* to act for the incapacitated individual if a power of attorney had not been executed.

Limited Power of Attorney

The owner of a closely held business may want to grant a limited power of attorney to a business associate. This limited power of attorney can be either durable or springing. In either case, the limited power of attorney restricts the powers granted to the agent to certain functions relating to the business operation. This power of attorney may be executed in addition to the power of attorney drafted to handle personal financial affairs. A limited power of attorney allows the trusted business associate to continue the operation of the business interest without interruption from family members and courts who are not familiar with one's business. Care must be taken in drafting these powers of attorney so as to avoid any overlapping of powers between the limited power of attorney and the durable or springing power of attorney.

Power of Attorney and Gifting

The ability to provide your beneficiaries with annual exclusion gifts during your lifetime is a key element of estate planning. If, however, you become incapacitated, you may want the attorney-in-fact to be able to continue to distribute annual exclusion gifts during the period of incapacitation. Accordingly, the power of attorney should include explicit language that allows the agent the power to make gifts to family members or others.

The absence of language expressly authorizing your attorney-in-fact to make gifts can have severe consequences. Courts have consistently taken the position that gifts made under a durable power of attorney are invalid for tax purposes unless the power of attorney authorizes the agent to make gifts. The power to gift will not be allowed under general language that authorizes the agent to conduct all activities on behalf of the principal.

Another reason for inserting such language is if a principal, while incapacitated, requires the assistance of a nursing home. If such an event were to take place, his or her agent may need to fill out a Medicaid application. In doing so, the agent may need to gift certain of the principal's assets in order for the principal to qualify for Medicaid assistance. For this purpose, a principal may also wish to grant to the agent the power to disclaim an inheritance, to convert assets to those allowable under Medicaid rules and regulations, and to change domicile to another state with more favorable Medicaid eligibility rules.

Selecting an Attorney-in-Fact

Any competent adult can serve as your agent. As with a trustee, you will want someone who is responsible, who can be trusted, and who has the competence to manage your affairs. This may or may not be just one person. Often it is best to appoint a trusted family member, such as a spouse or child, and a third party with special expertise, such as your lawyer, an accountant, a colleague, a friend, or your financial planner as coagents.

The principal should also appoint an alternate in case the primary agent is unable or unwilling to accept the responsibility of being the agent.

Possible Abuses

As in all cases where financial assets are at stake, be aware of potential abuses in executing a power of attorney. In 1996, *Probate & Property* magazine published an article about such abuses. In writing this article, David M. English and Kimberly K. Wolff surveyed estate planning attorneys regarding abuses of powers by agents. They found that abuse was infrequent but such abuses were significant. They also found that the alternatives (guardian-ships, joint bank accounts) were no less risky. Additionally, 98% of the respondents concluded that the advantages of a power of attorney outweigh the risks. The message is clear: Having a power of attorney is worthwhile, but you should exercise great care in appointing your agent or coagents. Proceed with caution and vigilance when granting, limiting, or conditioning their authority, but don't leave loved ones stranded—execute the appropriate power of attorney.

Advance Directive for Health Care—Your Living Will

Ignoring Right-to-Die Orders

On June 2, 1996, an article appeared in the *New York Times* regarding a 38-year-old woman who as a result of serious illness had spent four years in agony, screaming and thrashing about each day during this ordeal. A seizure had left Brenda Young unable to care for herself. As a result, she required around-the-clock medical supervision. She needed to be fed, bathed, diapered, and tied into bed each night so that she did not push herself over the padded bed rails and injure herself. Her only words were "water" and "bury me." Mostly, she just emitted continuous screams.

It was precisely this kind of existence that Brenda Young had sought to avoid. On her doctor's advice, she had signed an advance directive for health care just one month before suffering the seizure that left her helpless. Brenda had been warned that the seizures might worsen. Therefore, she named her mother as agent under the terms of a living will if she became incapacitated. The day of reckoning came with her last seizure. Against her wishes, she was put on a ventilator, tube fed, and maintained throughout a two-month coma.

All the while, her mother protested to both the hospital and the doctors that Brenda did not want life support. She even had the living will to prove her daughter's specific wishes, but to no avail. Brenda's mother sued the hospital for failing to abide by the terms of the advance directive for health care, and the result was astonishing. The family won a $16.5 million verdict against the hospital.

Although this 1996 Michigan case was one of the first of its kind, other lawsuits have since been filed seeking to hold hospitals, nursing homes, and doctors liable for ignoring living wills. If nothing else, Brenda Young's nightmare may help others when dealing with hospitals, doctors, or health-care workers who fail to respect a person's intent in executing a living will.

Every person has the right to determine what medical care he or she receives, and each U.S. citizen has a constitutional right to refuse medical treatment. However, in many cases, people who require medical care are unable to communicate their wishes to their health-care providers. To ensure that your wishes are known and followed, you should take two important steps:

1. First, execute a document that makes clear your desires regarding different medical treatments under different circumstances.

2. Second, execute a document authorizing someone you trust to make medical decisions for you if you are unable to do so.

The first document is often referred to as a living will or an instruction directive, while the second document is known as a health-care power of attorney, proxy directive, or appointment of health-care agent. Both are referred to as advance directives for health care. However it may be titled, the goal of such a document is to provide instructions regarding medical care and the appointment of an agent or proxy to make decisions on your behalf if unfortunate and/or unforeseen situations should arise. Your long-term goals are multidimensional:

- To prevent doctors, courts, or others from acting in ways that are contrary to your desires.

- To ease the burden on your friends and family.

- To prevent disagreements between friends and family regarding these difficult and heart-wrenching decisions.

The importance of executing a living will cannot be underestimated. Medical technology is rapidly changing, and many treatments can be extremely costly. Some treatments may also be very painful and have undesirable side effects. Treatment may cause you physical pain and cause you and your loved ones emotional pain for months or perhaps years. In addition, end-of-life care can generate expenses that jeopardize your financial affairs as well as the financial affairs of your loved ones. As a result, a living will is a critical component of your overall estate plan. The laws of each state differ and laws often change, so you should always consult your attorney when composing your living will.

Instruction Directives or Living Wills

As previously stated, an instruction directive is the same as a living will. As its name denotes, the intent of a living will is to state, as clearly and precisely as possible, the types of medical care you do or do not want under specific circumstances. A living will represents the best evidence reflecting your personal desires with respect to medical treatment. If your living will is properly prepared and clear, it is legally binding on a hospital or doctor. The hospital and doctor are, in turn, immune from liability when they act in accordance with your instructions as set forth in a properly drafted living will.

One of the primary issues addressed in a properly drafted instruction directive is the "right to die" consideration, which is usually put into effect when a patient is terminally ill (generally less than a year to live) and either is permanently unconscious or is conscious but has irreversible brain damage (no ability to make decisions).

The instruction directive should set forth one's views regarding such things as your religious convictions and the minimal quality of life you would deem acceptable. Cardiopulmonary resuscitation should be addressed in the instructions, as should directions regarding the administering of pain medication, even if it will hasten one's death. Furthermore, one should specify the treatment one *does* want as well as the treatment that one does not want.

You should also specify whether and under what circumstances you want artificial nutrition and hydration. Most states (although not New Jersey) require specific instructions regarding nutrition and hydration, while a few states deny the right to refuse nutrition and hydration altogether. In such states your wishes will not be respected if your request is to refuse artificial nutrition and hydration. These differences in state laws make it essential that you contact an attorney before executing any advance directive for health care.

With regard to religious considerations, you should make sure to consult your clergy. If you decide on a course of treatment (or nontreatment) contrary to or inconsistent with the tenets of your religious faith, your instruction directive should address this issue. Also, it is recommended that you provide the name and address of clergy to be consulted for interpretation of your religious beliefs. For Orthodox Jews, a Halachic living will includes designation of a rabbi to approve the decisions of the agent, as well as alternate rabbis in case the first is unavailable to perform this duty.

Proxy Directives

The health-care proxy directive, sometimes referred to as a health-care power of attorney, is extended by you to your agent and gives your agent the authority to make medical decisions on your behalf. It also ensures that your wishes will be carried out during any period you are unable to make your own medical decisions. Appointing your own health-care agent eliminates the need for the court to appoint one for you, thereby avoiding a potentially costly and messy procedure.

Some people make the mistake of believing a proxy directive is not necessary because they have an instruction directive. However, it is impossible to foresee and make detailed contingency plans for every possible circumstance. It is almost inevitable that someone will have to make some decisions for you if you are unable to do so. It certainly helps to have someone fighting for you to carry through your wishes.

Your health-care proxy directive takes effect when you are judged unable to make decisions. This determination is usually made by your attending physician and any additional physicians required by law. The health-care proxy directive lapses as soon as you regain the ability to make decisions. And, like a last will and testament, an advance health-care directive is freely amendable and revocable while you are of sound mind.

The rights you extend to your agent through a health-care proxy directive are often broad and far-reaching. You can give your agent the authority to consent, refuse to consent, or withdraw consent from any care, treatment, or procedure designed to maintain, diagnose, or treat a physical or mental condition. The document should state what decisions your agent may or may not make.

In your proxy directive you may include instructions and guidelines for your health-care agent, but it is generally a better idea to express your wishes in two legal documents (your proxy directive and your instruction directive). In so doing, you always want to be sure that each document is consistent with the other.

Appointing a Health-Care Agent

When choosing a health-care agent, you should carefully decide who would be the best person to serve as your agent. The person you choose should know you well and be familiar with your beliefs regarding different treatments under different circumstances. For this reason, most people often choose a spouse or other loved one. However, be sure that whomever you choose will be capable emotionally and physically of handling the stress and carrying out the wishes expressed in your instruction directive. Be sure to discuss your wishes with your potential agent before you name him or her in the document. Even if that person agrees to your terms, make sure to name an alternate in case your primary agent is unavailable to act as your proxy if the need arises. It is also a good idea to discuss these matters with your family, attorney, doctor, and clergy.

Despite laws and lawsuits, doctors and hospitals sometimes fail to carry out a patient's wishes as expressed in a living will. For this reason, you should ask your doctor and hospital what they require in an advance health-care directive and how they feel about the termination of life. This candid discussion will increase the chances that your wishes will be honored. Also, if the conversation raises doubts in your mind, it will give you the chance to find alternative medical personnel and facilities. In some states, if a doctor tells you he or she is unwilling to honor your wishes, the doctor is required to assist in transferring you to the care of another doctor who *will* honor your wishes.

Formalities

Formalities differ from state to state, but generally two disinterested, nonfamily member witnesses are required to sign an advance health-care directive. Some allow for a notary public's signature as a substitute, but at least two witnesses' signatures are best. Except for specific clauses that violate substantive state law, your advance health-care directives are likely to be honored if utilized in a state other than the state in which the health-care directive was prepared. Yet you must realize that there is no guarantee and no substitute for advance planning.

Conclusion

Reasons for having a living will range from the humanitarian to the economic. On the humanitarian front, for most people the thought of being trapped indefinitely in a hospital bed on life support with no reasonable expectation of recovery is simply unacceptable. Additionally, a spouse or other family member may not have closure and may be unable to move on with their lives. Economically, not only may medical bills mount, but income may decrease if one is incapacitated and life insurance benefits will not vest since the individual is still alive. Any type of retirement planning or estate planning must also be put on hold. By executing a living will, you give loved ones the opportunity to carry out your intent. Without a living will, one does not have such options without judicial intervention. Most planners agree that incorporating a living will into one's estate plan is essential.

Utilization of the Lifetime Gift Exemption, Deathtime Exemption, and Annual Exclusion Gifts

Introduction

The centerpiece of George W. Bush's presidential election campaign was to enact tax cuts that would put money back in the hands of Americans and ultimately stimulate the economy. Part of the proposed tax cuts included repealing the so-called "death tax," more commonly known as the estate and gift tax. Only days after President Bush's inauguration, he made it clear that his first priority was to work with Congress to enact the tax cuts mandated by the voters. The result was the passage of the Economic Growth and Tax Relief Reconciliation Act of 2001, which was signed into law by the President on

June 7, 2001. Part of the $1.35 trillion tax cut included a repeal of the estate tax in year 2010.

Prior to its enactment, however, Congress debated over whether there should be estate tax repeal or estate tax reform. Supporters of estate tax reform sought to increase the exemption against the estate tax and decrease the rate of tax. Supporters of repeal sought to repeal the estate and gift tax and replace it with a carryover basis system that would instead tax realized gains. The result of the debate was the passage of a Tax Act that created an amalgamation of the "repeal" theory and the "reform" theory.

Essentially, over the next eight years, commencing January 1, 2002, the deathtime exemption against the estate tax will increase, and the rate of tax will decrease. At the end of this eight-year span the estate tax will be repealed and replaced with a carryover basis system. However, the estate tax repeal and new carryover basis system have only a one-year life span and then, absent an affirmative act of Congress and the President, the law sunsets and the current estate and gift tax system comes back to life. Not only is this new Tax Act confusing and complex, but unfortunately it does not provide solid ground that people can rely on to plan their estates. It does not ultimately and reliably increase the exemption against the estate tax nor decrease the rate of tax for anything more than a brief period of time (one year), after which the same onerous estate and gift tax system becomes once again the law of the land. This is not relief, but rather prescribed chaos. All too often, when Congress seeks to provide the taxpayers with relief, the result is hundreds of pages of legislation with back-ended cuts and qualifications. History has repeated itself, and the age-old adage "The more things change, the more they remain the same" holds true.

Fundamental estate tax planning historically rotates around one central tenet: to thoughtfully provide for loved ones in a tax-efficient manner. Now, more than ever, one must be proactive in creating an estate plan. A commonsense approach must be the central theme in preparing an estate plan, and the plan must be reviewed by a cabinet of advisers as time passes and the laws change again (which in all likelihood will occur well before 2010).

Prior to the Economic Growth and Tax Relief Reconciliation Act of 2001 we had a unified estate and gift tax system, which is summarized in Table 5.1. Now we no longer have a unified estate and gift tax system, but rather the amalgamation of transfer tax systems best summarized in Table 5.2.

One must compare and contrast Table 5.1 (the Taxpayer Relief Act of 1997) to Table 5.2 (the 2001 Tax Act) to fully appreciate where we were, where we are, and where we are likely to be in the future.

Table 5.1 Taxpayer Relief Act of 1997

Year	Exemption Amount	Gift Tax Exemption	Applicable Credit	Maximum Estate Tax Rate
1997	$600,000	$600,000	$192,800	55%
1998	$625,000	$625,000	$202,050	55%
1999	$650,000	$650,000	$211,300	55%
2000	$675,000	$675,000	$220,550	55%
2001	$675,000	$675,000	$220,550	55%
2002	$700,000	$700,000	$229,800	55%
2003	$700,000	$700,000	$229,800	55%
2004	$850,000	$850,000	$287,300	55%
2005	$950,000	$950,000	$326,300	55%
2006	$1,000,000	$1,000,000	$345,800	55%

Back-Ended Deathtime Exemption Increases

Both Table 5.1 and Table 5.2 back-end the increase in the deathtime exemption against the estate tax. More specifically, Table 5.1 effectively increased the deathtime exemption equivalent from $600,000 to $700,000 over six years from 1997 to 2002. The increase in the exemption has been so slow that it has barely kept up with the inflation rate. Moreover, if one's asset base of $1 million appreciated at the rate of 12% per year for these six years, the value would be almost $2 million, resulting in an asset base that has grown faster than the increase in the deathtime exemption from estate taxation. Similarly, the new law, as set forth in Table 5.2, accelerates the exemption to $1 million, but within two years (2004) the increase in the deathtime exemption rises to $1.5 million, and then again in two years (2006) to $2 million, where it remains over a three-year period. Once again, if $1 million grows at the rate of 12% per year, in six years the value will be almost $2 million. The Table 5.1 back-ended deathtime exemption increase lasted only four short years before Table 5.2 was enacted. Query: Will Table 5.2 last beyond four years?

Table 5.2 Economic Growth and Tax Relief Reconciliation Act of 2001

Year	Deathtime Exemption Amount	Lifetime Gift Tax Exemption	Applicable Credit at Death	Maximum Estate and Gift Tax Rate
2002	$1,000,000	$1,000,000	$345,800	50%
2003	$1,000,000	$1,000,000	$345,800	49%
2004	$1,500,000	$1,000,000	$555,800	48%
2005	$1,500,000	$1,000,000	$555,800	47%
2006	$2,000,000	$1,000,000	$780,800	46%
2007	$2,000,000	$1,000,000	$780,800	45%
2008	$2,000,000	$1,000,000	$780,800	45%
2009	$3,500,000	$1,000,000	$1,455,800	45%
2010	Estate tax repealed	$1,000,000	N/A	Estate tax repealed; gift tax at 35%, with $3,000,000 basis step-up to spouse and $1,300,000 basis step-up to others
2011	$1,000,000	$1,000,000	$345,800	55%

Tax Rates Still Onerous

Tables 5.1 and 5.2 also share the honor of setting forth onerous transfer tax rates. The estate tax earned a dubious distinction as being the highest tax rate in the country. Even after the estate tax rate reductions are fully phased in, the estate tax will remain the highest tax rate nationwide at 45%. Accordingly, the tax simply cannot be ignored, and neither Table 5.1 nor Table 5.2, both of which were intended to provide relief, leave one feeling relieved.

Use It or Lose It

The deathtime exemption against the estate tax is still a "use it or lose it" technique that requires proactive planning to take advantage of the law. A simple "I love you" will, wherein one spouse leaves his or her entire estate outright to the surviving spouse, is often an estate tax trap for the client who is uninformed or otherwise unwilling to plan. Accordingly, both of the transfer tax systems set forth in Tables 5.1 and 5.2 require the consideration of either exemption equivalent trusts or disclaimer trusts for married couples seeking to reduce their potential estate tax liabilities.

The comparisons of the old Table 5.1 and the new Table 5.2 systems are, however, overshadowed by perhaps the most significant structural and theoretical shift in the ideology of taxation that we have seen in almost 30 years. The concept of taxing the transfer of wealth either during one's lifetime through gift taxation or at death through estate taxation dates back to 1916 in the United States, and as far back as centuries ago in Europe. The transfer tax system, albeit much maligned, has developed into a well-entrenched body of law. Estate tax liability could be either avoided entirely, or at least minimized, with careful planning.

However, under the new Tax Act of 2001, the transfer tax system will be repealed on December 31, 2009, and will be replaced with a "new" tax and a new philosophy in taxation, shifting from a transfer tax to a tax on realized capital gains. (Of course, it is a given that the U.S. Treasury will lose hundreds of billions of dollars of revenue in this shift in ideology.) Not only does taxing gains presume that (1) there must be a gain, and (2) it must be realized, it also presumes that you (and your heirs) have diligently tracked your cost basis, enabling your heirs to compute the tax due. And yes, this is the same carryover basis philosophy that had an ill-fated one-year life span in 1976. And so, too, will it have an ill-fated life span again, but this time, in all likelihood, even before its gestation period.

Until it is changed, however, understanding the 2010 one-year carryover basis system is important. At death, the basis of assets received from a decedent will carry over to the heirs and be subject to capital gains tax upon sale, with two exceptions. The first $3 million of assets passing to a spouse will be stepped up to fair market value basis at date of death. Additionally, $1.3 million of assets passing to anyone else will receive a similar step-up in basis. Not all property, however, is eligible for a step-up. Property acquired by a decedent by a gift from a nonspouse less than three years before death is excluded from these step-up rules. The purpose of this three-year rule is to prevent gifts of low-basis assets to someone whose time is limited, with the hope that the assets will be bequeathed back with a new fair market value basis.

Unlikelihood of Estate Tax Repeal

Accountants, bankers, lawyers, insurance professionals, and financial planners have read the new Tax Act of 2001, attended seminars, talked with their clients, and almost without exception agree that estate tax repeal, as scheduled in 2010, will never occur.

There are at least five compelling reasons to support this not so bold prognostication.

Decreasing Surplus + Increasing Spending = Deficit Spending

First, one need only read the front page of the morning newspaper to find an article citing decreasing surpluses, increased federal spending, and the fear that funds held sacred for Social Security, Medicare, and Medicaid may be at risk. To give one example, the July 6, 2001, front page of *USA Today* reported, "In January the Congressional Budget Office (CBO) estimated that the 2001 surplus would be $96 billion, not counting funds Congress has pledged to reserve for Social Security and Medicare. But the CBO now says that the 10-year $1.35 trillion tax cut enacted in June, along with a slowing economy, has reduced the surplus to $16 billion." The *New York Times* headline on July 12, 2001, added, "Declining Surplus Renews Debate over the Budget Outlook," which may have been fueled by Senate Budget Committee chairman Kent Conrad's comments that the $1.35 trillion tax cut coupled with current spending levels have already caused the budget to dip into the Medicare Part A trust fund surplus. On October 1, 2001, the *New York Times* reported that analysts both inside and outside the government have determined that the large federal budget surpluses of recent years will likely give way to a deficit in the 2002 fiscal year brought on by the weakening economy and the costs of the campaign against terrorism. Deficit spending is rearing its ugly head again, and a movement for tax increases (or at least stabilization) will ultimately follow in the years to come. Eliminating a several-hundred-billion-dollar tax break to the wealthiest 2% in the country sits out there like an oversize piñata, and the stick-wielding Congress won't be blindfolded.

Carryover Basis

Second, if a carryover basis tax system is going to generate any revenue that the U.S. Treasury can rely on, there must be gains realized. Holding assets with built-in gains doesn't trigger the capital gains tax; only selling such assets and realizing the gains triggers a tax. (But what, pray tell, is your cost basis?)

Every investment vehicle spawns its own basis cobweb. Take, for example, mutual funds that automatically reinvest dividends. With every dividend that is reinvested your basis changes. Some investors have their paychecks debited to fund their mutual fund accounts automatically. Twenty-six times a year the investor must record the purchase price of the purchased units to track the basis. If Johnny Diversified invested in a family of five different mutual funds scheduled for automatic dividend reinvestments and he contributed 10% of each paycheck every year for 20 years, his basis would be . . . his best guess. But that's Johnny's problem. Under the current law, when Johnny dies the mutual funds get a step-up in basis—his heirs receive the funds cleansed of basis issues. Under the carryover basis system set for 2010, though, when Johnny dies it's his heirs' problem.

Mutual funds present one set of basis issues, while stocks present another. If Johnny was a buy-and-hold guy he might own securities such as IBM, Intel, GE, Procter & Gamble, and Pfizer. Assume Johnny has held each stock for 10 years and held true to his philosophy that when any stock split, he bought a corresponding amount. If each stock split five times, each time by a different ratio, and at each split Johnny bought more stock, his basis would be . . . Johnny's best guess. But that's his problem. If Johnny dies under the carryover basis system, though, it's his heirs' problem. I hope his brother's not a day trader.

Not to belabor the point, but what about collectibles, such as stamps, coins, jewelry, artwork, and other such bric-a-brac? Try finding the check Aunt Bess wrote for each of her 1,100 miniature porcelain dolls or Uncle Jacques' checks for his prized baseball card collection numbering over 10,000 cards. Virtually impossible.

Closely held businesses or commercial real estate holdings bring unique problems such as depreciation rules or capital improvement rules. Tracking basis adjustments in a closely held business is just not what one routinely does. The step-up in basis rules were a way of cleansing issues at death. The new rules proposed to take effect in 2010 bring back the 1976 nightmare. It's "déjà vu all over again."

Furthermore, if the estate tax system were replaced with a carryover basis system, tax revenues would be generated only if and when individuals actually sold appreciated assets, an event that is difficult, if not impossible, to predict. Accordingly, a historically predictable (and growing) source of federal tax revenue (i.e., the federal estate tax) would be replaced with a highly unpredictable, and therefore difficult to budget, source of federal revenue (i.e., taxation of capital gains).

The United States Treasury requires a steady stream of tax revenues, and, unfortunately, waiting around for future generations to liquidate investment portfolios earned by their parents (and perhaps grandparents) will not supply the needed funds to keep the government going. Thus, it is logical to assume that Congress will once again realize (as it has done for the past 85 years) that the estate tax system remains a necessary source of revenue to help offset the enormous amount of funds required to run the country, and will once again act to ensure its continued existence.

Sunset Provisions

Third, the carryover basis system is not only unmanageable, it has only a one-year life span. To ensure compliance with the Congressional Budget Act of 1974, none of the provisions of the new Tax Act apply after December 31, 2010. What this means is that absent an affirmative legislative act, including a supermajority vote of the Senate, approval by the House of Representatives, and the then President's approval, all changes promulgated in the 2001 Tax Act disappear or sunset on January 1, 2011.

Quite a hurdle, and since we don't know who our President will be, the makeup of Congress at that time, or what the economic climate will be, you certainly can't rely on such a legislative act. But without this legislative act, the current estate and gift tax system, with all of its warts, reappears. Thus, the repeal of the estate tax and implementation of the carryover basis system would be a transient one-year shift until the estate and gift tax system, for better or worse, once again becomes law. Even the ostrich knows when not to stick its head in the sand.

State Estate Revenue Losses

Fourth, while it's true the estate and gift tax system generates substantial federal revenues for the U.S. Treasury, the states also rely heavily on state estate tax revenues. However, under the new Tax Act, state estate tax revenues will be reduced by 25% beginning in year 2002 and will continue to decrease until the states' estate tax revenues end in year 2005. Reports indicate the revenues generated by the states from state inheritance taxes range between 2% and 3% of total revenues. Potential lost revenue to the states could be in the billions of dollars. Lost revenue must be made up somewhere, leading to increased property taxes, sales tax, income taxes, or perhaps a revised state estate tax. As senators and representatives begin to lose revenue in their home states and federal reserves dwindle, the groundswell to reverse or otherwise change the new Tax Act will pick up steam.

Future Elections

Fifth and finally, just as President Bush made tax issues a centerpiece of his campaign, so too will future presidential candidates, senators, and members of Congress. In fact, between now and when the law is due to sunset, there will be two presidential elections and five congressional elections. In light of the uncertainty built into the current Tax Act, there's no doubt that further reform will become the centerpiece of future elections, especially as we get closer and closer to repeal and then sunset.

How Do I Plan While Acknowledging the Law Is Likely to Change?

Don't rely on repeal. It's fool's gold. Plan for the system as it currently stands through 2009. Plan sensibly, with flexibility after reviewing all of the issues with your cabinet of advisers. Utilizing the exemption equivalent as a cornerstone to tax planning remains prudent. The deathtime exemption equivalent and the lifetime gift exemption are still the cornerstones of proper estate tax planning and, in light of the new law, will merit either disclaimer trusts or exemption equivalent trusts (also known as bypass or credit shelter trusts), together with a planned gifting program.

Deathtime Exemption Equivalent Planning

The lifetime gift exemption equivalent can be used only on an inter vivos basis (during one's lifetime), and the deathtime exemption equivalent can be used only on a testamentary basis (at death). Creating wills for a husband and wife who have an asset base over the then exemption equivalent amount requires that their wills carve out either a deathtime exemption equivalent trust or a disclaimer trust. If you are married, the determination of which technique to utilize depends on your needs, concerns, and asset base.

The exemption equivalent technique directs the executor to carve out the amount of the then applicable deathtime exemption equivalent and hold it in trust. That trust can be for the benefit of the surviving spouse exclusively and provide all of its income for that spouse, as well as provide for principal invasion rights for his or her health care, education, maintenance, and support. In fact, in many states the surviving spouse can be the trustee of his or her own exemption equivalent trust.

Alternatively, the exemption equivalent trust can be for the benefit of the surviving spouse and/or children, and income and/or principal can be distributed to them under the trustee's absolute discretion. The language that directs the disposition of both income and principal must be carefully considered with the cabinet of advisers in order to assure that the surviving spouse's needs and/or children's needs are well provided for.

While each case is different, as a general rule arranging for the distribution of income and sometimes principal to the surviving spouse provides many couples with a comfort level that the trust assets will not be withheld from the surviving spouse. If exemption equivalent trusts are created in both spouses' wills, it is important that both spouses consider equalizing their estates so that assets will be available to fund an exemption equivalent trust regardless of which spouse dies first.

Estate Equalization

Estate equalization, which is required to properly fund mandatory exemption equivalent trusts, is a method whereby the cabinet of advisers reviews a couple's asset base to determine whether the titles and ownership of certain assets needs to be equalized to ensure that each spouse has the full exemption equivalent amount in his or her name. By way of example, assume that Veri and Jen Oriss have a total asset base of $2 million. The assets are titled as shown in Table 5.3.

If the assets are all titled jointly, as illustrated, and the husband dies first, all of the assets would pass to the surviving spouse by operation of law. That is, jointly owned assets pass to the survivor regardless of how the decedent's will may direct the disposition of assets. Since the jointly owned assets would pass to the spouse by operation of law, the husband's will does not govern the distribution of assets held jointly. Therefore, even if Veri's will has exemption equivalent provisions, the exemption equivalent trust would not be funded because all of the assets would pass directly to Jen by operation of law. In order to avoid losing the exemption equivalent amount, Veri and Jen Oriss should retitle their assets as shown in Table 5.4.

Example 1

Assume that Veri and Jen Oriss have assets as set forth in Table 5.3 but have executed only simple wills whereby their entire estate passes to the surviving spouse and upon the surviving spouse's death to their three children equally. If Veri and Jen both die in 2002, their children will inherit $1,565,000 and the re-

TABLE 5.3   Assets Before Estate Equalization

Asset	Title	Value
House	Joint	$500,000
Stocks, bonds, mutual funds	Joint	$1,000,000
Shore house	Joint	$500,000
Total		$2,000,000

TABLE 5.4   Assets After Estate Equalization

Asset	Title	Value
House	Tenants in common	$500,000
Stocks, bonds, mutual funds	Husband	$500,000
Stocks, bonds, mutual funds	Wife	$500,000
Shore house	Tenants in common	$500,000
Total		$2,000,000

maining $435,000 of their $2 million will be used to satisfy the state and federal estate tax liability (see Figure 5.1).

Example 2

Now, assume that Veri and Jen Oriss have met with their estate planner, who has drafted wills to address the potential estate tax problem in Example 1. Veri and Jen each execute wills with exemption equivalent provisions and equalize their assets (see Table 5.4). The result is that the federal estate tax liability is completely eliminated (see Figure 5.2).

Deathtime Disclaimer Planning

For those with assets that significantly exceed the deathtime exemption equivalent, or for those who want assurance that the deathtime exemption equivalent will ultimately pass to their loved ones, mandatory exemption equivalent trusts may be the preferable technique to reduce estate tax exposure. However, for couples whose asset base is or is expected to be in the $1.5 million to $3.5 million range, and who are confident that the surviving spouse will ensure that the marital assets will ultimately pass to the couple's mutual loved ones, disclaimer trusts created in their wills may be the more appropriate technique to protect against estate taxation.

This disclaimer approach provides the surviving spouse with the flexibility of calling an "audible" upon the first spouse's demise as to whether to fund an exemption equivalent trust. More specifically, if a husband dies in 2004 leaving an asset base of $800,000 and his wife has her own asset base of $500,000, there may be no need to fund an exemption equivalent trust as the

For: Oriss, Veri & Jen
Report Name: Basic—Flowchart
Plan: Plan1   Scenario: All to Spouse
1st Death: 2002   2nd Death: 2002   Gifts: No   Discounts: No

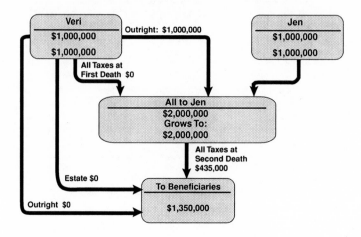

Death Tax Detail		
	Veri	Jen
Federal tentative tax	$ 0	$ 780,800
Unified credit + gift tax paid	(345,800	(345,800)
State death tax credit	(0)	(74,700)
Other credits	(0)	(0)
Net federal tax	$ 0	$ 360,300
NY state tax	0	74,700
Income tax on retirement plans	0	0
Generation-skipping transfer tax	0	0
Total tax	$ 0	$ 435,000
TOTAL TAX FOR BOTH DEATHS:	$ 0	$ 435,000

FIGURE 5.1 Example for Husband and Wife

Reproduced with permission from CCH Incorporated, 2700 Lake Cook Road, Riverwoods, Illinois 60015.

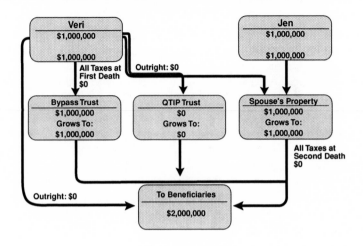

For: Oriss, Veri & Jen
Report Name: Basic — Flowchart
Plan : Plan2   Scenario: Optimum Marital
1st Death: 2002   2nd Death: 2002   Gifts: No   Discounts: No

Death Tax Detail				
		Veri		Jen
Federal tentative tax	$	345,800	$	345,800
Unified credit + gift tax paid	(	345,800)	(	345,800)
State death tax credit	(	0)	(	0)
Other credits	(	0)	(	0)
Net federal tax	$	0	$	0
NY state tax		0		0
Income tax on retirement		0		0
Generation-skipping transfer tax		0	$	0
Total Tax	$	**0**	$	**0**
TOTAL TAX FOR BOTH DEATHS:			$	**0**

FIGURE 5.2 Example for Husband and Wife

Reproduced with permission from CCH Incorporated, 2700 Lake Cook Road, Riverwoods, Illinois 60015.

then deathtime exemption equivalent will be $1.5 million (i.e., more than their combined asset base). The surviving spouse could take the husband's $800,000 outright because these assets, combined with her own $500,000 asset base, would total only $1.3 million, which is still less than the $1.5 million deathtime exemption. For estate tax purposes, there is no need to fund the exemption equivalent trust.

Alternatively, if the surviving spouse is only 55 years old and has both significant earning capacity and likely longevity, then the $1.3 million growing at the rate of 7% for 10 years, plus future additions to the asset base, may warrant her to disclaim her husband's $800,000 in favor of funding the exemption equivalent trust created under his will. In such a case, it behooves her to protect her husband's $800,000 with the exemption equivalent trust rather than taking the assets outright and having those assets includable in her estate. Her "audible" within nine months of her husband's demise should be to disclaim all or a portion of his assets in order to fund the exemption equivalent trust, which could provide her with both an income stream and rights to invade principal for her health, education, maintenance, and support.

The decision whether to recommend a mandatory exemption equivalent trust or a disclaimer trust in one's will may best be summarized as follows:

EXEMPTION EQUIVALENT TRUST	DISCLAIMER TRUST
• Combined assets exceed both current and projected deathtime exemption equivalent of both spouses. • Assurance is needed that assets will ultimately pass to intended loved ones. • Comfort in knowing the estate tax issues are addressed.	• Combined assets may be under the current and projected deathtime exemption equivalent of one spouse. • There is total confidence that each spouse will ultimately pass the assets to their mutual loved ones. • Flexibility to make estate tax decisions at first spouse's death, not now.

Lifetime Gift Tax Exemption

The Economic Growth and Tax Relief Reconciliation Act of 2001 bifurcated what was once a unified estate and gift tax system. Under the new act, the lifetime gift tax exemption is increased to $1 million but remains at that level, while the deathtime exemption continues to incrementally increase through 2009. This increase to $1 million, however, provides individuals with larger estates a tremendous opportunity to transfer wealth to loved ones free of gift tax. These lifetime gifts are over and above the annual exclusion amounts. Leveraging the lifetime gift tax exemption by utilizing, as an example, family limited partnerships, grantor retained annuity trusts, and insurance trusts is a prudent course of action for those seeking to significantly reduce their taxable estates above and beyond the $1 million lifetime gift exemption cap.

Annual Exclusion

When determining the total value of assets that can be gifted in any one calendar year, it should be noted that the lifetime gift tax exemption is in addition to the annual gift tax exclusion. That is, each donor also has the ability to gift, over and above the lifetime gift tax exemption amounts, the sum of $11,000 per donor per donee. (Beginning with the 1997 Tax Act, this gift tax annual exclusion is adjusted for inflation rounded down to the next lowest multiple of $1,000, which increased the annual exclusion to $11,000 beginning in year 2002.) Consider the following example to illustrate gift tax planning for some very generous parents.

Example 3

Veri and Jen Oriss are still married, and their three children, Ruby, Saffire, and Pearl, have grown into responsible, appreciative adults. Veri and Jen can each gift $11,000 to each child for a total of $66,000 in year 2002. In addition to that, they may also gift their lifetime gift exemption amounts so that the total gift from the parents to the children could reach $2,066,000, consisting of $1 million (lifetime gift exemption in year 2002), plus $33,000 in annual exclusion gifts, from Veri, and $1 million (lifetime gift exemption for year 2002), plus $33,000 in annual exclusion gifts from Jen.

It is important to note that the donor is responsible for filing a gift tax return, known as IRS Form 709 (see Figure A.2 in Appendix A). The tax return needs to be filed for any calendar year in which the donor makes gifts, other than those gifts that come within the annual exclusion amount or those which qualify for the marital deduction. The return is due on or before April 15th following the close of the calendar year, although an extension of time granted for filing the income tax return also serves as an extension of time for filing the gift tax return. If a tax is due, it is due and payable by the donor at the time fixed for filing the return without extensions. Taxable gifts will first be offset by the lifetime exemption equivalent until exhausted, after which the donor must pay the tax. If, however, the tax is not paid by the donor when due, the donee is personally liable for the tax to the extent of the value of the gift.

The gift tax is imposed on the value of any gifts made in the calendar year after subtracting the allowable exclusions and deductions. The $11,000 annual exclusion is available for gifts to any number of donees and for an unlimited number of years. Married donors can exclude gifts of up to $22,000 per year to each donee if each spouse consents to the combined gifts (a technique known as "gift splitting"). Thus, tax-free gifts to an unlimited number of beneficiaries can be doubled with the consent of the donor's spouse.

Gifting for Education and Health Care

In addition to the lifetime exemption amount and the annual exclusion, a qualified transfer for education or health care is not considered a gift for gift tax purposes as long as the transfer is made directly to an educational institution for tuition, or directly to a person or institution that provides medical care as payment for medical services. Thus, in addition to the $11,000 annual exclusion gifts, you may gift an unlimited amount for the benefit of any donee for his or her education, as long as the checks are made payable directly to the educational institution, not to the donee. Similarly, you can pay for the medical care of a loved one as long as the payments are made directly to the medical care provider. Reimbursing a child or beneficiary for tuition or medical payments already paid will not qualify as being exempt from gift tax.

Choosing the Appropriate Assets to Gift

When implementing a gift-giving program, one must carefully consider what assets should be gifted. It is important to remember that when a donor makes gifts to a donee, the donee retains the donor's cost basis. Therefore, a donor may want to look through his or her portfolio to find securities that have a basis as close as possible to the fair market value of the securities at the time of the gift. Otherwise, the donee would receive the donor's tax basis and incur a capital gains tax liability upon the sale of the securities regardless of whether the securities appreciated in value following the gift. However, even if a capital gains tax would ultimately be realized when a donee sells the securities, the top federal capital gains tax rate for capital assets held longer than 12 months is only 20%, as opposed to the highest gift tax rate, which is 50% for 2002.

The key to utilizing the exemption equivalent and annual exclusion during one's lifetime is to gift assets that the donor is reasonably confident will appreciate over time. Two key elements, appreciation and duration, make lifetime gifting a powerful estate planning tool. Accordingly, the age and health of the donor must be considered, as well as the economic climate, before embarking on a gift-giving program. For example, if a donor is 92 years old, even if reasonable appreciation is anticipated, the limitation of life expectancy may minimize the beneficial effect at such a mature age. In fact, it may be prudent not to gift appreciated securities, but rather to allow the holdings to get the step-up in basis upon a donor's demise. This step-up simply means that for tax purposes the basis of assets held by the decedent at the time of his or her death gets stepped up to the value at date of death. If, however, a substantial portion of the portfolio is in cash or cash equivalents, you should consider utilizing the annual exclusion to reduce the estate value as well as possibly gifting the lifetime gift exemption amount.

Example 4

Grandpa Bud is 92 years old and full of vim and vigor. His assets are as follows: (1) stocks with a basis of $1 million that have appreciated to a fair market value of $2 million and (2) $1.2 million in cash and cash equivalents, for a total estate of $3.2 million. He lives on his pension and Social Security. With two children plus eight grandchildren, all of whom are in private schools or college (eight grandchildren times tuition of $25,000 per year totals $200,000), Grandpa Bud should consider gifting cash, not appreciated securities, to his kids and grandkids. The securities have $1 million of gains that will be stepped up upon his demise and thus would be better as testamentary bequests.

However, Gandpa Bud should also utilize his annual exclusions to the fullest. Perhaps he should gift $11,000 of cash to each child and grandchild for a total of $110,000 per year plus paying for his grandchildren's schooling, as long as the payments are made directly to the educational institutions. By so doing, Grandpa Bud can reduce his estate each year by $310,000 and still preserve his deathtime exemption equivalent. Should the gifting program continue for four years, his estate tax liability could virtually be eliminated. Additionally, the donees are not saddled with Grandpa Bud's low basis in his stock portfolio.

Conclusion

Deathtime exemption equivalent planning, lifetime gift exemption planning, and annual exclusion gifts, including educational and health care gifting, are the primary estate and gift tax planning tools that should be considered by anyone seeking to prepare a comprehensive and efficient estate plan. Once the course of lifetime gifts is agreed upon, it must be recognized that there are a number of different ways that gifts can be made. That is, a gift does not have to be made by husband and wife outright to their children, but rather the assets can be gifted in trust for their children, as addressed in Chapter 9, "Transferring Wealth to Minors." In addition, limited partnership interests in a family limited partnership or certain business interests can be discounted so that exemption equivalent or annual exclusion gifts can be leveraged to maximize amounts of wealth that can be transferred without incurring an estate or gift tax. See Chapter 21, "Family Limited Partnerships."

Finally, if you have a team of advisers to assist in the preparation of the estate plan, each adviser will bring a particular skill set to the table to optimize and coordinate the estate plan. More specifically, over and above providing investment management services and retirement planning advice, the financial planner can help in the retitling of the investment accounts; the accountant can help determine what the exemption equivalent is for that particular year and what assets should be gifted after reviewing the capital gains tax implications and perhaps filing a gift tax return together with the appropriate valuations; the estate planner will develop estate planning strategies and draft the appropriate documents; over and above servicing lending needs and private banking requirements, the banker can also assist in balancing the fiduciary appointments; and the life insurance professional can help with respect to analyzing the viability of existing policies, ownership and beneficiary designations, and the opportunity and need for new coverage or for the policies to be transferred to an irrevocable trust (as fully set forth in Chapter 7, "Irrevocable Life Insurance Trusts." The team approach is the key ingredient to creating a commonsense, tax-efficient, flexible plan that is tailored to one's unique needs.

Spousal Planning

ne of the many perks of marriage is that the Internal Revenue Service
(IRS) treats spouses as one economic unit for estate and gift tax purposes.
Generally, there is no estate or gift tax exposure upon the transfer of
wealth between spouses. This immunity is called the unlimited marital deduction and may be utilized either during your lifetime or at death through a
number of different transfer techniques.

In the event a spouse dies leaving his or her estate (hopefully, less an exemption equivalent trust) to the surviving spouse, the tax on that transfer is deferred until the second spouse's demise. The IRS's logic for allowing
taxpayers to defer the estate tax is that the interest deferred will be includable
in the estate of the second spouse (unless expended during his or her lifetime)
and the IRS will most assuredly be around upon the second spouse's demise to
collect the tax on an asset base that hopefully has appreciated.

Generally, transfers to spouses at death may occur in any of the following
forms: (1) an outright transfer, (2) a qualified terminable interest property
(QTIP) trust, (3) an estate trust, (4) a qualified domestic trust, or (5) a power of
appointment trust. It is important to recognize that the aforementioned marital
transfer techniques serve only to defer estate taxation. Therefore, to the extent
that the asset base of spouses exceeds the exemption equivalent amount, an
estate plan should first consider the utilization of exemption equivalent trusts

to exempt that amount from estate taxes rather than simply deferring the tax through the use of the unlimited marital deduction.

Outright Transfer

We have all heard the phrase "simple will." Generally, a simple will is one that distributes all assets to the surviving spouse and upon that spouse's demise to the children. Other transfers that pass outright to the surviving spouse and qualify for the unlimited marital deduction include IRAs, life insurance, real estate titled as tenants by the entirety, or other assets held in joint name.

The tax consequence of a simple will can be harsh. More specifically, assume a husband dies leaving his entire asset base of $1 million to his surviving spouse (who has a like-sized estate of her own). Although the estate tax on the husband's assets will be deferred according to the unlimited marital deduction rules, his estate will lose the benefit of the $1 million exemption equivalent. Therefore, while the unlimited marital deduction rules are a staple of estate planners, the deduction should generally be utilized in conjunction with the exemption equivalent amount for taxable estates.

However, if both spouses' estates combined are under the exemption equivalent amount and the asset base is not expected to increase above the exemption equivalent amount, then relying exclusively on the unlimited marital deduction may be appropriate. In such a case, when the second spouse dies the estate size will still be under the exemption equivalent, resulting in no estate tax.

Qualified Terminable Interest Property Trust

Creating a last will and testament that distributes assets outright to the surviving spouse is one way to take advantage of the unlimited marital deduction. However, the surviving spouse then has the ability to utilize those assets as he or she sees fit as well as to dispose of them through his or her last will and testament. While in many cases such freedom of disposition does not create a problem or controversy, in an era of prolific litigation, multiple marriages, and longevity, many spouses prefer to restrict the use and benefit of wealth passing to their respective spouses through the use of a trust known as a qualified terminable interest property (QTIP) trust. The purpose behind the QTIP trust is to assure that the surviving spouse enjoys all of the income from the trust plus, if included in the language of the QTIP, the right to invade the corpus of the trust for reasons such as health, education, maintenance, and support, subject to the trustees' approval.

However, the reason that the QTIP trust has become a staple among estate planners is that the ultimate disposition of the QTIP trust assets is not governed by the last will and testament of the surviving spouse, but rather is generally governed by the last will and testament of the spouse who died first. Therefore, if the surviving spouse remarries, while he or she may enjoy the income from the QTIP trust, the trust principal will not go to the new spouse but rather to the children or heirs of the first spouse.

The rules of a QTIP trust, while not complex, must be strictly adhered to. In order to qualify for QTIP trust status: (1) the wealth that passes from one spouse to another must pass from the decedent to the surviving spouse; (2) the surviving spouse must be entitled to all the income from the entire property interest payable at least annually for life; (3) no other individual may have any power to appoint any of the property of the trust to any person other than the surviving spouse during that spouse's lifetime; and (4) the executor must elect on the estate tax return that the interest in the QTIP trust be treated as a QTIP, and therefore be ultimately includable in the second spouse's estate for estate tax purposes.

Furthermore, the assets of the trust must be income-producing property or the surviving spouse must have the power to make the trust property productive. A QTIP trust must also provide that all accrued and unpaid income be paid to the spouse's estate. When utilizing a QTIP trust, one cannot restrict the disposition of income or principal in an attempt to coerce or change behavior. For example, a QTIP trust would not qualify for the marital deduction if it provided that it would terminate in the event that the surviving spouse remarried.

While the QTIP trust may solve certain problems, it also creates others. Assume that Barney and Betty Boulder, both age 60, were married for 40 years and had one child, Rocco, currently 35 years old (and a chip off the old block). Two years after Betty's demise, Barney married Sally Stone, age 40, who had two children of her own. Several years later Barney died. While the QTIP trust created under Barney's will may provide for his new spouse, Sally, for her lifetime, such planning may lead to the scenario where Barney's son, Rocco, is waiting around for Sally to die to receive his inheritance. Rocco is now relegated to looking over Sally's shoulder, watching every dollar she spends and objecting (possibly as trustee) to every request for a principal invasion that Sally makes. Accordingly, before creating qualified terminable interest property trust provisions under one's last will and testament, it is important to consider the differential between the new spouse's age and the ages of the ultimate beneficiaries, the relationship between the new spouse and the ultimate beneficiaries, and who the trustees will be.

As to the nomination of trustees, while it may seem reasonable to name as cotrustees the second spouse together with one of the first spouse's children, such a fiduciary schematic may often lead to frustration and litigation. For example, every time the second spouse requests a principal invasion of the trust corpus, the interest of the residuary beneficiaries (i.e., the children) declines. In the event that the request for a discretionary invasion is not approved by one of the trustees, the surviving spouse has the right to file a summons and complaint in the appropriate court of law, seeking to overturn the trustee's decision not to make the discretionary invasion. For this reason, naming an independent trustee of a QTIP trust may help to create a harmonious administration of the trust while simultaneously protecting the interests of the surviving spouse, as well as the interests of the residuary beneficiaries.

Naming an independent trustee does not, however, solve Rocco's problem. Providing for the second spouse should be balanced by providing for a distribution to the children of the first marriage upon their own parent's demise. While such a distribution may cause estate taxation, the disposition could be structured to utilize all, or a part, of the exemption equivalent.

Estate Trust

Another technique utilizing the unlimited marital deduction is the estate trust. With a QTIP trust, all current income must be distributed at least annually to the surviving spouse. However, the surviving spouse may not need this income, so the utilization of an estate trust should be considered in the planning phase. Under the estate trust scenario, the income can be accumulated within the trust during the surviving spouse's lifetime. At death, the accumulated income and principal are distributed to the spouse's probate estate. Such a technique does not violate the unlimited marital deduction rules because ultimately the trust assets will become part of the surviving spouse's estate.

Qualified Domestic Trust

The IRS is willing to defer collecting estate taxes until the second spouse's demise for good reason: The IRS will outlast the life expectancy of the surviving spouse. However, Congress was concerned that surviving spouses who are not U.S. citizens would return to their own countries and move all of the assets outside of the United States in an attempt to avoid U.S. estate tax upon their ultimate deaths. Therefore, Congress enacted legislation that denies the marital deduction for non-U.S. citizen spouses unless such property passes from the decedent to a qualified domestic trust (QDOT).

While the qualified domestic trust rules are not difficult, they must be strictly adhered to. In this regard, the trust document must include the following six requirements:

1. At least one trustee of the trust must be an individual citizen of the United States or a domestic corporation. This is logical in that if the noncitizen spouse wishes to return to his or her own country, the assets would remain in the United States and the U.S. citizen trustee or the domestic corporation would be responsible for not only the trust's administration but for the collection and payment of any estate taxes that may become due.

2. No distribution, other than the distribution of income, can be made from the trust unless the trustee (who must be an individual U.S. citizen or domestic corporation) has the right to withhold from such distribution the appropriate estate tax that would be due on such distribution.

3. Any regulations promulgated in order to ensure the collection of any estate taxes must be strictly adhered to.

4. The appropriate estate tax election must be made by the executor.

5. The trust must be created and maintained under the laws of the United States and any state.

6. The property must pass from the decedent in a manner that qualifies for the marital deduction. If the assets of the QDOT exceed $2 million, the trust must require that (1) either the U.S. citizen trustee be a domestic bank or a bond be furnished in an amount equal to at least 60% of the fair market value of the trust corpus as of the date of the decedent's date of death, or (2) an irrevocable letter of credit be issued equal to 65% of the trust corpus. If the assets are less than $2 million as of the date of decedent's death, the trust must either contain the same requirements as stated for a QDOT of over $2 million or require that no more than 35% of the fair market value of the assets determined annually consist of real property located outside the United States.

The election to treat a trust as a QDOT created under one's last will and testament must be made on the estate tax return if filed on or before the due date thereof or, if not filed at that time, on the first return date filed thereafter, but in no event may it be made more than one year after the due date, including extensions.

Since the QDOT will require that its assets remain in the United States, it will ultimately be subject to estate tax upon the surviving spouse's demise.

Then the only concern of the IRS would be if the non-U.S. citizen spouse requested discretionary invasions during his or her lifetime, thus depleting trust assets. Therefore, estate tax is imposed each time a taxable event occurs. A taxable event occurs (1) when distributions of principal are made to the spouse during the spouse's lifetime (other than for hardship distributions), (2) upon the surviving spouse's demise, or (3) if the trust assets cease to qualify as QDOT assets. The tax that is due is equal to the amount that would have been taxed to the estate of the decedent if the marital deduction had not applied.

In order to determine how much of the exemption equivalent a non-U.S. citizen spouse will be entitled to, a distinction must be made between the three taxpayer classifications—citizens, residents, and nonresident aliens. With limited exceptions, the estate and gift tax rules apply equally to U.S. citizens and U.S. residents. A U.S. citizen is a person born or naturalized in the United States and subject to its jurisdiction. A noncitizen is considered a permanent U.S. resident if he or she resides within the geographical limits of the United States and, most importantly, intends to remain indefinitely. A noncitizen who is domiciled in the United States but does not intend to remain in the United States indefinitely is classified as a nonresident.

It is important to note the distinction when one is classified as a U.S. resident for income tax purposes and a nonresident for estate tax purposes. For estate tax purposes, a U.S. citizen and resident is entitled to the full exemption equivalent that can be applied against federal, state, and gift taxes. In contrast, however, a nonresident alien is allowed only a $13,000 exemption equivalent against U.S. federal estate taxes. This credit exempts the first $60,000 of the estate from estate tax and is not applicable to gift transfers. Accordingly, for estate tax purposes, whether one intends to remain in the United States is a pivotal question.

The unlimited gift tax marital deduction is available only if the recipient spouse is a U.S. citizen. If a nonresident alien transfers property to a noncitizen spouse, the unlimited marital deduction is not available. However, the annual exclusion is increased to $103,000 for gifts between the spouses. Additionally, nonresident taxpayers cannot "gift split" (a provision allows a married couple to treat a gift made by one spouse as having been made one-half by each) because the statute requires that both the donor and the spouse be United States citizens or residents. Additionally, no exemption equivalent is available to nonresident aliens to offset U.S. gift taxes. As to the annual exclusion, whereas nonresident aliens are not entitled to the gift tax exemption equivalent amount, they are allowed the $11,000 per donee annual gift tax exclusion.

If it is determined that a spouse is a nonresident and the estate planning team has determined that a qualified domestic trust should be utilized, the planners must be sure that assets that frequently pass by operation of law such as life insurance, joint accounts, and qualified plans should be directed to pass through the qualified domestic trust rather than passing outright by operation of law. Accordingly, the titling of assets can be crucial to the successful funding of a QDOT upon the first spouse's demise. That is, bank accounts, brokerage accounts, and life insurance policies should be reviewed to structure the ownership so that the assets do not pass by operation of law, but rather are eligible to fund the QDOT.

While a QDOT, properly administered, defers estate taxation, it also restricts distributions of the principal and relegates the spouse to making requests for principal invasions only for hardship purposes without triggering estate taxation. Additionally, even if a discretionary invasion is approved, estate tax is assessed on the payment. If discretionary invasions were requested from a QTIP trust and the distributions were spent without receiving assets of value in return, ultimately there would be no estate tax on those assets, whereas with a QDOT the estate tax is due upon the trust's distribution. Also, unlike a QTIP trust, the property remaining in the trust upon the spouse's death is subject to estate tax at the first spouse's incremental rate, thereby preventing the benefits of a potentially lower estate tax bracket upon the death of the surviving spouse. Finally, under the terms of the 2001 Tax Act, even if the estate tax is repealed, if a noncitizen spouse dies prior to January 1, 2010, with a will that created a QDOT trust, an estate tax will be due for the period up through January 1, 2021.

Power of Appointment Trust

A power of appointment trust is similar to a QTIP trust in that both trusts require that the surviving spouse be entitled to all income from the trust, payable at least annually, for life. However, the two trusts differ in two ways: (1) with a power of appointment trust the surviving spouse must have the power to appoint the trust property to him- or herself or to his or her estate, and (2) that power to appoint (or direct) can be exercised only by the spouse.

For practical purposes, a QTIP trust is often utilized in multiple marriage situations. Conversely, a power of appointment trust is most often utilized not to ensure that the children from a prior marriage inherit, but rather to allow the surviving spouse to call an "audible." More specifically, the surviving spouse has the ability to observe the growth and maturity of the marital children and may alter the percentage of distribution of the trust assets accordingly. For example, a surviving spouse, dismayed with her son's lack of morals and work ethic, may exercise the power of appointment granted to her under her husband's will and direct that the QTIP trust under his will not be distributed outright to the son, but rather be governed by an income-only trust created under her will, then upon her son's demise pass to his children, subject to the generation-skipping transfer tax rules.

Conclusion

The use of the unlimited marital deduction is one of the primary tools utilized by estate planners. However, in order to create an estate plan that protects both the surviving spouse as well as the members of the decedent's family, the following factors must be considered:

- How much wealth should be transferred to the surviving spouse and how much wealth should be transferred to other family members.

- Whether the transfer of wealth should be outright to the surviving spouse or in trust for the benefit of the surviving spouse.

- The extent to which the unlimited marital deduction should be utilized to defer estate taxation.

- The extent to which the surviving spouse should have control over the ultimate distribution of wealth.

- The relationship between the surviving spouses and any children from prior marriages.

- Any outstanding obligations from a divorce decree.

- The provisions of a prenuptial agreement, if any.

Accordingly, both the individual, as well as his or her spouse, must meet with the members of the estate planning team before implementing a plan or utilizing any of the structures discussed in this chapter.

Irrevocable Life Insurance Trusts

Probably one of the easiest ways for wealthy individuals to help reduce the national debt (if they were so inclined) would be to own life insurance in their own personal names. If you own life insurance individually you should recognize that approximately half of the insurance proceeds will ultimately go to benefit the U.S. Treasury, not your loved ones for whom you bought the policy.

Yes, it's true: Although life insurance is exempt from income tax, it is includable in one's estate for estate tax purposes and subject to estate tax. But day after day, for one reason or another, individuals continue to buy and own substantial amounts of life insurance to protect their families without realizing that the U.S. Treasury is the unnamed beneficiary of up to 50% of the death benefit. Even if you name your spouse as the beneficiary (thus deferring the estate tax via the unlimited marital deduction), make no mistake about it: When both you and your surviving spouse are gone, the death benefit of the life insurance policy, plus any growth, is subject to estate tax.

Enter the irrevocable life insurance trust. With a stroke of the almighty pen, life insurance may be removed from your estate for estate tax purposes and pass to your intended beneficiaries according to the terms of the life insurance trust document. With careful planning and utilizing the team approach, the death benefit of life insurance does not have to be subject to estate taxation. In an era when a $1 million life insurance policy is almost protocol, this fundamental estate planning technique must be considered and generally implemented.

Factors to Consider Before Creating an Irrevocable Life Insurance Trust

A comprehensive review of the following 10 factors must be undertaken before determining whether a life insurance trust is appropriate for you:

1. The reason the insurance was purchased (or is about to be purchased).

2. The type of insurance purchased (or to be purchased).

3. The term of the life insurance policy.

4. The existing cash value or interpolated terminal reserve (cash value plus any unused premiums).

5. The performance of the cash invested in the life insurance policy.

6. The value of your estate with and without the insurance death benefit.

7. The need for liquidity to provide funding for your loved ones, as well as for the payment of estate taxes.

8. The existing premiums or illustrated premiums viewed in conjunction with your gifting program utilizing the annual exclusion.

9. The health and insurability of the insured.

10. The cash flow of the insured (i.e., whether the premiums are affordable).

Once these issues have been flushed out, the estate planning team will be armed with the requisite knowledge to determine whether an irrevocable life insurance trust is appropriate. If an irrevocable life insurance trust is recommended, the life insurance policy may become an asset of the trust in one of two ways: either (1) by assigning or transferring an existing policy into a newly created irrevocable life insurance trust, or (2) by purchasing the policy through a newly created irrevocable life insurance trust so that the trust will serve as the owner and beneficiary of the insurance policy from the outset.

The Three-Year Look-Back

When an existing life insurance policy is assigned or transferred into an irrevocable life insurance trust, the death benefit will not avoid estate inclusion until three years from the date the policy is actually transferred into the trust. This "three-year look-back" rule does have merit. If every patient, upon hearing the bleak prognosis of Dr. Grim Reaper, quickly transferred one's insurance policies into an irrevocable life insurance trust and avoided estate tax, the estate tax system would have a gaping hole. Therefore, an individual assigning or transferring a life insurance policy into an irrevocable trust should be reasonably sure that the odds of surviving the three-year period are favorable. If you fail to survive the three-year term (whether by illness or by getting hit by the proverbial Mack truck), the death benefit will be includable in your estate for estate tax purposes. If, however, the trustee of an irrevocable life insurance trust purchases the life insurance policy from the beginning and names the trust as beneficiary, the death benefit is not subject to the three-year look-back rule and is thus not subject to estate taxation unless the grantor retained certain incidents of ownership.

Incidents of Ownership

Whether a life insurance policy is assigned to a life insurance trust or the trustee purchases the policy from inception, if the IRS determines that the grantor retained incidents of ownership, the policy will be includable in the grantor's estate. The IRS may find that incidents of ownership exist in the event the grantor retains certain rights, including the right to change the beneficiaries, the right to surrender or cancel the policy, the right to assign the policy, the right to revoke an assignment, the right to pledge the policy for a loan or borrow against the policy, the right to change contingent beneficiaries or to receive benefits after the primary beneficiary's death, or the right to change the time or manner of payment of the proceeds to a beneficiary.

In two recent cases, however, rulings have been issued that stand for the proposition that the grantor of an irrevocable life insurance trust may retain the power to change the trustee of the life insurance so long as the successor trustee is not related or subordinate. The term "related or subordinate" includes spouses, parents, descendants, siblings, and employees, but not nieces, nephews, in-laws, or partners. Accordingly, if the trustee is failing to perform his or her duties as trustee, the grantor should be able to replace that trustee with an independent trustee who will dutifully carry out his or her fiduciary responsibilities.

Crummey Notices

The payment of premiums by the grantor into an irrevocable trust is considered a gift to the beneficiaries of the trust and is therefore subject to gift tax. Grantors seeking to avoid gift tax exposure may look first to the $11,000 annual gift tax exclusion for relief. However, in order to apply the gift tax exclusion toward the payment of premiums or any other contribution to the trust, the IRS requires that the transfer into the trust be a present-interest gift to the beneficiaries of the trust. This means that the beneficiaries must have the legal right to withdraw the deposits made into the trust account before the trustee sends a check to the insurance company. Generally, the trust agreement should provide the beneficiaries with between 30 and 60 days in which they have the right to withdraw the funds contributed. These notices are called Crummey notices after a case called *Crummey v. Commissioner*, 397 F.2d 82 (1968), in which the court concluded that if a beneficiary of a trust has the immediate right to withdraw assets gifted to the trust, the beneficiary will have a present interest in the gift which will then qualify for the annual exclusion. After each gift is made to the trust, the beneficiaries must receive a Crummey letter notifying them of the gift and entitling them to withdraw all or a portion of the gift if they so desire.

The issuance of Crummey notices not only is an administrative burden to the trustee, but it can also be a confusing undertaking. If the grantor's contribution into the irrevocable life insurance trust is made once a year, and the trust is for the benefit of two adult beneficiaries, the burden is light. The trustee will issue the Crummey notices to the beneficiaries after the gift is made into the trust checking account allowing the beneficiaries 30 to 60 days to exercise the power or allow such power to lapse. At the expiration of the notice period, if the beneficiaries have allowed the power to lapse, the trustee may then pay the insurance premium out of the trust checking account. At all times, the trustee will maintain records of the Crummey notices being sent. Not so difficult. However, if premiums are due quarterly so that contributions into the trust are made quarterly, then the trustee should issue Crummey notices quarterly. If contributions are made monthly, now the trustee must issue 24 Crummey notices every year for the life of the trust and maintain records. If there are four beneficiaries, that's 48 Crummey notices a year.

The administrative burden to the trustee is compounded if the trust holds two or three life insurance policies, each with different premium dates, and grantor gifts are made 30 to 60 days before each premium due date, perhaps one monthly, one quarterly, and one annually. Worse yet, any beneficiary who is a minor must have an authorized agent, not the grantor or trustee, to receive the notices. Accordingly, when considering who the trustee of an irrevocable trust should be, be sure to nominate an individual or trust company ready, willing, and able to assume this responsibility.

Hanging Powers

The grantor's enthusiasm for utilizing the annual exclusion by virtue of issuing Crummey letters must be tempered by the potential gift tax implications to the beneficiary who has the right to withdraw contributions from the trust but declines to do so. Declining to withdraw the funds so provided in the Crummey letter is considered a lapse of a general power of appointment. That is, since the beneficiary has the power to take or appoint the trust funds to himself or herself but fails to do so, then other beneficiaries of the trust may benefit, and thus the beneficiary has technically made a gift. This gift occurs only if the beneficiary predeceases the grantor, because a beneficiary who survives the grantor will receive the trust property. But if the beneficiary predeceases the grantor and thus does not receive the trust property, then the gift tax liability may be realized.

Some relief to this potential gift tax exposure is provided by what's known as the "five and five" power. The Internal Revenue Code (IRC) provides that the lapse or release of a general power of appointment is not a taxable gift except to the extent it exceeds the greater of $5,000 or 5% of the trust funds. Thus, for example, if a grantor has three children as beneficiaries of an irrevocable life insurance trust, transfers $15,000 into the trust, and the trustee issues Crummey notices which the beneficiaries allow to lapse, there is no gift tax exposure to the grantor because of the use of $5,000 of the annual exclusion for each beneficiary. In addition, since the $15,000 gift into the trust is apportioned among the three beneficiaries, each having a $5,000 withdrawal right, there is no gift tax to the beneficiaries, either, since the gifts to each beneficiary do not exceed $5,000.

What if the grantor's gift into the trust is not $15,000 but rather $30,000? The grantor still does not have gift tax exposure ($11,000 annual exclusion times three), but the beneficiaries may have exposure since $30,000 divided by three is $10,000, and that's $5,000 over the "five and five" power. Accordingly, if a beneficiary predeceases the grantor, then the amount of contributions allocated to such beneficiary each year in excess of the "five and five" power will be includable in the deceased beneficiary's estate.

Enter the "hanging Crummey power" or "hanging power." A hanging power drafted into the trust agreement allows the excess of the "five and five" to accumulate for withdrawal in future years, perhaps when the grantor stops funding the irrevocable life insurance trust. Accordingly, if the grantor in this example transfers $30,000 into the trust for 10 years and then makes no further contributions (perhaps because the premiums have vanished), the hanging power would eliminate the potential gift tax exposure to the beneficiary's estate 10 years after the grantor stops making contributions into the trust ($5,000 per year for 10 years).

Example 1

Assume that Bill and Mary Smith have combined assets of $2 million. Figure 7.1 demonstrates the effect of Bill's purchase of a life insurance policy with a face value of $1 million. With Bill as owner and insured of this policy, the proceeds are subject to estate taxes. Without planning, their combined estate of $3 million would create an estate tax liability of $930,000.

Example 2

Figure 7.2 details what would happen if, before purchasing the new life insurance policy, Bill and Mary execute new wills with exemption equivalent trusts and arrange for the purchase of the insurance policy through an irrevocable life insurance trust. As shown, the $930,000 tax liability is eliminated.

Administration of the Life Insurance Trust

The manner in which an irrevocable life insurance trust was formed and the way it was administered may be closely scrutinized by the IRS in an estate tax audit upon one's demise. Accordingly, strict adherence to the rules and regulations surrounding insurance trusts is imperative. In order to properly administer a life insurance trust, the following six procedures must be closely followed:

1. Obtain a tax identification number for the irrevocable trust.

2. Open up a trust checking account in the name of the irrevocable trust with the trustee being the only signatory.

3. Be sure that contributions into the trust exceed the premiums due.

4. Issue and retain copies of the Crummey notices in the trustee's files for future reference.

For: Smith, Bill & Mary
Report Name: Basic – Flowchart
Plan: Plan2   Scenario: All to Spouse
1st Death; 2002   2nd Death: 2002   Gifts: No   Discounts: No

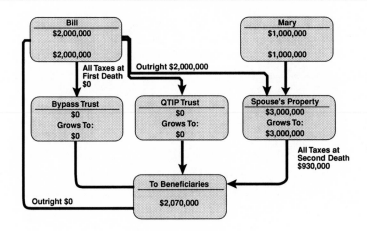

Death Tax Detail				
		Bill		Mary
Federal tentative tax	$	0	$	1,275,800
Unified credit + gift tax paid	(	345,800)	(	345,800)
State death tax credit	(	0)	(	136,500)
Other credits	(	0)	(	0)
Net federal tax	$	0	$	793,500
NY state tax		0		136,500
Income tax on retirement		0		0
Generation-skipping transfer tax		0		0
Total Tax	$	0	$	930,000
TOTAL TAX FOR BOTH DEATHS:			$	930,000

FIGURE 7.1   Example 1

Reproduced with permission from CCH Incorporated, 2700 Lake Cook Road, Riverwoods, Illinois 60015.

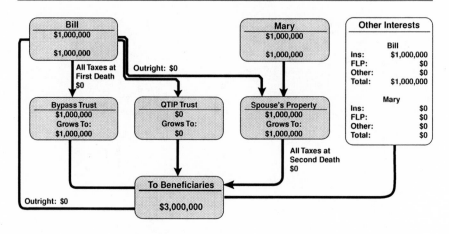

Tax Detail		
	Bill	Mary
Gifts to beneficiaries	$ 1,000,000	$ 0
Total gift tax paid through life	0	0

Death Tax Detail		
	Bill	Mary
Federal tentative tax	$ 345,800	$ 345,800
Unified credit + gift tax paid	(345,800)	(345,800)
State death tax credit	(0)	(0)
Other credits	(0)	(0)
Net federals tax	$ 0	$ 0
NY state sax	0	0
Income tax on retirement plans	0	0
Generation-skipping transfer tax	0	0
Total tax	$ 0	$ 0
TOTAL TAX FOR BOTH DEATHS:		$ 0

FIGURE 7.2   Example 2

Reproduced with permission from CCH Incorporated, 2700 Lake Cook Road, Riverwoods, Illinois 60015.

5. Ensure that the trustee pays the insurance premiums, if any, out of the trust account; do not pay insurance premiums out of personal or business checking accounts directly to the insurance company.

6. Coordinate with your accountant any necessary tax filings for the trust (Form 1041).

Second-to-Die (Survivorship) Life Insurance Trust

If the primary purpose of the life insurance trust is to provide your heirs with liquidity to pay estate taxes, it may be prudent for the trustee to purchase a "second-to-die" (or survivorship) life insurance policy. With a second-to-die policy, the death benefit is paid only upon the death of the second spouse. For estate tax purposes this is usually when liquidity is needed, as there are usually no estate taxes due upon the death of the first spouse to the extent that the estate plan takes complete advantage of the unlimited marital deduction. Upon the death of the second spouse, the estate tax is due and payable within nine months. That is when the insurance proceeds can really come in handy to help pay estate taxes.

Postponing the payment of estate taxes until the second spouse dies is generally one of the fundamental options of a properly planned estate. However, deferring estate taxation until the second spouse's demise can prove a sobering experience without the proper planning. This experience sometimes has been referred to as the "second death tax wallop." A properly designed second-to-die life insurance policy can be acquired to provide the liquidity when these estate taxes are due. Further, by allowing the insurance company to postpone the payment of death benefits on the life insurance policy until the second spouse's death, both spouses' life expectancies are used in the actuarial calculation, which can dramatically reduce the insurance premiums. There are some considerations, however, to second-to-die life insurance policies. Consider the following four factors before committing to a second-to-die policy inside an irrevocable life insurance trust:

1. Be sure the surviving spouse will have the necessary cash flow to continue to support the premium payments after the first spouse's demise.

2. Be sure that the premiums due will not unknowingly cause taxable gifts since one spouse's annual exclusion will be lost upon his or her demise

(reducing the available annual exclusion gifts from $22,000 to $11,000 per beneficiary).

3. Determine what happens in the event of a divorce.

4. As both spouses are treated as the grantors of a second-to-die trust, neither spouse should serve as a trustee (otherwise, the entire death benefit of the insurance policy could be included in the estate of the second to die).

Provisions to Include in the Life Insurance Trust

In order to use the irrevocable life insurance trust to pay estate taxes, the trust document should authorize the trustee to make loans to the estate and/or purchase assets from the estate. The trustee cannot pay the estate's debts directly or give the cash to the estate because the life insurance policy could be considered part of the estate and could be taxed as such. The trustee should be able to furnish the executor with cash by purchasing assets from the estate for fair market value. Because the tax basis of assets held in the estate is stepped up to their fair market values at date of death, no gain would be realized upon the sale of assets by the estate to the trust. The executor can then use the cash to pay debts and estate taxes.

Besides arranging for your trustee to provide your estate with liquidity, it is important for an irrevocable trust to contain some built-in flexibility in its terms because you will not be able to change the terms later. Take into consideration the consequences of divorce, remarriage, or other personal events, and provide your trustee with the directions and flexibility to adequately respond to changing circumstances. For example, with regard to children, use language that is flexible enough to include future children. The trustee should also be given the flexibility necessary to respond to changes in the tax law.

Although the trust is irrevocable and cannot be changed once executed, the trust may be drafted so that upon the insured's demise the assets are distributable to the beneficiaries according to age-terminating trust provisions similar to those provisions found in a will. For instance, perhaps one-third of the trust assets could be distributed when the beneficiary attains age 25, one-half of the remaining balance at age 30, and the balance at age 35. Additionally, the trustee could be given discretion to invade principal on behalf of a beneficiary for his or her health, education, maintenance, and support over and above the age-terminating triggering dates.

Alternatively, the irrevocable life insurance trust could be created such that the trustee has full discretion when and if to remit income and/or principal to the beneficiaries. More specifically, if the trustee has the discretion to remit or withhold distribution of income and/or principal and the trustee believes that a beneficiary is acting irrationally or proves incompetent (or simply that the distribution of trust funds is not in the beneficiary's best interest), the trustee may have the discretion not to remit income and/or principal, but rather to wait until such beneficiary proves himself or herself worthy.

An irrevocable life insurance trust may be blended with the generation-skipping transfer (GST) tax provisions to leverage transfers to future generations. More specifically, an irrevocable life insurance trust may be created for the benefit of grandchildren. As more fully set forth in Chapter 8, "Generation-Skipping Transfer Tax," there is currently a $1,060,000 exemption from the generation-skipping transfer tax subject to a cost of living adjustment. With the use of an irrevocable life insurance trust established for the benefit of grandchildren (and future generations), the exemption amount can be used against the premium payments, thus exempting the death benefit from the GST tax.

For instance, assume each year the grantor makes a contribution into an irrevocable life insurance trust created for the benefit of grandchildren. The contribution into the trust each year necessitates the filing of a gift tax return. The annual contribution into the trust should be allocated against the GST tax exemption amount. Accordingly, if the grantor contributes $20,000 a year for five years into an irrevocable life insurance trust created to acquire a $1 million life insurance policy for the benefit of grandchildren, the $1,060,000 exemption is reduced by only $100,000 ($20,000 × 5), and the death benefit of the life insurance policy passes to the grandchildren free of GST tax.

Irrevocable Trust versus Beneficiaries Owning the Life Insurance Policy

A simple alternative to an irrevocable life insurance trust may be to have your beneficiaries own the insurance policy on your life directly. For federal estate tax purposes, it does not matter who owns the policy provided it is not owned by either the decedent or his or her spouse. If you have only a few children and they are adults who act prudently, individual ownership should be considered. The simplicity and lack of expense are attractive. However, although this arrangement avoids the estate tax, there are a number of advantages to having the policy owned by a trust:

First, there is greater certainty that the proceeds will be used for their intended purpose if a trust is created and a trustee named who understands the estate plan. The beneficiaries might otherwise use the funds imprudently or borrow excessively against the cash value in the policy prior to the death of the insured individual. Additionally, upon one's death, the policy proceeds will go, in one lump sum, directly to the beneficiaries if they own the policy; they might spend the proceeds before estate taxes are due (or fail to cooperate when the taxes are due).

Second, if one or more of the beneficiaries own the policy and predecease you, some of the value of the policy will be included in their estates.

Finally, the trust terms can shield the death benefit from the claims of your childs' creditors or spouse's equitable distribution demands in the event of a divorce. A trust could also offer a measure of protection from the implications of incompetent or otherwise unreasonable beneficiaries.

Life Insurance Planning in Anticipation of Estate Tax Reform

As has been stated throughout this book, under the terms of the Economic Growth and Tax Relief Reconciliation Act of 2001, the exemption equivalent is scheduled to increase and the rate of tax will decrease until the tax, in theory, will be repealed. However, estate tax repeal may last exactly one year (January 1, 2010, to December 31, 2010). So, unless you have it on good authority that your time will come during this brief 12-month period eight years from now, you must continue to plan for the payment of estate taxes, particularly in light of the fact that on January 1, 2011, the entire estate tax system currently in place is due to be reinstated with all of its current onerous provisions (including a top federal estate tax rate of 60%).

As a result, it is more imperative than ever that you plan for your estate today, and this includes the full utilization of life insurance trusts. Under the terms of the 2001 Tax Act, the deathtime exemption equivalent is due to increase to $1.5 million in 2004, $2 million in 2006, and $3.5 million in 2009 with the estate tax rate reduced to 50% in 2002 and going down to 45% by 2007 (which will still represent a premium of approximately 10% over the highest income tax rate at that time). Although these increasing exemption amounts will help offset the very high rate of tax imposed on estates during this period, estate tax planning will continue to be necessary for families of means. This is particularly true if you take into consideration the fact that family wealth does not stand still. A $5 million estate can easily double to $10 million if prudently invested over a 10-year period. Even with the full utilization of both a husband's and a wife's exemption amounts, an estate of that size would be subject to estate tax exposure of approximately $3.5 million until year 2004, $3 million until year 2006, and $2.5 million until 2009. Even in 2009, a husband and wife would be facing estate tax of almost $1.5 million on a combined $10 million estate. On January 1, 2011, one year after repeal (remember, repeal will last only from January 1, 2010, to December 31, 2010), the same couple would again face an estate tax of as much as $5 million.

In face of this uncertainty, life insurance held in a properly structured insurance trust exempt from estate tax remains a cornerstone of a well-designed estate plan. However, like any estate planning that needs to be performed in the face of estate tax reform, insurance planning must be structured to be as flexible as possible. Accordingly, it is recommended that every individual meet with his or her team of advisers to structure the right insurance planning in the face of the uncertain fate of estate tax reform. This may entail the utilization of insurance products different than those which have been historically recommended. For instance, convertible term insurance or a decreasing death benefit policy may be warranted rather than a whole-life policy, particularly in the case of a second-to-die (survivorship) life insurance trust designed specifically to pay estate tax liability. In any case, it is the individual's particular situation that will ultimately determine the best route to take. These facts must be presented to the insurance professional as well as the estate tax attorney for their consideration and input. It is only then that truly informed and knowledgeable advice can be extended to the client for his or her ultimate decision on the matter.

Conclusion

Numerous articles by estate planning commentators have highlighted the 10 most common estate planning mistakes. A common thread throughout these articles is that individuals whose estates exceed the exemption equivalent often own life insurance in their individual names, ultimately exposing the death benefit to unnecessary estate taxes. Creating an irrevocable life insurance trust to own the insurance and be the beneficiary of the death benefit can remove the asset from one's taxable estate. The cost to set up such a trust and the annual administration thereof are almost universally worth the expenditure and the effort. Furthermore, as highlighted throughout this book, creating an estate plan and, in particular, deciding whether an irrevocable life insurance trust is right for you, must be discussed at length with your team of advisers. This is especially true in light of the uncertain environment created by the Economic Growth and Tax Relief Reconciliation Act of 2001.

CHAPTER 8

Generation-Skipping Transfer Tax

The concept of estate planning has existed for centuries. So, too, has the idea of transferring wealth from a grandparent directly or indirectly to a grandchild or grandchildren. Through the ages, wealthy families have traditionally avoided or substantially reduced estate taxes by transferring property to or for the benefit of grandchildren or even great-grandchildren, thus skipping a generation (or two) and the consequent estate taxes on one or more generations. Simply stated, when you transfer wealth across generations, any estate taxes that would have otherwise been imposed on the skipped generation are avoided.

In order to address this potential estate tax windfall, Congress enacted the generation-skipping transfer (GST) tax on the transfer of assets to grandchildren, as well as great-nieces, great-nephews, and younger generations. Such transfers now potentially trigger the GST tax even if they may be exempt from estate or gift taxes.

Assume, for instance, a grandfather who establishes a trust to provide income to his child for life, and, upon the death of the child, for the assets to pass to his grandchildren. The amount held in trust (the "trust corpus") would not be included in the child's estate for estate tax purposes because the child had no rights to the trust other than the income paid out. Therefore any estate taxes on the trust would not be due until the death of the grandchildren, thus postponing the estate tax liability for an entire generation.

Prior to the imposition of the GST tax, these assets could have continued to grow without estate liability until the grandchildren's demise. However, Congress was aware of such transfers, and in 1986, in an attempt to prohibit such attempts at skipping a generation (and thus an additional level of transfer tax), Congress enacted the GST tax.

The thought of a 37% to 50% federal estate tax is already enough to make your heart skip a beat. However, when you learn about the GST tax, resuscitation may be required. The GST tax is imposed on transfers made after October 22, 1986, at a rate equal to the highest gift and estate tax rate. Currently, that means a flat GST tax of 50% over and above the already onerous federal estate tax.

That's the bad news. The good news is that with comprehensive estate planning, opportunities still exist to transfer wealth from a grandparent to grandchildren without the imposition of the GST tax. To begin with, every individual may transfer up to $1,060,000 (the GST exemption amount beginning in year 2001) without triggering the GST tax.

This GST exemption amount will be increased by a cost of living adjustment in 2002. Furthermore, under the terms of the Economic Growth and Tax Relief Reconciliation Act of 2001, the GST exemption amount is due to increase starting in 2004 by the same amount as the unified credit exemption amount, and a reduction in the GST tax rate will correspond to the reduction in the highest estate tax rate during such period. (See Table 8.1.) As a result of this coordination of the GST exemption amount and the unified credit exemption amount, planning for the minimization of the generation-skipping transfer tax and estate tax has been made simpler. Prior to this unification, because the GST exemption amount was greater than the unified credit exemption amount, it was necessary to establish a series of trusts to ensure that the GST exemption was fully utilized. Now one can plan for the GST exemption amount by allocating such amount to a unified credit exemption trust, thus taking full advantage of the increasing GST exemption, as well as the unified credit exemption in the same testamentary trust established under one's last will and testament.

As in the case of the estate tax, the GST tax is due to expire in 2010. However, as also is the case with the federal estate tax, in 2011 the GST tax is then to be reinstated with all of the same provisions currently in effect (including

TABLE 8.1	Generation-Skipping Transfer Tax Rates	
Year	GST Exemption Amount	GSI Tax
2001	$1,060,000	50%
2002	$1,060,000*	49%
2003	$1,060,000*	48%
2004	$1,500,000	47%
2005	$1,500,000	46%
2006	$2,000,000	46%
2007	$2,000,000	45%
2008	$2,000,000	45%
2009	$3,500,000	45%
2010	Repealed	Repealed
2011	$1,060,000*	55%

*Increased by the applicable cost of living adjustment.

the existing 55% GST tax). Accordingly, well-to-do individuals who are interested in planning for the well-being of their grandchildren (and perhaps their grandchildren's grandchildren) cannot wait (and hope) that repeal will actually take place. If they fail to act, they could be met with the same onerous GST tax provisions that currently exist.

Generally, the imposition of the GST tax is triggered when wealth is transferred by a transferor (person transferring the assets) to a "skip person" (someone in a generation at least two generations below that of the transferor). Under the GST rules, there are three events that trigger the imposition of the GST tax: a direct skip, a taxable termination, and a taxable distribution. The amount and timing of tax due depend in part on which GST event occurs.

In order to understand if and when a direct skip, taxable termination, or taxable distribution has occurred, it is necessary to first define the term "skip person." A skip person is a natural person or a trust assigned to a generation two or more generations below that of the transferor. If the beneficiary is two or more generations below the transferor, he or she is considered a skip person.

Anyone who is not a skip person is considered a nonskip person. Generational assignments are summarized as follows:

GENERATIONAL ASSIGNMENTS—FAMILY MEMBERS

- Grandparents, siblings, spouses.
- Parents, siblings, spouses.
- Children, siblings, spouses.
- Grandchildren, nieces, nephews, spouses.

For transfers that are made to beneficiaries who are nonfamily members of the transferor, the determination of whether the beneficiary is a skip person depends on the difference in ages between the transferor and the beneficiary. Generational assignments for nonfamily members are summarized as follows:

GENERATIONAL ASSIGNMENTS—NONFAMILY MEMBERS

- If the beneficiary is not more than $12^{1}/_{2}$ years older or younger than the transferor, the beneficiary is in the same generation.
- If the beneficiary is more than $12^{1}/_{2}$ years younger but not more than $37^{1}/_{2}$ years younger than the transferor, the beneficiary is one generation lower.
- If the beneficiary is more than $37^{1}/_{2}$ years younger than the transferor, the beneficiary is two or more generations lower.

Direct Skips

Anytime an individual transfers property to a skip person, the GST tax will be imposed. Such a transfer may be made by gift, by inheritance, or otherwise. The direct skip is the least complicated transfer that results in the imposition of GST tax. It is simply the transfer of an interest in property to a skip person.

This transfer may be in the form of an outright gift to such person or in a trust solely for such person's benefit. A trust is a skip person only if: (1) all interests in the trust are held by one or more skip persons at the time of the transfer, or (2) no person holds an interest in the trust at the time of the transfer, but future distributions can be made only to skip persons. Thus, a transfer in trust for the sole benefit of a grandchild is treated as a direct skip, whereas a transfer in trust to a child for life with the remainder going to a grandchild is not treated as a direct skip because the trust will not be treated as a skip person. A direct skip may be made during a transferor's lifetime or at death and is taxed only once regardless of how many generations are actually skipped.

For direct skips, the GST tax will be computed on a "tax-exclusive basis," which means that the 50% GST tax rate is imposed on the amount of the transfer in order to determine the tax due. When a direct skip occurs during the lifetime of the transferor, he or she is generally responsible for any GST tax imposed, even though the GST tax paid by the transferor will be treated as an additional gift to the skip person for gift tax purposes. When a direct skip occurs at death, the GST tax is payable by the decedent's estate. The GST tax imposed on a direct skip through the use of a trust is payable by the trustee out of trust proceeds.

Taxable Terminations

Both taxable terminations and taxable distributions take place in the context of trusts established for the benefit of both nonskip and skip persons. Unlike direct skips, taxable terminations and distributions generally do not take place at the same time estate or gift taxes are due. The event triggering either the estate or gift tax has generally already taken place upon the establishment of the trust or at some later time but prior to the event triggering the taxable termination or distribution.

A taxable termination generally occurs when a nonskip person's interest in a trust is terminated and immediately thereafter only skip persons have any interest in the trust. For example, when a child's interest in a trust terminates and the trust property then benefits only grandchildren, a taxable termination has occurred. Unlike direct skips, a taxable termination results in a tax-inclusive GST tax, with part of the trust assets being used to pay the taxes, even though the tax liability was computed on the entire trust corpus.

There exist three situations in which a termination will not result in the imposition of the GST tax:

1. The transfer of the property held in the trust at the time of termination is subject to federal estate or gift tax.

2. Immediately after the termination, a nonskip person has an interest in the trust.

3. At no time after the termination can any distribution be made from the trust to a skip person.

Taxable Distributions

A taxable distribution occurs whenever a trust distributes income or principal to a skip person and such distribution does not otherwise constitute a taxable termination or direct skip. A common situation involves a grandparent who creates a trust and gives the trustee the discretionary power to provide income or principal to the grandparent's issue. Any distribution of income or principal to a grandchild (or any other skip person) would trigger the GST tax as a taxable distribution.

As in the case of a taxable termination, the GST tax on taxable distributions is computed on a tax-inclusive basis, which means that the amount of the transfer to a skip person will include the amount of the tax due, and ultimately reduce the total transfer amount (although not the GST tax).

Predeceased Ancestor Exception

When immersed in the intricacies of the GST, it is always important to note that in certain circumstances the death of a middle-generation (nonskip) beneficiary may allow a skip person to move up the generational ladder, precluding the imposition of the GST tax. Generally this occurs when an individual has a deceased child and transfers assets to the deceased child's children. Alternatively, if the transferor has no living descendants, and transfers assets to children of a deceased niece or nephew, the predeceased ancestor exception will apply.

Example 1

Linda is a grandparent. She creates an irrevocable trust and pays the gift tax on the transfer of wealth to the trust. The trust provides that the income be paid to her brother, Phil, during his life.

On Phil's death, the income then goes to Linda's children for life. Finally, upon the trust termination, the trust corpus passes to Linda's grandchildren, which transfer would generally be subject to the GST tax.

If one of Linda's children (who was alive at the time the trust was created) dies before she does, the grandchildren do not move up the generational ladder, and no predeceased ancestor exception is available.

Example 2

Now, let us assume that Linda (as a grandparent) creates a revocable living trust (not subject to gift tax at the time of its creation), retains an interest in the trust for her lifetime, and provides that on her death the trust will be transferred to her children for life and then to her grandchildren.

Now, if one of her children dies before she does, that child's children move up the generational ladder precluding the GST tax as to those grandchildren.

The distinction between the two examples turns on when the middle generation beneficiary dies. The exception applies only when the predeceased ancestor was not living at the time the transfer was subject to gift or estate tax.

Annual and Lifetime Exclusions from GST Tax

There are certain exceptions to the imposition of the GST tax. The first is that every individual has a $1,060,000 exemption (as of the year 2001), which may be used during his or her lifetime or at death. (This amount will be increased in 2002 by a cost of living adjustment.) For married couples, this would have allowed up to $2,120,000 to be sheltered from the GST tax in year 2001.

In addition to the $1,060,000 exemption per spouse, transferors have the ability to exclude certain payments made for the benefit of skip persons' educational and medical needs. In this regard, tuition payments made directly to an educational institution for the education and training of an individual are not subject to the GST tax. The payments must be made directly to the educational institution and are limited to tuition; such payments cannot include room and board at the educational institution. There is no limit, however, to the funds that can be expended for such tuition, which include payments for tuition for private day school education, college education, and postgraduate education.

Similarly, payments made for any person's medical care are excluded from GST tax considerations. Again, these payments must be made directly to the provider of the medical care. Such payments can include not only services rendered by a physician or hospital but also the payment of medical insurance.

Another exemption from the GST tax rules includes the ability for the transferor to gift $11,000 annually under the annual gift tax exclusion. The ability of a husband and wife to gift increases the transfer to $22,000 per skip person. Although at first blush this exception does not appear to amount to much of a tax break, these annual exclusion amounts may result in the transfer of significant wealth to skip generations over an extended period of time, provided the transferor utilizes his or her annual exclusion gifts each year.

The transferor has two options in utilizing the $11,000 annual gift tax exclusion for the purpose of transferring wealth to a skip generation. Although the simplest transfer would be an outright $11,000 gift to a grand-child or other skip person, such a transfer may not always be appropriate, depending on the skip person's age and ability to handle money. Therefore, consideration must be given to transferring the $11,000 annual exclusion into a trust.

However, in order for such a gift to be exempt from the GST tax under the annual exclusion exemption, such transfer must qualify as a direct skip to a qualifying trust. In this manner, the transfer must be to a trust in which the skip person is the only person who has a present interest in the trust. The trust must have only one individual as the beneficiary. During the life of such individual, no other person can benefit from the trust, and if such individual dies prior to the termination of the trust, the trust assets must be includable in such individual's taxable estate. The skip person must have a present interest in the trust principal and income.

As an alternative, the trust can include the skip person as a permissible current recipient of trust principal or income, or provide for trust income or principal to be used to satisfy individual support obligations. Accordingly, transfers to an irrevocable life insurance trust where discretionary beneficiaries include not just skip persons, but also, potentially, the transferor's spouse or children (a typical life insurance trust scenario) will not be exempt from the GST tax by reason of the nontaxable gift exclusion.

Computation of GST Tax Liability

One must also be aware that the computation of the GST tax will vary depending on whether the transfer is a direct skip, a taxable termination, or a taxable distribution. The computation of the GST tax is complex. However, for the brave of heart, a brief explanation of how to compute the GST tax follows. For this purpose, definitions of the following are essential:

- Applicable fraction
- Inclusion ratio
- Applicable rate

Applicable Fraction

The applicable fraction is the amount of a transfer, either in trust or outright, that is actually exempt from the GST tax. In this regard, if the applicable fraction is 1, then all of the property being transferred is exempt from the GST tax. In the alternative, if the applicable fraction is 0 all of the property is subject to the GST tax, whereas if the applicable fraction is between 0 and 1 a tax on a portion of the distribution is due.

The following formula may be helpful.

$$\text{Applicable fraction} = \frac{\text{GST tax exemption allocated to property transferred}}{\text{Fair market value of property at time of transfer}}$$

Inclusion Ratio

The inclusion ratio is the amount of the transfer, whether in trust or outright, that is actually subject to the GST tax. If the applicable fraction is 0, then the inclusion ratio is 1, and the entire amount of the property transferred is subject to the GST tax. The inclusion ratio is computed as follows:

$$\text{Inclusion ratio} = 1 - \text{Applicable fraction}$$

A trust will generally maintain its inclusion ratio until the grantor makes additional transfers or allocates additional GST tax exemption to the trust, or until the trust pays GST tax.

Applicable Rate

The inclusion ratio is utilized to calculate the applicable rate of the GST tax as follows:

$$\text{Applicable rate} = \text{Inclusion ratio} \times \text{Flat GST tax rate}$$

The flat GST tax rate is the maximum estate/gift tax rate in effect at the time of the transfer. The taxable amount will depend on which of the three GST tax events has occasioned the tax.

Effective Use of the Lifetime GST Tax Exemption

If a donor were to transfer the $1,060,000 generation-skipping exempt amount into an inter vivos GST trust, future generations could be spared the burden of additional estate taxes.

Dynasty Trust

The purpose of creating a generation-skipping transfer tax trust with the exempt $1,060,000 sum is to create a long-term trust that will benefit your children, as well as grandchildren and more remote descendants, for generations to come. This form of planning vehicle is frequently referred to as a dynasty trust or descendant's trust.

The transferor may fund a trust for his or her descendants with up to $1,060,000 or, in the event of a gift split with a spouse, $2,120,000, without incurring any GST tax. Again, this amount is exempt from only the GST tax amount, not estate or gift taxes. Accordingly, any assets transferred into a GST-exempt trust may be subject to gift tax at the time of transfer to the extent it exceeds the donor's (and/or spouse's) available exemption equivalent.

A dynasty trust may be structured to last for the maximum period of time permitted by state law. Some states measure this period by the lifetimes of everyone alive at the time the trust is established plus 21 years. However, other states allow the life of the trust to run in perpetuity. During this time, the trust corpus is not subject to any further estate, gift, or generation-skipping transfer taxes. If the trust corpus were to double every 10 years appreciating at the rate of 7% annually, you can begin to understand how money left to grow at such a level in perpetuity can, in fact, create a dynasty. In this respect, trustees of a dynasty trust generally seek to preserve the trust corpus rather than making distributions to beneficiaries, which would serve only to reduce the size of the trust corpus.

GST Trust and Life Insurance

In determining the types of assets that should be transferred into a generation-skipping transfer tax trust, you should consider funding such a trust with life insurance. However, in so doing, you must also recognize that if, in fact, the only asset of the generation-skipping transfer tax trust is a new insurance policy, only the premiums added to the trust each year would be allocated to the generation-skipping transfer tax trust.

Accordingly, it may be prudent for the trustee of an irrevocable generation-skipping life insurance trust to acquire permanent insurance. If this is done, transfers into the trust each year may qualify, depending on their amount, for the $11,000 annual exclusion. If the premiums exceed such amounts, the annual gift tax return should allocate the premium against the $1,060,000 exemption.

This is important because if the trustee acquires term insurance, at the expiration of the life insurance contract the GST tax exemption amount that was used to fund premiums may have been used up with no resulting assets in the trust, whereas with permanent insurance, depending on assumptions and interest rates within the life insurance policy, there should come a point in time when the life insurance has either vested due to the death of the insured or the premiums have been offset by either dividends or cash value for the balance of the insured's lifetime. If, in fact, permanent insurance has achieved this premium offset, then the utilization of the GST tax exemption may have turned out to be a prudent investment.

Technical Relief Under the Economic Growth and Tax Relief Reconciliation Act of 2001

The Economic Growth and Tax Relief Reconciliation Act of 2001 also provided certain relief from many of the more technical provisions of the GST tax that have caused problems for years. These new provisions take effect as of January 1, 2002:

1. *Deemed allocation of exemption to certain lifetime transfers.* Under prior law, if an individual made a direct gift to a skip person, the GST exemption automatically applied, preventing the transferor from inadvertently subjecting the gift to the GST tax (at least up to the exemption amount). Under the new law, if an individual makes an indirect skip during life, any unused GST exemption amount will also automatically apply. This new provision will help protect taxpayers who have failed to make an allocation of GST exemption to an indirect skip transaction (which happens in many cases) on an otherwise timely filed gift tax return.

2. *Retroactive allocation of exemption.* The new law also permits a retroactive allocation of the GST exemption when an unnatural order of death occurs. Thus, if a trust provides for a child to receive certain property at a particular age, with the property to go to the child's issue if he or she were to die before reaching such age, the GST exemption will be automatically allocated upon the death of the child if such child were to die prior to reaching the predetermined age.

3. *Severance of trust.* Under prior law, there was no way to break a trust into separate parts for purposes of allocating the GST exemption. Under the new law, if a trust is broken down into two or more parts for GST purposes, the resulting trust will be treated as separate trusts, allowing for the GST exemption amount to be allocated to the portion of the trust that the transferor wishes to exempt from the GST tax.

4. *Relief from late election to allocate exemption.* Under the new law, regulatory authority is now provided for granting extensions of time for purposes of allocating the GST exemption. As provided in the new law, when determining whether to grant relief, the IRS may take into account all relevant circumstances, including evidence of intent contained in the trust instrument. If relief is granted, the value of the transfer can be used to determine a GST exemption allocation.

5. *Substantial compliance with allocation of exemption.* Under prior law, substantial compliance with the requirements for allocating GST exemption could not establish that such exemption was allocated to a particular transfer or trust. Under the new law, an allocation of the GST exemption that "demon-

strates an intent" to allocate GST exemption will be accepted. Accordingly, substantial compliance with the requirements will suffice to establish that the GST exemption was allocated to a particular transfer or trust.

Practical Considerations

Once you have mastered the intricacies of the GST tax, you must then make a determination as to whether utilizing the GST tax exemption and creating a dynasty trust are appropriate. You must recognize that creating massive wealth for generations yet unknown could, potentially, have the opposite effect of what you have sought to create. More specifically, perhaps your grandchildren or great-grandchildren may become so reliant on the income from the trust that they will not be motivated to fully develop and educate themselves and may lose the initiative to excel in their careers. Further, some beneficiaries may fall victim to vices such as drugs, gambling, or alcoholism. Without the reality check of having to go to work and pay bills, which helps one develop mentally, emotionally, and spiritually, a person's bad habits may, in fact, be funded by the massive income stream generated by such a trust.

Many believe that it is important for children and grandchildren to have "the eye of the tiger"—that is, that every individual should try to reach his or her maximum potential, whether that potential be a vocation, a profession, or the ownership of a business. Reaching one's potential is a goal worth striving for. If creating massive amounts of wealth for beneficiaries yet unknown frustrates your perception of this self-actualization theory, then perhaps you need to revisit these issues before creating a vehicle designed to perpetuate your wealth for generations to come.

Alternatively, you may seek to anticipate all of the problems that may crop up and add enough flexibility in the trust document to give the trustees the appropriate amount of latitude to sprinkle income or withhold income from beneficiaries who are undeserving. However, once income is withheld from one sibling but not from others, family squabbling (and perhaps litigation) may result.

You would need a crystal ball to forecast what types of problems might occur for grandchildren or great-grandchildren yet unborn. Accordingly, even if you have mastered the intricacies of the GST tax, mastering your intent should be the focal point—the true heart of your estate plan.

Transferring Wealth to Minors

Introduction

To the extent that you have the ability to transfer wealth to children during your lifetime, the next consideration should be how to transfer the wealth so that it helps your children as they mature, rather than stifles their growth (both spiritually and financially). To help accomplish this objective, you should review with your estate planning team the advantages and disadvantages of each of the following five transfer techniques specifically designed for minors:

1. A Uniform Gifts to Minors Act (UGMA) or Uniform Transfers to Minors Act (UTMA) account.

2. A trust created under IRC 2503(c).

3. A trust created under IRC 2503(b).

4. A Crummey trust.

5. A qualified tuition program (IRC 529 plan).

Uniform Gifts to Minors Act Account

Once the estate planning team has reviewed these gift transfer vehicles, it is not unusual for them to conclude that the Crummey trust and/or a qualified tuition plan are the best alternatives. However, it is appropriate to start the analysis with the Uniform Gifts to Minors Act (UGMA) account or Uniform Transfers to Minors Act (UTMA) account, because it is so frequently used and just as frequently misunderstood. Every state has different rules governing these accounts. However, all are consistent in providing that once the children have reached their age of majority, the assets contained in such accounts belong to them outright.

One of the factors that will vary from state to state is the age at which the minor is mandated to receive the money, usually 18 or 21. The UGMA requires that a fiduciary (referred to as the custodian) be appointed to hold the assets for the minor until that child reaches the age of majority. However, once the minor attains the age of majority, he or she has the right to demand that all assets in the account be transferred directly to him or her.

Assume Peter and Paula Merry begin transferring $11,000 per year per spouse into a UGMA account for the benefit of their child, Lucas, starting at infancy. If, in fact, $22,000 were transferred into the UGMA account from birth through age 18, the total dollars contained in that account by age 18 (assuming 8% growth per year) would be approximately $900,000. At the ripe old age of 18, Lucas, the Merrys' wayward son, demands the funds so he can explore the world—first-class all the way. The Merrys, short of judicial intervention, are powerless to prevent Lucas from doing so.

Perhaps it was the Merrys' intent that the funds would be used for Lucas's college or graduate school and that Lucas would begin a career before a significant amount of wealth was transferred to him. However, with a UGMA account, a rebellious 18-year-old can turn his or her back on the morals and ethics of one's family and find instead a religious cult, motorcycle gang, or commune more satisfying than hard work. Years of hard work and savings for a child's benefit can be squandered by that same young adult in a flash.

Parents have little or no recourse to prevent such a catastrophe. Therefore, if you have any concerns that, at the age of 18, your child could demand the money and not use the funds as you would wish, think twice about utilizing a UGMA account or using it as your primary gift-giving vehicle.

Finally, many people are unaware of another booby trap that comes with a UGMA account—namely, the parent is custodian of that fund. If the parent dies prior to the child's attaining the age of majority, the assets contained in the account are includable in the parent's estate for estate tax purposes.

Trust Created Under Code Section 2503(c)

The second technique created for the transfer of wealth to minors is the creation of a trust that has been legislatively sanctioned under Section 2503(c) of the Internal Revenue Code. A trust agreement can be entered into during a parent's lifetime for the benefit of a minor child. The parent can then transfer his or her $11,000 annual exclusion into the trust or, by gift splitting, combine the transfer for a total of $22,000 per minor beneficiary. The parents (as grantors) cannot be the sole trustees but will usually nominate an independent cotrustee to help administer the trust. If the parents served as the sole trustees, the assets in the trust would be includable in their estates for estate tax purposes.

Generally, the trustee must be authorized, but not mandated, to spend all of the income and principal for the benefit of the minor child. In fact, if the trust document limits the trustee's ability to use the property for the benefit of the child in any way, such restriction may prevent the trust from qualifying as a 2503(c) trust.

However, the biggest concern a parent may have when creating a 2503(c) trust parallels the concern discussed regarding a UGMA account. As in the case of a UGMA account, the beneficiary of a 2503(c) trust must either receive the property held in trust for his or her benefit or at least have the right to demand the property no later than age 21.

You can, however, build into the trust document a time frame and deadline for the child's right to demand the withdrawal. When the minor reaches the age of majority, he or she can demand the assets but only during this window of time. For instance, the defined window might be as little as 30 days. If the child does not demand the assets during this time period, the assets remain in trust pursuant to the trust terms.

However, the problem arises when a child does demand the money because that child may use the money in a way that the parents would not deem appropriate. Usually, the children who demand the money are the same children the parents are concerned about in various other aspects of their lives. Therefore, with regard to these types of children, the 2503(c) trust does not adequately address the issue of keeping the money out of the hands of problem children.

Simply not telling children about their rights in the trust is not a viable solution. If the child were to petition a court, demanding that the property in the trust be transferred over, the court would, in almost all cases, require the trustee to transfer the money. While the 2503(c) trust does create a bit more flexibility in the investment management and utilization of funds held for the benefit of a child, the beneficiary does have the right to demand the money upon attaining age 21.

Trust Created Under Code Section 2503(b) (Mandatory Income Trust)

A 2503(b) trust (mandatory income trust) is similar to the 2503(c) trust as previously explained, with one significant difference. It requires mandatory distribution of the income annually to the minor. The distribution can be either outright to the minor or to a UGMA account created for the minor's benefit. However, once the child reaches majority, the distributions must go to the child.

A 2503(b) trust requires the donee to have a present interest in order for a gift to qualify for the $11,000 annual exclusion. The beneficiary may receive an income interest for a fixed term or even for life. The actuarial value of the income interest in a 2503(b) trust qualifies for the gift tax annual exclusion, but the remainder is a gift of a future interest. Accordingly, a gift tax return must be filed each year a gift is made to a 2503(b) income trust, and gift tax must be paid or exemption equivalent expended for any amounts in excess of the annual exclusion amount.

Another rule that governs 2503(b) trusts is the requirement that the income earned by the trust be paid out at least annually. The income interest in the beneficiary must be an absolute right. If the trustee has the ability to accumulate income during the beneficiary's minority, then the beneficiary's interest will be deemed to be a future interest and the actuarial tables cannot be used to value that interest for annual exclusion purposes.

One of the main disadvantages of creating such a trust is that the income distribution is mandatory. Parents are generally more comfortable in creating a trust for a minor that gives the trustee discretion to distribute income and/or principal for the beneficiary's health, education, maintenance, and support. The parents may ultimately regret the fact that the income must be distributed as opposed to being accumulated in the trust. Even if the child is using the funds in ways that are contrary to the parents' wishes, the trustee is required to continue annual distributions.

Unlike a 2503(c) trust, because the trustee does not have the power to invade principal, the grantor may serve as sole trustee without—as with a 2503(c) trust—the assets being includable in the grantor's estate for estate tax purposes.

Crummey Trust

The Crummey trust is named after the rather infamous case, *Crummey v. Commissioner*, 397 F.2d 82 (1968). Under the terms of a Crummey trust, the trust document will provide that when money is transferred into the trust, usually funded by annual exclusion gifts, the beneficiaries of the trust (or their legal guardian or other agents if they are minors) are given the right for a limited period of time to withdraw the contributions made into the trust, or they can waive that right.

Once this right has been waived, the contributions to the trust qualify as present interest gifts up to the $11,000 annual exclusion ($22,000 for combined gifts from a husband and wife). The ability to withdraw the contributions made into the trust each year (thereby qualifying the gifts for the annual exclusion) is known as the Crummey power. Once this right to the annual contributions has been waived, the assets held in the Crummey trust grow estate tax free outside the grantor's estate.

The Crummey trust, while it does have its own administrative burdens, seems to be one of the most appropriate techniques for parents to utilize the annual exclusion to transfer wealth for the benefit of minor children. What makes the Crummey trust potentially superior to UGMA accounts, 2503(b) trusts, and 2503(c) trusts is that the trustee of a Crummey trust is not required to distribute the money when the minor reaches his or her majority, as required with these other gift-giving vehicles.

Furthermore, the terms of the trust can specify at what ages and under what circumstances the principal and income of the trust becomes available to the child. For instance, the trust agreement can provide for one-third of the trust assets to be distributed at age 25, one-half at age 30, and the balance at age 35, or any other ages or fractions that the grantor believes would be appropriate for the minor beneficiary (see discussion of age-terminating trusts in Chapter 7).

The Crummey trust, however, is not without its own administrative responsibilities, which must be considered when creating a strategy for the utilization of annual exclusion gifting to minors. For instance, when the contribution is made into the trust, a Crummey letter must be issued by the trustee to the minor, or more appropriately, to the minor's legal guardian or authorized agent. (See Figure 9.1.) It generally provides the minor's guardian or agent between 30 and 60 days to withdraw the contribution made into the trust.

If a determination is made by the minor's guardian or agent not to withdraw the sum, then the transfer into the trust by the parent is deemed to have qualified for the annual exclusion. Although technically the guardian or agent serving on behalf of the minor does have the option to withdraw the contributed sums, in the event such a withdrawal is made, it may be the last contribution into the trust the grantor ever makes, which of course is not in the beneficiary's best interest.

Additionally, the Crummey trust is a taxpaying entity, requiring that a tax identification number be obtained and tax returns be filed annually. Unfortunately, the income tax rates for income accumulated within the Crummey trust are compressed when compared to individual income tax rates (see Appendix B). More specifically, a trust or estate will reach the top marginal bracket of 38.6%

FIGURE 9.1 Sample Crummey Letter

To: _____

Address: _____ Date: _____

Re: Trust Withdrawal Rights

Dear (beneficiary, or agent for beneficiary if a minor):

As you know, a trust has been created entitled "The John Smith Family Trust," naming (beneficiary) as a beneficiary.

Under Article Second of the Trust, you, as Agent for (beneficiary), are entitled to withdraw on an annual basis the lesser of $11,000 or the amount actually contributed to the trust for (beneficiary's) benefit. This year, the total withdrawal amount is $_____. Article Second of that Trust gives you the unrestricted right to withdraw such part or all of this amount as you wish, to use for (beneficiary's) uses and purposes.

If you wish to exercise the withdrawal rights conferred upon (beneficiary), you must do so within thirty (30) days from the date of this letter.

If you do not intend to exercise the withdrawal rights granted to (beneficiary), please so indicate by signing on the appropriate line.

Please return signed copy to me.

Should you have any questions, please don't hesitate to call me.

Sincerely yours,

Mary Smith, Trustee

I acknowledge receipt of this notice of right to withdraw property transferred to the Trust, but decline to do so.

Signed: _____

I acknowledge receipt of this notice of right to withdraw property transferred to the Trust and wish to withdraw such funds.

Signed: _____

---

on income earned over $8,900 in 2002. Married individuals filing jointly don't reach the 38.6% bracket until their taxable income exceeds $297,350 in 2002.

However, the trust document may provide the trustee with the ability to distribute the income, thus reducing the taxable income of the trust by the amount distributed. In fact, distributions could be made into a UGMA account for certain expenditures to benefit the child during each calendar year. Any amounts in the UGMA account would be taxed at the minor's bracket. Prior to reaching the age of 14, minor children are generally taxed at their parents' bracket. However, at the age of 14 they obtain their own tax bracket, which can result in substantial tax savings.

In determining whether to spend the time and money establishing Crummey trusts for children, it is important to do a complete analysis of how best to utilize your $11,000 annual gift exclusion per child ($22,000 for married individuals utilizing gift splitting). Assume, for instance, that a husband and wife have created one irrevocable life insurance trust for the purpose of holding a life insurance policy on the life of the husband. Assume also that the life insurance premiums being paid into this irrevocable trust are $11,000 per year. Further, in order to provide liquidity for the payment of estate taxes, the husband and wife have created a second-to-die life insurance trust that has an independent trustee. The husband and wife, as grantors of the second-to-die trust, contribute an additional $11,000 annually into the trust for the payment of premiums on the second-to-die policy.

Assuming that the husband and wife have two children, the maximum amount of money they can gift in accordance with the annual gift tax exclusion is $44,000 through gift splitting. They have already used $22,000 of their gift tax exclusion by virtue of funding the premiums for both life insurance trusts. Therefore, if the parents want to fund a Crummey trust for each of their children, the maximum amount they can contribute to each trust is $11,000 per year.

In the event that the life insurance premiums on either the life insurance policy insuring the husband or the second-to-die policy insuring the husband and wife vanish or are paid in full, then those transfers can be redirected into the Crummey trusts, allowing each trust to be funded with up to $22,000 per year gift tax free.

Qualified Tuition Programs (529 Plans)

The cost of putting children through college can be overwhelming. Accordingly, any help Congress can provide to ease this burden should be well received. Section 529 plans may be the most effective legislation Congress has enacted to enable parents to save for skyrocketing college costs. Qualified tuition programs, as authorized under Section 529 of the Internal Revenue Code, are programs established state by state for the purposes of investing for tuition as well as room and board expenses on a tax-advantaged basis. There are generally two programs: (1) the prepaid tuition plan program, as well as (2) the higher education savings account plan program. Under the prepaid tuition plan program, participants can make contributions to a qualified trust operated by either a state or a private institution that allows the participants to prepay tuition and fees at a particular institution. However, the more popular program involves the higher education savings account plans that allow participants to contribute to a state savings account that generally is managed by one or more mutual fund companies on behalf of a designated beneficiary (the college-bound student) and can be used at any higher education institution.

The amounts contributed to the savings plan grow tax free and can be used for tuition expenses, as well as reasonable room and board expenses at any college or other qualified learning institution. The donor of the account may choose among the mutual fund selections offered by the state. Another one of the principal benefits of a 529 plan is that there are no income limitations on the donor. An individual is not restricted from investing in a 529 plan if such individual's income is more than a certain amount, unlike other college savings vehicles such as the education IRA. Furthermore, a transfer from one account benefiting one designated beneficiary to another account benefiting another designated beneficiary is not taxable if the beneficiaries are members of the same family, including siblings and even first cousins.

Contributions to a 529 plan are treated as gifts to the named beneficiary for gift tax and generation-skipping transfer tax purposes. Accordingly, a donor's contribution can qualify for the annual $11,000 gift tax exclusion. Furthermore, for purposes of 529 plans, a donor can make a contribution of anywhere between $10,000 and $50,000 for a designated beneficiary in a single year and elect to treat the contribution as having been made over a five-year period. Thus, a married couple can contribute up to $100,000 to a 529 plan in a single year without any adverse gift tax consequences (including the reduction in their exemption equivalents). However, once such a gift has been made, the donor is prevented from utilizing the annual gift tax exclusion. Accordingly the 529 plan must be reviewed in conjunction with any existing irrevocable life insurance trusts which also require the utilization of the annual exclusion for the following five-year period.

Prior to the enactment of the Economic Growth and Tax Relief Reconciliation Act of 2001, as the money came out of a 529 plan it was subject to taxation at the beneficiary's tax rate. Furthermore, if the donor were to withdraw amounts for any purpose other than to pay for qualified tuition expenses, the state sponsor would impose a "more than *de minimis*" monetary penalty. Pursuant to the 2001 Tax Act, distributions from 529 plans are now excludable from gross income to the extent such distributions are used to pay for qualified higher education expenses for tax years beginning after December 31, 2001. Furthermore, if a withdrawal is made from a 529 plan for other than qualified higher education expenses, the penalty is now set at 10%. Thus, if the donor is required to withdraw funds for hardship or other purposes, the donor can determine the exact costs associated with such a withdrawal.

The 2001 Tax Act also revised the definition of eligible room and board and eliminated the dollar amount limitations on such expenses that were originally established. The original dollar amounts were very low and did not accurately reflect the actual cost of student housing. In effect for 2002, room and board costs are now defined as follows: (1) for students living at home with parents, an amount determined by the particular learning institution; (2) for students living in housing provided by the school, an amount based on what most of the school's residents are normally charged; and (3) for students not living in student housing, the amount of expenses "reasonably incurred" by students for room and board. It should be noted that the definition of qualified higher education expenses has also been expanded to include expenses of special needs beneficiaries necessary in connection with their attendance in particular institutions.

A 529 plan will be treated as an asset of the account owner (generally the parent) for student aid purposes and should be taken into consideration when calculating a student's eligibility for subsidized loans, work study programs, or other grants provided by federal or state governments or by the college itself. It also should be noted that like every other benefit provided under the 2001 Tax Act, the specific benefits are currently set to disappear for years beginning after December 31, 2010. Accordingly, if the 2001 Tax Act is allowed to expire, the provisions set forth in Section 529 prior to its enactment would be reinstated. This would include specifically the reinstatement of the provision that taxes amounts withdrawn from a 529 plan even if used for qualified higher education expenses; these amounts would be subject to taxation at the beneficiary's (i.e., the student's) tax rate.

Conclusion

A Uniform Gifts to Minors Act (UGMA) account, 2503(b) trust, 2503(c) trust, Crummey trust, and 529 plan each have advantages and disadvantages. The estate planning team should therefore review the purpose for transferring wealth to children, the children's apparent maturity levels, and the parents' asset base before choosing which, if any, tool should be utilized to make gifts to the children and how that tool should be incorporated into the estate plan.

Integrating Retirement Planning with Estate Planning

Introduction

During your wealth accumulation years, a substantial portion of that wealth may result from the accumulation of assets in tax-deferred accounts, including IRAs, 401(k) plans, as well as other qualified plans. It is not unusual for this wealth to grow during the wealth accumulation phase to the point where assets invested in qualified plans make up a substantial part of an individual's total asset base. One of the most common estate planning mistakes is failing to integrate this wealth with your estate plan.

During the wealth transference phase of one's life, the account owner should review the beneficiary designations of his or her qualified plan assets with the team of advisers. Through this review process, the account owner can maximize the income tax–deferral techniques provided within these plans and ensure that, upon his or her death, the plan assets will be transferred to the intended beneficiaries in the most tax-efficient manner possible. In some cases, utilizing trusts as intended beneficiaries may provide both estate tax benefits and nontax benefits, including the proper identification of the ultimate beneficiaries of the plan assets after both plan owner and spouse are gone. In order to determine the most appropriate beneficiary designation for you, and whether utilizing trusts may be advantageous in your particular situation, a review of the basic rules is required. These rules have long been considered too complex and inflexible, often leading to disastrous consequences for both IRA participants and their intended beneficiaries. As a result, on January 11, 2001, the IRS came out with newly proposed regulations designed to simplify the rules and reduce or alleviate much of the confusion resulting from the complexity of the prior system.

Required Beginning Date

Under the new IRA and retirement plan rules, you are still required to begin taking distributions starting on your "required beginning date." An IRA account owner's required beginning date is defined as April 1 of the calendar year following the year in which the owner attains age $70\frac{1}{2}$. For example, if Les Tupass was born on May 31, 1931, his required beginning date will be April 1, 2002. Under the prior rules, once Les reached the beginning date, he would have had to have calculated his required minimum distributions from his qualified assets using one of several complex formulas provided in the regulations. The amount of these required minimum distributions depended not only on his life expectancy but, in many cases, on the life expectancy of the account beneficiary. Thus, such amount could vary significantly depending on the formula chosen, as well as who was chosen as intended beneficiary or beneficiaries.

Lifetime Minimum Distributions

Under the new regulations, lifetime required minimum distributions are calculated each year based on a uniform table provided in the regulations. (See Table 10.1.) The account balance of the IRA owner at the end of each year is then divided by the applicable age-based factor in the table.

The only exception to this general rule is if the account owner has named his or her spouse as the sole beneficiary and such spouse is more than 10 years younger than the account owner. In such case, a separate table is used to calculate the minimum distributions.

Postdeath Distributions

If the owner of an IRA or retirement plan were to die prior to the end of the distribution payout period, the new set of rules has been designed to simplify the manner in which the remaining IRA or retirement fund balance will be

| | Distribution | | Distribution |
Age	Period	Age	Period
70	26.2	93	8.8
71	25.3	94	8.3
72	24.4	95	7.8
73	23.5	96	7.3
74	22.7	97	6.9
75	21.8	98	6.5
76	20.9	99	6.1
77	20.1	100	5.7
78	19.2	101	5.3
79	18.4	102	5.0
80	17.6	103	4.7
81	16.8	104	4.4
82	16.0	105	4.1
83	15.3	106	3.8
84	14.5	107	3.6
85	13.8	108	3.3
86	13.1	109	3.1
87	12.4	110	2.8
88	11.8	111	2.6
89	11.1	112	2.4
90	10.5	113	2.2
91	9.9	114	2.0
92	9.4	115 and older	1.8

TABLE 10.1   Lifetime Minimum Distributions

distributed to the owner's beneficiaries. First, if there is a named beneficiary, the distribution period is simply the remaining life expectancy of the beneficiary. If the account owner has failed to name a beneficiary and dies before the required beginning date of the minimum distributions, the account balance must be distributed within five years of the account owner's death unless one or more beneficiaries are named by December 31st of the year following the year in which the account owner dies. If the account owner dies after the required beginning date but has failed to name a beneficiary, the account balance will be distributed over what would have been the remaining life expectancy of the owner. If the designated beneficiary of the account

owner is his or her estate, the distributions will be made to the estate beneficiaries based on the owner's remaining life expectancy.

Beneficiary Designations

Under the old rules, the account owner had to designate his or her beneficiary
or beneficiaries prior to the required beginning date and could not change the
beneficiaries after such date once the required minimum distribution amounts
were established. Thus, even the account owner who did in fact change the actual beneficiaries of an IRA would still be required to take distributions in accordance with the original calculation (unless, of course, changing the
beneficiary designation decreased rather than extended the payout period, in
which case the beneficiary would be required to take distributions that would
be made over the shortened payout period).

Under the new regulations, a named beneficiary (such as a spouse) can disclaim all or a portion of an IRA in order to pass the benefits to children (or
even grandchildren) with longer life expectancies, thus stretching out the term
over which the IRA or retirement plan can be paid out. For instance, if Les Tupass died leaving a substantial balance in his IRA, and his wife, Hope, had no
need for the IRA distributions, she could disclaim her right to the IRA and
pass the IRA benefits to the Tupass children to enjoy over their lifetimes.

In addition to naming one or more individuals as beneficiaries, an account
owner can also name a trust as the beneficiary of his or her IRA or retirement
plan. As under the prior rules, if a trust is named as a beneficiary, the trust beneficiary can be treated as a designated beneficiary for purposes of the minimum distribution rules. Furthermore, unlike the old rules, the deadline for
providing proper trust documentation identifying the beneficiaries of the trust
is no longer nine months after the death of the account owner but rather the
end of the year following the year in which the account owner died.

Estate Planning with Retirement Plan Assets

As if the rules governing plan distributions from qualified plans are not complicated enough, you must also determine how you want to integrate your retirement plan assets into your estate plan. In this regard, you should begin to
consider the utilization of trusts as designated beneficiaries of the plan assets.
Two issues must be addressed in making this determination. The first issue is
whether the plan assets are necessary in order to fully fund an exemption
equivalent trust. The second issue is whether a qualified terminable interest
property (QTIP) trust can be utilized to preserve the qualified plan assets for

the surviving spouse, and upon the spouse's demise, distribute the assets to the account owner's children and/or other heirs.

Only individuals and beneficiaries of certain trusts will qualify as designated beneficiaries under a qualified plan. The law permits trusts to serve as designated beneficiaries if the following four requirements are met:

1. The trust must become irrevocable upon the death of the account owner.

2. The trust must be valid under state law.

3. The beneficiaries must be identifiable from the trust instrument itself.

4. A copy of the trust or certified list of the trust beneficiaries, as well as a description of their interests, must be provided to the plan custodian no later than the end of the year following the year in which the plan owner died.

In certain situations, naming an exemption equivalent trust under your will can serve a number of purposes. Assume Les and Hope Tupass are both 60 years old, happily married, and have two children. Les owns marketable securities of $500,000 and an IRA in the amount of $1.5 million. Inasmuch as Les's IRA names Hope as his designated beneficiary, if Les should die the IRA will pass to Hope, who in all likelihood will roll the IRA over into her own IRA. While this will defer the estate tax on the qualified plan through the use of the marital deduction, the only other asset that Les has in his taxable estate is the $500,000 investment management account. Therefore, if Les has not used any of his exemption equivalent in year 2002 (the exemption equivalent is $1 million in year 2002), he has used only $500,000 of his $1 million exemption, leaving $500,000 of assets subject to estate taxes upon Hope's demise.

In order to remedy this situation, Les Tupass should consider naming Hope as the beneficiary of his IRA and an exemption equivalent trust created under his will as the secondary beneficiary. Thus, if Les predeceases Hope, she would have the option of disclaiming up to $500,000 of Les's IRA. Should Hope opt to disclaim the $500,000, the assets would be payable to an exemption equivalent trust created under Les's will free from estate taxes upon Hope's death.

If Les Tupass had $1 million of marketable securities in his own name outside of his IRA, he would want to use those assets, rather than the IRA, to fund his exemption equivalent trust. This is because the trust must provide for all of the trust income, including income earned within the IRA, to be distributed to the surviving spouse with the greater of the income earned in the IRA or the required minimum distribution to be distributed from the IRA to the trust, at least annually. Ordinarily, the most prudent way to fund an exemption equivalent trust is with assets that you anticipate will appreciate because they will grow estate tax free.

Thus, the downside of a spouse disclaiming IRA assets to fully fund an exemption equivalent trust is that the trustee is required to remit to the spouse the greater of the income earned or the minimum distribution amount. Accordingly, the usual goal of encouraging capital growth within the exemption equivalent trust will be hindered by this minimum distribution requirement. However, if there are no other assets to fund the exemption equivalent trust, this technique should be considered.

Funding a QTIP Trust with Plan Assets

An individual who has children from a prior marriage (or marriages) may wish to provide a spouse with the benefit of receiving distributions from an IRA or qualified plan, but simultaneously ensure that, upon the surviving spouse's demise, the children from prior marriage(s) will be the ultimate beneficiaries of the IRA or 401(k) plan assets. If, however, a spouse is named as beneficiary, then upon the account owner's demise the spouse will have the benefit of receiving the qualified plan and may also have the ability to roll the account into the surviving spouse's own IRA, subsequently naming his or her own beneficiaries, which may or may not be the original account owner's children. In order to remedy this potential problem, an account owner may wish to consider utilizing a qualified terminable interest property (QTIP) trust as the beneficiary of the qualified plan.

Assume Les Tupass dies in year 2002 and is survived by his second wife, Hope, and two children from a prior marriage. A copy of the will, which contains a QTIP trust, and a list of the beneficiaries are provided to the custodian of the IRA within nine months following Les's death. The IRA will be includable in Les's estate for estate tax purposes. However, after conferring with the team of advisers, the executor of Les's will determines that it is in the best interest of all parties to transfer Les's IRA into the QTIP trust.

Because the trust requires that all of the trust income (including distributions from the IRA if contributed to the trust) be distributed to Hope at least annually, the trust may qualify for estate tax deferral under the marital deduction rules. The amount of the annual minimum distribution from the IRA required each year may be calculated by dividing the account balance of the IRA as of December 31 of the year preceding Les's death by the remaining distribution period. On Hope's death, any undistributed balance of the IRA will remain in the QTIP trust over the remaining distribution period and be distributed to the named beneficiaries of the trust rather than leaving the ultimate distribution of the IRA to Hope.

Charitable Remainder Trust

Perhaps your IRA or 401(k) plan contains a substantial amount of assets but is not a significant part of your estate plan. For instance, assume Les's estate is valued at $7 million and of that amount $2.5 million is in an IRA. Assume further that Hope has either predeceased Les or has no need for his IRA assets. In an effort to reduce the tax exposure, and provide a stream of income to loved ones while at the same time providing for his favorite charity, Les may opt to name either the charity or a charitable remainder trust as the beneficiary of his IRA. By so doing, he will reduce if not eliminate the income tax that would otherwise be due upon the distribution of the IRA assets, and the estate will be entitled to a charitable deduction to the extent of the interest belonging to the charity. As a result of this type of charitable planning, the estate will be entitled to a charitable deduction, income tax liability will be reduced, a stream of income to loved ones can be guaranteed, and a charitable cause is funded. Truly a win-win-win.

If the account owner has designated more than one beneficiary, the general rule is that the distributions must be made over the life expectancy of the oldest beneficiary. However, this rule can be sidestepped by creating separate accounts. Furthermore, an account owner can name a charity or a charitable trust as a beneficiary of one or more IRA accounts. Thus, if the account owner has named multiple beneficiaries, one of which is a charity or charitable trust, the account allocated to the charity can be "cashed out" and the charity share can be distributed to the charity by the end of the year following the year in which the account owner died so that the distributions to the other beneficiaries will not be affected.

Conclusion

Integrating retirement assets with an estate plan requires the consideration of the following seven factors:

1. The account owner's cash needs during retirement.

2. The age of the account owner.

3. Whether there is a spouse, and if so the spouse's age.

4. If there is a spouse, the spouse's income needs.

5. Whether there is a second spouse, and if so whether there are children from a prior marriage.

6. Whether the account owner is charitably inclined.

7. If there is no spouse, the ages of the intended beneficiaries.

All of these factors should be considered with the estate planning team in order to determine the most tax-efficient method of distributing the assets while simultaneously ensuring that the wealth transference that is being effected is in accordance with the account owner's intent. Only after these factors have been thoroughly analyzed can the account owner determine whether a trust should be incorporated into one's retirement and estate plans.

CHAPTER

11

Charitable Planning

Introduction

Paying estate taxes is optional. Charitable planning is often referred to as the "silver bullet" because the combination of reducing tax exposure, guaranteeing a stream of income, and providing for a charitable cause can satisfy and balance the need for self-preservation with an altruistic desire.

If you are not charitably inclined, you may be after completing this chapter. If any one of the following considerations applies to you, then charitable planning should be considered in the creation of your estate plan:

■ You have an asset base that includes highly appreciated securities paying low dividends and you have a desire to liquidate the holdings to generate greater cash flow but a hesitancy to do so due to the capital gains tax exposure.

■ You have substantial amounts of wealth in qualified plans such as IRAs and 401(k)s and are concerned about both the estate tax liability and income tax liability on the qualified plans.

■ You want to reduce income tax liability.

■ You want to reduce estate tax liability.

- You would like to supplement your or your family's cash flow in the form of fixed payments over the course of years or for their lifetimes.

- You have a genuine desire to want to help charities and perhaps to have children or loved ones participating in helping the social causes near and dear to you.

Common Forms of Charitable Planning

Charitable planning can be accomplished either during one's lifetime or at death. If charitable planning is utilized during one's lifetime, an income tax deduction is available, while if charitable planning is used at death, an estate tax deduction is available. The most common forms of charitable planning include the following:

1. Outright gifts to charity during one's lifetime.

2. An inter vivos or testamentary charitable remainder annuity trust (CRAT).

3. An inter vivos or testamentary charitable remainder unitrust (CRUT).

4. An inter vivos or testamentary charitable lead annuity trust (CLAT).

5. An inter vivos or testamentary charitable lead unitrust (CLUT).

6. A private family foundation.

7. Qualified plans passing to a charitable trust.

These planning tools may be used individually or melded together to accomplish numerous objectives. Accomplishing these objectives should be undertaken after counsel with the cabinet of advisers to design a plan that accomplishes your objective.

Outright Gifts to Charity During One's Lifetime

An outright gift can be made during one's lifetime, in which case the donor receives an income tax deduction. Alternatively, an individual can create an outright bequest to a charity in one's will and the estate will be entitled to an estate tax deduction.

Charitable Remainder Annuity Trust

An inter vivos (during one's lifetime) or testamentary (at death) charitable remainder annuity trust is one that can be created either during one's lifetime to receive an income tax deduction or at death to receive an estate tax deduction.

An individual donates property to the charitable remainder annuity trust during his or her lifetime or at death. The trust asset is then valued, and a fixed percentage of the fair market value of the trust assets will be remitted to non-charitable beneficiaries at least annually. The annual payout must be at least 5% of the initial net fair market value of the trust. The term of the trust may be for one or more beneficiaries' lifetimes or for a term but not to exceed 20 years. At the expiration of the lifetime, lifetimes, or term, the trust will terminate and the trust assets will be paid over to the charitable organization.

A charitable remainder annuity trust includes the word "annuity" because the noncharitable beneficiaries will receive a fixed percentage of the fair market value of the assets during the term, and that amount will remain fixed regardless of whether the account appreciates or depreciates. Since the trust is valued only once at inception, no subsequent contributions may be made into the charitable remainder annuity trust. Since the payment is a fixed annuity, it is more frequently utilized when the noncharitable beneficiary may require a fixed income stream to live on as opposed to payments that vary as the trust assets fluctuate.

Charitable Remainder Unitrust

An inter vivos or testamentary charitable remainder unitrust is also one that can be set up during one's lifetime or at death. However, unlike the charitable remainder annuity trust, a charitable remainder unitrust will require the trustee to value the assets every year. After the assets are valued, a fixed percentage of not less than 5% of the fair market value of the trust assets must be paid to the noncharitable beneficiary.

Accordingly, the trustee of the charitable remainder unitrust will value the assets once each year and then pay a fixed percentage of the fair market value of the trust assets for that year to the noncharitable beneficiary. Each succeeding year during the trust term, the trust assets will be revalued and the trustee will remit the fixed percentage of the fair market value of the assets to the noncharitable beneficiaries for that year, and so on through the life of the trust. If the assets appreciate, the income stream will increase. Conversely, if the assets depreciate, the income stream will decrease.

Unlike a charitable remainder annuity trust, a charitable remainder unitrust is permitted to receive additional contributions so long as the trust-governing instrument allows for additional contributions and has a formula for determining the contribution, generally on a prorated calendar year and as a percentage.

There are several variations within the charitable remainder unitrust category, such as net income charitable remainder trusts, net income makeup charitable remainder unitrusts, and flip unitrusts.

A net income charitable remainder unitrust (NICRUT) provides that in the years where the charitable remainder unitrust net income is less than the required annual payout, the trustee pays the lesser amount of the net income or the regular annual payment without recovery in later years.

Conversely, a net income makeup charitable remainder unitrust (NIMCRUT) is similar to a NICRUT, but provides that in years that the net income exceeds the unitrust required payout, the excess income can make up for any prior years in which the unitrust amount was not fully paid due to insufficient income.

Another variation is the flip unitrust. This technique may begin as a NICRUT or NIMCRUT, but upon a date specified in the trust document or upon a triggering event, it converts to a straight charitable remainder unitrust. For example, if you contribute unmarketable securities that produce minimal income until sold, upon a sale (the trigger event), a one-time conversion to a CRUT is permitted. Permissible triggering events are marriage, divorce, death, birth of a child, or sale of an unmarketable asset.

The Taxpayer Relief Act of 1997 also requires that a charitable remainder trust cannot have a payout greater than 50% of its fair market value for charitable remainder trusts created after June 18, 1997. Additionally, the value of the remainder interest for the benefit of the charity must be determined on the day the charitable remainder trust is created and must be at least 10% of the value of the property contributed. The reason these two limitations were placed on charitable remainder trusts is that over the years taxpayers have used charitable remainder trusts so as to avail themselves of the ability to sell appreciated assets without the imposition of capital gains tax while at the same time receiving the assets back, requiring the trustee to pay 50% of the fair market value of the trust to the grantor every year. Such planning was determined by the IRS to be abusive, thus the imposition of these rules.

Capital Gains Treatment of Trusts Created Inter Vivos

When appreciated assets are transferred to an irrevocable inter vivos charitable remainder trust, the trustee can sell the trust assets without incurring any tax on the capital gain. Accordingly, this is attractive for individuals who have highly appreciated securities but are receiving little income yield from these securities. Accordingly, after such assets are contributed to a charitable remainder trust, the assets can be sold and reinvested in assets that have a more significant income yield. This is especially attractive for an individual who has a portfolio that consists in part of highly appreciated securities, when one may not want to sell the assets and incur the capital gains tax. An inter vivos charitable remainder trust enables the trustee to sell the appreciated securities and pay income tax only on the income received. If, however, the income is insufficient to meet the required payout, then capital gains tax may be realized, but only to the extent paid out.

Charitable Lead Trust

A charitable lead trust is essentially the inverse of a charitable remainder trust. Utilizing an inter vivos charitable lead trust, the donor can transfer property to the trust, which requires the trustee to pay out a percentage of the fair market value of the trust to the charity first for a term of years or for the life or lives of individual(s). At the end of the term, the charity's interest ceases and the trust assets are then distributable to the donor or the donor's heirs as provided in the trust document.

If created during one's lifetime, the charitable contribution income tax deduction is available only when the donor is treated as owner and is taxable on the trust income that is paid to the charity. Accordingly, trustees may invest the trust assets in tax-exempt securities. A charitable lead trust, like a charitable remainder trust, may be either an annuity trust or a unitrust. Charitable lead trusts do not need to meet the 5% payout rules applicable to charitable remainder trusts.

Private Family Foundations

Individuals can transfer property either during their lifetimes, at death through their wills, or as beneficiary of a charitable remainder trust to a private family foundation. Advantages of a private foundation are that the donor may retain control of the foundation during his or her lifetime, and at death provide for a board of trustees to operate the foundation in accordance with a mission statement written by the donor.

Private foundations have proven to be an attractive planning tool for individuals who would like their family members to continue to perpetuate both the charitable interests of the donor and the donor's legacy. A private foundation must devote most of its earnings and assets directly to the conduct of its intended charitable purposes.

Qualified Plans

Qualified plans such as IRAs and 401(k)s are subject to income tax exposure. This tax is known as income in respect to decedent (IRD) and is triggered upon the death of the account owner in the event such individual dies without having received the income and paid the tax. Since such assets are ultimately subject to both estate tax and IRD, it is often advantageous to designate a charity as the beneficiary of an IRA or other qualified plan, thereby both creating an estate tax deduction and avoiding the income in respect to decedent. Accordingly, since there is no IRD and the charitable bequest may be fully deductible for estate tax purposes, it is an attractive estate planning technique.

Alternatively, assets such as IRAs or 401(k)s that would otherwise trigger the income in respect to decedent may name the beneficiary of the account to be a charitable remainder trust. Since there will be no IRD, the noncharitable beneficiaries of the charitable remainder trust may actually receive more income than if the qualified plan had passed outright to them without a charitable trust. Why? Because the dollars that would otherwise have had to go for both estate taxes and IRD taxes could be reinvested within the trust and be included as a percentage of the payout to the noncharitable beneficiaries.

Qualifying Charities

The Internal Revenue Code Section 170(a) provides guidelines for the charitable contribution income tax deduction for payment to some types of charities. To qualify as a "public charity" the organization must be one of the following:

- A church, a convention, or an association of churches.

- An educational organization with a regularly scheduled curriculum, a regular faculty, and enrolled students, including primary, secondary and postsecondary institutions; colleges and universities; early childhood centers; and trade schools.

- A hospital organized as a not-for-profit organization and created for the purpose of operating a facility for the care of the sick.

- A community chest, corporation trust fund, or foundation intended for charitable, religious, educational, scientific, or literary purposes; for the prevention of cruelty to animals or children; or to foster amateur sports competition.

- A governmental unit.

- A publicly supported organization.

Once it is determined that the organization you intend to contribute to is in fact a charity, it is important to determine whether the charity is a public charity or a private foundation. This determination will affect both the income tax deduction and the estate tax deduction in accordance with Table 11.1.

TABLE 11.1 Charitable Contribution Deduction Limitations

Type of Property (1)	Donee (2)	Valuation Limitation (3)	Donee (4)	Valuation Limitation (5)	Individual Carryover (6)	Tax Treatment (7)
		Percentage Limitation				
(A) Cash	Public charity	50%	Private foundation	30%	5 years	Full deduction
(B) Long-term capital gain property (except for tangible personal property)	Public charity	30% or 50%*	Private foundation	20%	5 years	Full deduction for fair market value (gain is a tax preference)
(C) Ordinary income property	Public charity	50%	Private foundation	30%	5 years	Deduction limited to basis
(D) Tangible personal property						
(1) Use-related	Public charity	30%	Private foundation	30%	5 years	Full deduction for fair market value
(2) Use unrelated to exempt purposes of donee	Public charity	50%	Private foundation	50%	5 years	Deduction limited to adjusted basis

*The 50% deduction limitation applies only if donor makes election and reduces the deductible amount by amount of gain donor would realize if property were sold at fair market value.

How Do You Determine the Amount of the Charitable Deduction?

The amount of the charitable contribution deduction that will be allowed for income tax purposes depends on five factors, as follows:

1. *Type of property given away.* Types of property include cash, long-term capital gain property, ordinary income property, and tangible personal property.

2. *What type of organization you are gifting to.* It may be either a public charity or a nonpublic charity, often referred to as a private charity or private foundation. Table 11.1 illustrates in detail how to determine the applicable percentage for charitable deductions for both a public charity and a private foundation.

3. *Identity of the donor.* If the donor is an individual, the deduction would be limited to specific percentages of the individual's contribution base; if a corporation, limited to a deduction based on the percentage of its taxable income.

4. *Amount of property given away.* Both individuals or corporations may carry over contributions over their deductible limits for up to five years.

5. *Place where the contribution is used.* More specifically, gifts made to a U.S. charity are treated more charitably than gifts to most foreign charities.

The deduction limitations are referenced in Table 11.1. In reviewing Table 11.1, you will note that cash, long-term capital gain property, ordinary income property, and tangible personal property are treated differently for deduction limitation purposes. The treatment as to the most common types of property contributed is as follows.

Cash

If cash is contributed by a donee to a public charity, the deduction ceiling is 50% of the individual taxpayer's contribution base or 30% if to a private foundation. Contributions by individuals to either charitable entity in excess of the deductible limit for the taxable year may be carried over a period of up to five years. However, a full deduction of up to the percentage limitation—50% of the contribution base for individuals who itemize deductions—is allowed for gifts of cash.

Long-Term Capital Gain Property

Intangible personal property such as stocks and all real property held for the long-term period may not exceed 30% of your contribution base if gifted to a public charity or 20% of your contribution base if gifted to a private foundation. If the gift exceeds this limitation, you may carry the excess deduction over up to five years, including up to the full fair market value of the gift. However, to the extent the excess of the value of the capital gain over and above its basis may be considered an item of tax preference, the alternative minimum tax must be considered.

Finally, you have an election to make with respect to the deduction limitations. The 30% limit can be increased to 50% if you are willing to reduce the value of the gift by potential gain, essentially basis. This election may prove beneficial either when your income fluctuates from year to year or when the amount of appreciation is small.

Ordinary Income Property

Ordinary income property is composed of:

- Assets held less than the requisite long-term period at the time contributed.

- Certain stock dividends.

- Works of art, books, letters, and musical compositions, but only if gifted by the person who created them or prepared them or for whom they were prepared.

- A businessperson's stock-in-trade and inventory that would result in ordinary income if sold.

Ordinary income that is given to a public charity by an individual is deductible subject to a 50% contribution base and is limited to 30% if given to a private foundation. However, the deduction limitation for ordinary income is generally limited to the donor's basis for the property (unless a corporation gifts to a charity or private foundation for use in its exempt purpose for the care of the ill, the needy, or infants).

Tangible Personal Property

Tangible personal property includes items such as cars, jewelry, sculpture, books, and artwork. Such gifts are entitled to either a 30% deduction or a 50% deduction, depending on use. If the tangible personal property gifted will be used to further the cause of the charity, one can deduct up to 30% of adjusted gross income and deduct the full fair market value of the asset. If, however, the tangible personal property gifted is unrelated to the charity's purpose, then the donor can deduct 50% of the taxpayer's contribution base or adjusted gross income, although the deduction is limited to basis.

A Win-Win-Win

Since the preceding substantive analysis doesn't illustrate the economic virtues of charitable planning, perhaps the following illustration will. Assume our heroe's, Veri and Jen Oriss, both age 70, seek to very generously provide for their three daughters, Ruby, Saffire, and Pearl, ages 50, 48, and 46. While all three daughters have accumulated substantial asset bases themselves, Veri and Jen want to supplement their retirement funds, reduce their estate tax liability, and provide for their favorite charity, Greenpeace. The couple's assets are summarized in Table 11.2.

Their federal estate tax liability in year 2002, assuming no estate planning, is $5,430,000, as shown in Figure 11.1.

However, if deathtime exemption equivalent trusts are utilized, and the life insurance is not deemed viable and is replaced in a life insurance trust, the estate tax is reduced to $3,930,000, as shown in Figure 11.2. A savings for sure, but not enough.

If the Orisses passed $5 million through a testamentary charitable remainder unitrust to run for 15 years while paying 7% of the trust's fair market value as determined annually to their daughters, the estate tax liability will be reduced to $3,262,035 and Greenpeace will ultimately receive $5,000,959, as shown in Figure 11.3. Ruby, Saffire, and Pearl, however, don't yet see this plan as a real gem. After all, their parents are giving away their rightful inheritance. A closer examination reveals that this plan is not just any gem, it's flawless. Here's why.

TABLE 11.2　The Orisses' Asset Base		
Asset	**Title**	**Value**
Home	Tenants by the entirety	$1,000,000
Stocks, bonds, mutual funds	Joint tenants	$8,000,000
Life insurance	Husband to wife	$2,000,000
Treasuries	Joint	$500,000
Vacation home	Joint	$500,000
Total		$12,000,000

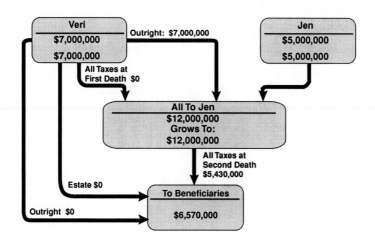

For: Oriss, Veri & Jen

No Tax Planning

	Death Tax Detail		
		Veri	Jen
Federal tentative tax	$	0	$ 5,775,800
Unified credit + gift tax paid	(	345,800)	(345,800)
State death tax credit	(	0)	(1,040,100)
Other credits	(	0)	(0)
Net federal tax	$	0	$ 4,389,900
NY state tax		0	1,040,100
Income tax on retirement plans		0	0
Generation-skipping transfer tax		0	0
Total tax	$	0	$ 5,430,000
TOTAL TAX FOR BOTH DEATHS:			$ 5,430,000

FIGURE 11.1

Reproduced with permission from CCH Incorporated, 2700 Lake Cook Road, Riverwoods, Illinois 60015.

For: Oriss, Veri & Jen

Exemption Equivalent and Irrevocable Trust Planning

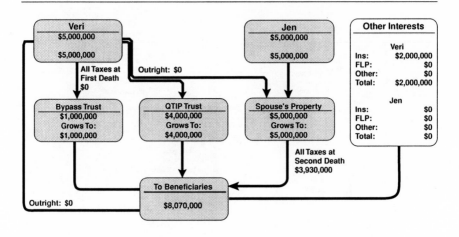

	Tax Detail		
	Veri		**Jen**
Gifts to beneficiaries	$ 2,000,000		0
Total gift tax paid through life	0		0
	Death Tax Detail		
	Veri		**Jen**
Federal tentative tax	$ 345,800	$	4,275,800
Unified credit + gift tax paid	(345,800	(	345,800)
State death tax credit	(0)	(	687,300)
Other credits	(0)	(	0)
Net federals tax	$ 0	$	3,242,700
NY state sax	0		687,300
Income tax on retirement plans	0		0
Generation-skipping transfer tax	0		0
Total tax	$ 0	$	3,930,000
TOTAL TAX FOR BOTH DEATHS:		$	3,930,000

FIGURE 11.2

Reproduced with permission from CCH Incorporated, 2700 Lake Cook Road, Riverwoods, Illinois 60015.

For: Veri and Jen Oriss

Scenario: Unitrust
Gift Date: At Second Death
Duration: Term Only—Years: 15

Value of Gift $5,000,000
Payout Rate: 7.0%
AFR: 5.6%

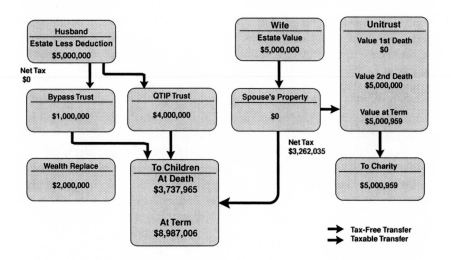

FIGURE 11.3

Reproduced with permission from CCH Incorporated, 2700 Lake Cook Road, Riverwoods, Illinois 60015.

Reduction in Children's Estate Tax Liability

Assume the Orisses will live their actuarial life span of another combined 14 years. When the charitable remainder unitrust is funded upon the death of the second spouse, Ruby will be age 64 , Saffire age 62 , and Pearl age 60 . The three have all seen their respective asset bases double twice. Now having estate tax issues themselves, they realize that incorporating their parents' assets (less estate taxes paid) into their estates will only subject the assets to estate taxation again in their estates at their respective deaths. This simply doesn't make sense.

Increased Cash Flow

Then they realize the second practical benefit. If they did inherit Mom and Dad's assets, reduced by estate taxes, what would they do with the assets? Answer: They generally would invest in the stock market and either take dividends and income or simply reinvest the yield. Having been advised by their financial planner that dividend income of 2% and growth of 7% has historic support, they realize the 2% dividend income does little to supplement their lifestyles while the 7% growth is just compounding their projected estate tax liabilities.

The virtues of the testamentary CRUT begin to shine (see Figure 11.4). Now Ruby, Saffire, and Pearl receive 7% of the fair market value of the trust principal every year ($5 million subject to market adjustments every year) for 15 years! Distributions of $350,000 a year for 15 years or $5,250,000 as income will surely supplement their retirement funds. Additionally, the daughters will receive the exemption equivalent trust plus growth from the trust created under the will of the first parent to die, the exemption equivalent amount from the estate of the second deceased parent, plus the life insurance trust, all estate tax free.

Now Veri and Jen secure a significant estate tax deduction—they win; the daughters will receive a substantial income stream for 15 years—they win; and Greenpeace preserves our oceans for generations to come—we win.

Conclusion

How much is enough? That is, charitable trusts are generally not utilized when the estate tax can be eliminated by virtue of the exemption equivalent and/or the utilization of annual exclusions. But, assume that one has an asset base not of $2 million (the exemption equivalent amount for both husband and wife), but rather $10 million or $20 million or more. If an individual has two children, how much is enough?

One of the fears of passing one's entire wealth base to children is that re-

For: Veri and Jen Oriss

Scenario: Unitrust
Gift Date: At Second Death
Duration: Term Only—Years: 15

Value of Gift: $5.000,000
Payout Rate: 7.0%
AFR: 5.6%

Primary Flowchart

Donor makes a gift of $5,000,000 to unitrust.

Donor(s)

To Unitrust

Trust returns payments of 7.00% of trust to income beneficiaries each year.

Payments to income beneficiaries

Donor(s) are entitled to a tax deduction of $1,787,210.

Charitable Deduction

Remainder to Greenpeace

At end of unitrust term, all remaining trust passes to Greenpeace.

FIGURE 11.4

Reproduced with permission from CCH Incorporated, 2700 Lake Cook Road, Riverwoods, Illinois 60015.

ceiving such large amounts of money may take away the "eye of the tiger," since many successful individuals believe that much of their success may be attributable to that insatiable hunger for success and the lucrative benefit that attaining such success may yield. Removing such a carrot from one's children's future could potentially hinder their growth and maturity.

Accordingly, when considering charitable trusts, many individuals find both the income tax and the estate tax benefits attractive, but also appreciate the fact that their beneficiaries or heirs may receive only a fixed percentage of the assets for a term of years or a lifetime. Such an amount would not, in effect, take the eye out of the tiger but rather could be used for the basics of life such as food, clothing, shelter, education, and health. Loved ones must earn their keep, not live off inherited wealth.

Additionally, when balancing the priorities between wealth transference and encouraging one's heirs to continue to grow and succeed as individuals, the percentage of the payout to the noncharitable beneficiary and the term of years can be altered so as to both affect the income and/or estate tax deductions and set the amount of the payments to your heirs. As a general principle, the longer your heirs' interest or the higher the percentage of the fair market value paid to your heirs, the smaller the income or estate tax deduction. Conversely, the shorter the trust's term for heirs and the smaller the percentage of the payout to your heirs, the larger the income or estate tax deduction.

Charitable planning either may be just a part of the entire estate plan or, for larger estates, may serve as the cornerstone to the estate plan. These most difficult and personal decisions must be made with a cabinet of advisers in order to ensure that your income tax deductions are appropriate to your adjusted gross income so that no deductions are lost, and that the income stream of an inter vivos charitable tool used is appropriate for your needs or that on a testamentary basis the estate tax deduction is appropriate for the estate's needs. Charitable planning may truly be the silver bullet and one of the most important facets of creating an individual's estate or business succession plan.

Supplemental Needs Trusts

A family seeking to provide for a loved one who is mentally or physically challenged generally has two major fears: (1) the fear that the assets set aside for the disabled beneficiary will wind up going directly to a health care facility and never really benefit the loved one, and (2) the fear that the assets set aside for the disabled loved one may inadvertently disqualify him or her from any benefits that would otherwise be provided through federal, state, or local governmental agencies.

Unfortunately, as a result of these fears, the parents may do nothing, or worse, they may decide to cut off the disabled beneficiary from inheriting any assets at all. Parents may hope that their other children will pool their resources and assume responsibility for their disabled sibling. It may work, but it's a hope, not a viable plan. With proper planning, however, disabled individuals can still enjoy assets left to them, still remain eligible for governmental assistance, and benefit from the support system established to see the plan through.

For most people, the very idea of disinheriting a disabled child in order to preserve governmental medical benefits is simply unacceptable. However, the parents (as well as other benefactors) of a disabled loved one need to structure their estate plans so that they will not jeopardize the disabled beneficiary's access to governmental medical assistance benefits. Proper planning can preserve the governmental benefits while simultaneously providing comprehensive asset management of any assets gifted to the disabled child in order to complement such governmental programs, provided the necessary steps are taken during the parents' lives.

A supplemental needs trust is one such planning tool. A supplemental needs trust is a discretionary trust created either during a parent's lifetime or by a testamentary trust created by a will. The trust document directs the trustee to use the trust income and/or principal for the benefit of the disabled individual, but only for those purposes not already covered by public assistance programs.

In fact, the supplemental needs provided for by the trust may be restricted to those needs that make life more enjoyable for the disabled beneficiary. In such situations, the trust document can be drafted to provide that trust assets can be used only for expenditures not considered basic necessities otherwise covered by federal, state, and local government programs. In this regard, the trustee can exercise discretion to apply trust funds for such expenditures as travel, recreation, training programs, summer camps, education, and so on, but be prohibited from expending trust assets on services already provided through a governmental agency.

For example, if a beneficiary does not have the ability to walk or use one's extremities, the trustee could invade the trust principal for the purpose of purchasing a computer with voice recognition capacity to draft letters, play games, or bring the outside world to the beneficiary through the Internet. In so doing, the trustee could provide the beneficiary with activities not otherwise covered by governmental funds without jeopardizing the beneficiary's right to governmental assistance.

Safeguarding the Trust

The trust instrument must be carefully drafted. Primarily, it must not provide the trustee with any powers that would allow him or her to direct trust income or principal for the purpose of providing the beneficiary with benefits that could overlap those benefits funded through governmental agencies. If the trustee were directed to use trust assets for items such as food, clothing, or shelter, the trust could jeopardize those same benefits that would otherwise be provided by governmental agencies.

Ordinarily, the trust document for a supplemental needs trust should provide a definition of the special needs of the disabled beneficiary and prohibit the trustee from making any distributions that would jeopardize governmental benefits specific to an individual possessing that type of disability. Furthermore, the trust document can provide for the use of any and all such programs for such individual. In this regard, the trust document should direct the trustee to utilize whatever benefits are offered through public agencies such as supplemental security income (SSI) and Medicaid for the disabled beneficiary.

Medicaid

Medicaid regulations provide that income and resources are considered available both when actually available and when the applicant or recipient has a legal interest in a liquidated sum and has the legal ability to make such sum available for support and maintenance. However, the federal Medicaid statute, Title XIX of the Social Security Act, 42 U.S.C. Section 1396 (1982), does not require that states withhold public funds from a mentally or physically disabled person simply because a trust has been set up for that person's benefit. Rather, the federal Medicaid statutes provide that state law governs the availability of public funds provided through the federal Medicaid program.

Under most state benefits laws, the state can deny medical assistance benefits based on a determination that trust assets are available resources. For example, if the trust language authorizes the trustee to invade the income and/or principal of the trust in such a way that the beneficiary is deemed to possess assets in excess of the income and resource availability levels set forth in the Medicaid provisions, benefits could be denied in whole or in part. Accordingly, specific language must be inserted in the supplemental needs trust document to ensure that the trust assets will not be characterized as available resources for Medicaid programs.

Sources of Funding

A variation of the supplemental needs trust is a special needs trust. If the source of funds to establish the trust already belongs to the disabled person, perhaps as a result of assets gifted to the individual, accumulated during the individual's working years prior to the onset of the disability, or as the result of a personal injury action against the party that may have caused the disability, a special needs trust should be created. If the source of funds to establish the trust is from parents or other benefactors of the disabled person, a supplemental needs trust should be created. The distinction between these two sources has important ramifications in how the trust will be treated under federal law.

In the case of a trust created with the assets of the disabled person (a special needs trust), federal law provides that the trust will not disqualify that person from government assistance if specific conditions are met:

- The trust contains the assets of an individual under age 65 who is disabled. An individual is considered disabled if he or she is unable to engage in any substantial gainful activity by reason of any medically determinable physical or mental impairment that can be expected to result in death and which has lasted, or can be expected to last, for a continuous period of not less than 12 months or in the case of a child under the age of 18, if he or she suffers from any medically determinable physical or mental impairment of comparable severity.

- The trust was originally established for the benefit of the disabled individual by a parent, grandparent, legal guardian of the individual, or court, but is currently treated as assets of the disabled person.

- The state will receive all amounts remaining in the trust upon the death of such disabled individual up to an amount equal to the total medical assistance paid on behalf of the individual under a state plan.

A special needs trust that meets these conditions can provide for the needs of the disabled beneficiary without jeopardizing governmental funding. The trust may continue even after the beneficiary attains age 65, but the trust cannot be added to or otherwise augmented after the disabled beneficiary attains age 65.

When a supplemental needs trust is established by a third party with assets that never belonged to the disabled beneficiary, the applicable rules are different, and the trust must be carefully drafted to avoid any pitfalls.

- The trust should grant broad discretion to the trustee rather than providing for mandatory distributions for categories such as health, maintenance, or support, or for specific items such as clothing or shelter.

- The trustee should be directed to make distributions only for extras that are not supplied by governmental programs, such as travel, vacations, and similar items.

- It is also advisable that there be a specific expression of the grantor's intent that the income and principal be used only to supplement public benefits, and that the trustee cannot in any way utilize the income or principal of the trust in such a manner as to overlap with or supplant public benefits.

- Finally, a supplemental needs trust should contain an escape clause that will terminate the trust and distribute the assets to the disabled beneficiary's siblings (or charity if there are no living family members) if there is any serious risk that the government agency will force the trustee to invade the trust and deny the disabled beneficiary the benefits of such programs.

In this manner, if the trust document is carefully drafted the assets will be available to help benefit the disabled beneficiary without disqualifying him or her from governmental benefits.

Choosing a Testamentary Trust

When creating an estate plan that will benefit a disabled child, parents frequently utilize a testamentary supplemental needs trust as part of their wills. By utilizing a testamentary supplemental needs trust, the parents will be able to provide for their disabled child after they are gone; the trust will ensure that a support system has been put in place for their disabled loved one.

With respect to funding a testamentary supplemental needs trust, the question arises as to how much of the parents' estates should be held in trust for the benefit of the disabled beneficiary when compared to amounts to be left to the disabled beneficiary's siblings. While there is no right or wrong answer to this question, it is not unusual for parents ultimately to distribute their estates in equal shares to their children. Assets that pass to or for the benefit of the disabled child will pass through the supplemental needs trust with the remaining amounts passing to the disabled child's siblings.

Parents may also wish to determine the percentage of their estate that should pass to the supplemental needs trust by backing into an equation of need. In this manner they can determine how much money is required annually to support the disabled child and provide a sum of money which, when multiplied by a specific return (e.g., 7%), would generate the amount necessary to continue this level of benefits. The remaining assets in the parents' estates would then be left to the disabled child's siblings.

For example, if a disabled child requires $30,000 a year, the parents could fund a supplemental needs trust with approximately $430,000. If this sum were invested to yield 7%, the trustee would then have sufficient income to continue the financial support of the disabled child with access to principal, if necessary, for emergencies. The remaining estate (as well as the remainder interest in the trust) could then be left to the disabled child's siblings. As discussed earlier, however, it is important that the trust not direct that all income be distributed to the disabled person, because that could result in disqualification from government benefits. This method is appropriate only for the purpose of determining the amount to fund the trust; the trust instrument must give the trustee the discretion in determining how much of the income or principal should be distributed.

Problems may arise when the amount of money necessary to provide such a cash flow is significantly greater than the percentage of the estate that would go to the disabled child's siblings. In these situations, the parents might consider the use of an irrevocable life insurance trust to fund all or a portion of the disabled child's needs. In this manner, the trustee could purchase a life insurance policy for the entire amount needed (or a lesser amount if additional assets were available partially to fund the special needs trust) with the death benefit payable to the supplemental needs trust. The trustee, at his or her discretion, could utilize the income and/or principal for the disabled child's needs subject to the terms of the trust document, and the remaining assets of the parents' estates, devisable by will, could then pass to the other siblings without controversy.

The mere establishment of a testamentary supplemental needs trust does not reduce the size of the parents' estates for estate tax purposes. A supplemental needs trust, created on a testamentary basis, will be subject to estate taxes in the same manner as if the parents had left money outright to the disabled child. However, a testamentary supplemental needs trust may be funded out of, or as part of, an exemption equivalent trust, which would be exempt from estate taxes. Also, the creation of a supplemental needs trust as an irrevocable life insurance trust, funded with a second-to-die life insurance policy, would completely remove the trust proceeds from the parents' taxable estates, and, therefore, would have the benefit of estate tax exclusion, as well as providing for the needs of the disabled child.

Trustees

Another issue that merits serious consideration in the creation of a supplemental needs trust is who should be named as trustee. Parents should consider the disabled child's siblings, relatives, trusted family advisers or corporate fiduciaries. However, in deciding who should serve as trustee, the parents must recognize that a supplemental needs trust confers a broad range of discretion upon the trustee. There are potential land mines every time a trustee makes a distribution. An individual trustee unfamiliar with the uniqueness of a supplemental needs trust may inadvertently make a distribution deemed to be a basic need, rather than a supplemental need, thus exposing the trust income and/or principal to the claims of a governmental agency.

The trustee must know the disabled beneficiary and be aware of the particular needs of the beneficiary. Naming a corporate fiduciary (a bank or trust company) as cotrustee, together with an individual cotrustee, may provide the best of both worlds. An individual named by the parents as a trustee will presumably be familiar with the unique needs of the disabled beneficiary and will be in a position to provide the warmth and personal attention that the beneficiary will need after the parents are gone. However, the asset allocation, tax reporting, and distribution requirements require financial skills and a degree of objectivity that the individual may not possess.

Therefore, by creating a cotrustee relationship between an individual and a corporate trustee, the parents will have provided for the emotional love and support that the disabled beneficiary will need, as well as the asset management skills and tax advice the trust will require to operate on a day-to-day basis. Accordingly, such a cotrustee relationship between an individual trustee and the trust department of a well-respected financial institution should provide the beneficiary with a trust administration team capable and desirous of working together for the common cause—helping one in need.

CHAPTER

13

Qualified Personal Residence Trust

A qualified personal residence trust (QPRT) is a type of trust designed to provide a tax-efficient way to transfer a personal residence or vacation home to heirs while simultaneously maintaining control of the property at least during the term of the trust (and quite possibly well beyond the trust term). A QPRT is actually a type of grantor retained income trust (GRIT) in which the corpus of the trust is a residence or vacation home transferred by the grantor and the "retained income" is the right of the grantor to remain in the house rent-free for a term of years. In this manner, a QPRT is often referred to as a "house GRIT."

A QPRT is a simple concept and easy to understand. It works like this:

The grantor places a house in a QPRT for a term of years (e.g., 15 years). At the end of the term, the house is transferred to the grantor's children or other beneficiaries. The primary tax benefit of placing the residence in the QPRT stems from the fact that the gift tax, which is due upon creation of the QPRT, is based on the value of the house at the time of the transfer reduced by the actuarially determined value of the grantor's retained interest (i.e., the term of years during which the grantor will retain possession of the property). The value of the gift is further reduced by the grantor's contingent reversion interest (i.e., the possibility that the grantor may die before the end of the term, which would result in the house reverting back to the grantor's estate). In addition, because the gift is considered complete at the time the house is placed into the QPRT, any further appreciation of the residence's value during the trust term escapes estate taxes.

Thus, a QPRT allows the grantor to make a present gift of the house, eliminate its value from the grantor's estate for estate tax purposes, and continue to live in the house rent-free for a term of years. Furthermore, with respect to the gift tax due when the house is placed in the QPRT, although the $10,000 annual gift tax exclusion is not available, all or any portion of the $1 million lifetime gift exemption can be utilized to offset any gift tax due on the transfer. For this purpose, the grantor and the term holder (the person who gets rent-free occupancy for the length of the QPRT's term) do not have to be the same person.

The Savings You Can Expect

To give you an example of the savings involved, here are some hypothetical numbers. Assume the fair market value of your house is $400,000 and you have paid off the mortgage. If you put it into a 15-year QPRT and specify that it reverts to your estate in case you die within the 15-year term, by utilizing applicable IRS tables, the value of the gift at the time the house is placed in the QPRT would be $128,932 for gift tax purposes. The $128,932 figure results from subtracting the combined value of your 15-year rent-free occupancy of the house ($214,468) and the reversionary interest ($56,600) from the value of the house at the time the house is placed into the QPRT ($400,000).

Value of the house	$400,000
Value of rent-free occupancy of the house	($214,468)
Reversionary interest	($ 56,600)
Gift tax value	$128,932

In other words, you can make a $271,068 tax-free transfer ($400,000 less $128,932) and save $135,534 in estate and gift taxes ($271,068 multiplied by 50%, the gift tax rate). Also, if you utilized a portion of your $1 million lifetime gift tax exemption, there would be no gift taxes payable either at the time the QPRT was created or at the end of the 15-year term. Furthermore, your estate tax savings are actually much greater if you take into consideration the value of your house at the end of the 15-year term. The example in Figure 13.1 assumes that Landis Baron owns a house with a fair market value of $500,000 and no mortgage, which he places in a 10-year QPRT. The example assumes further that the value of the house will increase nearly threefold over the re-

**Qualified Personal Residence Trust
for Landis Baron**

Transfer Date 09/21/2000   Discount Pct .00%
Straight term   AFR 7.6%

Current Value of Residence	$500,000
Value of 10 Year Term	.51929
Equals Retained Value	259,646
Value of Gift	240,354
Gift Tax on Transfer of Remainder	0
Value of Residence at Death in 23 Years (without Transfer)	$1,557,011
Less Gift Value Amount Taxed at Death	240,354
Value Removed from Estate	1,316,657
Times Marginal Estate Tax Rate	.55
Projected Estate Tax Savings	$724,161

FIGURE 13.1   Qualified Personal Residence Trust for Landis Baron
Reproduced with permission from CCH Incorporated, 2700 Lake Cook Road, Riverwoods, Illinois 60015.

maining 23 years of the grantor's life. Accordingly, by placing the house in a QPRT, Landis will have saved $724,161 in estate taxes.

The value of your 15-year rent-free occupancy and of your reversionary interest is tied to the yield on U.S. Treasury obligations for the month the trust is created. This is usually higher than prevailing market rates. In addition, retained interests in homes tend to be overvalued because the valuation method assumes assets to be income producing. It should be noted, however, that IRS regulations regarding QPRTs are stringent and must be adhered to verbatim. The regulations give you only 90 days from the due date of your gift tax return to reform any defects in the QPRT trust.

The Drawbacks

Qualified personal residence trusts have a few drawbacks, but they are minor compared to the benefits of creating a QPRT.

First, because the gift is considered complete when the property is transferred into the QPRT, it is valued for capital gains tax purposes at the time the QPRT is created, not at the time the QPRT ends when your beneficiaries actually receive the property. In other words, your beneficiaries will not get a stepped-up basis in the house. If they decide to sell, they must pay capital gains tax (top federal rate of 20%) on all of the appreciation in the value of the house above the grantor's original cost basis in the property (unless one of them decides to take up residence in the house after the expiration of the QPRT term, at which point the personal residence exemptions may apply).

However, the benefits of the QPRT can still outweigh this potential capital gains tax hit because the estate taxes otherwise payable on the appreciated value of the house in the future (assuming your estate is greater than $1 million, or the then deathtime exemption equivalent) start at 37% and rise quickly to 50% currently, while the top capital gains tax rate is relatively modest at 20%.

Another possible drawback occurs if you die before the QPRT term ends. If death occurs prior to the end of the trust term, the value of the residence is included in your estate. If you paid gift taxes at the time of the creation of the QPRT, your estate will receive a credit on your estate tax return equal to the gift tax previously paid. However, this would still result in essentially prepaying the estate taxes due on the value of the house. Accordingly, the term of the QPRT should not exceed that number of years it is reasonably anticipated that the grantor will comfortably survive.

Furthermore, putting a residence into a QPRT can have the potential of negatively affecting your creditworthiness because you no longer can use your residence as collateral. However, if you live in a state without a homestead exemption, a QPRT can protect your residence from creditors. Your creditors will not be able to force a sale or eliminate your children's future interest in the residence. The most they might be able to reach is your right to occupy the residence rent-free during the QPRT term, which is of questionable value.

A note on jointly owned residences: It might be best to split the residence into two half interests as tenancies in common and create two separate QPRTs rather than putting the house into a single QPRT. You lose flexibility with the jointly owned single trust, and the current gift value will be greater than the sum of two separate QPRTs. You might also receive a valuation discount on the half interests in the tenancies in common because of the lack of marketability of such tenancies.

You should avoid using a QPRT for generation-skipping purposes. This is because you cannot allocate your generation-skipping transfer (GST) tax exemption until the end of the QPRT term or your death (whichever comes first) and not at the time you create the QPRT. This means that your GST exemption has to cover any appreciation in the value of your residence during the term. Thus, the use of a QPRT as a generation-skipping vehicle is a highly inefficient use of your GST exemption. It is better to use this exemption elsewhere. You can use your will or other gifts and trusts to correct any inequities this may cause.

Personal Residences

In order for a home to qualify as a personal residence for purposes of establishing a QPRT, the home must be either your principal residence or one other nonprincipal residence (vacation home) in which you resided for either 14 days during the previous year or 10% of the days you rented the residence during the year, whichever is greater. A nonprincipal residence will also qualify as a personal residence if it is unoccupied and available at all times for your use as a personal residence. A house will qualify for a QPRT as long as the structure's primary use is as a personal residence. A secondary use (or nonprimary) business or trade use (such as a home office) will not otherwise disqualify a qualified residence. The IRS approaches this question of determining the primary use of a residence on a case-by-case basis. For instance, the IRS recently ruled that the rental of a 500-square-foot unit within a 4,000-square-foot structure (the remaining 3,500 square feet constituting the grantor's personal residence) did not disqualify the structure for QPRT treatment.

A houseboat, a house trailer, or a tenant's stock in a cooperative housing corporation, among other things, can qualify as a personal residence. A personal residence includes the adjacent land as long as the land is not in excess of what is reasonably appropriate for residential purposes. The size and location of the residence is taken into account when making this determination. A personal residence does not include personal property such as household furnishings.

Determining whether two structures constitute separate residences can sometimes be tricky. In one case, a significantly smaller guest house was considered part of a vacation residence since guests paid no rent. This can become an important analysis because a person can put only one other property in addition to his or her principal residence into a QPRT (and you can have only one principal residence), for a total of two QPRTs. Each QPRT can hold only one residence. If you and your spouse share a principal residence, you can transfer a total of only three residences via QPRTs between the two of you (one principal residence and one secondary residence in each of your respective names).

Another planning strategy, particularly with a valuable residence, is to create multiple QPRTs, each containing a fractional interest in the residence, with staggered term periods.

Death of the Grantor Prior to the End of the QPRT Term

If the grantor does not survive the specified term of the QPRT, the house in the QPRT reverts back to the grantor's estate for estate tax purposes at the value of the residence at the time of death. However, the gift tax paid or the portion of the exemption equivalent expended when the QPRT was created is credited to the estate, so that you are basically back where you would have been if you had never tried the QPRT strategy.

In order to avoid this result, it is best to use a term for the QPRT that is half, or perhaps two-thirds, of the estimated normal life expectancy of the grantor, taking into consideration the health as well as current situation of the grantor. Of course, the shorter the term, the smaller the tax benefits (although each additional year produces a smaller tax benefit than the year before). To allow for the possibility of dying before the QPRT term expires, the grantor could consider purchasing term life insurance for the length of the QPRT term in the amount of the QPRT's expected tax benefits. The policy should be owned by an irrevocable life insurance trust or the grantor's beneficiaries so that it is not included in the grantor's estate.

During the QPRT Term

In order to retain the income tax benefits of being the homeowner (i.e., mortgage interest and real estate tax deductions), the grantor must retain the status as owner of the QPRT's principal. In other words, the QPRT must be a "grantor trust" for income tax purposes. If the grantor serves as the term holder (the person who will live in the house until the QPRT term ends) and holds a reversionary interest in the house (if the grantor dies before the term ends it reverts to his or her estate), the QPRT will be treated, for tax purposes, as a grantor trust. The only additional requirement is that the value of the grantor's reversionary interest must exceed 5% of the trust's total value. This requirement should not be difficult to meet unless the QPRT term is significantly less than the grantor's estimated life expectancy. If this is the case, the trust agreement may need to be supplemented, giving the grantor the power to substitute assets of equal value for the residence at any time during the term period in order for the QPRT to continue to qualify as a grantor trust.

The Expense Factor

A QPRT is relatively inexpensive to establish and maintain. Costs involved are basically limited to the legal costs of establishing the trust and any costs associated with transferring the property into the trust. The grantor may serve as the trustee during the QPRT term, as long as he or she does not retain certain "incidents of ownership" as trustee. For instance, the grantor-trustee is prohibited from retaining the power to change beneficiaries once the QPRT is in effect and from distributing trust assets to himself or herself (if these actions were permitted, the trust would be treated, for gift tax purposes, as an incomplete gift).

Also, the trust is not required to have its own separate taxpayer identification number, trust checking account, or separate income tax return. The grantor need not provide an accounting to the beneficiaries. The grantor may pay all the expenses on the property (mortgage payments, taxes, maintenance, insurance) directly or through the trust. For this purpose, the trust can hold assets besides the residence. However, the value of these other trust assets cannot exceed what is needed to pay reasonable trust expenses (including the cost of improvements) that have already been incurred or are reasonably expected to be incurred during any upcoming six-month period. Any excess funds in the trust have to be distributed to the grantor at least on a quarterly basis. No income or principal from the trust can be distributed to anyone besides the grantor during the QPRT term.

Please note that some payments made by the grantor during the trust term may have gift tax implications. While what counts as a taxable gift ultimately depends upon the particular statutes of the state in which the grantor resides, there are some general rules of thumb.

Payments for real property taxes, insurance, routine maintenance, and mortgage interest should not be considered taxable gifts because the grantor is the current beneficiary of those payments in his or her role as term holder. But payments for mortgage principal and capital improvements (including certain capital repairs) will also benefit those who get the property after the end of the QPRT term and most likely will be considered taxable gifts to the trust beneficiaries. The value of these improvements as gifts will, however, be discounted for purposes of establishing the value of the grantor's retained interest in accordance with the number of years remaining in the QPRT.

In this regard, some advisers recommend against putting property encumbered by a mortgage into a QPRT. It is probably best to pay off the mortgage or transfer the loan to another property before putting it into a QPRT. If you do put encumbered property into a QPRT, you will need the approval and cooperation of the mortgage holder. In the alternative, you can retain the debt and transfer the property, unencumbered, to the QPRT.

Sale, Destruction, or Damage of the Residence

If the residence is sold during the QPRT term, the grantor can maintain the QPRT status by purchasing another residence of equal value during a period equal to the lesser of two years following the sale or the remaining term of the QPRT. If the residence is damaged or destroyed, the grantor has the additional option of repairing or rebuilding the original house within the same period. If the house is sold, the grantor is liable for any capital gains tax due, since the QPRT remains a grantor trust for income tax purposes. However, if the house serves as the grantor's primary residence during the trust term, he or she will be eligible for the capital gains exemption available on the sale of a primary residence ($250,000 for single taxpayers and $500,000 for married couples filing jointly) and will get a step-up in the basis of the house.

If the house is sold or destroyed, the grantor retains the option to convert the QPRT into a grantor retained annuity trust (GRAT) and receive an annuity for the remaining term of the trust. The size of the annuity is determined through a complicated formula discussed in Chapter 22, "Grantor Retained Annuity Trusts and Grantor Retained Unitrusts," and is independent of the sum received on the sale of the residence. The annuity is fixed and must be paid from income, principal, or both. Commutation of the annuity (prepayment of the term holder's interest) is prohibited.

Post Survival of the QPRT Term

At the end of the QPRT term, the trust terminates and the house becomes the property of the children or other named beneficiaries outright. A grantor who wishes to continue to reside in the house after the end of the QPRT term must enter into a written lease agreement.

If you take this route, you must pay full and fair market rent to the new owners of your home—your children. However, there is a benefit to this arrangement. The rent you pay to your children is a transfer that, in essence, reduces the size of your estate and thus escapes gift and estate tax. Because it removes wealth from your estate without gift tax, you and your beneficiaries have a mutual interest in negotiating a fair market rent.

But be careful: If the rent is below fair market value, it could cause the entire value of the house to be included in your estate; if it is too high, the excess could be subject to additional gift tax. Because some people are uncomfortable becoming tenants in their own homes and being in a tenant-landlord relationship with their children, many put only their vacation homes into a QPRT.

An option that used to be available was for the grantor to buy back the house from the trust just before the QPRT term ended (the trust would then distribute the proceeds from the sale, tax free, to the trust's beneficiaries—i.e., the children). This option has now been closed by the IRS. In fact, now the QPRT agreement must affirmatively state that the trust may not sell the residence back to the grantor or the grantor's spouse.

Today, if your children agree, you can always negotiate to buy back the house from them after the term of the trust ends and then put it into another QPRT if you so choose. However, if your property has appreciated since you put it into the trust, your children will have to pay capital gains tax on the appreciation. The lack of capital gains tax when the trust sold the house back to the grantor was perhaps one of the reasons the IRS objected to the repurchase option; that it ran contrary to Congress's purpose in creating the QPRT (i.e., to facilitate the generational transfer of personal residences) was probably another reason.

QPRT Planning After the New 2001 Tax Act

If the estate tax is going to be repealed, why create a QPRT trust? While there are nontax reasons for creating a QPRT trust such as asset protection and dispositive clarity, a QPRT trust's main purpose is to reduce estate tax exposure. If estate tax repeal was a certainty, QPRT planning would be limited to those not likely to survive until repeal in 2010 but likely to survive a brief QPRT period (three, four, or five years). But estate tax repeal is not a certainty. In fact, it is a virtual certainty we will *not* see estate tax repeal. Accordingly, for those with an asset base considerably more than the deathtime exemption in 2009 ($3.5 million), a QPRT trust must be considered. However, one must structure the transaction so the gift portion is offset by the lifetime gift tax exemption of $1 million. Avoid paying gift tax. In this regard, utilizing a cabinet of advisers is a must in weighing the strengths and weaknesses of qualified personal residence trusts.

Integrating the Titling of Assets with the Intent of the Estate Plan

Introduction

One of the most common estate planning mistakes is for an individual to spend the time, effort, and money in having wills, living wills, powers of attorney, and trusts drafted without recognizing the significance of how the titling of assets may control the ultimate distribution of assets upon one's demise. In order to avoid this pitfall, the estate planning team should begin the estate planning process by filling out a last will and testament fact sheet, a copy of which appears as Figure 2.1. By completing this fact-gathering form, the estate planning team and the client will, among other things, focus on how each asset is titled and seek to integrate the titling of assets with the intent of the estate plan. Consider the following hypothetical case, which illustrates the importance of properly titling one's assets.

Titling Faux Pas

Manny and Mary Fopa have been married 10 years and have accumulated assets worth $2 million, as shown in Table 14.1.

The Fopas spent the time, effort, and money necessary to create wills that include exemption equivalent trusts for the benefit of both spouses with the intent of shielding the $1 million (as of year 2002) deathtime exemption equivalent amount from estate taxes. But if the Fopas never retitle their assets, their intent would be frustrated. Why? In the event Manny Fopa died first, the house would pass by operation of law directly to Mary Fopa because the house is titled as tenants by the entirety. The stocks, bonds, and mutual funds, also titled jointly, would also pass to Mary Fopa, as would the life insurance. Similarly, the IRA account would be rolled over by Mary Fopa into her IRA account. While Manny Fopa's will directs the executors to transfer the then-current exemption equivalent amount into the exemption equivalent trust, the executor has no assets with which to fund such a trust because the assets pass directly by operation of law to Mary. The only potential relief would be to file disclaimers within nine months after the first spouse's death to protect the exemption equivalent trust.

In completing the fact-gathering form, the estate planning team should counsel the Fopas to equalize the assets up to the exemption equivalent amount. More specifically, the estate planner might recommend that: (1) the house be retitled from tenants by the entirety (rights of survivorship) to tenants in common; (2) the stocks, bonds, and mutual funds be retitled one-half in

TABLE 14.1 Assets of Manny and Mary Fopa		
Asset	**Title**	**Value**
House	Tenants by the entirety	$500,000
Stocks, bonds, and mutual funds	Joint	$500,000
Life insurance	Husband to wife or, in default, children equally	$500,000
IRA	Husband to wife or, in default, children equally	$500,000
Total		$2,000,000

Manny Fopa's name and one-half in Mary Fopa's name; and (3) either one of two methods be used with respect to the life insurance: The estate planner could recommend either naming the exemption equivalent trust created under the last will and testament of Manny Fopa as the beneficiary of the life insurance, or perhaps, better yet, assigning or recreating the insurance in an irrevocable trust so as to completely remove it from Manny Fopa's estate (subject to the three-year look-back if assigned).

The example of Manny and Mary Fopa is a fairly typical fact pattern that illustrates just how critical the process known as estate equalization is. Through a fairly simple process of equalizing the Fopas' assets, their intent could have been carried out. A brief, fundamental review of the different ways in which property may be titled follows.

Jointly Held Property

A joint tenancy is a form of ownership wherein the cotenants own a whole, or unified, interest in the entire property. Each joint tenant has the right, subject to the right of the other joint tenants, to possess the entire interest in the property. The common-law definition of a joint tenancy requires the presence of four unities: (1) unity of interest, which means each joint tenant must have an identical interest; (2) unity of title, which means the same will, deed, or other document must confer title to all joint tenants; (3) unity of possession, which means that each owner has the right to possess the entire property interest; and (4) unity of time, which means that the rights of each joint tenant must vest at the same time.

Property owned jointly is frequently referred to as a will substitute, meaning that the will does not control the disposition of the asset, but rather the form of ownership governs the distribution of the asset. Joint property, or joint property with rights of survivorship, most frequently occurs with respect to bank accounts, brokerage accounts, and real estate. Not only do some institutions provide their clients with the ability to name the account ownership as joint tenants with rights of survivorship, which may frustrate one's intent to have those assets qualify for the exemption equivalent, but frequently the institution's forms also allow one to name a successor beneficiary, which most married couples utilize to name their children equally.

In the event that your children are minors, the result may be disastrous. The assets that pass by operation of law to the children (and thus are not governed by your last will and testament) go directly to the children who are minors. Inasmuch as a surrogate's court will not allow assets to pass to a minor, the surrogate's court will impose restrictions as to both investment options and distributions to the children. The investments may be forced to be liquidated and converted into money market accounts and/or certificates of deposit, held in various banks. Further, anytime the minor has financial needs requiring invasion into the account, a guardian would be required to petition the court to seek the release of those funds. Thus, not only would the assets' growth be limited, but the ability to gain access to the assets would become a costly and cumbersome process.

Therefore, one may be best advised to have the stocks, bonds, and mutual funds retitled from a joint tenancy form of ownership to one-half of the assets being titled in the husband's name and one-half of the assets being titled in the wife's name. The assets are then eligible to fund an exemption equivalent trust upon one spouse's demise, but if both spouses die, the assets may fund age-terminating trusts for the benefit of the minor children, managed by a trustee qualified both to invest the funds prudently and to distribute the funds as needed pursuant to the will, not a court order. However, before retitling the account holders as such, one should consider the following issues.

Before transferring real estate or brokerage accounts from tenants by the entirety to tenants in common (discussed in next section), an analysis of potential creditors should be undertaken. If either of the spouses is embroiled in litigation that is likely to result in a judgment being entered against that spouse, and if the asset is titled as a joint tenancy with rights of survivorship, the creditor may not be able to force the sale of the home in order to recover on its judgment or attach a jointly owned property. However, if the real estate is titled as tenants in common rather than tenants by the entirety, then a judgment creditor may be able to seek an action called "partition," which essentially allows the judgment creditor to force the sale of the house or attach one-half of a brokerage account, enabling the creditor to recover at least one-half of the equity in the house or one-half of the brokerage account to satisfy its judgment.

Another issue that one should consider prior to transferring jointly owned assets to husband and wife as tenants in common, is capital gains tax implications. It is important to recognize that when individuals acquire marketable securities, they have a basis in the account equal to its cost at the time the equity was purchased. If there is significant gain, there is of course capital gains tax exposure upon the sale of the equity. However, upon a spouse's demise, to the extent that the spouses own the equity jointly, there is a step-up in basis as to one-half of the equity. The step-up in basis essentially provides that the basis of that spouse's marketable securities will be stepped up to the fair market value at the date of death.

Accordingly, if assets are owned jointly by husband and wife and there is a likelihood due to one spouse's illness or the age differential that one spouse's demise is likely to occur first, but not within one year, it may be advisable not to transfer the assets from joint tenants to tenants in common for the purpose of creating an exemption equivalent trust, but rather, transfer the title to the spouse's name most likely to die first. Thus, the executor will have the ability to fund the exemption equivalent trust and at the same time achieve a step-up in basis as to all of the assets placed in such person's name as opposed to just half of the assets.

Tenants in Common

The tenancy in common arrangement allows an individual to gift during his or her lifetime or devise at death an undivided interest in a property. Thus, it may be advisable, if there are no other assets available to fund an exemption equivalent trust upon the first spouse's demise, to transfer real estate from jointly owned or tenants by the entirety to husband and wife as tenants in common. This change of ownership will allow the first spouse to pass one-half interest in certain property, such as the marital home, to the exemption equivalent trust.

However, one must be cognizant of the *Gallenstein* rule. If an individual dies at any time after 1981 owning a joint interest created prior to 1977, the entire property interest gets a step-up in basis. Thus, to transfer the deed from a joint tenancy established prior to 1977 to husband and wife as tenants in common would defeat this step-up benefit. However, if no other asset is available to fund the exemption equivalent trust and since the estate tax brackets are substantially greater than the capital gains tax brackets, such a transfer requires a balancing of consequences.

Pay-on-Death Accounts

Other forms of ownership that have a similar effect as joint tenancy are accounts known as in-trust-for accounts or pay-on-death accounts, which may pose some of the same problems discussed earlier, as well as some new ones. An in-trust-for account or a pay-on-death account is often referred to as a "poor man's trust," meaning that a trust document was never drafted, but upon one's demise the account passes to the named beneficiary. Such an arrangement presents a number of problems.

First of all, much like a joint tenancy account, if the asset is passing to a spouse, the asset is not available to fund an exemption equivalent trust. The second problem is that if the asset is not passing to the spouse but is passing to a child and the will directs that the assets are to be distributable equally to the children, inequities may arise. Siblings who were once amicable could become adversarial because the child who receives the pay-on-death account or in-trust-for account receives that asset as well as an equal amount of all assets passing under the will, thus causing a disproportionate distribution.

To make matters worse, if the will directs the estate tax to be borne by the residuary estate, not including assets passing by operation of law, the estate taxes would be paid equally even though the wealth was distributed inequitably. The siblings who are not the pay-on-death or in-trust-for beneficiary may feel that it is inequitable to have to pay estate taxes on assets that they didn't receive. In fact, unless the will directs otherwise, that may be the result.

As if those two considerations do not create enough problems within the estate administration process, it is also not unusual for a client to pass the assets in the form of a pay-on-death account or in-trust-for account to either a minor or someone who, at the time of the individual's demise, is not fiscally responsible to manage the asset base. Once again the asset will become subject to the jurisdiction of the surrogate's court, and the guardian may be required to invest in certificates of deposit or money market accounts, and invasions of principal will require judicial intervention. Once the beneficiary attains the ripe old age of 18 or 21 (depending on the jurisdiction), the asset will be distributed outright, regardless of the fiscal maturity of the child, unless a court directs otherwise.

Life Insurance

Another mistake that estate planners routinely see is life insurance owned individually, with the spouse—or in default, children—serving as the beneficiary(ies) of the life insurance policy. As discussed in Chapter 7, "Irrevocable Life Insurance Trusts," life insurance is an asset that is includable in one's estate for estate tax purposes. If the spouse is named as beneficiary, the estate tax will be deferred through the unlimited marital deduction until the surviving spouse's demise. However, at that time the insurance proceeds to the extent not spent, plus any growth, will be subjected to estate tax. If the spouse predeceases the insured spouse/owner, minor children or adult fiscally irresponsible children may be the beneficiaries.

Revocable Inter Vivos Trusts

In many states individuals create revocable inter vivos trusts for the purpose of avoiding probate and maintaining privacy, since revocable trusts are not probated and therefore do not become public records. In that regard, an individual may retain an estate planning attorney, prepare a revocable trust, and retitle the assets in the name of the revocable trust so that upon one's demise these assets would not be subject to probate. The problem is that over the years, new assets will be acquired and must be titled in the name of the revocable trust. Thus, the only way an individual's intent of avoiding probate will be realized is if he or she continues to meet with the estate planning team on a regular basis to review the asset base again to make sure that any new assets have been properly titled in the name of the revocable trust.

If the individual's assets are not properly titled in the name of the revocable trust and he or she dies, then just what the individual sought to avoid, namely probate, will become a necessity. Although in many states the probating of assets is not expensive or time-consuming, in other states it is. Therefore, if one's intent is to avoid making public one's asset base and to reduce costs associated with probating a will, a revocable trust may be prudent, but the titling of assets must be consistently reviewed to accomplish the goal.

UGMA Accounts

While Uniform Gifts to Minors Act (UGMA) accounts are covered in more detail in Chapter 9, "Transferring Wealth to Minors," suffice it to say that transferring wealth into such accounts, while exceedingly simple and well-intentioned, creates two concerns. The first is that to the extent that the parent is a custodian and then dies before the custodianship ends, the assets are includable in that parent's estate.

Additionally, when the minor reaches age 18 or the age of majority in that particular state, the assets become distributable outright to the beneficiary. All too often the beneficiary, while deemed an adult by law, is not yet ready to properly manage the assets held in the UGMA account, and the risk is that money that had been building for years may be squandered. As discussed more fully in Chapter 9, alternatives exist that, while more time-consuming, eliminate many of the risks inherent in Uniform Gifts to Minors Act accounts.

Life Insurance in Matrimonial Actions

It is an unfortunate statistic that roughly 50% of all marriages, many of which involve minor children, end in divorce. Generally, a divorce decree may require that alimony payments or child support payments are to be made for a period of years, frequently until the child reaches age 18 or 21. Courts recognize that the potential exists for a husband or wife to die prior

to completing the alimony or support payments, and therefore it is not unusual for courts to require that life insurance be taken out to provide the necessary liquidity for such payments. Without proper counsel, a number of
problems may occur regarding the ownership of the insurance and designation of the beneficiaries.

With respect to the question of ownership, if the spouse's estate is subject to
estate taxes, then while the divorce decree requires that a fixed sum be paid,
the life insurance could be subject to estate taxes. It is also not uncommon for
divorce decrees to require that the death benefit be paid to the ex-spouse as
trustee for the benefit of minor children. Unfortunately, insurance paid in such
a manner does not create a trust, and therefore the surviving parent would be
named beneficiary without the benefit and/or restrictions that may be necessary to safeguard the funds for the benefit of the minor children. Again, without a trust that directs the funds to be distributed as children attain certain ages
or for specific causes, the funds may have to be paid to children at an inappropriate age.

Divorce decrees frequently require that the life insurance that one spouse
must buy pursuant to the divorce decree be a fixed sum. Practically speaking,
however, when the court directs the spouse to obtain insurance, he or she may
buy the life insurance policy and continue to pay the premiums over the
course of many years. Depending on the type of insurance, the death benefit
may increase over time. Therefore, what happens if the death benefit, which
was originally $250,000 pursuant to the divorce decree, has, due to market
conditions, increased to $380,000 upon the insured's demise? Who is to re-
ceive the $130,000 excess? Is it the ex-spouse for the payment of the alimony
obligation or is it the children in the form of child support payments? Ambiguity is the foundation for litigation, delays, and costs.

IRAs and Qualified Plans

Structuring the distribution of qualified plans is more fully set forth in Chapter
10. However, it is important to note that—as with life insurance, brokerage accounts, jointly owned accounts, and Uniform Gifts to Minors Act accounts—
beneficiary designations of IRAs and qualified plans must be incorporated into
the estate plan. Whether one intends to pass tax-deferred wealth into an exemption equivalent trust, a qualified terminable interest property trust, an age-
terminating trust, or a charitable trust, or simply outright to your spouse, the
decision should be one made after all relevant factors have been considered by
the estate planning team.

Conclusion

The examples set forth in this chapter regarding the titling of assets provide further evidence of why it is imperative to create an estate planning team consisting of your estate planning lawyer, accountant, life insurance professional, financial planner, and banker. In this regard, your team can help you identify and implement the following:

■ Check that assets are properly titled to assure that exemption equivalent trusts are able to be funded.

■ Assure that assets passing outside the will to children are directed into the appropriate trust.

■ Increase the likelihood of obtaining a step-up in basis.

■ Avoid inequity unless intended.

■ Avoid ambiguity, costs, and delays.

■ Avoid unnecessary estate taxes.

The failure to review the titling of each asset to ensure that it is integrated into the intent of the estate plan surely will cause just what one seeks to avoid when creating an estate plan. Furthermore, it is not enough to coordinate the titling of assets during the initial estate planning process; one should reassemble the estate planning team at least once every two to three years or upon changed circumstances to review the entire plan and retitle assets as necessary.

Business Succession Planning

Introduction

If ever there was a case that underscores the need for comprehensive business succession planning it would be the estate of Elizabeth Boyer, as reported in the *New York Times* on October 31, 1999. What started as a small summer camp in Winnipesaukee, New Hampshire, turned into a multimillion-dollar tax lien assessed by the IRS for estate taxes, interest, and penalties. Why? In part because Elizabeth Boyer failed to create a business succession plan. As a result, upon her death the summer camp and property were fully includable in her estate for estate tax purposes. Elizabeth Boyer's executors valued the business interest on Ms. Boyer's IRS Form 706 at $860,000. The IRS came up with its own valuation, a whopping $4.9 million, and then assessed a $3.9 million estate tax deficiency, including interest and penalties. Levies, tax liens, and court battles ensued, leaving the family members heartbroken and financially devastated. Had a comprehensive business succession plan been completed during Elizabeth Boyer's lifetime, this nightmare could have been avoided.

Many consider family-owned businesses to be the fabric of the U.S. economy. In fact, it is a widely reported fact that of approximately 18 million businesses in the United States, more than 80% are family owned. Family owned and operated businesses account for more than 50% of the nation's employment and over 50% of the country's gross national product.

Remarkable statistics, but even more remarkable is that over the next five years, an estimated 43% of the nation's family-owned businesses will pass from one generation to the next. Yet the majority of these family-owned businesses will not make it past the business owner's demise. Why? Because the family members will fail to put in place a workable business succession plan.

The key to the successful transfer of a family-owned business is not only to structure the transfer in the most tax-efficient manner, but also to structure the transfer in such a manner as to simultaneously promote family harmony, continuity, and leadership. The implementation of a successful plan assures the safe passing of the torch.

Unfortunately, business succession is not an easy task. In fact, only 30% of family-owned businesses survive through the second generation, and less than 15% pass successfully to the third generation. Improper planning, taxation, the failure to provide for leadership roles, and the inability to understand the process as a whole are generally the primary causes that lead to such startling statistics.

What Is Business Succession Planning?

Business succession planning is planning that fosters both the succession of leadership and the orderly transfer of control of a family business to the next generation. Business succession planning incorporates all of the tax and nontax considerations that a business owner must assess when determining whether, and, if so, how the family business is to be passed to the next generation and generations to come. In this regard, a number of factors should be analyzed when determining whether to make a transfer of all or part of the business interest to children (or grandchildren). The considerations include:

- Estate and gift tax ramifications.

- The business owner's willingness to let go.

- Family members' willingness to commit to the business.

- Maintaining equity when making distributions to participating and nonparticipating family members.

- Timing.

- Value of the business.

- Incorporating the business succession plan into the estate plan.

- Effect of the business succession plan on retirement planning.

- Maintaining an income stream, if necessary.

The orderly transfer of control in a family business should be of primary importance in evaluating when and to whom to make such gifts. Because the considerations are many and may be difficult to evaluate, a business owner should undertake a thorough and reasonable assessment of the advantages and disadvantages associated with any such transfer before gifting an interest in the family business. Finally, business succession planning is not a one-time event, but rather an ongoing process that should be analyzed on an annual basis and modified with each changing circumstance.

Who Is Responsible for Planning?

All too often, the senior members of the family are so immersed in the day-to-day operations of the business that they fail to realize the importance of implementing an effective business succession plan. It is easy for the business owner to put off business succession planning. Many owners have strong personalities and feel more comfortable remaining in control. The idea of passing the torch may be perceived as a threat to that control. Other business owners are aware that they need to plan for their succession but have a natural reluctance to begin the process.

Often, the process begins only after the owner realizes that his or her life's work is at risk and that the significant value created is in jeopardy because of a failure to plan for the future. With the highest incremental federal estate tax rates currently at 50%, it is not unusual for the ongoing value of a family business to be cut in half upon the death of the senior family member.

Conversely, once the business owner begins the process of putting a business succession plan into place, it often invigorates both the members of the family and the business. Creating a business succession plan may also give the owner the comfort and security of knowing that, as retirement approaches, the business is well positioned to pass to the next generation and the owner's income is secure for the duration of retirement.

Commitment and Execution Are Pivotal

In order to take the first step in establishing a successful business plan, a business owner must acknowledge that establishing a successful plan can effectively perpetuate the business owner's legacy while promoting family harmony. The owner must also recognize that his or her life's work is at risk without such a plan.

Dealing with leadership transition issues is just as important as dealing with tax and other financial issues that arise with any transition. To understand what is at stake, the owner should:

■ Commit to creating and carrying out a business succession plan.

■ Work with professional advisers to determine the market value of the business and the estate and gift taxes that would result without planning.

■ Work with these advisers to structure such a plan and create a workable timetable for moving the plan forward to completion.

■ Understand that the owner is pivotal for the purpose of both establishing and carrying out the plan.

■ Recognize that succession planning should take on the same level of importance as the day-to-day operation of the business and that it, too, will be an ongoing responsibility that takes time and attention.

■ Empower and educate successors so that they understand the responsibility associated with taking over the reins and carrying out the day-to-day responsibilities of running the business.

Seeking Professional Counsel

By committing to the creation of a business succession plan, the business owner may have undertaken the first and perhaps the most important step for the purpose of ensuring the ongoing success of the business. The second, and perhaps equally important, step is to assemble the cabinet of advisers—the business succession planning team—to help create and carry out the plan. This cabinet of advisers should include:

■ An accountant.

■ An estate and business succession planning attorney.

■ A professional life insurance agent.

■ A Certified Financial Planner (CFP).

■ A banker.

■ Any family members who are involved in the business.

■ *Accountant.* It is imperative that the company's accountant be involved in creating an effective succession plan. However, it is equally important for the business owner to realize that, while the accountant who has prepared the company's tax returns over the years will be an integral part of creating an effective plan, it is not unusual for another accounting firm or valuation company to be retained for the purpose of valuing the company for gifting purposes.

■ *Attorney.* Over the years, the business owner may have used an attorney to assist with general corporate matters. However, for the purpose of creating an effective business succession plan, the business owner must retain the services of an attorney whose expertise is in the area of estate and business succession planning. Attorneys who are well versed in the estate and business succession planning area are accustomed to working with companies' counsel, who generally have a good understanding of the history of the firm. In this way, the company's corporate counsel and the business succession specialist can work closely together to implement a succession plan that is best suited for the needs of the company.

■ *Insurance agent.* Early in the development of the business succession plan, one of the most common problems is outdated or inappropriate life insurance. Such life insurance policies can be owned improperly, bought for a specific purpose that is no longer required, or contain death benefits that have not kept up with the value of the business. Therefore, it is critical to bring in a life insurance agent who is familiar with estate and gift taxation and the business succession planning area as a whole. After choosing a life insurance professional, the business owner should present copies of all the life insurance contracts for the agent to review. As the business succession planning process unfolds, the agent can then report to the business owner and other advisers the agent's findings and insurance recommendations to facilitate the plan.

■ *Certified financial planner (CFP).* As part of the business succession team, a certified financial planner can work with the business owner in helping to develop the plan that works best for the owner. The CFP generally brings expertise in the areas of finance, tax, and law and can provide the team with his or her experience in working with companies in similar situations.

■ *Banker.* Many business owners have long-term relationships with banks regarding credit facilities and lines of credit, including asset-based loans, as well as day-to-day business checking and savings accounts. A banker brings financial acumen to the advisory team that is invaluable to the planners. The banker may, in fact, be able to provide the next generation with a credit facility and help finance the buyout or other transition planning devised by the family. Additionally, the banker may offer fiduciary talent as an executor or trustee to help carry out the terms of the business succession plan.

■ *Family members.* Finally, and most important, the business succession planning team must include both the senior and junior family members. The ongoing success of the business as well as the business owner's security in retirement are dependent in large part upon the success of the business, which may rest in the hands of the next generation. Only after the business owner, the advisers, and the succeeding owners have all met and aired their thoughts and concerns can a meeting of the minds take place and a plan begin to develop.

At this point, two of the most important steps in the creation of a business succession plan have occurred:

1. The business owner has realized the importance of the process and is committed to implementing the plan (as well as seeing it through to fruition).

2. The business owner has put together an effective team of advisers who have the skills and dedication to assist the business owner in creating a plan that is right for the particular circumstances.

Now the team's job is to help create a plan based on the unique circumstances of the business and the goals of the owner (and the successors) and to incorporate those intentions in the most tax-efficient, harmonious, and practical plan possible.

As the new Tax Act of 2001 increased the lifetime gifting exemption to $1 million per spouse, increased the deathtime exemption equivalent, decreased the rate of tax (as more fully set forth in Chapter 5), and phased out the qualified family owned business deduction (see Chapter 20), now, more than ever, the team of advisers must thoroughly review the business owner's intent, incorporate the tax law changes into the plan, and then monitor the plan closely as time passes.

CHAPTER

16

Start with a Business Valuation

General Valuation Comments and Observations

The business owner is now committed to the creation of a business succession plan and has assembled a team of advisers. The next step is to determine the value of the family business that the owner intends to transfer. Once the value of the business has been determined, it will be relied upon to effectuate one of several business transfer techniques.

In order to help facilitate the valuation process, the owner of a closely held business should have an understanding of the valuation process. In this manner, one can take a proactive role in helping to value the company. Moreover, the appraiser and/or business valuation expert will be relying on the information provided by the business owner, as well as data from other available sources.

Estate and Gift Tax Implications

A brief overview of the tax laws is necessary to understand the importance of valuing the company for estate and gift tax purposes. For estate tax purposes, a decedent's gross estate generally includes the fair market value of all property owned by the decedent on the date of death. For gift tax purposes, the value of a gift is its fair market value on the date of the gift. Under Revenue Ruling 59-60, the term "fair market value" is defined as the amount at which property would change hands between a willing buyer and a willing seller when (1) the buyer is not under any compulsion to buy, (2) the seller is not under any compulsion to sell, and (3) both parties have a reasonable knowledge of all relevant facts.

Closely held entities are generally owned by either a small number of individuals or members of a family (or a combination thereof). As a result, there is a limited (if any) stock trading history to assist in determining the fair market value of any ownership interest in the entity. Furthermore, the fair market value of the closely held entity may vary with market conditions. Accordingly, it is important for estate and gift tax purposes that a valuation be completed each time that shares in the business are transferred to family members.

Fundamental Factors of the Business Valuation

The valuation of a closely held company requires a thorough understanding and analysis of all relevant facts surrounding the company, past, present, and future. There is no general formula that applies to any specific industry or type of business; rather, the approach to valuation must be adjusted to fit the particular type of business and the current economic conditions.

In order to maximize the tax benefits of a business succession plan, all valuations used for estate and gift tax planning must comply with the applicable tax law provisions. In this regard, the Internal Revenue Service provides in Revenue Procedure 59-60 a list of the eight fundamental factors it considers essential in providing a proper valuation of a company:

1. The nature of the business and the history of the enterprise from its inception.

2. The general economic outlook, as well as the specific condition and outlook of the industry engaged in by the subject company.

3. The book value of the company's stock and the financial condition of the business.

4. The earning capacity of the company.

5. The dividend-paying capacity of the company.

6. The company's goodwill and any other intangible assets of the business.

7. The prior sales of the company's stock and the size of the block of stock to be valued.

8. The market price for stock of corporations that are engaged in the same or similar lines of business, the stock of which is actively traded on the open market (either on an exchange or over-the-counter).

Nature of the Business and History of the Enterprise

The history of a corporate enterprise from its inception will show its past stability or instability, growth or lack of growth, diversity or lack of diversity in its operations, and other facts needed to form an opinion of the degree of risk involved in the business.

When an enterprise has changed its form of organization but carries on the same business as its predecessor, the history of the former enterprise should be considered. The history includes the following data:

- The nature of the business.

- The type of products or services.

- The business's operating and investment assets.

- The business's capital structure.

- The facilities used to carry on the business, especially significant manufacturing plants or factories and the like.

- The sales records.

- The management of the business, with due regard to recent significant changes.

The valuation is closely linked to future expectations for the business. Favorable past events that are unlikely to happen in the future are generally discounted for purposes of the valuation process. Conversely, positive events that are likely to reoccur generally provide a premium to the valuation.

Economic Outlook and Condition of the Industry

A sound appraisal of a business must consider current and projected economic conditions as of the date of the business valuation. The economic analysis must go beyond the line of business the company is in, and should include the national economy and industries related to the business of the company. Price trends in the markets for labor, commodities, and other materials used in the business can play an important role in this factor.

It is also important to examine the company in comparison with its competitors. Is the company more or less successful than its competitors in the same industry? Does the company maintain a stable position with respect to its competitors? Greater significance may be attached to the ability of the company to compete in its industry. For example, previous high profits due to the novelty of the company's products may not be sustainable as competition increases.

Many factors can affect the future expectations of the business and must be taken into consideration in valuing the company. The loss of a key manager or employee in a small business may have a devastating effect on the value of the company, particularly if the company does not have the personnel in place capable of succeeding the lost employee.

On the other hand, there may be factors that offset the loss of a manager's services. The nature of some businesses and their assets may not be impaired by the loss of a manager. Furthermore, the economic loss caused by the death of a key manager may be covered by life insurance, or new management may be readily available outside the company.

Book Value of the Stock and Financial Condition of the Business

If the company has maintained formal accounting records, the owners should provide the balance sheets of the company to the valuation experts. Most valuation experts compare annual financial statements for at least the five-year period immediately preceding the desired appraisal date, as well as the monthly balance sheets for the most recent months preceding the valuation.

The financial statements of a company will usually disclose the following data:

- Liquid position of the company (ratio of assets to current liabilities).
- Gross and net book value of the company's principal classes of fixed assets.
- Working capital.
- Long-term indebtedness.
- Capital structure.
- Net worth or book value.

Any balance sheet descriptions that are not self-explanatory, as well as items composed of multiple assets or liabilities, should be explained in detail by supplemental information provided by the company.

Consideration should be given to nonessential assets, such as investments in securities, real estate (if unrelated to the business), and so on. In general, assets not required in the operation of the business will be considered separate from operating assets.

In computing the book value per share of stock, investment assets should be revalued on the basis of their market value. Comparison of the company's balance sheets over several years may reveal developments such as the acquisition of additional production facilities or subsidiary companies, improvement in financial position, and changes in the capital structure of the business.

If the corporation has more than one class of outstanding stock, the explicit rights and privileges of the various classes of stock must be examined, including:

- Voting powers.

- Preference as to dividends.

- Preference as to assets in the event of liquidation.

Earning Capacity of the Company

Detailed profit-and-loss statements should be obtained and considered for the period immediately prior to the business valuation, preferably for five or more years. Statements should show the following information:

- Gross income by item.

- Principal deductions from gross income including: major expenses; interest paid on each item of long-term debt; depreciation and depletion deductions taken by the company; officers' salaries (in total if they appear to be reasonable or in detail if they seem to be either excessive or understated); charitable contributions (whether or not deductible for tax purposes); and taxes paid (including income and excess profits taxes).

- Free cash flow available for dividend payments.

- Rates and amounts paid on each class of stock.

- Surplus amounts.

- Adjustments to and reconciliation with surplus as stated on the balance sheet.

- The percentage of earnings retained by the company for business expansion.

With the availability of detailed profit-and-loss statements, the valuation expert should be able to separate recurrent from nonrecurring items, to distinguish between operating income and investment income, and to ascertain whether any line of business in which the company is engaged has operated consistently at a loss and might be abandoned with benefit to the company.

Potential future income is a major factor in valuing a closely held business. All information concerning past income and its effect on predicting the future should be obtained. Prior earnings records usually are the most reliable guide as to future expectancy. The use of arbitrary 5- or 10-year averages, without regard to current trends or future prospects, may not produce a realistic valuation. If, for instance, a record of progressively increasing or decreasing net income is found, greater weight may be accorded the most recent years' profits in estimating earning power, rather than profits from earlier years.

Dividend-Paying Capacity

In general, a business valuation will also focus on the dividend-paying capacity of the company. However, in closely held family companies, the historic dividends paid by the company are generally not a good measure of the company's value. This is because the past payments of dividends in a small business (if any) are often related to the needs of the stockholders and may be dictated by income tax planning considerations.

Furthermore, if a controlling ownership interest in a company is to be valued, the dividend factor is even less significant since the payment of dividends is at the discretion of the very interest being valued. The controlling party can substitute salaries and bonuses for dividends to reduce net income, thus understating the dividend-paying capacity of the company. It follows, therefore, that dividends are a less reliable criterion of fair market value of a closely held family business than other applicable factors.

Goodwill and Other Intangible Assets

In the final analysis, goodwill and other intangible assets are tied to the company's earning capacity. Goodwill may be viewed as the capitalized value of the excess amount of the company's net earnings over a fair return on the company's tangible assets. Other factors such as the prestige and reputation of the business, the ownership of a trade or brand name, and a record of successful operation over a prolonged period in a particular locality should be considered in determining the value of a company.

Sales of the Stock

Prior sales of stock in a closely held corporation should be carefully investigated to determine whether they represent fairly negotiated transactions. Forced or distress sales do not ordinarily reflect fair market value, just as isolated sales or sales of stock in small amounts do not necessarily reflect an accurate measure of value. This is especially true if the valuation involves either a large controlling interest (on the one hand) or a small minority interest (on the other hand).

Sales of stock in comparable corporations should also be factored into the valuation. In selecting corporations for comparison purposes, care should be taken to use only corporations engaged in the same or similar lines of business as the appraised company to avoid comparisons with companies that are in higher- (or lower-) growth industries.

All relevant factors must be considered when analyzing sales of comparable companies. For instance, a corporation having one or more classes of preferred stock in addition to its common stock should not be considered directly comparable to an entity with only common stock. Likewise, a company with a declining business and decreasing markets is not comparable to a business with a record of earnings growth and market expansion.

The size or "block" of the ownership interest itself is also a relevant factor to be considered in the valuation process. A minority ownership interest in an unlisted corporation's stock is more difficult to sell than a similar block of listed stock. It is equally true that a controlling interest in a corporation may justify a higher value for a specific block of stock.

All of the foregoing factors and any other offsetting considerations should be carefully considered and weighed by the appraiser. Once the value of the overall business is determined, the final step in the valuation process is to determine whether any of the discounting techniques discussed next apply to the subject company.

Valuation Discounts

A business owner should recognize that if one owns publicly traded stock, there is a ready market for such securities and the current price of such securities can be easily determined. However, with respect to the sale of a closely held business interest, there may not be a ready market for the sale of an interest in the business. Accordingly, the valuation expert can discount the value of the company based on any number of factors unique to the owner's closely held business, including, specifically, the absence of a ready market for the shares of stock in the company.

For estate and gift tax purposes, discounts serve to decrease the value of any ownership interest transferred by gift to family members. This effectively achieves a leveraged effect by maximizing the use of the owner's $11,000 annual gift tax exclusion and/or exemption equivalent for purposes of passing interests in the family business to the owner's heirs.

When assessing the valuation discount associated with the transfer by gift of stock in a family-owned business, it is imperative for the business valuation expert to assert a reasonable position in determining how great a discount is warranted in light of the specific circumstances surrounding the family-owned business. Taking too great a discount may have the potential for inviting an IRS audit that may lead to protracted litigation and potential reduction in the discounts originally taken. Such a result is costly and can severely hinder future gifts by the senior members of the family-owned business.

Although courts generally consider the valuation opinions of expert appraisers, they have also demonstrated a willingness to disregard the experts and render their own opinions as to valuations. In *Mandelbaum v. Commissioner, T.C. Memo 1995–255*, the United States Tax Court sought to value the shares of a family-owned corporation in New Jersey. In that case, the taxpayer's experts had assessed a 70% discount on the shares of stock transferred to the owner's heirs because of an absence of a market for the shares. The IRS challenged the 70% discount and the battle ensued.

The Tax Court considered numerous factors regarding the corporation, including specifically the ability to trade the shares of stock in a free and open market. In its opinion, the Court found that the corporation's ability to make substantial dividends, with a strong and proven management team, and the fact that the corporation was considered a leader in its industry did not coincide with the taxpayer's position that the stock warranted such a substantial discount. Rather, based on the factors set forth in the case, the Court determined that a 30% discount for lack of marketability was appropriate. This discount appears reasonable in light of the surrounding facts. It was the taxpayer's experts' valuation report that was ultimately considered unreasonable.

Different Types of Valuation Discounts

There are several types of discounts, including, but not limited to, the following:

- Lack of marketability discounts.
- Minority interest discounts.
- Information access and reliability discounts.
- Key manager or thin management discounts.
- Comparability discounts.
- Investment company discounts.
- Market absorption or blockage discounts.
- Built-in capital gains discounts.

The lack-of-marketability and the minority discounts are the two discounts most generally applied in valuing the stock of closely held companies. However, several other adjustments or discounts should also be routinely considered when determining the value of shares in a closely held business for gifting purposes.

Marketability Adjustments

One of the most frequently used discounting techniques is the adjustment for lack of marketability. This lack-of-marketability discount is based on the fact that stock in a closely held business is not readily transferable, and thus it is not as attractive to potential investors.

As a result, stock in a closely held corporation is more difficult to sell than publicly traded stock and is thus worth less than readily tradable stock. Accordingly, the valuation expert may discount the value of the stock in a company by the fact that a ready market does not exist for the stock in the company.

The determination of the lack-of-marketability discount should incorporate the findings of various published studies that provide a basis for selecting such a discount. These studies typically revolve around four methods of quantifying the discount associated with the lack of marketability for the stock:

1. Comparison of private placements of restricted stock of otherwise publicly traded securities of the same company. (Since the difference between restricted stock and publicly traded stock in the same company is based solely on the ability to trade the security on a public exchange, the discount for lack of marketability is established by the price difference between the restricted and unrestricted stock.)

2. Comparison of sales of closely held stock subsequently brought public.

3. The cost (or "float") of publicly offering the stock.

4. Close analysis of court cases.

Based on these studies, it has been determined by experts and confirmed by the courts that a lack-of-marketability discount is generally warranted for stock in a closely held company. Based on these facts, it is not unusual for a lack-of-marketability discount to reduce the value of the shares of stock in a closely held business being transferred by as much as 20% to 50%.

Minority Interest Discounts

Another important consideration when determining the value of stock in a closely held company is the minority interest discount. When executing a business succession plan, it is typical for the owner to transfer a minority (noncontrolling) interest in the company to heirs and for the process to be continued over a period of time. The Internal Revenue Service recognizes that stock that does not reflect a controlling interest in a company is not worth as much as the stock held by the stockholder who retains control. Accordingly, this lack of control has a direct bearing on the value of the stock being transferred.

If the recipients of such stock have no rights over the control of the operation of the company, including specifically any rights to make distributions to themselves as shareholders, this aspect has a direct bearing on the value of the stock being transferred. The minority discount is recognized because the beneficiaries lack control over corporate policy, cannot direct the payment of dividends, and cannot compel liquidation of the company. Because of this lack of control, a willing purchaser of such an interest would pay far less for it on a pro rata basis than for a controlling interest.

The idea of the minority discount can best be illustrated by a hypothetical example of the Acme Corporation, owned by four shareholders: John, 25%; Freda, 25%; Michael, 25%; and Gloria, 25%. The corporation has been valued at $10 million, and Michael is seeking to transfer his 25% to members of his family.

If the accountant who prepared the valuation of Michael's shares simply took the $10 million valuation and multiplied it by Michael's 25%, then clearly his interest would be valued at $2.5 million. However, if the accountant recognized that Michael is merely a minority shareholder (without the ability through his 25% vote to declare distributions of profits, approve sales or control the vote on any corporate issue), Michael's shares would clearly be eligible for the minority discount. Consequently, the valuation expert may affix a discount to Michael's 25% interest in Acme. In this manner, if the expert were to affix a 40% discount to Michael's shares, the value of the gift could be decreased by 40% and the $2.5 million value would be reduced to $1.5 million.

Observe that the marketability discount and minority discount are different concepts. The lack-of-marketability discount will nearly always apply in the case of a closely held company even when the shares involved represent a controlling interest, whereas the minority adjustment will apply only when a noncontrolling interest is being transferred to each beneficiary.

Information Access and Reliability Adjustments

A valuation is based on the information available to the valuation expert as of the date of the business valuation. The hypothetical willing buyer and willing seller have reasonable knowledge of the relevant facts, but do they have assurances that the financial details relating to the enterprise will be made available in the future?

Much of the information used by a valuation expert is provided by the business owners themselves. Closely held businesses do not always maintain formal records such as financial statements prepared in accordance with generally accepted accounting principles. The information provided to the valuation expert on a particular company can range from the extensively detailed statements maintained by companies subject to the securities laws and stock exchange requirements to unaudited financial reports kept by company bookkeepers. Interestingly enough, this very uncertainty regarding the reliability of the data provided can be a basis for an additional valuation adjustment. The valuation expert has to take the quality of the information provided into account when valuing the business of a closely held company.

Key Manager or Thin Management Adjustments

There is greater risk (and thus a lower value) for a company whose future is dependent on one or only a few key managers when compared to a company with a management team tied to the company. This key manager discount often applies to closely held or family businesses because the ongoing success of the company is many times dependent on only one or two key individuals.

Comparability (Small Company) Adjustments

Comparability or small company discounts may be warranted when large, publicly traded companies are used as the standard for valuation. The same factors warranting marketability and thin management adjustments may be present here, but the main element is that the higher return demanded by investors from smaller companies is reflective of the financial risk of investing in smaller companies, which have less financial clout in terms of access to capital through public offerings or lenders. A smaller company may not have the same ability to survive a business or financial reversal or economic downturn, adding to the risk involved. Thus, when valuing a small closely held company, the valuation expert will assign a discount to the stock to reflect these risks.

Investment Company Adjustments

Investment company adjustments are usually applied in situations when the valuation of a private investment company (such as a financial, real estate, or natural resource company) is based on the market values of the underlying assets owned by the company rather than its earnings. From a pragmatic viewpoint, in order to obtain the value of the company's assets, the company may have to expend time and money to sell its assets. Buyers of such assets may not be easily found, and taxes will be due on such sales. Accordingly, a discount may be assigned to the stock of such a company to reflect the costs and uncertainties surrounding the potential realization of the value in the company.

This discount reflects the delay and expenses of realizing any profit from the company's assets. It also reflects the observation that although there is data establishing the underlying value of the assets owned by such a company, there is an entirely separate market for the buying and selling of ownership interests in investment companies themselves. In contrast to the minority discount, even a near 100 percent owner may be entitled to this discount.

Market Absorption (Blockage) Adjustments

A market absorption or blockage discount is generally applicable when the size of a block of stock to be sold is so large in comparison to the daily volume in an otherwise active market that it cannot be absorbed in the normal course of trading. The size of a blockage discount will reflect the value of the block of stock as determined by the price an underwriter would get on behalf of the seller through the sale of the block of stock outside normal market channels.

When an owner seeks to sell an unusually large block of stock in a company, the size of the block will depress the market for the stock and consequently reduce the price the seller would otherwise receive in an open market. This blockage discount differs from the lack-of-marketability discount discussed earlier, which is premised on the absence of a ready market for the stock. In the case of a blockage discount, there is a market but it cannot absorb the block of stock being offered for sale. Obviously, this type of analysis rarely comes up when valuing the stock of a closely held business.

Built-In Capital Gains Discounts

The capital gains discount is premised on the fact that many family-owned businesses were created and initially capitalized decades ago with low or minimal funding. Fortunately, over the years, the company has significantly appreciated in value. However, as a result, if there was a sale of the stock in the company, significant capital gains tax would be due. The fact that such a tax liability exists will have a direct impact on what the value of the business would be in the event of a sale and thus on the value of the stock in the company.

As this discount has only recently been recognized in a decision rendered by the Second Circuit Court of Appeals, there is little precedent as to what the applicable discount for the built-in capital gains liability might be. However, the accountant or the valuation expert should be able to establish the potential tax liability and apply a reasonable discount accordingly.

Multiple Discounts

These discounts do not exist in a vacuum, but rather more often overlap each other. Accordingly, the valuation expert will be able to combine the various discounts to reflect the value of the stock to be gifted, further reducing the value of the gifts. However, multiple restrictions may increase discounts only marginally. For example, a minority discount will have less of an impact on the value of the stock being transferred if a lack-of-marketability discount has already been taken into consideration. In this fashion, each discounting factor will have only an incremental effect on the value of the stock being transferred. Thus, in valuing the stock, the valuation expert will look to the discounts in concert and arrive at a valuation only after analyzing all of these discounts together.

Conclusion

The business owner, committed to the process of a business succession plan, has now completed the valuation and must make a determination as to how many shares should be transferred to his or her successors. The business owner must now work with advisers to make this determination. In this regard, legal and accounting advisers should provide the owner with information as to the gift tax implications of any plan and the appropriate estate and business succession planning tools to implement the plan. The business succession planning attorney must review any existing buy-sell agreements that govern restrictions on transfers of shares and ensure that any such agreements represent the current status of the corporation and allow for the transference of business interests. The review, creation, and modification of the buy-sell agreement is crucial to the business succession planning process and is discussed at length in the next chapter.

Buy-Sell Agreements

Introduction

As if creating a successful business isn't hard enough, now add the dilemma of what happens if one of your partners or shareholders dies, becomes disabled, or wants to retire. Generally, what most business owners do not see as a viable solution is having the spouse of the deceased, disabled, or retired shareholder become a new partner in the business. Nor does the spouse of such deceased, disabled, or retired shareholder generally want to jump into such a role.

Typically, in the event a shareholder dies, the spouse of the deceased shareholder is generally looking for only one thing—to be bought out of the deceased spouse's interest in the company, generally for cash. In the event that a shareholder becomes disabled, hopefully the business will continue to exist, but the remaining partners who are operating the business on a day-to-day basis will generally feel a little put-upon by the disabled partner who is no longer contributing to the business and yet continues to receive a full share of the profits. Also, the disabled partner may generally feel a sense of guilt by continuing to maintain ownership in the business and pulling out profits for which he or she is not contributing any value.

A partner-shareholder who is ready to retire and reap the rewards of many years in the business may be looking to the other partners to buy his or her share in the business. However, if the business does not have the liquidity to buy out the retired partner, once again inequities may arise if the retired partner is no longer contributing to the business yet continues to demand a share of the profits.

A buy-sell agreement is intended to address the issues of what happens upon the death, disability, or retirement of a partner or shareholder in a closely held business. Thus, in order to effectively draft a buy-sell agreement to address these issues, a comprehensive review must be undertaken to accurately determine the company's purpose, the partner's or shareholder's needs, the value of the business, and the events that will trigger a buyout. As touched upon earlier, a well-drafted buy-sell agreement is designed to address many of the problems associated with creating a business succession plan for a family-owned business.

The four primary issues that should be dealt with in an effectively drafted buy-sell agreement are:

1. Setting the terms for any future purchases or sales of stock by and between the current owners and their successors or other family members.

2. Establishing the purchase price or a formula for calculating the purchase price for any such future transfers of stock between the shareholders upon death, disability, or retirement.

3. Imposing restrictions on any transfers of stock, whether to outside third parties or to other family members.

4. Specifying whatever arrangements are necessary if a shareholder were to die, become disabled, or retire, including specifically the terms upon which any buyout will take place. In this regard, one of the primary issues to be addressed is whether, upon the death of a shareholder, the deceased owner's stock should be purchased by the surviving owners (referred to as a "cross-purchase agreement") or by the business itself (referred to as a "redemption agreement").

Use of a Buy-Sell Agreement upon the Death of a Shareholder

Although a properly drafted buy-sell agreement will address the buyout of a stockholder upon either death, disability, or retirement, the primary focus of this chapter will be the use of such an agreement upon the death of a stockholder. However, many of the concepts discussed in this chapter apply equally to the issues arising upon the disability or retirement of the shareholder.

Most buy-sell agreements are designed to serve certain common purposes in dealing with the death of a shareholder in a closely held business. A primary purpose of the buy-sell agreement is to maintain the continuity of management of the business and to prevent the deceased owner's family from creating conflicts that might injure the business or infringe upon its ongoing success following the death of a shareholder. A properly drafted buy-sell agreement allows the surviving owners to continue to manage the business without interference from the family and other heirs of the deceased owner.

A second purpose of the buy-sell agreement is to provide cash to the deceased owner's estate and/or family. Unlike publicly traded securities, stock in a closely held business generally has no ready market. The buy-sell agreement will provide for the purchase of a deceased owner's shares, either by the surviving shareholders through a cross-purchase agreement or by the company itself through a redemption agreement. By providing for this acquisition of stock from the decedent's estate, the buy-sell agreement in essence converts the deceased owner's unmarketable securities into readily available cash and/or a long-term income stream. This use of a buy-sell agreement thus provides the decedent's estate and family with much-needed funds to pay for ongoing living expenses and taxes as well as funeral and estate expenses.

Use of a Buy-Sell Agreement in Determining Price for the Stock of a Deceased Shareholder

The buy-sell agreement should help establish the value of the deceased owner's interest in the closely held business for buyout, as well as estate tax purposes. Through the use of a buy-sell agreement, the owners of a closely held business are able to utilize any one (or a combination) of several alternative methods for the purpose of establishing the price for which the survivors, either directly or through the company, will acquire the deceased owner's interest. This chapter will examine some of the more common pricing methods.

Agreed Value Method

The owners of a closely held business are usually in the best position to know the true value of their business. Under the agreed value method, the owners agree in advance to a specific purchase price. If an owner dies, that interest will be purchased from the estate for a specified dollar amount, no matter when the death occurs. Since the purchase price is fixed, there will be less uncertainty resulting from the death of an owner, and the parties will have ample opportunity to provide for funding sources to complete the acquisition.

This agreed value method can be perceived as a very simple method to implement once the shareholders have mutually determined a price at which they agree to receive (or pay) for a decedent's stock. However, if the business experiences any substantial changes over time (as every business does), this method may eventually result in a price that is either too high or too low.

One solution is for the buy-sell agreement to require the owners to periodically review and update the agreed value based upon changes in the business. Since typical owners often forget to update the agreed value set forth in their buy-sell agreement, the buy-sell agreement can also include a provision allowing the owners to reject the agreed value if it has not been updated for several years.

The primary benefit of using an agreed value method of valuation is that it provides a simple and inexpensive way to eliminate uncertainty in the value of a closely held business. The primary disadvantage of using this method is that it may result in an inaccurate price for the owners of a business with a fluctuating value. Furthermore, the value agreed upon by the owners of the business need not be respected by the IRS, resulting in a buyout price substantially below the amount the IRS may think the company is worth at the death of a shareholder. This can result in higher estate taxes for the estate of the deceased shareholder, yet insufficient funds to pay those taxes.

Formula Value Method

The formula value method is frequently found in more sophisticated buy-sell agreements because the formula value method, by its very essence, is designed to address the very changes that take place as a business builds and grows with each passing year. In arriving at a formula value, the owners should take into consideration the unique qualities of their business. Formula values can be based on book value (with certain adjustments), a multiple of earnings (net or gross), or a combination of any number of reasonable factors.

Book value is frequently a poor measure of a business's value since it generally represents historical valuations (adjusted for depreciation), which usually bear little or no resemblance to the current fair market value of a company's ongoing business. Book value fails to take into consideration a business's earning capacity or the value of its goodwill as an ongoing concern.

Capitalization of earnings, which multiplies the earnings of a business by a predetermined factor, takes into consideration the business's earning capacity and goodwill, but it may not take into consideration the true value of the assets owned by the business. Thus, it is imperative that the business owners work together with their advisers to develop a formula that reflects the true nature of their business. However, as in the case of the agreed value method, the owners should revisit their predetermined formula on a periodic basis to ensure that it still reflects their business model.

Appraisal or Arbitration Value

Under the appraisal or arbitration value method, the owners agree in advance that, upon the death of an owner, the value of the company will be determined either by an appraisal of the business or by arbitration.

Utilizing the appraisal or arbitration method to determine the value of a business is costly and time-consuming, but may result in a value that is closer to the fair market value of the decedent's shares at the time of death than certain other methods discussed here. For instance, under the appraisal method, both the estate and the surviving member(s) of the business are generally advised to seek separate appraisers. If the two appraisers cannot agree on a value, the parties are generally required to agree on a third appraiser whose decision will be final (unless the two sides sue each other). The parties have now paid for three appraisals of the business, each of which can be very expensive.

Furthermore, the value determined by the appraisers (or by an arbitrator) may be totally contrary to what the shareholders would have actually agreed upon had they all been alive at the time. Thus, because of all of the uncertainties, costs, and burdens placed on the business and the surviving members of the business (as well as the family of the deceased member), this valuation method is generally not recommended when drafting a buy-sell agreement.

Acceptance of Price Determination Methods by the IRS

For estate and gift tax purposes, an agreed value, formula value, or appraisal/arbitration value that is established pursuant to the terms of a preexisting buy-sell agreement will generally be respected by the IRS as the value of the business interest of the deceased shareholder, provided that:

- The buy-sell agreement was negotiated and entered into by the parties at arm's length.

- The decedent's estate is bound by the agreement to sell the decedent's interest to the remaining shareholders of the company (or the company itself).

- The purchaser (whether the surviving owners or the business) is obligated to purchase the decedent's interest or has an option to do so.

- The business interest could not have been disposed of during the lifetime of the decedent without first offering it to the company or to the other shareholders at a price no higher than the one fixed at the time of the decedent's death.

- The method used closely parallels the value of the company, as best calculated by all of the parties while alive, and the price specified in the agreement is fair and adequate as of the time the agreement is entered into by the parties.

On the other hand, if the buy-sell agreement is between related parties and the IRS determines that it consists of nothing more than a device designed to pass on a decedent's interests to "the natural object of his or her bounty for less than full value," the agreed price may not be binding for tax purposes.

Cross-Purchase versus Redemption Agreements

If, under the terms of a buy-sell agreement, when a business owner dies, his or her shares are required to be bought by the surviving owners of the business, the agreement is generally referred to as a cross-purchase agreement. If, however, under the terms of the agreement, the decedent's shares are required to be purchased or redeemed by the business itself, the agreement is generally referred to as a redemption agreement. A determination as to whether to utilize a cross-purchase agreement as opposed to a stock redemption agreement depends on the unique facts and circumstances of the business, including the type of entity involved—that is, a corporation, partnership, or limited liability company.

Corporate Buy-Sell Agreements

In determining whether a cross-purchase or redemption agreement should be utilized in a corporate setting, many factors should be considered, including the following.

Tax Consequences

In certain circumstances, a cross-purchase agreement may be preferable to a stock redemption agreement. For instance, with a cross-purchase agreement, the surviving shareholders get a cost basis in the stock equal to their purchase price, whereas with a redemption agreement they do not get a step-up in the basis of their shares because the company is deemed to have acquired the stock of the deceased shareholder.

For example, A and B each own 50% of the stock of a corporation. The tax basis of each 50% interest is $100,000, and the fair market value of each 50% interest is $500,000. Under a stock redemption agreement, if A dies, B's basis in his stock of the corporation (which now constitutes a 100% ownership interest), remains at $100,000 because B simply owns the same shares he owned prior to the redemption.

However, under the terms of a cross-purchase agreement, B is required to purchase A's stock directly from A's estate for $500,000. As a result, B's basis in the stock he acquires from A's estate ($500,000) is added to the $100,000 basis in the shares he already owns for a total basis of $600,000 in all of the stock he now owns after A's death. If it appears likely that the surviving shareholder will sell the business after the death of the other shareholder, serious consideration should be given to structuring the buy-sell agreement in the form of a cross-purchase agreement rather than as a redemption agreement.

In most instances, the form of agreement makes no difference to the deceased shareholder's estate for federal income tax purposes. In either case, the sale will result in no gain or loss because the estate will have received a new or stepped-up basis for the stock of the deceased shareholder equal to the purchase price (whether bought by the company or by the surviving shareholders). However, this favorable tax treatment applies to a redemption agreement only if the redemption is treated as a capital transaction rather than as a dividend taxable as ordinary income. In this regard, the general rule is that any distribution of money or property by a corporation to a shareholder (including a deceased shareholder's estate) will be taxed as a dividend to the extent of the corporation's earnings or profits, unless one of the following four exceptions apply:

1. The redemption payment completely terminates the stockholder's ownership interest in the corporation.

2. The redemption of stock is not being made on a proportionate basis for all stockholders and therefore is substantially disproportionate to the interest of the shareholders.

3. A distribution results in a partial liquidation of the corporation.

4. The distribution is not essentially equivalent to a dividend.

The most common method used to avoid the treatment of a distribution as a dividend at the time of the death of a shareholder is to have the redemption qualify as either a complete or "substantially disproportionate" redemption. In satisfying the tests for disproportionate or complete redemption, the rules of "constructive ownership" set forth in the Internal Revenue Code are applied in determining the number of shares a shareholder owned both before and after the redemption. For this purpose, living shareholders are deemed to own the stock of their spouses, children, grandchildren, and parents, in addition to their own stock.

In addition, stock owned by a beneficiary of a deceased shareholder's estate is considered to be constructively owned by the estate and such stock is considered as owned proportionally by its beneficiaries regardless of whether they are related to the deceased shareholder for purposes of applying the tests. As a consequence, if one of the beneficiaries of the deceased shareholder's estate already owned stock in the corporation, the estate may be considered, for tax purposes, as owning such stock, resulting in ordinary income treatment to the extent of earnings and profits of the corporation, rather than as a tax-free capital transaction. Thus, care must be taken to ensure that a buy-sell agreement structured as a redemption agreement does not inadvertently cost the estate of a deceased shareholder increased taxes that could otherwise have been avoided by structuring the buy-sell agreement as a cross-purchase agreement. The shareholders of a closely held family business should work with the firm's accountants and attorneys to avoid this tax trap.

Unequal Ownership

In those situations in which the shareholders of a company do not own equal shares in the company, it may be inequitable for the buy-sell agreement to be structured as a redemption agreement, since in such instances the majority shareholder may end up paying a disproportionate share of the costs associated with a buyout.

For example, assume a closely held business has two shareholders, A and B. A owns 70% and B owns 30% of the stock in the corporation. Under a stock redemption agreement funded with insurance, the premiums are generally paid for out of the earnings of the company. In such instances, but for the buy-sell agreement, A would have received 70% of the amount that went to pay for the insurance premiums and B would have received 30%. Thus, A ends up paying a disproportionate amount of the premiums for the insurance used to buy up B's 30% of the company. Under a cross-purchase agreement, each shareholder will typically use his or her own funds to purchase the other's stock, so that these disproportionate payouts can be avoided.

Number of Shareholders

If there are a significant number of shareholders in the corporation, and the buy-sell agreement is to be funded with life insurance, a redemption agreement may be preferable to a cross-purchase agreement. In such instances, the use of a redemption agreement will reduce the administrative burden associated with structuring the acquisition of life insurance. A cross-purchase agreement requires each stockholder to purchase life insurance on the other stockholders.

For example, if a corporation with 10 shareholders adopts a redemption agreement, only 10 life insurance policies will need to be acquired by the corporation. However, if the shareholders have entered into a cross-purchase agreement, each of the shareholders would have to acquire nine policies, one on each of his fellow shareholders' lives, making a total of 90 life insurance policies necessary to fully fund the agreement. A stock redemption agreement doesn't involve the administrative problems of dealing with so many policies. In the alternative, shareholders who insist on using a cross-purchase agreement should consider establishing a partnership for the purpose of holding the policies on each other's lives.

State Law Restrictions on Redemption

If a stock redemption agreement is adopted by the company, it may be necessary to satisfy certain requirements of state law before making the necessary redemption at the time of a shareholder's death. For example, in some states, stock may be redeemed only out of earned or other specifically designated types of surplus. If the purchase is not funded with life insurance (thus providing the needed surplus or retained earnings under state law requirements), it may be necessary, when state law causes a redemption problem, to provide that if the corporation cannot legally redeem all of the decedent's stock, the surviving shareholders will either be compelled or have the option to purchase such stock.

Partnership or Limited Liability Company Buy-Sell Agreements

With regard to a buy-sell agreement for either a partnership or a limited liability company, there exists a major tax distinction between a cross-purchase agreement and a redemption agreement in the treatment of goodwill. With a cross-purchase agreement, the portion of the interest in the business attributable to goodwill is treated as a capital asset for tax purposes. Thus, the payment of the portion of the purchase price attributable to such goodwill is not deductible by the partnership or limited liability company. Since the partnership or limited liability company interest acquired by the surviving owners of the company will receive a new tax basis on the deceased owner's death equal to the purchase price, the portion of the purchase price attributable to goodwill, which is treated as part of the capital transaction, will not be included in the taxable income of the deceased owner's estate.

On the other hand, if a redemption agreement is used, the partners or members have a choice. If the agreement states that a specific amount is to be paid for goodwill, the payment for this amount is treated as the payment for a capital asset. If the agreement is silent as to the amount of the redemption price allocable to goodwill, the portion of the purchase price allocable to goodwill may be considered as an income item and may be taxable as ordinary income to the deceased owner's estate and be deductible by the surviving partners of the partnership or surviving members of the limited liability company, as the case may be. In return for receiving this income tax deduction, the parties may be willing to have the buy-sell agreement provide for a larger goodwill payment than they would otherwise.

Another important tax issue regarding the issue of a buy-sell agreement in the context of a partnership or limited liability company involves the tax consequences of interest earned by the deceased partner on any obligations in the year of death. Unless there is a buy-sell agreement to the contrary, the death of a partner may not close the partnership or limited liability company's tax year. Accordingly, when a partner or member dies, that person's share of income or loss for the tax year ending after the death will be included in the estate income tax return rather than in the deceased owner's final income tax return. Depending on whether a lower or higher income tax results from reporting the deceased owner's share on the estate income tax return rather than on the decedent's final return, there may be a substantial benefit or detriment, depending on the particular facts and circumstances. However, when there is a buy-sell agreement terminating the decedent's interests at the time of death, the partnership or limited liability company's tax year (with respect to the deceased owner) will close as of the date of sale. If the sale under the buy-sell agreement occurs as of the date of death, then the tax year is deemed to close on the date of death and the deceased owner's share of income or loss will be included in the decedent's final return.

Conclusion

As you can see from the issues identified in this chapter, numerous questions surrounding the death, disability, or retirement of a business owner can and should be addressed in a properly drafted buy-sell agreement. In this regard, it is imperative that the owners of a business sit down with their advisers and go through all the various issues unique to their business before entering into such an agreement. However, once a properly thought-out agreement has been reduced to paper, it can save numerous headaches if and when one member of the business should pass away, become disabled, or decide it is time to head for the retirement community.

Funding Buy-Sell Agreements

Introduction

Having established the value of the business and drafted a buy-sell agreement, the shareholders of a company need to consider how to fund the sale of shares in the event of death, disability, or retirement of any or all of the shareholders. Depending on their financial means, the shareholders may agree that upon a triggering event such as the death of a shareholder, the surviving shareholders (under a cross-purchase agreement) or the corporation itself (under a redemption agreement) will simply buy out the decedent's shares from the deceased shareholder's estate using either corporate assets or their own personal resources.

However, the value of the deceased shareholder's interest as determined by the terms of the buy-sell agreement may be substantial, and corporate assets or an individual's own resources may not be either available or adequate. The surviving shareholders (or the corporation itself) could borrow the funds necessary to satisfy the terms of such an all-cash buyout. However, it would be far more advantageous to the surviving shareholders if the buy-sell agreement also provided for payments to be stretched out over a period of time. In such an event, the surviving shareholders could, for example, put down a lump sum (10% or 20%) and pay the remaining obligation under the terms of an installment agreement set forth in the buy-sell agreement, which could run for a number of years at an agreed-upon interest rate.

Shareholders should consider several factors before agreeing to an all-cash purchase or installment note obligation. First, the heirs of the deceased shareholder may need to live, at least in part, on the value of the decedent's shares. In this regard, the surviving spouse may not be able to support a family on the payments provided under a long-term installment obligation. On the other hand, the surviving shareholders may not be able to make the note payments under the installment agreement throughout the term of obligation, particularly if the deceased shareholder was key to the ongoing success of the business, potentially reducing the earnings of the company following the key manager's death.

Can Life Insurance Help?

In order to avoid the financial uncertainty of a long-term installment note buyout, the business owners' advisers may recommend that the buy-sell agreement be funded with life insurance purchased on the lives of the respective shareholders. With a cross-purchase buy-sell agreement, each shareholder purchases a life insurance contract on the lives of the other shareholders. For example, assume the Warren Corporation has four shareholders, John, Fred, Chris, and Phil:

- John, Fred, and Chris would purchase life insurance on Phil.

- Fred, Chris, and Phil would purchase life insurance on John.

- Chris, Phil, and John would purchase life insurance on Fred.

- Phil, John, and Fred would purchase life insurance on Chris.

Structuring a buy-sell agreement under the cross-purchase method provides the funds necessary to immediately buy out the shares held by the deceased shareholder's estate without having to assume the obligations of an installment agreement. Under such an agreement, the surviving shareholders are obligated to buy, and the estate of the deceased shareholder is obligated to sell, the shares held by the deceased shareholder at the time of death. The life insurance policies are purchased to ensure that the surviving shareholders have sufficient cash to make the necessary payment in one lump sum. In order to simplify the acquisition of life insurance in situations where there are multiple shareholders, it may be prudent to place the insurance policies in a partnership made up of all the shareholders, providing for the distribution of any life insurance proceeds to the estate of a deceased shareholder.

If the value of the decedent's shares subsequently grows beyond the size of the insurance policy, the agreement should provide for the payout and terms of the remaining amounts due under the buy-sell agreement (generally under an installment plan). The life insurance agent who previously reviewed the insurance policies of the company and the shareholders will have the ability to propose the appropriate type of insurance, as well as the size of the death benefit necessary to fund the cross-purchase buy-sell agreement. Ideally, the company should be revalued every year so that the policies' death benefits are current, thereby negating the need for an installment note.

The shareholders must recognize that life insurance premiums are not a deductible expense. Rather, the business owners have the option to bonus the life insurance premiums to each of the shareholders who, in turn, will individually make the life insurance premium payments to the insurance company. The shareholders, however, must understand that the bonuses used to pay the insurance premiums will be included in wages on their individual tax returns.

It is not uncommon for business owners to object to picking up this tax liability. Therefore, the business, depending on its own cash flow requirements, may utilize a program known as "double bonusing" or "grossing up" the bonuses. By so doing, the business would make bonuses to the shareholders not only in an amount to cover the premiums to be paid under the life insurance policies, but also for the tax liability that the business owners would recognize on the amount bonused.

Disability Buyout Insurance

The death of a shareholder is only one of the triggering events that may cause a shareholder's interest to be bought out. Disability may also serve as a triggering event forcing a company to buy out a shareholder's stake in the company. Too often, shareholders overlook the concept of disability buyout insurance. Most business owners are familiar with the concept of disability insurance, and may have a policy that provides for all or part of their incomes to be paid by their insurance carrier during a period of disability. Few business owners, however, possess disability insurance that actually provides the company or nondisabled shareholders the economic means to acquire the shares of a stockholder-employee if such shareholder should become permanently disabled.

Disability buyout insurance is a unique insurance funding vehicle. It provides that upon the disability of a shareholder, as defined in the buy-sell agreement, the insurance is paid to the existing shareholders so that they have the funds to buy out the disabled shareholder's shares. Just as in funding the life insurance premiums, the shareholders must report the disability buyout premiums on their tax returns, and once more, the bonusing program discussed in the previous section is applicable.

Retirement

Shareholders must also provide a funding mechanism to buy out a retiring shareholder's interest in the company. Under a buy-sell agreement, the shareholders who are to remain may have the ability to buy out the retiring shareholder's interest by using a down payment of 10% or 20% and structuring the balance as an installment agreement to be paid over a period of years at an agreed-upon interest rate. However, they may also, through the use of life insurance, seek to provide a cash value that will build within the life insurance contract. Properly structured, the life insurance program may permit the remaining shareholders to borrow against the cash value in the life insurance policy and use those funds to help buy out the retiring shareholder's interest, in whole or in part.

However, a myriad of issues must be analyzed before buying life insurance to fund a buyout. Only after the team of advisers considers the following 15 issues can the structure of the buyout take shape:

1. What form of entity is involved—partnership, S corporation, C corporation, or limited liability company?

2. How many owners are involved?

3. How is the health of the owners?

4. What are the ages of the owners?

5. Do any of the owners plan on retiring within five years? Ten years?

6. Has a valuation of the business been completed?

7. Are the shares, units, or partnership interests owned equally?

8. Do the insurance illustrations project enough cash buildup for each owner to be bought out upon projected retirement dates?

9. Will the business bonus the premiums to the owners?

10. If premiums will be bonused, have potential inequities been addressed? For example, if shareholder A owns 80%, is 35 years old, and healthy, while shareholder B owns 20%, is 65 years old, and a smoker, does A object to the company bonusing out premiums to B?

11. If a buyout is contemplated for retirement, is the death benefit going to lapse or be purchased by the business, the insured, or other owners?

12. If the entity has three or more shareholders and one dies, becomes disabled, or retires, will the survivors need to recalculate their interests and adjust the insurance policies?

13. Are additional owners likely to join the entity?

14. Are any of the owners uninsurable?

15. Is disability buyout insurance to be purchased?

Only after the team of advisers together with the business owners have considered the issues may a determination be made as to whether the buy-sell agreement should be a cross-purchase, stock redemption, or wait-and-see agreement (allowing the shareholders to determine at the time of triggering event to either purchase the shares or have the company redeem them).

Valuation Updates

Finally, the shareholders must recognize that the value of their company changes from year to year. A common mistake in business succession planning is to complete the valuation and not revisit it again over subsequent years. Shareholders run the risk that several years later, when a triggering event occurs, the life insurance originally purchased does not reflect the value of the company at the time of the triggering event, which can only lead to disgruntled heirs and potential litigation. Accordingly, both the business owners and their advisers should annually update the business valuation, and alter life insurance used to fund the buyout accordingly.

Transference of Business Interests

A number of factors should be taken into consideration when determining whether to make gifts of a closely held business interest to family members or other individuals. These factors include not only the typical tax, business, and other financial issues normally addressed in such circumstances but also the effect that such a gift or series of gifts will have on both the beneficiaries and the company.

The primary tax and business considerations include the donor's ability to reduce the size of his or her taxable estate for estate tax purposes, to provide for the orderly succession of the business to the next generation, and to ensure that any future appreciation in the business takes place in the name of the children and/or other family members rather than in the current owner's estate. However, nontax considerations, including the desire to provide the beneficiaries of such gifts with the incentive and opportunity to become involved in the operations of the company, are equally important.

Factors to Be Considered Before Gifting Company Stock

Making plans for the orderly transfer of control in a family business in a manner that both ensures the success of the business and fosters the personal growth of the successors should be of primary importance in determining when and to whom to make such gifts. A business owner should undertake a thorough in-depth analysis of the advantages and disadvantages associated with creating a gifting program of company stock. In this regard, the following factors should be considered before making a gift of company stock.

Reduction in Total Transfer Taxes

One of the most important reasons for considering the gifting of stock in a closely held family business is to enable the donor to reduce the ultimate estate tax liability.

Annual Gift Tax Exclusions

Each U.S. citizen may exclude the first $11,000 of gifts (other than gifts of future interests in property) made to any number of recipients during each calendar year. This annual exclusion is applied to all qualifying gifts to each recipient during the year in the order in which they are made until the $11,000 limit per person is exhausted. A gift tax return is required to be filed by an individual donor only if the annual gifts to any one person exceed $11,000 or if a husband and wife utilize gift splitting (as discussed in the following paragraphs). Thus, the owner of a closely held business may make annual gifts of up to $11,000 worth of stock per recipient without any gift tax consequences.

Furthermore, the advantages of annual-exclusion gifts can be doubled if the donor is married and both spouses utilize their annual exclusions. Each spouse can transfer separate interests in company stock or they can utilize gift splitting. Under gift splitting, the double exclusion can be obtained when one spouse owns and gifts all of the stock provided the other (nondonor) spouse consents to treat the transfer as if made one-half by each spouse.

A gift made by one spouse to any person other than the other spouse is considered made one-half by each spouse if both consent to split all gifts made by either while married during the calendar year. The effect of this provision is to permit one spouse to use the other's annual exclusion along with his or her own, thus increasing the annual exclusion from $11,000 to $22,000. Spouses may elect to split gifts only if both are citizens or legal residents of the United States. Gift tax returns may be required if gift splitting is utilized.

However, the utilization of the annual exclusion to facilitate the transfer of business interests must be made as part of one's overall gifting program. More specifically, one should determine whether the annual exclusion is required in any other facet of the estate plan such as irrevocable life insurance trusts, Section 529 plans, qualified personal residence trusts, or Crummey trusts.

Example

Husband owns 100% of the Puppy Company and wishes to transfer stock to his two children and four grandchildren. Husband, individually, could gift up to $66,000 (6 × $11,000) total each year. If wife consents to gift splitting, the couple, collectively, could gift up to $132,000 (6 × $22,000) of Puppy Company stock to be transferred gift tax free each year through the use of annual exclusion gifts.

Lifetime Gift Exemption

In addition to the $11,000 annual gift tax exclusion, the owner of a closely held company should also consider utilizing all or a portion of his or her applicable credit in order to gift larger amounts of company stock during his or her lifetime. The Internal Revenue Code currently provides for a lifetime exemption equivalent against gift tax of $1 million. Unlike the estate tax exemption, which increases to $1.5 million in year 2004, $2 million in 2006, and $3.5 million in year 2009, the lifetime gift tax exemption is fixed at $1 million.

Furthermore, if the business owner is married, the spouse's exemption equivalent can also be utilized, allowing a husband and wife together to transfer, in the years 2002 through 2004, $2 million of company stock (before utilizing any discounting techniques) to their beneficiaries without the imposition of federal gift taxes. If the lifetime gift exemption is to be utilized by the taxpayer during his or her lifetime, a gift tax return must be filed.

Removal of Posttransfer Appreciation

Once shares of stock have been transferred, all postgift appreciation (the appreciation that occurs after the gift of stock has been made) is removed from the donor's taxable estate. If the company then grows in value after the gift, all future appreciation of the gifted shares takes place in the estate of the beneficiary. So the donor removes from his or her estate tax base not only the value of the gifted shares but also all future appreciation in the value of the shares arising after the date of the gift.

Income Tax Savings

The donor can also achieve income tax savings by transferring shares of stock to his or her beneficiaries (who often are in a lower marginal income tax bracket than the donor). Thus, after the donor has transferred shares of stock to beneficiaries, all dividends and/or other distributions of income associated with such shares will be allocated to the beneficiaries, thereby reducing the taxable income of the donor.

Be aware, however, that if a beneficiary is younger than age 14, the "kiddie tax" may apply. This provision of the Code subjects a child under the age of 14 to taxes at the same rate as the parents, thus reducing the benefit of allocating income (and thus the income tax) to young children. However, once children reach the age of 14, they obtain their own tax brackets.

Capital Gains

In addition to removing the current income associated with such shares of stock from the donor's tax base, the removal of all future appreciation in the value of the gifted stock (both prior to and following the transfer) may also result in substantial tax savings for the donor. Under the Code, the recipient of a gift of appreciated assets generally takes the same tax basis as the donor. Thus, if the beneficiary of a gift of stock subsequently sells the stock, the gain is realized by the beneficiary and not the donor.

If the recipient subsequently disposes of the stock, he or she generally realizes the same amount of gain as would the donor. However, depending on the income tax bracket of the recipient, he or she may pay fewer taxes on the gain than would the donor.

Capital Losses

Although gains may be shifted from the donor to the recipient, losses may not be shifted. Loss basis rules set forth in the Internal Revenue Code operate to preclude the transfer of losses from a donor to a recipient. Under these rules, the recipient's basis in stock for determining losses is the lesser of the donor's basis in the stock or the fair market value of the stock on the date of the gift. If the stock has a fair market value at the time of the gift that is less than the donor's adjusted basis, the recipient's (donee's) basis is the fair market value at such time.

Ensuring Company Success

In an effort to reduce estate taxes, don't lose sight of the other goal of succession planning—business continuity. When structuring the gifting program, several issues must be addressed to help ensure that the gifting program is also in the company's best interest. The first issue is to determine whether the shares being gifted should be voting or nonvoting shares. If the shares gifted are voting, determine whether the child—who may become a swing vote—

has the mental maturity and financial sophistication to alter the course of the business for the better. If not, consider gifting nonvoting stock.

Many gifting programs utilizing the annual exclusion call for equal transference of stock to the children. However, if only one of the children is involved in the business, perhaps the participating child should receive voting stock, and the nonparticipating children should receive nonvoting stock. The key point is to gift shares of the business in a manner that reduces estate tax while simultaneously providing for the transition of leadership to help ensure the company's future success.

Willingness

Creating a business succession plan too often presumes that the child wants the shares. If a child has no interest in joining the family business, the shares could still be gifted but perhaps should be nonvoting shares given either outright or in trust for the child's benefit. If, on the other hand, the child is ready, willing, and able to join the family business, perhaps the transference of stock should be completed during an apprentice period. Accomplishing the transfer of stock via the annual exclusion could foster this phasing-in concept.

Many businesses operate with bank credit lines or where the principals have personally guaranteed obligations of the company, including leaseholds. Whatever the potential liability may be, beware of transferring stock to children without first discussing the pros and cons of the transfer. Many businesses have risk, and the company should want only those who are willing to embrace the risk to share, hopefully, in the eventual reward.

Equality

If one child is involved in the family business and the others are not, should shares be gifted equally among all of the children? If so, in the event that the business dramatically appreciates due to the participating child's blood, sweat, and tears, then the other children will share equally in the success of the business. Is that equality? While there exists no one right way to address this issue, several options are available.

Perhaps the nonparticipating children should be beneficiaries of a life insurance trust having a death benefit equal to the value of the shares gifted to the participating child. Alternatively, cash or securities could be gifted to the nonparticipating children instead of the business interest. Communication, teamwork, and flexibility combined with a sensitivity to the issues will help ensure that equality, if not achieved, was at least sought.

Enhanced Estate Liquidity

Estates of significant value often are exposed to hardship because the major assets of the estate may be illiquid, such as shares of stock in a closely held business. When the owner of a company dies, the estate may be liable for numerous expenses, including substantial estate taxes. To avoid the problem of leaving an estate consisting primarily of illiquid assets such as closely held stock, the gifting of stock during one's lifetime serves two purposes:

1. It reduces the value of the estate by the value of the stock when gifted (as well as any postgift appreciation in the stock gifted).

2. It increases the percentage of liquid assets in the estate as compared to the illiquid assets (such as any shares of stock remaining in the estate of the deceased shareholder following such gifts).

This analysis should be carefully considered in light of certain postmortem planning techniques available to the heirs of one's estate.

Planning for Control of Family Business

Providing for an orderly transfer of control in a closely held business is an important issue to be addressed when preparing the estate plan of an owner of a family business. If a person owns a successful business, the estate tax due upon death may be substantial. Furthermore, distribution of the ownership interests in the business after the person's death may generate disagreement among the beneficiaries if control of the business was not prescribed by the decedent prior to death or through a will. Thus, the owner can avoid many potential family problems by initiating a plan for the transfer of a controlling interest in the company to the children intended to run the business after the business owner is gone.

Example

Gary and Leslie are the sole owners of stock in a closely held corporation. The value of the stock constitutes one-half of their estate; the other half consists of marketable securities. The couple has four children, two of whom have worked in the business for several years and have expressed an interest in continuing the business following the retirement of their parents. The other two have no interest in the business.

Gary and Leslie would like to transfer control to the two children involved in the business and give the rest of their property to the other two children.

Lifetime gifts may be used to start the process of transferring both types of assets in an orderly fashion, as well as reducing the size of their estate for estate tax purposes.

For instance, one method would be for Gary and Leslie to maximize use of their exemption equivalent to transfer shares in the company to the two children interested in running the business after their parents are gone, and then provide an equalization clause in their wills to make up any difference to the two children not interested in running the business. Such a strategy would have the effect of increasing the liquidity of Gary and Leslie's estate and help prevent the need to liquidate the company to pay estate taxes.

Loss of Step-Up in Basis

As mentioned earlier, the Internal Revenue Code generally provides that the recipient of a lifetime gift inherits the tax basis in transferred property equal to the donor's basis (a "carryover basis" in the property). The Code also provides, however, that the tax basis of property received from a decedent at death equals the fair market value of the property on the date of death ("stepped-up basis"). Any appreciation in the value of property gifted before death is not eligible for this step-up in basis.

The loss of the stepped-up basis resulting from making lifetime gifts rather than postdeath transfers is an important factor to consider when determining whether to make lifetime gifts of company stock. However, currently the top marginal federal income tax rate on long-term capital gains is 20%, whereas the top federal estate and gift tax rate is 50%. This differential in capital gains versus estate tax rates should be carefully analyzed by business owners and their financial and tax advisers before determining whether lifetime gifts make economic sense.

As has been stated throughout this book, all estate and business succession planning must be performed with one eye on Congress. Under the terms of the Economic Growth and Tax Relief Reconciliation Act of 2001, the estate tax is due to be phased out over the next eight years. If this phaseout were ever actually to take place, the current estate tax system, which provides for the step-up in basis of the assets of a decedent, would be replaced by a carryover basis system in which generally (with certain limited exceptions) all assets of a decedent would retain their historic bases. Thus, the basis differential between lifetime gifts and gifts at death set forth before would be lost. The only exception is if you were to use company stock to take advantage of the $3 million step-up in basis to a spouse or the $1.3 million step-up for gifts to persons other than a spouse. Accordingly, if you have started a lifetime gifting program involving equity interests in the family business and repeal actually does take place, the generally accepted downside of such a gifting program (i.e., loss of step-up in basis) would no longer exist. Thus, it is even more economically imperative that you start such a program, or continue such a program if already started, in the face of estate tax. There is little, if any, downside.

Loss of Control over Property

After the stock has been transferred outright, free of trust, the donor no longer has any ownership rights. Furthermore, if the transferred property is income producing, the income no longer belongs to the donor. Without any of the planning structures discussed in the chapters to follow, the IRS may deem a transfer to be incomplete if the donor is able to control the property or treats it as his or her own following such a transfer. Thus, when making lifetime gifts it is imperative that donors relinquish control over the gifted shares and no longer treat them as their own.

Methods of Transfer

Once a determination has been made that a business succession plan must be implemented, the method of transferring the interest must be considered. The following techniques are available for this purpose:

- Outright transfer of voting stock.
- Outright transfer of nonvoting stock.
- Family limited partnership (see Chapter 21).
- Grantor retained annuity trust (see Chapter 22).
- Grantor retained unitrust (see Chapter 22).
- Intentionally defective grantor trust (see Chapter 23).
- Self-canceling installment notes (see Chapter 25).
- Private annuities (see Chapter 25).
- Trusts, including specifically qualified subchapter S trusts (QSSTs) and electing small business trusts (ESBTs).
- In the case of failure to implement a gifting program during one's lifetime, partial tax relief under IRC Sections 6166 and 303.

Qualified Subchapter S Trust

A trust can serve as a shareholder in an S corporation provided it satisfies the requirements of a qualified subchapter S trust (QSST). A QSST can have only one current income beneficiary, and all income earned by the trust must be distributed currently to the beneficiary. If the trust fails to meet this income distribution rule, the status of the trust as a QSST terminates on the first day of the next taxable year after such disqualifying event occurs. Furthermore, any principal distributed by the S corporation during such beneficiary's life must also be distributed to that beneficiary. If the trust terminates during the current income beneficiary's life, the trust assets must be distributed to such beneficiary. Upon the death of the beneficiary, a QSST must terminate and distribute all of its assets to the beneficiary's estate. The beneficiary of a QSST must be a U.S. citizen or resident, and must cooperate in the planning since the election to treat a trust as a QSST can only be made by such beneficiary. The election, once made, is irrevocable.

Failure to qualify the trust as a QSST—or as an electing small business trust (ESBT), as discussed in the next section—can have dire consequences to the status of the corporation as an S corporation. If a trust owning stock in a corporation fails to so qualify, the corporation will not qualify as an S corporation and will lose its ability to flow through profits to its shareholders. Instead, the corporation will be subject to taxation as a separate legal entity (i.e., a C corporation). Without proper planning, such a result can have adverse consequences on both the corporation and its shareholders, including the trust established as the gifting vehicle for all or a portion of the stock.

Electing Small Business Trust

In 1996, seeking to provide more planning opportunities for S corporations, Congress created the electing small business trust (ESBT), which can also serve as a shareholder of an S corporation. The trustee of an ESBT must file with the Internal Revenue Service an election for the trust to be an ESBT.

Unlike a QSST, an ESBT can provide for multiple beneficiaries and discretionary payments of income between the multiple beneficiaries, as well as between future unborn beneficiaries. A trust can qualify as an ESBT if no interest in the trust was acquired by purchase and all of the beneficiaries are either individuals or estates that would otherwise qualify as S corporation shareholders (except charitable organizations, which may hold contingent remainder interests as well as current interests in the trust). However, unlike a QSST, the portion of the ESBT consisting of S corporation stock is treated as a separate trust, subject to income tax at the highest individual rate in effect at the time.

In determining the tax liability with regard to the remaining portion of the trust (if any), the income from the S corporation stock is ignored. Although distributions from the trust on this portion are deductible in computing the taxable income of the trust, none of the income generated by the S corporation stock held by the trust is deductible. Thus, without careful planning, an ESBT can prove to be a highly inefficient vehicle for holding S corporation shares for income tax purposes. As a new type of planning vehicle, the ESBT provides more flexibility than a QSST, but the decision to use an ESBT must be carefully considered and analyzed.

Failure to Implement Gifting Program During One's Life— Partial Tax Relief Under Code Sections 6166 and 303

Even if you have failed to implement any of the previously referenced gifting techniques during your life, the IRS provides certain estate tax relief. If more than 35% of your estate consists of at least a 20% ownership interest in a closely held business, your executor may make a timely filed election under Section 6166 of the Internal Revenue Code to defer the payment of estate taxes applicable to such interest for a period of up to 14 years. If gifts were made within three years of death, this business interest must meet the same 35% test after adding such gifts back into the estate for purposes of making the computation.

Prior to the 2001 Tax Act, Section 6166 treatment was available only if such company had 15 or fewer partners or shareholders. Under the 2001 Tax Act, the number of business owners has been increased from 15 to 45. If Section 6166 is elected on a timely filed estate tax return, the portion of the estate tax liability due to the small business interest may be paid in up to 10 installments, with the first due no later than five years and nine months after the owner's death. However, during the period of deferral, interest must be paid annually (although at a favorable 2% annual interest rate) and the executor remains personally liable for the estate tax during the entire period of deferral. Any interest paid on such deferral cannot be deducted against the estate for estate tax purposes.

Furthermore, under Section 303 of the Internal Revenue Code, the redemption of stock to make payments of estate tax will not be treated as a dividend taxable to the estate as ordinary income, provided any such amount is actually utilized to pay estate tax liability and/or financial or administrative expenses of the estate. Absent Section 303, such redemptions would be treated as dividend income unless such redemptions generally resulted in the termination of the decedent's (and his or her entire family's) interest in the company. With

Section 303, there is rarely any tax on such redemptions because the stock being redeemed receives a step-up in basis so that the only taxable gain on a redemption of stock to pay estate taxes results from an increase in the value of the company following the death of the owner. Redemptions under Section 303 must generally be made within three years of the assessment of estate taxes against the estate of the deceased company owner. However, if the estate has made a timely filed Section 6166 election, these redemptions can be made during the time established for the payment of the installments set forth in the Section 6166 election.

Conclusion

Frequently, numerous techniques are utilized in conjunction with each other in an effort to meet multiple objectives, such as to help secure the retirement needs of a business owner, hedge against the risk factor of each tool, transfer the business interest over time, reduce estate tax, protect the gifted interest from claims of creditors, maintain equality, and provide for the transition of leadership over time. Accomplishing all of these objectives is a delicate balance requiring skill, patience, teamwork, and commitment.

CHAPTER

20

Family-Owned
Business Deduction

Introduction

Recognizing that family businesses are an integral part of the U.S. economy, Congress sought to provide estate tax relief for family business owners as part of the Taxpayer Relief Act of 1997. Prior to the enactment of the 1997 Act, however, there were discussions about completely exempting certain family-owned businesses from estate taxation, which was then watered down to a fixed $750,000 exemption from estate taxes for certain family businesses. This exemption amount was then further watered down to produce the Taxpayer Relief Act of 1997, as further revised by the Revenue Reconciliation Act of 1998.

The qualified family-owned business (QFOB) deduction has unfortunately provided little relief for small business owners, is difficult to implement, and places a heavy compliance burden on the survivors for years after the owners' deaths. Accordingly, while it is a tool available to help offset the estate tax attributable to a family-owned business, proactive planning outside the use of the family-owned business deduction is generally more advantageous than passively relying on the QFOB deduction with all of its associated complexities and qualifications.

The new 2001 Tax Act repealed the qualified family-owned business deduction for all estates where death occurs after December 31, 2003. Providing relief to business owners was a great idea, but the relief provided in the form of the QFOB deduction was a failure, and under the new act the deduction is repealed effective December 31, 2003. Until then, however, the supposed relief is available, and the mess Congress created is summarized next.

Deduction Amount

The first objective in trying to understand the QFOB deduction is to discern the actual amount of the deduction that is available. The QFOB deduction is limited to $675,000. The exemption equivalent is limited to $625,000, if the deduction is fully elected. If, however, the entire $675,000 QFOB deduction is not utilized, a greater amount of the exemption equivalent may be used. Accordingly, if all of the onerous QFOB requirements are met, the total amount that can be sheltered is $1,300,000. Even in year 2006, the applicable credit will still be $202,550 (exemption equivalent of $625,000) and the maximum QFOB remains at $675,000.

Initial Qualifying Rules

However, several complex requirements must be met before a family business will qualify for the QFOB deduction. The first requirement is that the decedent must be a citizen or resident of the United States at the time of death. Additionally, the principal place of the business of the family-owned company must be in the United States.

The 50% Test

Furthermore, the value of the decedent's interest in the qualified family-owned business must exceed 50% of his or her adjusted gross estate. In computing the value of the decedent's adjusted gross estate, you must start by calculating the decedent's gross estate, reduced by estate tax deductions and other claims against the estate (including debts) increased by certain gifts made by the decedent prior to death. These gifts include:

- Family-owned business interests that the decedent gave to family members and that are still retained by these family members at the time of the decedent's death.

- Gifts to the decedent's spouse during the 10-year period preceding the decedent's death (minus any gifts included in item 1).

- Gifts within three years prior to death (other than annual exclusion gifts).

Existence of Trade or Business

In making the determination as to whether a business qualifies for the family-owned business deduction, the business must first qualify as a trade or a business under the Internal Revenue Code. Excluded from this definition are passive assets, which include: (1) assets producing interest, dividends, rents, royalties, annuities, and other personal holding company income; (2) net gains from assets that are interests in a trust, partnership, or real estate mortgage investment entity that do not constitute an active trade or business; (3) net gains from assets producing no income; (4) assets giving rise to income from commodity transactions or foreign currency gains; (5) assets producing interest-like income; and (6) assets producing income from notional principal contracts or payments in lieu of dividends.

This passive asset test must be met at the time of the decedent's demise and during the postdeath 10-year recapture period following the decedent's death (other than a two-year window immediately following death). Although there is not a concise definition of what a trade or business is, the term was intended to require continuity and regularity of activity in which the owner or owners carry the risk of production and the risk of price change.

Once it is determined that the decedent was a U.S. citizen, that the family business's principal place of business is within the United States, that the value of the family-owned business exceeds 50% of the gross estate, and that the business is not deemed to be a passive entity, the next test is the ownership test.

Ownership Test

A qualified family-owned business interest includes an interest as a proprietor or an interest in an entity carrying on a business if at least 50% of the entity is owned directly or indirectly by the decedent or a member of the decedent's family. An interest in a business will also qualify as a family-owned business interest if at least 70% of the entity is owned by members of two families, and at least 30% is owned by the decedent or the decedent's family. Similarly, an interest qualifies as a family-owned business interest if 90% of the entity is owned by members of three families and at least 30% is owned by the decedent or the decedent's family.

Qualified Heir Test

Even if the value of the decedent's interest in the family-owned business exceeds 50% of the decedent's adjusted gross estate, it will qualify under the family-owned business deduction only if it, in fact, passes to the decedent's heirs at the time of death.

Furthermore, the interest being passed to a family member must be to a "qualified heir." Qualified heirs are the eligible individuals who may receive an interest in the closely held business in order for the family-owned business to qualify for the deduction. The term is defined as (1) members of a decedent's family who acquired the property or who received the property pursuant to the decedent's last will and testament, and (2) active employees of the trade or business to which the qualified family-owned business relates if they had been employed by such trade or business for at least 10 years before the decedent's death.

The term "member of family" is a term of art having a specific definition. That definition includes: an individual's spouse; lineal decedents of the individual, the individual's spouse, and the individual's parents; as well as the spouses of lineal decedents. However, in order for these family members to qualify for the family-owned business deduction, the decedent's family must have materially participated in the trade or business for at least five of the eight years immediately preceding the decedent's retirement, disability, or death. Additionally, the decedent or at least one member of the decedent's family must have owned the family business interest or interests for five or more of the last eight years prior to the decedent's death.

Material Participation

What is material participation, you ask. While there is no one test in determining what material participation is because material participation may mean different things for different businesses, generally it is considered physical work or participation in the management decisions of the business. This is a nebulous term at best, which will undoubtedly result in numerous differing interpretations (and probably much litigation).

Recapture Rules

In the event that the decedent's heirs have made it through the labyrinth of rules set forth so far, they are still not done. A number of events will trigger a recapture tax and reverse the benefits derived from qualifying the business as a family-owned business at the time of the decedent's death.

If the qualified heirs or members of the qualified heir's family cease to materially participate in the closely held business for more than three years during the eight-year period following the decedent's death, the recapture rules are triggered. The recapture rules will also be triggered if the principal place of business ceases to be located in the United States or if any qualified heir loses U.S. citizenship.

Another event that triggers recapture is if the family-owned business fails to pass the passive asset test or if an increase in the amount of passive assets after the decedent's results in the business no longer being treated as a "trade or business" under the applicable Internal Revenue Code provisions.

But perhaps the biggest burden for the qualified heirs or family members is the restriction that the business cannot be sold during the 10-year period following the decedent's death.

If any of the events set forth take place, triggering the recapture rules, estate taxes plus interest will be due in the following percentages:

YEAR	RECAPTURE PERCENTAGE
1–6	100%
7	80%
8	60%
9	40%
10	20%

Conclusion

One would need a crystal ball to determine whether a qualified heir or family member would remain actively involved in a family business 10 years after a parent's demise. In light of the fact that the qualifying rules for meeting the stringent requirements of the qualified family-owned business deduction are so complex and onerous, combined with the fact that upon the decedent's demise these recapture rules loom large, it is hard to get excited about the family-owned business deduction. The deduction will be repealed as of 2004.

The burdens viewed in conjunction with the few benefits of the family-owned business deduction lead most commentators to conclude that the family-owned business deduction is not a technique that you, the business owner, should plan for (although you may be fortunate enough to fall into it). If a business owner fails to proactively create a business succession plan, and if upon his or her demise (on or before December 31, 2003) all of the family-owned business deduction requirements are met, and if during the subsequent

10 years the recapture rules are not triggered, then the family-owned business deduction offers some relief from estate taxation, although it is doubtful.

Recognizing that the original goal of the legislators was to provide estate tax relief for family business owners, the family-owned business deduction legislation has fallen short of its goal. Accordingly, if it is your intention to preserve your family business for future generations, you should plan proactively during your lifetime and not rely on the family-owned business deduction.

Family Limited Partnerships

Introduction

Question: What wealth transference technique allows parents to:

■ Gift as much as 99.9% of an asset (or assets) to their heirs or other beneficiaries?

■ Retain control of the assets gifted?

■ Discount the value of the gifts for gift and estate tax purposes?

■ Retain control of the flow of income from the assets gifted?

■ Maintain flexibility in structuring the form of the gift and the timing of the gift?

■ Protect the assets gifted from claims of creditors?

■ Promote continuity of management to accomplish a business or other succession plan?

■ Reduce the inevitable estate tax burden?

Answer: The family limited partnership (FLP).

This chapter's discussion is limited to family limited partnerships (or FLPs). However, family limited liability companies (FLLCs) are becoming increasingly popular because of their asset protection attributes and can be used in many instances in lieu of family limited partnerships. An FLLC is established in much the same way as an FLP but is treated, for liability purposes, similar to a corporation, thus insulating all of the individual members from any liabilities of the FLLC.

Truly one of the estate planner's most powerful tools, the family limited partnership merits consideration in almost every high-net-worth estate and business succession plan. As this technique incorporates the principles of gift tax planning, estate tax planning, valuation discounts, and creditor protection all rolled into one ongoing strategy, the team approach is a must. While the cost to create and maintain a family limited partnership is not insignificant, the upside far outweighs the cost.

By conveying a family business or portfolio of family investments to a family limited partnership, the senior members of a family can share the value of their assets with their heirs while simultaneously maintaining control over the assets and lowering both their income taxes and their estate taxes. In addition, a family limited partnership can be an effective tool for introducing the younger members of a family to the family business or investment portfolio while limiting much of the downside risk generally associated with handing over the reins of the operation of such business or portfolio to other members of the family.

The use of a family limited partnership generally consists of two steps: (1) one or both parents create the partnership and serve as the general partner(s) of the partnership (either directly or through a wholly owned corporation or limited liability company), and (2) the parents then gift limited partnership interests to their children and/or grandchildren, who then serve as the limited partners. Initially, one or both parents hold both the general partnership and the limited partnership interests. The general partnership interest(s) can consist of as little as .1% of the total equity in the partnership assets with the limited partnership interests (which can be divided into a large number of units) accounting for the remainder of the equity in the partnership assets. The parents retain the general partnership interest(s) for an indefinite period of time and systematically assign the limited partnership interests to their heirs.

Who Controls the Partnership?

While holding as little as .1% of the equity in the partnership, the parents, as the sole general partners, can maintain full and complete control over the business or investments held by the partnership while gifting as many of the limited partnership units to their heirs as they desire. Thus, the parents can successfully shift much of the value of their assets to their children and/or grandchildren (thus reducing estate and income taxes) without giving up control of the assets inside the partnership.

Assume, for instance, that the parents have a large parcel of commercial real estate they wish to transfer out of their combined taxable estates. The net fair market value of the property is $1 million. The parents are interested in utilizing their $11,000 annual gift tax exclusions to provide gifts of a portion of the real estate to each of their three children. If they had to make gifts of the real estate outright, they would have to deed fractional interests to their children, a costly, time-consuming, and administratively burdensome affair.

In the alternative, the parents could contribute the real estate to a family limited partnership. The parents would serve as the general partners of the partnership, initially owning all of the general and limited partnership interests. They could then gift the limited partnership units to their children over a period of years, using their $11,000 annual gift tax exclusions. (The parents would combine gifts in order to give each child $22,000 worth of limited partnership units each year.)

To accurately reflect the value of the annual gifts, it is necessary to appraise the property owned by the partnership, then transfer that portion of the partnership interests to each of the children which accurately reflects the $11,000 (or $22,000 combined) annual gift. Assuming a value of $1 million (which remains constant over the gifting period), the parents could gift limited partnership units to their three children (valued at $66,000 per year) and remove the entire $1 million value from their taxable estates over a 16-year period without ever losing management control over the real estate. Alternatively, they could take advantage of a portion of each of their exemption equivalents ($1 million in year 2002 for a combined exemption equivalent of $2 million) to gift all of the limited partnership units in one year (a technique that can be beneficial in situations where the partnership assets are appreciating rapidly).

Discounting the Value of the Limited Partnership Interest

Furthermore, because the children do not control the operations of the partnership and do not have the right to assign their interests in the partnership without the general partners' consent, the parents are able to gift even more than $22,000 worth of assets each year by utilizing the limited partnership structure. For example, the net value of the property contributed to the family limited partnership outlined in the previous section is $1 million. However, the value of the limited partnership interests gifted to the children may be reduced or "discounted" since, as limited partners, they cannot vote, freely sell their shares, or participate in the decision-making process. Even if the limited partners have the right to sell their interests, generally there is no ready market to buy limited partnership interests in the family partnership (as is the case with publicly traded securities).

Each family limited partnership has its own unique characteristics, whether it is the property contributed to the partnership or the family members who participate in its administration. Accordingly, the following two discounting techniques must take into consideration the unique qualities of each partnership before the valuation expert or accountant can determine the appropriate discount for transferring limited partnership interests. Furthermore, as discussed in Chapter 16, these are not the only discounts available to the business valuation expert. (See, for example, the key manager and investment company adjustments set forth in Chapter 16).

1. *Minority interest discount.* Limited partners are prohibited by law from participating in the daily operations of a partnership. They generally may not appoint managers, decide on the future direction of the partnership, declare distributions, determine compensation, or force liquidation or sale of the underlying assets. Both the IRS and the courts have recognized that a minority interest ownership position such as a limited partnership interest is worth less than a proportionate percentage of the underlying assets because of this lack of control over the operations of the partnership. Not having direct access to the underlying assets of the partnership or the ability to control those assets allows for a discount when gifting limited partnership interests in the family partnership.

2. *Lack-of-marketability discount.* Another factor to consider in valuing limited partnership interests is the lack of marketability for such interests. Unlike a publicly traded security, there exists no ready market for limited partnership interests. Furthermore, in the context of a family limited partnership, the partnership agreement will generally provide additional restrictions on the transferability or disposition of limited partnership units, such as the right of first refusal by the general partners or an outright prohibition on the transferability of partnership interests without the general partners' consent. Thus, the limited partners' interests in the partnership should be assessed at an additional discount to reflect this lack of marketability.

The combined discounts for minority interests and lack of marketability can reduce the value of the limited partnership interests in a family limited partnership by as much as 20% to 50%, depending on the circumstances. Consequently, a larger percentage of the net equity of a family limited partnership can be gifted utilizing the annual gift tax exclusions and the applicable credits of the parents.

For instance, in our example, if the parents were advised to use a 33% combined discount for lack of marketability and lack of control, they could gift limited partnership interests that correspond to $33,000 worth of the underlying real estate ($33,000 discounted by 33% equals $22,000) to each of their three children, or $99,000 worth of real estate held in the family partnership each year, without any gift tax consequences. This would enable them to give away the entire value of the $1 million parcel in 10 years (as opposed to 16 years without discounting) utilizing only their combined $22,000 annual gift exclusions.

In the alternative, the parents could utilize a portion of their combined applicable credits to gift all of their limited partnership units in one year, using only $700,000 of their combined credits. In fact, in 2002, by utilizing only the couple's combined $2 million exemption equivalent and taking advantage of a 33% combined discount, the parents could remove $3 million of assets from their combined estates in a single year.

Since the value of property varies from year to year, it is important to review the value of the limited partnership interests on a periodic basis if annual exclusion gifts are being utilized. This exercise must be performed prior to making any gifts intended to qualify for the $11,000 annual gift exclusion or the applicable credit. Also, the amount of discounting available may be affected by the type of property owned by the partnership. If the partnership owns mostly marketable securities, the discounting allowable for the partnership units will usually be less than if the partnership owns primarily illiquid assets such as real estate. If the partnership owns a closely held business or a parcel of real estate, the discounts applied to the partnership units will most likely be higher.

Should You Form an Entity to Serve as the General Partner?

If the parents' intent is to direct the future control over the family assets placed into the partnership, they may do so by stating in their wills the disposition of the general partnership interests. Under state law, the death or bankruptcy of a general partner usually terminates a partnership (although the partnership agreement may permit a majority of the remaining partners to vote to continue the partnership if a general partner dies). Therefore, if the parents act as general partners in their individual capacities, there may be some limit on the ability of the partnership to continue. Accordingly, they may want to consider structuring the limited partnership with a corporation or limited liability company (LLC) as the general partner.

Instead of owning the general partnership interest individually, the parents can form a corporation or LLC to hold the general partner's interest. The parents would own the stock or membership interests in the general partner entity. Then, upon the death of either parent, the partnership would not terminate. This way, the parent(s) could direct future control of the business after they are gone by leaving the stock or membership interests to the particular family members they choose to run the business or manage the assets placed in the partnership. This may enable the parents to distribute the assets of their estates equitably to a group of children while still allowing them to vest control in one or more children who have expressed an interest and a willingness to continue to manage the assets held by the partnership.

Asset Protection

Another attractive feature of the family limited partnership is the ability to protect the partnership assets from the children's creditors, spouses, or other persons who may have claims against their assets. For instance, if any of the children were to declare bankruptcy or be put into receivership, the creditors would be severely limited in their ability to attach any of the partnership assets. The creditors could not order the liquidation of the partnership, disposition of partnership assets, or partition of any part of the partnership assets.

Often, the best result a creditor can expect is merely the right to receive distributions attributable to the limited partnership units owned by the debtor child, but only if and when any such distributions are made by the partnership. The parents, as the general partners (or owners of the entity serving as the general partner), have a great deal of control over the amount and timing of these distributions. As a result, creditors are hesitant to take partnership units that could result in their receiving "phantom" income for federal income tax purposes and no cash to pay the tax liability. Such limitations may facilitate the child's ability to reach a favorable settlement with creditors.

Furthermore, a limited partnership agreement can protect the integrity of a family business by giving the partners or the partnership the right to acquire the interests of any bankrupt or divorced partner. This may generally be accomplished by permitting the partnership itself or the other partners the right to acquire any assets that might otherwise fall into the hands of an outsider.

Conclusion

A family limited partnership can provide numerous benefits for both tax and business reasons. This is particularly true in light of the major revisions to the estate tax system under the terms of the Economic Growth and Tax Relief Reconciliation Act of 2001 (and even under the remote possibility of repeal in 2010). In fact, because of their almost limitless flexibility in both income and estate tax planning, family limited partnerships remain one of the most valuable tax planning tools available to taxpayers today (and will continue to remain so for years to come). However, the issues involved in establishing such an entity are numerous and complex. Accordingly, anyone considering setting up a family limited partnership should always consult his or her team of advisers in order to properly implement the techniques described in this chapter.

Grantor Retained Annuity Trusts and Grantor Retained Unitrusts

Introduction

Creating effective estate plans for high-net-worth, high-income individuals many times requires the use of more sophisticated estate planning tools. Such tools often rely on two basic estate planning concepts: the use of valuation discounts and the leveraging of gift transfers.

The use of these two estate planning concepts is particularly effective in the case of individuals whose net worth is concentrated, to a great extent, in privately held businesses such as real estate or closely held companies. Generally, the desire of such individuals is fourfold: (1) to continue to control their interests in such assets for as long as possible, (2) to enjoy the cash flow resulting from their assets, (3) to transfer assets eventually to their loved ones, and (4) to minimize estate taxes.

The use of a grantor retained annuity trust (GRAT) or a grantor retained unitrust (GRUT) may provide a solution to these seemingly contradictory objectives. By utilizing a GRAT or GRUT, an individual can retain control over assets for as long as possible, still enjoy the future income from such assets, and simultaneously transfer the assets to his or her heirs with a minimum of estate and gift taxes.

What Is a GRAT?

The underlying structure of a GRAT is relatively simple. The grantor (1) establishes an irrevocable trust, (2) transfers certain assets to the trust, (3) retains an interest in the trust for a defined period of time, and (4) transfers the trust assets to the intended beneficiaries (generally the grantor's children or heirs) at the end of the trust term. The grantor retains the right to a fixed annuity for a term of years, at the end of which the trust assets (as well as any appreciation) pass directly to the beneficiaries or to a continuing trust for their benefit.

The benefit of a GRAT from an estate and gift tax perspective is that the value of the gift to the beneficiaries is reduced by the present value of the annuity payments retained by the grantor. Thus, if the grantor gifts the remainder interest in certain assets, yet retains an annuity interest in the assets, the value of the gift is discounted according to certain actuarial tables established under the Internal Revenue Code. These tables are published by the IRS on a monthly basis and provide an interest rate based on the applicable federal rate for a mid-term debt instrument (three to nine years) multiplied by 120%.

Under the Treasury regulations, the trust instrument establishing the GRAT must set forth a fixed term of years and the specified annuity amount, payable at least annually to the grantor. The longer the term and the greater the annuity amount due the grantor, the smaller the gift and consequent gift tax liability due on the gift to the ultimate beneficiaries.

Therefore, the life expectancy of the grantor is critical when determining the likelihood of the GRAT running to term. If the grantor dies during the term of the GRAT, the entire value of the assets held in the trust is pulled back into his or her estate and is subject to full estate taxation. Thus, the term of the trust must be carefully established so that the grantor's odds of surviving the term are favorable. Even if a 70-year-old grantor is in good health, it may be imprudent to establish a GRAT with a term of 10 years, whereas if the donor is 60 years old a GRAT of 10 or even 15 years may be statistically prudent.

A grantor can also establish several GRATs of varying terms (sometimes referred to as "tiered GRATs"). For instance, a grantor could establish three separate GRATs of 5, 7, and 10 years. If the grantor then lived for 7 years after establishing such tiered GRATs, even though the assets in the 10-year GRAT would be pulled back into his or her estate, the assets (as well as any appreciation) in the 5-year and 7-year GRATs would have been successfully removed from the grantor's taxable estate.

A grantor should avoid utilizing a GRAT that may benefit grandchildren. Under the generation-skipping transfer tax provisions, interests in a GRAT are not deemed to be gifted at the time of the establishment of the GRAT. Rather, if the grantor dies prior to the GRAT term, the full value of the trust corpus is included in the grantor's estate, and if the beneficiaries are skip persons, the gift will be treated as a generation-skipping transfer upon termination of the GRAT. (See Chapter 8, "Generation-Skipping Transfer Tax.")

What Is a GRUT?

There are certain situations in which a grantor retained unitrust (GRUT) may serve as a more effective transfer technique than a GRAT. Under the terms of a GRUT, the grantor retains a fixed percentage of the trust corpus, as opposed to a fixed annuity interest as in the case of a GRAT. This type of arrangement requires the revaluation of the trust corpus on an annual basis, with a fixed percentage of the trust (e.g., 7%) payable to the grantor annually (or more frequently) regardless of the amount of income actually earned by the trust.

GRAT or GRUT—Which One Should You Choose?

When determining whether to use a GRAT or a GRUT, one thing to be aware of is that a GRUT will generally produce a lower remainder value than a GRAT if the annuity payout rate is less than the applicable federal rate. However, a GRAT will produce a lower remainder value than a GRUT if the annuity payout rate is greater than the applicable federal rate.

Also, with the use of a GRAT, the assets need to be valued only once (at the time they are placed into the trust). With a GRUT, the assets need to be valued each year. This annual revaluation may prove impractical and cost-prohibitive if the assets placed in the GRUT consist of real estate or equity interests in a closely held business. As a result, the use of a GRAT, rather than a GRUT, will generally be less expensive from an administrative standpoint.

In the case of either a GRAT or a GRUT, the grantor cannot retain an interest in "all income earned by the trust." Such a right to all of the income would result in the beneficiaries' interest being valued at zero and the full value of the trust corpus retained in the grantor's estate.

Assets to Be Placed in the GRAT or GRUT

A potential grantor can place almost any type of asset in a GRAT or a GRUT. However, interests in real estate or a closely held business have proven to be the most effective for purposes of reducing estate and gift taxes because of the use of minority and marketability discounts.

Real Estate or Fractional Interests Therein

Assume a potential grantor owns an apartment building valued at $1 million which generates $100,000 of cash flow per year. Assume further that the grantor creates a GRAT for 10 years, reserving $100,000 per year as an annuity payout. If the statutory rate is 8%, the value of the retained annuity interest is $608,110, and the gift will be equal to $1,000,000 minus $608,110, or $391,890. Thus, by creating a GRAT, the grantor is able to accomplish the following three goals:

1. The grantor retains the cash flow for a period of 10 years.

2. The grantor maintains control over the property as the GRAT trustee.

3. The grantor is able to remove the $1 million property from the estate, plus all its future appreciation, for a gift valued at $391,890, which can be offset through the use of the grantor's exemption equivalent.

For purposes of further leveraging the value of the GRAT, the grantor can contribute a fractional interest in the real estate rather than contributing the grantor's entire interest in the real estate. This technique may help justify a discount for the value of the fractional interest prior to valuing the retained interest for purposes of establishing the value of the gift portion of the GRAT. Fractional interests in real estate may be discounted, since a fractional interest in real estate is valued at less than the corresponding percentage of the entire parcel of real estate. However, the transfer of a fractional interest in real estate requires re-deeding the property and possibly subdividing the real estate, and could require zoning approval and additional costs in certain situations. Accordingly, careful analysis should be undertaken before considering the placement of fractional interests of real estate in a GRAT.

Family Limited Partnerships

One alternative to transferring fractional interests of real estate or other assets into the GRAT would be to create a family limited partnership. The grantor could then increase the leverage of the gift by transferring the assets into the family limited partnership and then transferring limited partnership interests into the GRAT. As discussed in Chapter 21, the value of a limited partnership interest in a family limited partnership may be reduced due to its lack of marketability and lack of control over the operation of the partnership. Thus, by transferring limited partnership interests into the GRAT, the grantor can take advantage of these discounts, further leveraging the value of the gift prior to transferring the asset into the GRAT, while simultaneously retaining control over the property through retention of the general partnership interest even after the end of the trust term.

Closely Held Business Interests

The owner of a closely held business can transfer a minority interest in the business to a GRAT and retain an annuity interest, thereby transferring substantial value in the business to intended heirs while retaining a predetermined cash flow.

Example

Will Grant is 60 years old and owns a business through an S corporation of which he owns 100%. The business is worth $2 million and earns $200,000 per year, which he distributes to himself on an annual basis.

If the business were to appreciate 20% a year for seven years, it would be worth approximately $8 million at the end of that seven-year period. Estate taxes could exceed $4 million. Will decides to transfer a 49% interest in the S corporation to a seven-year GRAT and retain a 10% annuity during that period. If the minority interest in the corporation is subject to a 30% minority interest discount (so that the value of the assets contributed to the GRAT is equal to approximately $700,000), the value of the retained interest will be equal to $351,750, thereby resulting in a gift equal to $700,000 minus $351,750, or $348,250. At the end of the seven-year GRAT term, he will have saved almost $2,000,000 in estate and gift taxes and created a succession plan.

Thus, a donor can retain control of the stock through his status as the trustee of the GRAT, retain as well the entire $200,000 income per year, and still transfer a substantial portion of the company to his children for a minimum of estate and gift tax consequences.

Qualified Annuity Interests/Fixed Term

In drafting the trust instrument for a GRAT, it is imperative that the trust provide for the retention of a "qualified annuity interest," which consists of the right to receive fixed amounts payable no less frequently than annually. Furthermore, the trust instrument must provide for a fixed term of years. As previously stated, if the grantor predeceases that fixed term, all of the trust corpus will be pulled back into the grantor's estate for estate and gift tax purposes. However, if the client is survived by a spouse, there will generally be no tax due, provided that the grantor's will provides a disposition for such interest which qualifies for the marital deduction.

Minimizing the Mortality Risk of a GRAT/GRUT

As stated earlier, if the grantor dies during the annuity term of a GRAT or a GRUT, the entire amount of the GRAT/GRUT property will be included in the gross estate of the grantor. Thus, despite the fact that the grantor may have paid a gift tax or used all or a portion of the lifetime exemption equivalent at the time the GRAT is created, all of the GRAT benefits will generally be lost.

In order to minimize this risk, the grantor could consider entering into an agreement with the beneficiaries of the GRAT (let's assume the grantor's children) by which the children would contract with the grantor to purchase the contingent reversionary interest (i.e., the assets of the GRAT if the grantor were to predecease the trust term) for fair market value. The grantor's estate would pay the children the value of any amount that it would receive from the GRAT if the grantor were to die before the GRAT term ends. Furthermore, all of the annuity payments that would have been paid to the grantor for the remaining term of the GRAT following the grantor's death would be a portion of the GRAT proceeds payable to the children under their agreement.

As provided in the Internal Revenue Code, an estate is entitled to a deduction for all claims against the estate, provided that such claims were contracted for with adequate and fair consideration in money or money's worth. Thus, the estate of the grantor may then be entitled to an estate tax deduction equal to the amount that the estate is required to pay the children upon the death of the grantor.

Under the terms of such an agreement, the children would agree to pay the grantor (the parent) a purchase price equal to the actuarial value of the grantor's contingent reversionary interest, as determined under the applicable IRS tables. Thus, the purchase price of the contingent reversion interest would, by definition, be equal to full and adequate consideration supporting the estate's deduction for such payment to the children at the time of the parent/grantor's death.

Although this structure is premised on the fact that the value of the grantor's contingent reversionary interest would not exceed the benefits to the children, such value can be substantial and the children would need the requisite funds to pay for the grantor's reversionary interest. This payment could be made as a lump sum at the time of the agreement, or, in the alternative, the children could agree to pay for the grantor's interest through a promissory note entered into on an arm's-length basis. However, the children would still need the requisite funds to make the debt service payments on the note. In order to make such funds available, the parent could make gifts to the children. In this regard, it is imperative that such gifts not be made at the same time that the debt service payments are due. The gifts should not correspond to the debt service payments either in timing or in amount. Furthermore, if the grantor survives the GRAT term, the children's acquisition cost of the contingent reversionary interest would be lost.

Detailed in Figure 22.1 is an example of a GRAT created by Maxwell Fobee. Maxwell transferred a $1 million property into a GRAT and retained an annuity of 10% per year for the shorter of life expectancy or 10 years. By retaining such a large annuity, the gift has been zeroed out; thus no gift tax will be due. If the asset appreciates at the rate of 10% through life expectancy (2023) and remains in the grantor's estate, the estate tax savings will be $4,881,091.

In general, such interest payments made payable to the parent/grantor will

---

**Grantor Retained Annuity Trust
for Maxwell Fobee**

Transfer Date 09/06/2000	AFR 7.59%
Based on Shorter of Life or Term (10 yrs)	Discount Pct .00%

Property Value	$1,000,000
Times Payment Percentage	.10000
Equals Annual Payment	$100,000
Times Annuity Factor	6.3583
Equals Value of Return to Donor	$635,830
Remainder (Gift)	364,170
Remainder (Gift) per IRS	364,170
Gift Tax	$0
Value of Property at Death in 2023	
(without Transfer)	$9,238,881
Retained Payments + Gift of Remainder	364,170
Property Transferred Tax Free	8,874,711
Times Marginal Estate Tax Rate	.55
Projected Estate Tax Savings	**$4,881,091**

FIGURE 22.1 Grantor Retained Annuity Trust for Maxwell Fobee

Reproduced with permission from CCH Incorporated, 2700 Lake Cook Road, Riverwoods, Illinois 60015.

be taxed to such parent as interest income. Thus, the grantor might consider establishing a trust for the benefit of the children that could be used to pay the interest on the promissory note. Such trust would be irrevocable and thus treated as the children's trust for estate tax purposes but could be structured as a grantor trust for income tax purposes. Interest on the note could then be paid by the trust to the parent/grantor and would be treated, for income tax purposes, as being made by the grantor/parent to himself or herself and thus not treated as interest received for tax purposes as there are no tax consequences that stem from the payment and/or receipt of income to/from oneself. The grantor/parent could then avoid income tax upon the receipt of the interest income from the trust.

The IRS could argue that the consideration paid for the grantor's reversionary interest would be equal to full and adequate consideration only if the price paid for such reversionary interest equaled not only the reversionary interest but the entire value of the assets in the GRAT (thus creating a gift aspect to the transaction). However, because the grantor's interest is only that of a contingent reversionary interest subject to valuation according to IRS tables, it appears that such an argument would not withstand the scrutiny of the courts. Accordingly, since the law is not yet established as to children buying the contingent reversionary interest, one must be willing to undertake a battle if the IRS challenges the transaction.

The estate tax cost associated with such a technique for reducing the mortality risk of a GRAT or GRUT is simply that the moneys paid to the parent for establishing such a guarantee would theoretically increase the size of the grantor/parent's estate. However, this cost may be more than offset by several factors, including the removal of the GRAT assets from the estate of the grantor should he or she predecease the GRAT term, as well as the ability of the parties to consider increasing the term of the GRAT without fear that the entire transaction would be lost if the grantor/parent were to die before the end of the GRAT term.

Sale of the GRAT Remainder Interest to a Dynasty Trust

As stated earlier, another general limitation to utilizing a GRAT as an effective estate planning tool is the fact that the grantor cannot allocate the generation-skipping transfer tax exemption (GST exemption) to the remainder beneficiaries at the time of the establishment of the GRAT. Under the applicable provisions of the Internal Revenue Code, because the value of the assets transferred to the GRAT would be included in the grantor's estate if he or she did not survive the GRAT term, the GST exemption rules would not apply, thus negating the benefit of a GRAT if the grantor wished to include grandchildren (and possibly great-grandchildren) in the pool of beneficiaries.

In such situations, the parties should consider the establishment of a GRAT with children as the remaindermen-beneficiaries who may then subsequently enter into an agreement to sell their remainder interest to a GST-exempt dynasty trust. This would allow for distributions to be made to successive generations without additional transfer taxes. In order to avoid the tax treatment of such a transfer as a gift by the children to their children for tax purposes, the purchase price must be the fair market value of the remainder interest as determined under the applicable tables of the Internal Revenue Code. Furthermore, because the grantor retains a contingent reversionary interest in the GRAT, the value of such reversion must be reflected in the value of the remainder interest. Accordingly, the price paid by the dynasty trust must take into account the value of the reversionary interest.

GRAT Planning After the Enactment of the 2001 Tax Act

With the uncertainty created by the passage of the Economic Growth and Tax Relief Reconciliation Act of 2001, there is a question whether the use of a GRAT is still warranted. In response to this question we would respond yes— in certain situations. First, until December 2008, there are not a lot of statutory changes that will affect tax planning for larger estates except for the phased-in increases to the exemption equivalent and a slight reduction in estate tax rates. Accordingly, GRATs still make sense in many situations. This is particularly true in light of the uncertainty that repeal will ever take place (and if it does, whether it will stay in place).

The same concept behind a GRAT of leveraging gifts to remove the assets from one's estate and allowing them to grow outside that estate still makes sense. In this regard, the new Tax Act actually increases the lifetime gift tax exemption to $1 million, thus providing the ability to remove even more assets from one's estate utilizing the GRAT or GRUT structure. However, in this environment of estate tax uncertainty, it is generally not recommended that one utilize a GRAT structure that goes beyond the current date of repeal (January 1, 2010), nor is it recommended that one make gifts valued in excess of $1 million thus incurring a gift tax at the time of the transfer to the GRAT. However, it still makes sense to enter into one or more short-term GRATs, including perhaps a tiered GRAT structure (of, say, three-, five-, and seven-year durations). Simply because Congress has acted (which, as we all know, Congress does at least once a year, and certainly every time there is an election) does not mean that you should stop planning. It is hard to imagine under what economic environment (let alone political environment) Congress will allow repeal to stand, or allow us to even get that far. In the meantime, you should consider planning with flexibility in case there is repeal, but also continue planning on a tax-advantaged basis in the more likely event that estate tax repeal never comes to fruition.

Conclusion

The use of a GRAT or GRUT as part of the estate plan for a sophisticated, high-net-worth individual or family can create significant estate and gift tax savings. However, the use of such a vehicle requires close analysis of the facts and a thorough understanding of the law underlying such techniques. Accordingly, it is imperative that an individual contemplating the use of this type of structure work closely with one's professional advisers to ensure that the benefits that are offered by such a structure are realized.

CHAPTER

23

Intentionally Defective Grantor Trusts

Introduction

So your annual exclusions are fully utilized, your exemption equivalents have been exhausted by both you and your spouse, and yet, having valued your assets, there is still substantial estate tax exposure. Moreover, you still own assets that are producing a steady stream of income and will continue to grow in value. For one who is desirous of continuing the gift-giving process to family members but is out of annual exclusions and exemption equivalents, the intentionally defective grantor trust (IDGT) may be the answer.

The concept behind an IDGT is simple. You create a trust for the benefit of your children and sell certain assets to the trust in return for a long-term installment note. By creating the IDGT and selling assets to the trust, you have, in essence, converted an appreciating asset (the asset sold) into an asset with a fixed value (the promissory note) while simultaneously retaining the right to receive a consistent stream of income from the long-term installment note for the purpose of securing your retirement income. Inasmuch as an intentionally defective grantor trust is not structured as a gift transaction, a gift tax return does not have to be filed, nor will any gift tax be owed so long as the asset is sold to the IDGT for fair market value.

The Major Benefit of an IDGT

The estate tax benefit of transferring the appreciating asset out of your estate may be incentive enough to enter into an IDGT, but what really makes an IDGT intriguing is its ability to take advantage of the discrepancies between the income tax and the estate tax provisions found in the Internal Revenue Code. Incredible as it may seem, the grantor trust rules in the income tax provisions do not coincide with those in the estate tax provisions. Thus, it is possible to design a trust that is treated as a grantor trust for income tax purposes but is not treated as a grantor trust for estate tax purposes.

If the IDGT is designed correctly, it will be treated as a grantor trust for income tax purposes and any transactions between the grantor (the creator of the IDGT) and the IDGT will be ignored under the income tax provisions of the Internal Revenue Code. However, the same trust agreement can be drafted so that the IDGT will not be included in the grantor's estate for estate tax purposes.

The typical structure of an IDGT involves the grantor's sale of appreciated assets to the IDGT in return for a long-term installment obligation issued by the IDGT. The obligation may provide for payment of interest only, with a balloon payment at the end of the note term. Because the IDGT will be ignored for income tax purposes, the sale of the assets by the grantor to the IDGT will not be subject to capital gains tax, and the interest payable on the note will not be subject to income tax. Instead, any income earned by the IDGT on the assets held by the trust, although creating value for the IDGT, will be treated as earned by the grantor. As a result, the income taxes paid by the grantor on the income earned by the IDGT will, in fact, have the effect of further reducing the size of the grantor's estate while creating additional value outside the grantor's estate.

However, during the period the grantor owns the installment note (which is fixed in value), the assets inside the IDGT continue to appreciate outside the grantor's estate. Thus, if the grantor has assets which are expected to appreciate greatly in future years, he or she can sell them to the IDGT in consideration for a long-term note. The grantor then sets the interest rate on the note at the lowest rate allowable under the tax law while still avoiding any gift tax consequences.

The value included in the grantor's estate will equal only the face value of the note, and the assets inside the trust will pass to the heirs according to the terms of the trust agreement. If the assets placed in the IDGT grow faster than the interest charged on the installment sale note, the net appreciation of the assets (in excess of the note payments back to the grantor) will take place outside the grantor's estate, thus reducing the estate taxes that would have been due on the appreciating assets if they had remained in the grantor's estate.

Implementation of an IDGT

In order to implement this structure, the grantor must first create the IDGT which, as described, will be structured as a grantor trust under the income tax provisions and as a nongrantor trust for estate tax purposes. Next, the grantor must capitalize the IDGT with sufficient assets to reflect its independent status. It is generally advised that the IDGT have amounts independent of those to be purchased from the grantor in an amount equal to approximately 10% to 20% of the value of the installment note. This can be accomplished by having the grantor prefund the trust with cash or other assets. The transfer of this small percentage of the eventual value of the IDGT will be treated as a gift to the grantor's beneficiaries for gift tax purposes.

Following the capitalization of the IDGT, the trustee of the IDGT then enters into the sales agreement for the purchase of the grantor's assets at their fair market value in consideration for an installment obligation. (A third party can guarantee the obligation to help support the legitimacy of the transaction.) In order for the transaction to withstand IRS scrutiny, it is imperative that the assets acquired by the IDGT are accurately valued for purposes of the sale. Otherwise, the transaction could inadvertently create a part sale, part gift situation.

For example, the owner of a closely held business with a fair market value of $1 million can create an IDGT designed as a grantor trust for income tax purposes but not for estate tax purposes. Assume the grantor's business has developed a product that will result in the substantial appreciation of the company and its stock in the future. The grantor creates the IDGT and sells the company stock to the IDGT for $1 million, taking back a $1 million installment note with a nine-year term and an interest rate equal to the minimum rate required under the tax law (in this case the mid-term applicable federal rate).

If the business is unable to generate sufficient income to pay the interest on the note, the grantor can fund the IDGT with sufficient cash to pay the interest on the note. Any amounts contributed to the trust by the grantor will, however, be treated for gift tax purposes as additional gifts by the grantor to the beneficiaries of the trust.

Nine years later, the product produced by the company has been a great success and the value of the company has appreciated from $1 million to $5 million, generating more than enough cash flow to enable the trust to pay back the $1 million principal on the note, and resulting in $4 million passing outside the grantor's estate.

In the alternative, the trust could contribute $1 million of the company's stock (now only 20% of the company's value) back to the grantor as repayment on the note. In either case, at least $4 million of the $5 million company is now owned by the IDGT for estate tax purposes and is excluded from the grantor's gross estate upon death. All transactions between the grantor and the IDGT remain exempt from income tax because of the trust's status as a grantor trust for income tax purposes.

In addition, if the IDGT pays back the grantor at the end of the note term with appreciated property (20% of the company stock in this example), the basis in the appreciated property now owned by the grantor will be stepped up at the time of death, resulting in additional income tax savings by the grantor's beneficiaries if and when they go to sell the stock following the grantor's death. In the alternative, the grantor may consider repurchasing the entire $5 million business, thus transferring cash to the trust and taking back the appreciated company stock, and perhaps creating a new IDGT (or equivalent vehicle) for the company at a later date. The cash inside the trust can then be used to acquire a diversified portfolio for the benefit of the trust beneficiaries (i.e., the grantor's heirs), which will continue to grow and appreciate outside the grantor's estate.

Drafting the IDGT Trust Agreement

It is imperative that the trust instrument creating the IDGT be carefully drafted to take advantage of this lack of symmetry in the Internal Revenue Code. Certain provisions must be put in the trust instrument so that it will be treated as a grantor trust for income tax purposes but not for estate tax purposes. These provisions may include giving the trustee (who can be the grantor's spouse) the discretion to apportion income and principal from the trust among the grantor's heirs without limiting the power by reference to an ascertainable standard. (For this purpose, limiting standards include restricting expenditures for specified purposes such as the beneficiary's health or education.) Because the grantor does not retain any powers that he or she can personally exercise, the transfer is deemed complete and the trust is not includable in the grantor's estate.

Another provision that can be placed in the trust agreement to take advantage of this lack of symmetry in the grantor trust rules is to provide the grantor or a nonadverse party (not a creditor or governmental agency) with the power (in a nonfiduciary capacity) to acquire trust property by substituting other property of an equivalent value. A number of other methods exist for creating this discrepancy between the income tax grantor trust rules and the estate tax grantor trust rules, but these two methods have proven to be the easiest to facilitate.

IDGT versus GRAT

Advantages of an IDGT over a GRAT

There are certain advantages inherent in an IDGT when considering the use of an IDGT as opposed to a GRAT. Unlike the grantor of a GRAT, the grantor of an IDGT need not survive the term of the trust in order to reduce the taxable estate. If the grantor predeceases the term of the installment note received in consideration for the sale of assets to the trust, the value of the note is simply included in the estate for estate tax purposes (rather than the value of the assets sold to the IDGT). If this is a concern, the note can be designed as a self-canceling installment note (SCIN), which would be automatically canceled at the time of the grantor's death (see Chapter 25, "Self-Canceling Installment Notes and Private Annuities"). Be aware, however, that if it is determined that a SCIN is appropriate, either the interest on or the principal of the note must be increased in order for the note to qualify as a SCIN.

Second, as discussed in Chapter 22, "Grantor Retained Annuity Trusts and Grantor Retained Unitrusts," the interest rate set by statute for a GRAT must be equal to at least 120% of the mid-term applicable federal rate (AFR). However, if an installment note with a three- to nine-year term were taken back by the grantor upon the sale of assets to an IDGT, the interest on such a note need equal only 100% of the mid-term AFR to avoid the imputed interest rules under the estate and gift tax regulations.

Furthermore, unlike a GRAT, an IDGT is perfect for generation-skipping tax planning. The IDGT can be generation-skipping transfer (GST) tax exempt, and the sale of assets in exchange for a note should not require an allocation of the grantor's GST $1 million exemption (see Chapter 8, "Generation-Skipping Transfer Tax") because it's a sale, not a gift.

Finally, with an IDGT, a grantor's spouse can be a beneficiary without adverse estate tax consequences, whereas if the grantor's spouse were the beneficiary under the terms of a GRAT instrument, the entire corpus of the trust would continue to be included in the grantor's estate, even after the termination of the trust.

Disadvantages of an IDGT versus a GRAT

However, as you might suppose, there are certain disadvantages in choosing an IDGT over a GRAT which should also be carefully analyzed before choosing one method over the other. One risk of using an IDGT over a GRAT is the potential for undervaluing the assets being acquired by the IDGT in consideration for the installment note. If the assets sold to an IDGT are not accurately valued, the IRS could argue that, at the time of the sale, the grantor actually created a part gift/part sale, resulting in gift tax consequences that might include penalties, interest, and assessed gift tax costs.

Furthermore, the IDGT is premised upon the assumption that the assets sold to the trust will appreciate in value over time. Accordingly, if the value of the assets placed in the IDGT actually decreases to an amount less than the face amount of the note taken back by the grantor, the IDGT would have insufficient funds to pay off the debt. Furthermore, the value of the note retained in the estate of the grantor could, in effect, be larger than the assets transferred out of the estate at the time of the sale of the assets to the IDGT.

Conclusion

The IDGT is an exceptional estate planning tool for one who has exhausted the traditional gifting techniques and still has tremendous estate tax exposure coupled with assets that are continuing to appreciate. Because the use of an IDGT as an estate planning tool involves the sale, rather than gift, of one or more assets to the trust, a gift tax return need not be filed. The utilization of an IDGT still serves as an effective tool for transferring assets to your loved ones at a fixed price in return for a steady stream of income to the seller (the senior family member), thus continuing to provide an effective estate and business planning tool for wealthy taxpayers. However, it is imperative that an individual looking to use such a vehicle work closely with his or her tax advisers and that the trust be closely monitored to ensure that it is respected both at the time of its inception and during the period in which it remains in existence. Unless one is relying on the remote chance the estate tax repeal will become a reality, an IDGT remains a staple as an estate and business succession tool.

Split Dollar Life Insurance

Introduction

Jean-Claude Pierre, fickle and temperamental, is the truly gifted chef at the famed restaurant La Crêpe. La Crêpe has developed a reputation throughout the city as the chic French restaurant with a six-month waiting list and home to the rich and famous. Prior to Jean-Claude becoming the head chef at La Crêpe, the restaurant was rarely full on weekends. In fact, the owners, Rudy "Flash" Ruden and Vito Molito, were thinking about closing the doors and absorbing their losses. But after they hired Jean-Claude and the customers began enjoying the finest crêpes east of the Mississippi, the restaurant began to blossom.

One Saturday night, Rudy and Vito were in the back room counting their money when Jean-Claude burst in demanding that he share in the profits and become a one-third partner in La Crêpe, Inc. Jean-Claude continued to lament that earning $65,000 per year with no upside in the restaurant was simply not enough, and unless they were to make him a partner, he was going to hang up his spatula and retire. After Jean-Claude left, Rudy and Vito knew this was a real problem. They did not want Jean-Claude to be their partner, but knew if he left they could be finished. They called their attorney, who told them that they might want to consider offering Jean-Claude a split dollar benefit package, which is a form of golden handcuffs.

The lawyer went on to summarize a split dollar plan by informing Rudy and

Vito that the plan would not grant Jean-Claude an ownership interest in the business but would provide him with what he really wanted—more money. In fact, the lawyer continued, the owners could provide Jean Claude with potentially hundreds of thousands of dollars that could grow tax free inside a life insurance policy and vest over a 5- to 10-year period. If Jean-Claude were to quit, he would not fully vest in the compensation program. Therefore, it would behoove Jean-Claude to remain as the head chef so that he could continue to vest in the split dollar plan. The best part, explained the lawyer, was that any monies laid out by La Crêpe, Inc., would ultimately be repaid to the owners upon death or termination, so whatever their out-of-pocket costs will be (insurance premiums), they would ultimately be reimbursed.

The owners explained this compensation package to Jean-Claude, while simultaneously advising him that if he were to be an owner he would have to sign personally on the lease as well as on the credit lines, and be responsible for the burdensome administration involved in running the business. Jean-Claude was quick to accept the split dollar compensation plan and was eager to finalize the arrangement, which he realized was a form of retirement planning that could help him retire comfortably as well as providing his heirs with a much-needed life insurance policy, without any significant sacrifices.

The term "split dollar life insurance" is often erroneously thought of as referring to a type of life insurance policy, but it is actually a method of financing the acquisition of life insurance rather than a type of policy. Specifically, the term "split dollar" refers to the manner in which the respective parties pay for the premiums on the life insurance. Historically, split dollar life insurance has been designed to provide key employees an added perk as part of their compensation packages.

In a typical split dollar arrangement, the premiums are split between the employer and employee. Generally, it is advisable when setting up such a split dollar plan that the parties utilize some type of permanent life insurance that can build cash value, such as individual and survivorship policies, whole-life, universal life, and variable life insurance. Note that term life insurance provides no buildup of cash value inside the policy and therefore is not advisable if the goal of the split dollar plan is to provide both retirement planning and estate planning benefits.

The Split Dollar Financing Arrangement

A typical split dollar financing arrangement involves the acquisition of a life insurance policy by the employer for one or more of its key employees. There are many variations. However, in a typical arrangement, the employer pays the larger share of premiums—that is, the costs associated with building up the cash value inside the insurance policy. The employee pays for or reports as compensation (if this amount is paid for by the employer) the cost of the pure life insurance (i.e., typically, the cost of acquiring an annually renewable term life insurance policy).

The cost of the pure life insurance is generally referred to as the "annual economic benefit cost." You may also have seen or heard this cost referred to as the "P.S. 58" cost for an individual life insurance policy, or the "P.S. 38" cost for a survivorship (or joint life) policy. The term "P.S. 58" referred to the government table used to determine how much the employee is required to report for income tax purposes as the pure cost of the death benefit associated with the life insurance policy acquired in the split dollar arrangement. The P.S. 58/P.S. 38 rates were based on mortality tables originally published in 1946. In 2001, the IRS published Notice 2001-10, in which it announced that the IRS will no longer accept the P.S. 58/P.S. 38 rates as a proper measure of the value of current life insurance protection for federal tax purposes. Instead, a new table has been created entitled "Table 2001," which the IRS will accept for taxable year 2001 and beyond. (See Table 24.1.) In the alternative, taxpayers may use an insurer's actual one-year term insurance rates, provided that such one-year term rates are actually charged as premiums to policyholders through

TABLE 24.1 Table 2001: Interim Table of One-Year Term Premiums for $1,000 of Life Insurance Protection

Attained Age	Section 79 Extended and Interpolated Annual Rates	Attained Age	Section 79 Extended and Interpolated Annual Rates	Attained Age	Section 79 Extended and Interpolated Annual Rates
0	$0.70	35	$0.99	70	$20.62
1	$0.41	36	$1.01	71	$22.72
2	$0.27	37	$1.04	72	$25.07
3	$0.19	38	$1.06	73	$27.57
4	$0.13	39	$1.07	74	$30.18
5	$0.13	40	$1.10	75	$33.05
6	$0.14	41	$1.13	76	$36.33
7	$0.15	42	$1.20	77	$40.17
8	$0.16	43	$1.29	78	$44.33
9	$0.16	44	$1.40	79	$49.23

(Continued)

TABLE **24.1** *(Continued)*

Attained Age	Section 79 Extended and Interpolated Annual Rates	Attained Age	Section 79 Extended and Interpolated Annual Rates	Attained Age	Section 79 Extended and Interpolated Annual Rates
10	$0.16	45	$1.53	80	$54.56
11	$0.19	46	$1.67	81	$60.51
12	$0.24	47	$1.83	82	$66.74
13	$0.28	48	$1.98	83	$73.07
14	$0.33	49	$2.13	94	$80.35
15	$0.38	50	$2.30	85	$88.76
16	$0.52	51	$2.52	86	$99.16
17	$0.57	52	$2.81	87	$110.40
18	$0.59	53	$3.20	88	$121.85
19	$0.61	54	$3.65	89	$133.40
20	$0.62	55	$4.15	90	$144.30
21	$0.62	56	$4.68	91	$155.80
22	$0.64	57	$5.20	92	$168.75
23	$0.66	58	$5.66	93	$186.44
24	$0.68	59	$6.06	94	$206.70
25	$0.71	60	$6.51	95	$228.35
26	$0.73	61	$7.11	96	$250.01
27	$0.76	62	$7.96	97	$265.09
28	$0.80	63	$9.08	98	$270.11
29	$0.83	64	$10.41	99	$281.05
30	$0.87	65	$11.90		
31	$0.90	66	$13.51		
32	$0.93	67	$15.20		
33	$0.96	68	$16.92		
34	$0.98	69	$18.70		

the insurance company's standard distribution channels. In the case of a typical term life insurance policy, the Table 2001 cost generally increases as the employee ages.

Thus, a careful analysis must be undertaken to ensure that the split dollar arrangement does not become cost prohibitive to the employee as he or she ages.

Under a typical split dollar arrangement, the employer receives a portion of the death benefit upon the death of the employee. That portion is equal to either (1) the amount of the premiums that the employer has paid out or (2) the cash value of the insurance as of the date of the termination of the policy. The employee's estate (or insurance trust if one has been established for holding the insurance policy) will receive the death benefit over and above the amount payable to the employer.

Benefits of a Split Dollar Arrangement

Why would an employer want to enter into a split dollar financing arrangement with certain employees? Because such an arrangement serves as an inducement for the employees to remain in the employer's business. In fact, offering an employee a split dollar insurance package is often done in lieu of providing the employee an interest in the company itself.

The employee will be interested in such an arrangement because, depending on age and health, he or she may pay only the costs as provided pursuant to Table 2001 as if the policy was term insurance and yet receive all the benefits associated with a permanent life insurance policy. These benefits include the right to cash value buildup inside the policy, even possibly the right to borrow against such cash value inside the policy on a tax-free basis.

A split dollar arrangement is most cost efficient when the employee is relatively young so that the cost of the annual term life insurance premium is low. Many times, as part of the split dollar plan, the employer will pay the employee a bonus equal to the amount of the employee's contributions, grossed up to include the anticipated tax on the bonus, so that the entire arrangement serves as a pure economic benefit to the employee.

A split dollar agreement may provide for a termination of the plan (generally referred to as a "rollout") at a specified time. At that time, the employee repays the employer for the amount of the employer-paid premiums and receives the insurance policy outright. A rollout is generally structured so that the transfer of the policy takes place only after the insurance has been fully funded. Thus, the employee will not have to pay any future premiums on the insurance policy.

Furthermore, the split dollar arrangement should be designed to ensure that there is sufficient cash value in the insurance policy to provide the necessary funds to repay the employer for the premium outlay. The employer and employee recognize that the timing of the rollout will coincide with retirement or just ensure the employee doesn't quit before vesting in the plan.

A variation of the rollout is the "crawl-out." Under a crawl-out arrangement, the employee continues paying the annual economic cost to the employer, even after the premiums have been offset by dividends, until the employee's cumulative contributions have fully repaid the employer for its outlay. When the employer is repaid, the plan terminates, and the employee has full ownership of the insurance policy. The reason for choosing a crawl-out over a rollout is that under the terms of a crawl-out the employee, rather than the policy, funds the repayment of the employer's premium outlay.

Tax Consequences

Prior to the publication of Notice 2001-10, the tax consequences of a split dollar arrangement were relatively straightforward. In general, the employee was treated as having received taxable compensation income each year equal to the annual economic benefit (the annual term cost of P.S. 58 cost), reduced by any amount paid on the annual premiums by the employee. However, in Notice 2001-10 the IRS provided that the employee must account for his or her rights in the cash surrender value of the life insurance policy in an equity split dollar arrangement.

Historically, in a typical split dollar arrangement, the employer would pay the employee an annual bonus equal to the P.S. 58 cost, plus an additional amount calculated to take care of the income tax on the entire amount paid by the employer. In this manner, the employee would receive the entire benefit without any offsetting tax detriment. The employee would then continue to work for at least the term of the premium pay-in period and upon retirement would own the life insurance policy with a substantial cash value. The employee could then borrow against the cash value of the life insurance policy, thus providing tax-free retirement funds, if necessary, or simply retain the full face value amount of the insurance policy for the benefit of his or her family.

Under the terms of Notice 2001-10, the IRS in essence has taken the position that this tax characterization of a split dollar arrangement fails to identify properly the employee's entire benefit upon receipt of the insurance policy. The IRS asserts that if the employee is receiving the economic benefit reflected in the cash value within the insurance policy, the employee must include such amount in his or her gross income at the time such benefit is substantially vested. Under the terms of the Notice, the employee would generally be required to take such cash value increases into gross income each year as compensation income, thus substantially reducing the tax benefits of the split dollar arrangement.

In the alternative, the IRS has specifically sanctioned the treatment of the split dollar arrangement, for tax purposes, as a loan pursuant to which the employer is treated as lending the employee the premium amounts on the insurance policy on an annual basis. The IRS then provides that, if the parties respect this loan arrangement, the employee need include only the imputed interest on the loan in his or her income each year, which rate of interest is determined pursuant to the applicable federal rates posted by the IRS each month. Then, at the time the employee gains unrestricted ownership of the life insurance policy, either he or she must reimburse the employer for the loans made to pay the premiums or, in the alternative, the employer can release the employee from the obligation to repay the premiums at that time. If the employee is released of the obligation to repay the amounts lent, he or she would incur gross income to the extent of such release, which the employer can bonus to the employee in order to pay the tax.

Ownership of the Life Insurance Through an Irrevocable Life Insurance Trust

After conferring with an estate planner and insurance professional, the employee may decide to create an irrevocable life insurance trust to own the policy. Thus, for estate tax purposes, the death benefit is removed from the taxable estate. However, when a life insurance trust owns the policy, the employee is treated, for estate and gift tax purposes, as having made a gift to the trust each year much in the same way you would if you had established an insurance trust for an insurance policy you would have otherwise acquired for yourself.

As in a typical irrevocable life insurance trust, the measure of the gift will be the annual premiums paid by the grantor (here, the employee). However, by placing the policy in trust, one can exclude from the estate the entire amount of the insurance proceeds and thereby reduce estate taxes at the time of the insured's death. Furthermore, because the measure of the gift (the annual economic benefit) is not the full premium on the permanent insurance policy, the insurance proceeds can be excluded from the estate with little, or no, gift tax cost. However, the ability to borrow against cash value may be prohibited by the trust document.

Different Types of Split Dollar Arrangements

There are several different methods for structuring the repayment of premiums to the employer through a split dollar arrangement. The two most common are the collateral assignment method and the endorsement method.

Collateral Assignment Method

In a collateral-assignment split-dollar arrangement, the employee (or an irrevocable trust established for holding the policy) applies for and owns the policy. A portion of the value of the policy is collaterally assigned, or secured, by the employee or his or her trust to the employer. This is done to ensure that the employer is repaid the premiums it has advanced during the pay-in period, since the employer does not own any part of the policy itself.

When the split dollar arrangement is terminated (at the time of the death of the employee or when the policy is cashed out or rolled out), the employer is reimbursed for the amount of the premiums that it has paid. Both the trustee of the insurance trust and the insurance company must honor the collateral assignment, which has a similar effect as a mortgage on real property. Before the death benefit is paid, or upon the employee's retirement or termination, the collateral assignment must be satisfied.

Endorsement Method

Under the endorsement method, the employer serves as the purchaser and owner of the insurance policy. A separate agreement is entered into between the two parties, spelling out the employee's rights to the insurance policy. The employer names itself as beneficiary of an amount equal to the cash value of the policy at the time of the insured's death and, by endorsement, provides that the insured employee or his or her assignee (such as an insurance trust) has the right to name and change the beneficiary of the portion of the proceeds in excess of the cash value.

Loans from the Cash Value in the Life Insurance Policy

Although the split dollar method is not free from tax cost, a properly designed split dollar arrangement can provide a substantial benefit, both by way of tax-free loans (which can be treated as additional retirement benefits), as well as by way of substantial insurance proceeds available upon the death of the employee to his or her heirs.

For example, assume a 20-year split dollar arrangement was created for Jean-Claude Pierre. Upon retirement, the policy would have a cash value of $1.6 million. Accordingly, for each of the next 17 years (his actuarial life expectancy) he could borrow, tax free, $65,000 (17 × $65,000 = $1,105,000) to invest and help secure his comfortable retirement while still having enough money to repay the crawl-out obligation to La Crêpe, Inc. subject to the amount due to La Crêpe, Inc. If he died, the collateral assignment would simply be repaid out of the death benefit. Note, however, that these types of payout models are based on insurance company projections, and the amount of money projected is not guaranteed; the reality will depend on the actual investment performance inside the insurance policy itself. Additionally, a split dollar agreement will govern the structure of the obligations between the parties.

Private Split Dollar

Private split dollar plans, sometimes referred to as family split dollar, consist of an insurance financing arrangement between a family member or a trust and the insured. Unlike employer-employee split dollar arrangements, it does not involve an employer. Rather, a third-party family member or trust assumes the role of the employer and provides the lion's share of the funds that go to pay the premiums for the life insurance on the insured. In a typical arrangement, private split dollar is set up on a collateral assignment plan where the owner of the policy (generally an insurance trust) owns the policy and collaterally assigns all of the cash value to the payer of the premiums, typically individuals related to the insured, such as the insured's spouse and children.

The primary benefit of a private split dollar financing arrangement is to provide for funding of insurance premiums without the limitation of the annual exclusion, while simultaneously providing the insured's family access to the cash value of the insurance policy. As discussed in Chapter 7, "Irrevocable Life Insurance Trusts," traditional insurance trust planning requires that annual gifts equal to the premium payment be made to the insurance trust, with the general goal of avoiding gift taxes through the use of Crummey withdrawal powers and the $11,000 annual exclusion gifts. As a result, with the increasing size of premium payments on large insurance policies or where the insured is getting on in years, the likelihood is greater that the premiums gifted to the insurance trust will result in taxable gifts.

In a private split dollar arrangement, a family member (usually the spouse) can pay a large portion of the premium payments (reducing the size of the premiums required to be gifted to and paid by the insurance trust), thus reducing or eliminating any taxable gifts. The trust is required to pay only the annual economic benefit cost, which is usually a small fraction of the entire premium to be paid and thus needs much less in the way of funding to pay its share of the premiums.

In two recent private letter rulings, this type of arrangement was ruled upon favorably by the Internal Revenue Service. In Private Letter Ruling 9636033 the insured's spouse entered into a split dollar arrangement with a newly created irrevocable life insurance trust pursuant to which the trust and the spouse each paid a portion of the premiums for a policy on the taxpayer's life. The IRS ruled that the payments would not result in a taxable gift to the trust by either the taxpayer or the spouse, and the death benefit payable to the trust would not be includable in the taxpayer's gross estate.

In the ruling, the trust purchased the policy and entered into a collateral-assignment split-dollar arrangement with the spouse by which the trust paid an amount of payments equal to the lesser of the P.S. 58 costs or the one-year term cost, with the spouse paying the balance of the premiums out of her separate funds. The taxpayer retained no powers over the trust, and neither the spouse nor the taxpayer served as a trustee of the insurance trust. As in the case with traditional split dollar, the spouse (in the role as the employer) was entitled to an amount equal to the greater of the premiums she paid or the net cash value of the policy according to the collateral assignment agreement at the time of her husband's death.

In the ruling, the IRS determined that there was no inclusion of the death benefits in the estate of the insured taxpayer because the insured had retained no incidents of ownership in the policy and no powers over the trust. Be aware, however, that under the ruling if the spouse (or whichever family member is advancing the funds to pay this portion of the premium) is entitled to receive only the premiums he or she paid, there is a risk that the equity buildup would constitute an additional gift to the trust or other family members.

In putting this type of arrangement in place, it is imperative that the will of the insured's spouse (or whichever family member is making the payments to the trust for the premiums) must provide that the spouse or such family member's ownership of the cash value of the insured's policy not be given to the insured or to a testamentary trust of which the insured is either a trustee or a beneficiary so that the insured will not be deemed to have any incidents of ownership in the policy.

In Private Letter Ruling 9745019, the IRS addressed similar issues with regard to a second-to-die life insurance policy placed in an irrevocable life insurance trust that was created by a husband and wife with one of their children as trustee. In that ruling, the husband and wife paid the premium above the P.S. 38 cost of insurance and then entered into a collateral assignment agreement with the trust by which they would receive out of the death benefit their interest in the split dollar arrangement. The IRS ruled that other than their rights under the collateral assignment arrangement, the husband and wife retained no incidents of ownership in the policy so that the death benefits were not includable in either the husband's or the wife's estate.

Conclusion

A split dollar arrangement can be a cost-efficient technique for bringing together an employer and an employee and providing the employee with an additional incentive to remain loyal to the employer. This type of an arrangement can serve as an efficient and effective compensation tool for an employee and may vest for over several years and create a form of golden handcuffs. Furthermore, it can also be effectively utilized in a family situation to address the need to fund increasing premium payments without the limitation of the annual exclusion.

The key is to analyze carefully the costs associated with providing these benefits with the desired result as to all participants. As in all cases, in order to provide a complete and accurate analysis of the situation, one should always utilize the services of a sophisticated insurance professional, as well as legal and accounting advisers.

Self-Canceling Installment Notes and Private Annuities

Introduction

As discussed in previous chapters, the lifetime transfer of appreciating assets to family members provides many benefits for avoiding or reducing onerous estate tax liabilities. However, gifting such property has a number of drawbacks. These drawbacks include the potential gift tax consequences for gifts over and above the lifetime gift exemption as well as the reduction in the income of the donor following such gifts, which may come at a time when such income may become necessary to sustain a donor's standard of living.

Selling Assets as an Estate Planning Tool

As an alternative, senior family members may wish to consider selling assets to junior family members rather than giving them away. This is generally accomplished through the use of a sale in consideration for a long-term installment note. Such a technique can provide income for the senior family members while still accomplishing the goal of transferring the future appreciation in the assets sold to the family members.

However, such a method has the effect of leaving the long-term note in the estate of the senior family member throughout its term, which can produce unwanted estate tax consequences should the seller die prior to the end of the note term. Two possible solutions are the self-canceling installment note (SCIN) and the private annuity. Both techniques provide income to the senior family member selling the assets during his or her lifetime, but with each technique the debt automatically terminates upon the death of the seller. Obviously, both the SCIN and the private annuity are most effective in situations where the senior family member is not expected to survive his or her actuarial life expectancy, has exhausted the exemption equivalent (and is not willing to pay gift tax), and is reasonably certain the asset will appreciate. In addition, the junior family members must have sufficient cash flow to fund the annual payments on the SCIN or private annuity.

Self-Canceling Installment Note

A SCIN is designed like any other installment obligation, but with a twist. As with other types of installment notes, a SCIN provides for an agreed-upon number of fixed payments at a specific interest rate over a set period of time. However, unlike the terms of other installment notes, a SCIN possesses a unique feature: It automatically cancels upon the death of the note holder.

This self-canceling feature creates a number of gift and estate tax issues that could technically recharacterize the installment sale as part sale, part gift. However, these issues can be successfully addressed by requiring the purchasers to pay a premium for the self-canceling feature. The premium can take the form of either an increased amount paid for the asset (with a corresponding increase in the note principal) or an increase in the interest rate payable to the seller on the installment note. Although the IRS has not provided any definitive regulations as to what this premium should be, the following factors must be taken into consideration:

- Seller's age at the time the note is executed.

- Probability of receipt of each note payment each year.

- Applicable federal rate.

As the probability of receipt goes down, the SCIN premium goes up. Generally, however, SCIN premiums tend to range between 2% and 4% over and above the Code Section 7520 rate, which is equal to 120% of the mid-term (three to nine years) applicable federal rate. This premium can be costly. Therefore, if the senior family member still runs marathons, eats gingerroot, and drives in the right lane, the junior family member might want to reconsider utilizing a SCIN.

A properly structured SCIN will be treated as an installment obligation under the applicable provisions of the Internal Revenue Code. Therefore, the senior family member will be subject to tax on the interest paid by the junior family member(s), as well as the capital gains tax on any gain recognized upon the sale of the appreciated assets over the term of the note. Assuming the selling family member is a cash-basis taxpayer, this gain will be picked up each time a principal payment is made and will equal the amount of principal payment received each year minus an allocable portion of the seller's basis in the assets sold.

To address this issue, the SCIN can also be structured so that the installment note provides for interest-only payments for a specific length of time, followed by a balloon payment of principal at or toward the end of the note term. Under such an arrangement, the seller would receive interest over the life of the note and pay tax on the interest as received. The junior family member/purchaser could deduct the interest paid on the SCIN, subject to the typical limitations on interest deductibility for investment acquisitions.

For estate tax purposes, the assets being sold by the senior family member will be excluded from his or her estate at the time of death if death occurs before the note's satisfaction, provided that the sale is treated as complete at the time the parties enter into the SCIN. In this regard, it is imperative that the premium paid for the self-cancellation feature be fair and reasonable; otherwise, the obligation could be treated as a transfer in which the transferor has retained a life interest. The result could be that the entire value of the assets sold would be included in the estate of the selling senior family member at the time of death.

To avoid this situation, both sides of the transaction must respect the sale of the assets and the term of the SCIN. Accordingly, the senior family member is prohibited from the use or enjoyment of the assets sold and should not in any way limit the buyer's rights over the property, although the assets can be used as collateral for the note. Under the installment obligation provisions of the Internal Revenue Code, the assets should not be resold by the junior family member for at least two years. To do so generally accelerates the tax consequences to the senior family member, requiring him or her to report the gain on the sale of the assets in the year subsequent to the sale by the junior family member.

As mentioned earlier, if the seller does not survive the term of the SCIN, the balance of the note is not included in the decedent's estate and the amount that the junior family member is required to pay for the assets is reduced by the number of installments left on the note. Furthermore, if the seller does die before the note matures, the junior family member has no recognition of gain since the buyer is deemed to have paid fully for the assets at the note's inception. However, the amount of gain on the sale of property that goes unrealized by the seller due to his or her premature death will still be treated as income in respect of the decedent, taxable to the seller's estate.

For example, a senior family member age 65 sells stock in the family business with a basis of $100,000 and a fair market value of $1 million to his son in exchange for a 10-year interest-only SCIN. If the father dies prior to the end of the term of the note, the son is not required to make any further payments on the note and owns the stock free and clear. Furthermore, the son receives a basis in the assets purchased equal to the fair market value at the time of the sale regardless of whether the father survives the term of the SCIN. However, the $900,000 gain ($1 million fair market value minus $100,000 basis) that would have been recognized by the father in year 10 (upon the due date of the balloon payment on the SCIN) will be treated as a capital gain in the decedent's estate.

Detailed in Figure 25.1 is an example of the potential estate tax benefits of Maxwell Fobee, who sold a commercial property valued at $2 million, to his children over a 15-year SCIN. If the asset remains in his estate until his actuarial date of death and appreciates at the rate of 10% per year, the SCIN approach may save over $10 million in estate taxes.

Private Annuities

A private annuity is similar to a SCIN in that (1) both the private annuity and the SCIN can provide the senior family member a stream of income in return for selling assets to the junior family members and (2) when the seller/senior family member dies the SCIN terminates and the annuity ends, neither being includable in the senior family member's estate for estate tax purposes.

However, there exist certain major distinctions between the two techniques. The primary nontax difference between the private annuity and the SCIN is that, in general, an annuity, by definition, lasts for the remaining term of a seller's life, regardless of how long he or she lives. Furthermore, under the terms of a private annuity, unlike a SCIN, the assets sold cannot be used as collateral for the annuity.

For income tax purposes, with both a SCIN and a private annuity, the

SCIN INT for
Maxwell Fobee

Transfer Date 09/21/2000	AFR 7.6%
SCIN Term 15 Years	Current Interest 6.3%
Interest Premium Is 3.3842%	Discount Pct .00%

Total Value of Property Sold	$2,000,000
Annual Note Payment	258,227
Value of Property at Death in 2023	
(without Sale)	$22,109,487
Value of Payment Retained	3,336,667
Property Transferred Tax Free	18,772,820
Times Marginal Estate Tax Rate	.55
Tentative Estate Tax Savings	$10,325,051
Less Income Tax at Death	$0
Projected Estate Tax Savings	**$10,325,051**

FIGURE 25.1 SCIN for Maxwell Fobee

Reproduced with permission from CCH Incorporated, 2700 Lake Cook Road, Riverwoods, Illinois 60015.

seller is treated as if the property were sold for a long-term obligation. However, if the seller receives a private annuity in consideration for the sale of assets, the term of the obligation is equal to his or her life expectancy, and the annual payment made to the annuitant (the seller) consists of three parts:

1. The return of basis portion.

2. The capital gain portion.

3. The ordinary income portion (which is generally equivalent to the interest portion on a SCIN).

Under the terms of a private annuity, the interest rate on the interest portion of the annuity must equal or exceed the statutory rate of 120% of the federal mid-term rate for the month the annuity contract is entered into. Unlike interest payments on a SCIN, the interest portion of an annuity is not deductible by the obligor. A private annuity is not treated as an installment sale under the Internal Revenue Code, and payments made to the annuitant by the purchasers are not deductible as interest. Furthermore, the obligor's basis in the assets remains open and is adjusted with each annual payment. Accordingly, each portion of an annuity payment characterized as either gain to or recovery of basis for the annuitant increases the obligor's basis in the property. If the annuitant dies before the full recovery of basis (based on the annuitant's life expectancy), the transaction will be deemed complete. However, unlike the SCIN, the obligor of a private annuity will recognize a gain in the year of the death of the annuitant to the extent of the unpaid obligation.

A properly structured private annuity will result in the removal of the assets sold from the estate of the senior family member/seller in accordance with the terms of the private annuity. No taxable gift will occur with a properly structured private annuity sale as long as the present value of the annuity is equal to or in excess of the fair market value of the property. However, as in the case of a SCIN, if the private annuity is not properly structured or not for fair market value, it may result in the sale being treated as part sale, part gift. Even worse, if the private annuity were treated as a retention of a life estate by the annuitant, it could cause the entire property to be included in the annuitant's taxable estate.

Be aware that IRS regulations prohibit the use of actuarial tables in establishing the value of the annuity if the annuitant suffers from a terminal disease and has at least a 50% chance of dying within one year. Also, as noted earlier, a private annuity will result in adverse gift and/or estate tax consequences if the assets sold are used as collateral for the annuity or if the annuity payments are in any way restricted by the income produced by the assets being sold. In addition, if the obligor is not personally liable on the annuity contract or if the facts and circumstances demonstrate that it was never feasible to make the annuity payments, the assets may be pulled back into the seller's estate for estate tax purposes.

Finally, unlike the finite term of a SCIN, a private annuity generally runs for the entire life of the annuitant. Thus, the seller can outlive his or her life expectancy, necessitating continuing annuity payments. To address this issue, the parties should consider drafting the private annuity to provide that payments will terminate on whichever occurs first: death of the annuitant or a set term of years. This issue should be carefully laid out for the parties so that the senior family member understands that the private annuity could run out prior to his or her death.

Detailed in Figure 25.2 is an example of a single private annuity created for Maxwell Fobee (age 61) based on a $2 million sale in exchange for an annual payment of $215,364 for Maxwell's life expectancy of 25 years. Note a projected estate tax savings of over $10 million.

Single Private Annuity for Maxwell Fobee	
Transfer Date 09/21/2000	AFR 7.6%
Age at Transfer 61	Discount Pct .00%

Value of Property	$2,000,000
Divided by Annuity Factor	9.286600
Equals Annual Annuity Payment	215,364
Value of Property at Death in 2023 (without Sale)	$22,109,487
Value of Payment Retained	3,406,016
Property Transferred Tax Free	18,703,471
Times Marginal Estate Tax Rate	.55
Projected Estate Tax Savings	**$10,286,909**

FIGURE 25.2 Single Private Annuity for Maxwell Fobee
Reproduced with permission from CCH Incorporated, 2700 Lake Cook Road, Riverwoods, Illinois 60015.

Conclusion

The use of SCINs and/or private annuities to augment an estate plan may provide additional estate and gift tax benefits. Since neither of these techniques involves gifts, a gift tax return need not be filed nor a gift tax paid. These tools should be carefully considered in situations where one or more senior family members do not anticipate living as long as the generally accepted life expectancy rates. However, such instruments cannot be used when individuals know that they will die within a short period of time. Such situations are treated as shams and ignored by the Internal Revenue Service.

Since both SCINs and private annuities are based only in part on estate tax savings, the utilization of these tools must make sense on a transactional basis independent of estate taxation in the unlikely event of estate tax repeal. As both techniques lock in a sales price, provide an income stream to the senior family member, step up basis to the buyer, and provide a mechanism for business succession planning, they remain viable business succession strategies. However, as in the case with all sophisticated estate planning tools, family members must look to their team of advisers before deciding whether such structures are right for their particular facts and circumstances.

Conclusion

Introduction

Each chapter in this book has been designed to identify and discuss at least one estate or business succession planning concept. The book is intended to provide the reader with a level of comprehension such that once each chapter has been completed, the reader should be in a position to determine whether that concept or technique applies in his or her particular situation. But it is not the use of one individual concept or technique that accomplishes the entire purpose of the book, but rather the melding of multiple concepts and techniques working together that produces the optimal result.

To create an estate and business succession plan that addresses your unique needs and provides a better future for your loved ones is an enlightening and rewarding experience. Hopefully, in reading this book, you have identified the tools and techniques that are appropriate for your particular needs, and now comprehend the importance of assembling a team of advisers to help complete and maintain the estate and/or business succession plan that is right for you.

In order to offer examples of how this melding of techniques can benefit you, we have designed certain fact patterns to help you envision just how creative estate and business succession plans can work. While the examples are by no means exhaustive, they are intended to demonstrate the limitless number of factors that need to be addressed in an estate or business succession plan and the level of creativity required to accomplish the objective. By going through these examples, we hope that you will realize the benefits that can be derived from the process.

Fact Pattern #1

ESTATE PLANNING TOOLS

- Last will and testament.
- Advance directive for health care.
- Durable power of attorney.
- Revocable trust.

Fact Pattern

Mel and Harriet Kingston are in their late 60s and are celebrating their 40th wedding anniversary. With mutual love and respect, they have reared their three children, who are now living independently with their respective spouses and children of their own. As planned, the Kingstons are the prototypical snowbirds, residing in the Northeast during the late spring and summer seasons and retreating to their Florida condominium in the late fall and winter seasons. With almost $14,000 a year in Social Security income, $30,000 a year in pension and IRA income for the lives of both spouses, and $20,000 a year in interest income, together with a modest lifestyle, the couple live comfortably on their income and the wealth they have accumulated over the years (see Table 26.1).

Mel and Harriet's first priority from an estate planning perspective is to take care of each other if one spouse should die, and upon the second spouse's demise to distribute the assets equally among their children. They have also inquired as to how they might structure a fund for their grandchildren's education.

In designing the clients' estate plan, the first step of the process is to undergo an intensive fact-gathering mission wherein the goal of the estate planner is to obtain all of the necessary information, including not only a summary of the Kingstons' asset base, but also an understanding of their relationship with their children (as well as the relationships with each

TABLE 26.1 The Kingstons' Asset Base		
Asset	Title	Value
New Jersey home	Tenants by entirety	$300,000
Bonds	Joint	$400,000
Florida condominium	Tenants by entirety	$150,000
IRA	Husband to wife	$150,000
Total		$1,000,000

other), and to determine who the fiduciaries should be. Along with the clients' accountant and estate planning attorney, an insurance professional and financial planner may be helpful. Although the Kingstons' assets will not be subject to estate taxes since the assets do not exceed their exemption equivalent, the advisers may help determine the proper beneficiary designations for Mel's IRA.

The estate planning documents that this couple should consider include: a last will and testament leaving their assets to each other outright, and upon the second spouse's demise, a bequest to each grandchild for college and the balance to their children in equal shares; an advance directive for health care so that in the event one spouse is unable to make health-care decisions, the agent under the advance directive for health care (the other spouse) can make the decisions for the incapacitated spouse; and a durable power of attorney wherein they would name each other as their agents. In the event neither spouse can serve in this capacity, their children can serve as successor agents.

Perhaps the tool that is most often overlooked in this process—but, when properly utilized, can mean the difference between an estate plan plagued with administrative delays and an estate that can be administered expeditiously—will be the utilization of a revocable trust for the Florida property. More specifically, if an individual dies owning property in another state, generally an ancillary estate administration will be required to be commenced in that other state—in this case, Florida—upon the second spouse's death. Ancillary estate administration proceedings can take time and be

costly, and may require the utilization of local counsel in the relevant jurisdiction.

This ancillary administration proceeding can be avoided if the clients execute a revocable trust, also known as a living trust, and transfer the deed to the
Florida property into the trust. By so doing, the asset would pass outside of
their probate estate(s) and be governed by the trust document carried out by
their two sons, as trustees. By completing their wills, advance directives for
health care, durable powers of attorney, and revocable trusts, the Kingstons
have an estate plan that, if reviewed periodically, will serve their needs well.

Fact Pattern #2

ESTATE PLANNING TOOLS

- Last will and testament with exemption equivalent provisions.

- Unlimited marital deduction outright.

- Living will.

- Durable power of attorney.

- Irrevocable life insurance trust.

Fact Pattern

Melanie and Charles Worth have been married for 40 years and have three
children: Damien, Sondra, and Whitney. Damien has proven to be a thorn in
the Worths' sides. For every value they have tried to instill in him, he has
gone in the opposite direction. His inability to adjust to the requirements of
growing up and making it in the real world still keeps the Worths up at night.
The fact that they survived his adolescent years is a testament to their strong
marriage.

The Worths possess a great deal of love and affection for each other, as well
as for their other two children. Their primary concern is establishing an estate
plan to provide for each other and for their three children, but they are concerned by the prospect of Damien getting hold of a substantial portion of their
estate after they are gone. Charles has worked for over 30 years as a manager
for a gourmet food store, and Melanie has been a teacher in the public school
system for as long as she can remember. Together they have managed to save
and conservatively invest their assets, resulting in the asset base shown in
Table 26.2.

The Worths currently do not have any estate plan despite having been

TABLE 26.2 The Worths' Asset Base

Asset	Title	Value
Marital home	Tenants by entirety	$500,000
Stocks, bonds, and mutual funds	Joint	$2,500,000
Cash, CDs, and Treasuries	Joint	$200,000
Life insurance	Husband to wife	$800,000
Total		$4,000,00

urged to create one by their accountant and financial planner. Now they are ready, willing, and able not only to put an estate plan in place but to address their bigger concern, one that causes Melanie tears almost nightly: Damien's defiance.

After helping the Worths prepare a detailed last will and testament fact sheet, the planner recommends that each client execute a last will and testament with exemption equivalent provisions. Inasmuch as the clients have an asset base of $4 million it is important to equalize their estates so that both of them have at least the current exemption equivalent amount in their names (in year 2002, $1 million per spouse). In order to do so, the clients transfer their brokerage account from a joint tenancy into two individually managed accounts, one in Melanie's name and one in Charles's name (or, if the financial institution will accommodate them, they could transfer the account from joint tenants with rights of survivorship to tenants in common) in order to fully fund the exemption equivalent trust upon the first spouse's demise.

Having equalized their estates and included exemption equivalent provisions in their wills, the next focus is what happens to assets over the exemption equivalent amount in the event Charles dies first. The Worths agree that any balance should pass outright to Melanie. They have the ability to utilize the unlimited marital deduction and pass the assets outright to Melanie or utilize a qualified terminable interest property (QTIP) trust. The determination as to which vehicle would be better is one that requires consideration of whether

Melanie is willing to assume the management role of the assets individually. Does she feel comfortable in so doing? Also, is there a concern that either spouse will remarry and ultimately name a new spouse as beneficiary?

The clients have expressed their desire to keep the plan as simple as possible and to utilize trusts only when necessary to reduce estate tax exposure. They have vowed to each other that their hard-earned wealth will remain in the family and, in pledging their enduring love to each other, have also indicated that they are soul mates and will never remarry. Accordingly, the planner may be comfortable utilizing the unlimited marital deduction outright so that all assets over the exemption equivalent amount pass outright to the surviving spouse. There is nothing wrong with making this decision if the clients have been informed of all their options and if this planning option makes them feel comfortable. If so, the goal has been accomplished.

However, the clients' last will and testaments would not be complete without the consideration of an *in terrorem* clause (no contest clause). That is, the clients have decided that inasmuch as Damien has been so difficult, he should not share in the wealth that the family worked so hard to amass. If the clients simply cut Damien out of their wills, there might be an increased likelihood that Damien would challenge the wills and perhaps claim that they lacked testamentary capacity when drafting the wills.

The mere filing of a summons and complaint making such allegations would result in an almost immediate freeze of the estate administration process, increased legal fees, and anxiety. Damien, in his evil ways, probably already knows this and intends to leverage such results into a settlement in his favor. Accordingly, the Worths may wish to consider creating a $100,000 bequest in Damien's name but with the inclusion of an *in terrorem* clause. The result would be that upon the second spouse's demise, Damien would receive the bequest—a lump sum of $100,000—but the will's *in terrorem* clause would provide that in the event Damien were to challenge the will the bequest would automatically lapse and he would lose the bequest outright.

Additionally, when the planner drafts the $100,000 bequest for Damien, the planner should indicate in the clause that the parents recognize that he is one of their three children, but inasmuch as he has not shown the love and respect that they had expected, nor has he shared in the value structure that they sought to confer upon him, he should not share equally in the residuary of the estate with his two siblings. Further, the Worths may indicate that they have given this issue considerable thought and are steadfast in their conviction that this clause be strictly enforced.

Including such language in the bequest for Damien accomplishes a number of things: First, the testator's intent has been clearly identified. Thus, in the event that a judge ever had to interpret the client's intent, the clause stands for itself. In addition, the *in terrorem* clause (no contest clause) should have a chilling effect on Damien's potential to gear up for a will contest. In the event he sought the advice of a lawyer to object to the will, upon learning that he may lose the $100,000 bequest simply by challenging the will and inasmuch as there is descriptive language in the will that explains why his interest was cut off, there is not much Damien can do. While the clients take no pleasure in drafting this clause, it would pain them even more to know that their assets would be distributed equally among their children and that the other children would be hurt to see that Damien shared equally.

The clients should also consider the utilization of a durable power of attorney and an advance directive for health care. In both cases they will need to consider who their backup agents are. Once again, this process will require the review of extended family relationships and close family advisers.

The couple acknowledge that they are not spenders and the assets are conservatively invested with the dividends and income being reinvested. Their monthly cash flow needs are covered through their pension and Social Security payouts. Accordingly, they reasonably expect their asset base to continue to build. The clients have utilized the annual exclusion and routinely gifted the maximum annual exclusion amount per year to their other two children, but not Damien, and intend to continue to utilize their annual exclusion gifts for those two children (as well as perhaps grandchildren). The clients feel that they have paid enough in taxes during their lifetimes and are willing to take whatever steps are necessary to pass as much of their estate to their children as possible estate tax free.

In this case, the clients should sit with their insurance professional and consider implementing an irrevocable life insurance trust to protect the existing $800,000 policy. This trust will shield the death benefit from estate taxation as long as Charles survives three years from the date the policy is assigned to the trust. The clients will utilize their annual exclusions for the payment of premiums and issue Crummey notices each year so the contributions into the trust qualify as present interest gifts.

The Worths will also execute durable powers of attorney naming each other as agent and their accountant as the backup agent. Additionally, in the event either spouse is unable to make health-care decisions, they should execute advance directives for health care (living wills) naming each other as agent and their two adult children, not Damien, as successor coagents.

By designing the plan in this fashion, the clients have: (1) protected their exemption equivalents; (2) assured the surviving spouse of financial freedom through the use of the unlimited marital deduction; (3) once and for all dealt with Damien's recalcitrance; (4) protected the $800,000 life insurance policy from needless estate taxes; and (5) finalized living wills and powers of attorney if ever necessary. Their goals having been accomplished, they now simply need to provide for a maintenance program to be reviewed periodically.

Fact Pattern #3

ESTATE PLANNING TOOLS

- Last will and testament with exemption equivalent provisions.
- Springing power of attorney.
- Qualified domestic trust.
- Advance directive for health care.
- Supplemental needs trust.
- Irrevocable life insurance trust.

Fact Pattern

David and Ingrid Johnson have been happily married for over 15 years. Ingrid, while not a U.S. citizen, intends to remain in the United States and has proven to be a great mother to their 10-year-old twins, Joshua and Jamison. Unfortunately, Jamison was born severely retarded and although Ingrid's care and patience are unending, the parents are concerned for Jamison's welfare after they are gone.

David is a human resources director who unfortunately has been passed over for promotion. Living frugally, however, the couple have amassed wealth as shown in Table 26.3. The following plan design may be recommended for the Johnsons: last will and testament with exemption equivalent provisions as well as qualified domestic trust provisions, a springing power of attorney, an advance directive for health care, a testamentary supplemental needs trust, and an irrevocable life insurance trust.

In this case, the clients' wills are the cornerstone of their estate plan. The inclusion of exemption equivalent provisions will enable them to protect the exemption equivalent amount, which in the year 2002 is $1 million per spouse. However, because Ingrid is a non-U.S. citizen, the lifetime marital

TABLE 26.3 The Johnsons' Asset Base

Asset	Title	Value
Marital home	Joint	$500,000
Stocks, bonds, and mutual funds	David's name	$1,500,000
Universal life insurance policy	David as owner, Ingrid as beneficiary	$500,000
401(k)	Husband to wife	$500,000
Total		$3,000,000

deduction is limited to $103,000 for year 2002. Thus, David should create a planned gifting program and each year move approximately $100,000 into Ingrid's name.

Additionally, inasmuch as David will have assets in his name over and above the exemption equivalent amount, if the assets were to pass directly to Ingrid they would not qualify for the marital deduction and therefore would be subject to estate taxes upon David's demise. Thus, David's will should include a qualified domestic trust (QDOT), requiring that at least one U.S. citizen serve as a trustee for the trust (either a U.S. individual or financial institution), together with the requirement that all income be distributed to Ingrid, that there be no conditions or contingent interests, and that the executor elect to qualify the trust as a QDOT on IRS Form 706 upon David's demise. By creating such a trust, David will have restored the marital deduction for Ingrid's benefit. Thus, if David dies first, the exemption equivalent amount will be protected from estate taxes and all of the assets passing to Ingrid (including the 401(k) since the beneficiary is now the qualified domestic trust) will qualify for the estate tax deferral mechanism provided under the unlimited marital deduction.

The other key planning technique that must be incorporated into the clients' wills are supplemental needs trust provisions. First, the Johnsons must determine what percentage should go to each child. To the extent that the Johnsons wish to provide for Jamison, the assets otherwise passing to him should instead be set aside through the use of a supplemental needs trust. The purpose of a supplemental needs trust is (1) to preserve the basic benefits that Medicare, Medicaid, and other state and local agencies may provide Jamison and (2) to supplement those basic benefit programs by providing the trustee the discretion to remit income and/or principal to Jamison for needs that are over and above those provided through the aforesaid agencies. Special attention must also be given to who will be named trustees and guardians under the will to ensure that Jamison as well as Joshua are well cared for if something should happen to both David and Ingrid.

Additionally, the Johnsons should execute an advance directive for health care for use in the event one spouse is unable to make health-care decisions for himself or herself, and a durable power of attorney, which will enable each spouse to make financial decisions for each other. However, in the case of the Johnsons, what will make the drafting of the durable power of attorney challenging is the naming of the second-tier agent. In the unlikely event that both spouses were alive but incapacitated, the testamentary supplemental needs trusts carefully drafted in their wills are not applicable because neither Johnson has died. Accordingly, whoever is named as successor agent pursuant to the Johnsons' powers of attorney must have the presence of mind, as well as the background, not only to satisfy the financial obligations of the parents, but also to provide for the needs of Jamison without jeopardizing any benefit program to which he is entitled.

The clients should also consider the utilization of an irrevocable life insurance trust. David has a $500,000 universal life insurance policy that he bought years ago to provide for Ingrid if anything were to happen to him. In an effort to still provide for Ingrid as well as to assist in both children's development, and inasmuch as their estate is over the exemption equivalent amount, the utilization of an irrevocable trust will remove the life insurance from David's taxable estate provided David survives the assignment of the policy by at least three years. David will need to coordinate the issuance of the Crummey notices each year. In this regard, David should consult with his advisers before naming Jamison as a Crummey beneficiary inasmuch as the right to demand the money may jeopardize Jamison's Medicaid eligibility.

The Johnsons have unique planning needs. Thus, by designing this plan in the manner set forth above, they will be able to pass wealth to their children in the most tax-efficient manner possible through the inclusion of the exemption equivalent, testamentary QDOT trust, and supplemental needs trust provisions in their wills as well as the establishment of an irrevocable life insurance trust to protect the life insurance proceeds from estate taxation. In this fashion, David and Ingrid now have the security of knowing that they have provided for each other, as well as taken care of their children after they are gone.

Fact Pattern #4

ESTATE PLANNING TOOLS

- Last will and testament with exemption equivalent provisions.

- QTIP trust.

- Generation-skipping transfer tax trust.

- Charitable remainder trust.

Fact Pattern

Jeff and Amy Ruble are in their mid-60s and are enjoying the fruits of their success. Married at 19 years old, now living in a beautiful home complete with an in-ground swimming pool, they are clearly each other's best friends. Their two wonderful children, Rebecca and Sam, are both professionals and have amassed their own individual wealth. The Rubles were also blessed with four grandchildren whom they adore. Jeff sold his printing business 10 years ago for $7 million and has invested the money wisely, resulting in the asset base shown in Table 26.4.

Inasmuch as the Rubles recognize that their children's need for wealth is minimal, the clients, although they certainly intend on passing a portion of their wealth to their children, are equally focused on providing for their grand-children, as well as their favorite charity, the Salvation Army.

Their wills should include exemption equivalent provisions which, after the second spouse's demise, fund generation-skipping trusts providing income to

TABLE 26.4 The Rubles' Asset Base

Asset	Title	Value
Marital home	Joint	$500,000
Stocks, bonds, and mutual funds	Jeff	$8,000,000
Term life insurance policy	Husband to wife	$1,000,000
Cash, CDs, and Treasuries	Amy	$1,000,000
Total		$10,500,000

their children for life with the remainder going to their grandchildren, estate and GST tax free. With assets over and above the exemption equivalent amount, their wills should direct the executors to fund a qualified terminable interest property trust for the benefit of the surviving spouse. Upon the second spouse's demise, the QTIP trust together with all assets over and above the then exemption equivalent amount, would fund the charitable remainder uni-trust to provide income to the children for 10 years (or longer if desirable). At the expiration of the trust term the assets would pass outright to the Ruble Family Foundation, intended to benefit the Salvation Army.

The clients have chosen a 10-year term because the two children are 30 and 35, respectively, and the clients have an anticipated actuarial life span of 25 years. Therefore, 25 years from now their children will be 55 and 60, respectively, and 10 years of income will help them prepare for retirement (although it is designed to only supplement their existing financial base). Additionally, the children will receive the income from the generation-skipping transfer tax trust created under each of the parents' wills, which, together with the income from the charitable trust, should adequately supplement their children's needs.

The clients have discussed this technique with their children, who are all in favor of the plan's creation and, in fact, are closely aligned with the Salvation Army, as well. Accordingly, the charitable remainder trust will provide a sub-stantial estate tax deduction, significantly reducing the Rubles' estate tax exposure while incorporating their fondness for their favorite charity into the plan. The Rubles' children can then serve as board members of the foundation to help carry on the family torch.

With respect to the $1 million life insurance policy, the clients recognize that they no longer need it and yet continue paying premiums on it. They have several options. They could simply stop paying the premiums and let the policy lapse, or replace the term policy with a second-to-die policy and place the policy in an irrevocable life insurance trust for the benefit of their children. In the alternative, they could opt instead to gift the policy to the Sal-vation Army now so that any premium payments made in the future would be treated as a charitable deduction against their taxable incomes. This could provide a win-win situation. This decision needs to be made by the team of advisers including the insurance professional.

In addition to planning their estate, the Rubles should also focus on future gifts. For instance, all of the Rubles' grandchildren currently attend private schools, of which the Rubles approve. In an effort to reduce their taxable es-tate, while at the same time benefiting their grandchildren, the clients can pay unlimited amounts for their grandchildren's tuition directly to the schools. It gives them great pleasure to do so, and the grandchildren recognize that their grandparents are paying for their schooling. The Rubles can continue to pay for tuition throughout their grandchildren's elementary, middle, and high school years, as well as college and beyond.

Fact Pattern #5

Estate Planning Tools

- Last will and testament.
- Living will.
- Durable power of attorney.
- Qualified personal residence trust.
- Valuation of business interest.
- Planned giving.
- Family limited partnership.

Fact Pattern

Jay and Lynne Fein, both age 55, have been married for 35 years and are quite proud of their three children, Adam, who is 33; Seth, 29; and Shay, age 27. Both Jay and Lynne were former partners at one of the Big Five accounting firms in Manhattan. After 20 years of sharpening their pencils, they decided it was time for a lifestyle change. Together they bought Plum Point Bluffs, a 20-acre tract on Lake George. The Bluffs consists of a 15-acre tract with 22 motel efficiency units, a small marina, and a restaurant called Lake Views. On the other five-acre tract sits a beautiful 3,000-square-foot lakefront home where the couple reside. Ironically, their three-bedroom Central Park West condo became their vacation home. Healthy, happy, and proud, the Feins were on top of the world until a visit to their estate planner exposed a whopping estate tax liability, unnecessary personal liability for owning the Bluffs in their personal names, and no business succession plan. The Feins were surprised upon the review of their asset base (Table 26.5) to discover how it had grown over the years and, unfortunately, what their estate tax liability would be if they did nothing.

The Feins want to protect each other in the event of either spouse's demise or incapacity, then pass their wealth to their children equally in the most tax-efficient manner and provide for their favorite charity, Animals and Oceans, which they founded 10 years ago. "Not a problem," responded

TABLE 26.5   The Feins' Asset Base

Asset	Value	Title	Growth
Central Park West condo	$1,000,000	Joint	6%
Five-acre lakefont residential property	$1,000,000	Joint	6%
Fifteen-acre business property	$5,000,000	Joint	6%
Stocks, bonds, and mutual funds	$3,000,000	Joint	8%
Life insurance policy (whole-life)	$2,000,000 death benefit ($60,000 cash value)	Jay—owner Lynne—beneficiary	—
401(k)	$500,000	Jay—owner Lynne-beneficiary	6%
Cash, CDs, and Treasuries	$500,000	Joint	3%
Total	$13,000,000		

Taks Wize, their estate planning attorney. After assembling the Feins' accountant, financial planner, and insurance professional, Wize proposed the following plan.

"First the basics," started Wize, and suggested a last will and testament with exemption equivalent provisions designed to flow into a generation-skipping trust upon the first spouse's demise, and the balance into a QTIP trust for the benefit of the surviving spouse. By so doing, the Feins could provide handsomely for their grandchildren, should they be so blessed.

In an effort to maintain harmony and provide expertise, Wize recommended a corporate executor and a corporate trustee. The Feins, familiar with a short but popular poem by Edgar A. Guest, "The Executor" (see Chapter 2), quickly agreed.

After including several bequests for friends and loved ones, and providing caretakers for their clumsy but lovable hound, Sophie, the Feins were confident their wills were starting to take shape.

Both the advisers and the Feins agreed that a durable power of attorney for financial matters and an advance directive and health care proxy were necessary. After a thoughtful conversation, the Feins decided to name their trusted accountant and their eldest son, also an accountant, as agents under the durable power of attorney. All three children would serve as agents under the health care proxy and would be so advised.

"Now for some intermediate tax planning," continued Wize. The Feins' current estate tax liability of over $6 million was simply unacceptable despite a patriotic spirit. The team agreed that the life insurance policy was performing well, the cash value was not part of their retirement plan, and the death benefit was not required to ensure Lynne's lifestyle. Therefore, the policy could be assigned to an irrevocable life insurance trust subject to the three-year look-back rule. The transfer of the cash value would be treated as a gift, but since Crummey letters would be issued by the trustee to the children, the gift would qualify for the Feins' annual exclusion. The insurance professional assumed the responsibility for obtaining the change of ownership and change of beneficiary forms and seeing the process through to conclusion. All agreed that since the Feins are young and healthy, a second-to-die life insurance illustration should be prepared for the team to review at the next planning meeting after the estate tax liability had been whittled down by other planning techniques.

"Advanced planning," Wize exclaimed, "is where the fun begins!" The Central Park West condo could be transferred into a qualified personal residence trust (QPRT) and the 15-acre tract in Lake George could be transferred into a family limited partnership with a planned giving program put into place. The icing on the cake is naming the Feins' foundation, Animals and Oceans, as the secondary beneficiary of the 401(k) assets after naming Lynne as the primary beneficiary. Each technique is then summarized with supporting estate tax calculations and easy-to-understand definitions. The plan would potentially save millions of dollars in estate taxes, insulate the Feins from personal liability, and help solidify the business succession plan since the family limited partnership agreement names Seth, who already manages the business, as the successor managing partner.

The accountant will assume the responsibility for preparing the valuation of the business and filing a gift tax return for gifts of the limited partnership units to the children, as well as the gift of the remainder interest in the QPRT. The financial planner will prepare an analysis of the current portfolio, and, based on the Feins' goals, risk tolerance levels, and current economic trends, demonstrate how the portfolio can be restructured to meet the Feins' objectives.

The estate planning team has done its homework. Most impressed, the Feins issued the edict to implement the plan. The advisers working together complete the plan and agree to meet at year's end to review the plan in its entirety with the Feins. Such review meeting should take place every year thereafter. One brisk autumn morning, Jay and Lynne are sitting on their balcony overlooking the most tranquil lake and agree that life couldn't be finer.

Conclusion

The estate and business succession plans set forth in this chapter were intended to address each of the clients' wealth transfer concerns. Providing for one's spouse, children, grandchildren, and other loved ones may be considered the crowning achievement and final planning strategy that started with the wealth accumulation years when these individuals first began their careers. As individuals travel through the journey of life and enter their retirement years, their goals shift from wealth accumulation to wealth preservation, leaving clients with feelings of pride for what they have accomplished over the years.

However, the focus of this book is that the effort cannot stop there. By spending a relatively modest amount of time in preparing an effective estate and business succession plan, the final point of the triangle can be completed; all that one worked for during one's life can be addressed in a plan designed to perpetuate values and pass on wealth to one's loved ones. Such a process can give the parents a sense of joy and pride in having been able to successfully complete the planning process, but it can also be used as a tool to demonstrate to children the importance of creating such an estate and business succession plan, with the hope that they, too, will provide for their children and grandchildren for generations to come.

Perhaps the most understated aspect of estate and business succession planning is that it can actually be educational and enjoyable. Assembling a team of advisers gives the individuals an opportunity to work with these professionals in a way that perhaps they have not done before—opening up and sharing their ideas and opinions with their advisers in order to solicit all of the combined experience and intelligence that these advisers bring to the table. Learning about all the different estate and business succession planning tools is often educational and enlightening. Once individuals become acclimated to the entire spectrum of estate and business succession planning tools, they can provide greater insight to the team of advisers in setting up a plan that addresses their particular needs and desires and those of their family and loved ones.

With this in mind, we trust that you have found this book informative and it has helped you to develop a wealth transfer plan that suits you. We hope that you enjoy your journey and that you put your heart into creating the estate and business succession plan that is right for you.

Estate and Gift Tax Rates

2001 Tax Rates

If the amount with respect to which the tentative tax to be computed is:	The tentative tax is:
Not over $10,000	18 percent of such amount.
Over $10,000 but not over $20,000	$1,800, plus 20 percent of the excess of such amount over $10,000.
Over $20,000 but not over $40,000	$3,800, plus 22 percent of the excess of such amount over $20,000.
Over $40,000 but not over $60,000	$8,200 plus 24 percent of the excess amount over $40,000.
Over $60,000 but not over $80,000	$13,000, plus 26 percent of the excess of such amount over $60,000.
Over $80,000 but not over $100,000	$18,200, plus 28 percent of the excess of such amount over $80,000.
Over $100,000 but not over $150,000	$23,800, plus 30 percent of the excess of such amount over $100,000.
Over $150,000 but not over $250,000	$38,800, plus 32 percent of the excess of such amount over $150,000.
Over $250,000 but not over $500,000	$70,800, plus 34 percent of the excess of such amount over $250,000.
Over $500,000 but not over $750,000	$155,800, plus 37 percent of the excess of such amount over $500,000.
Over $750,000 but not over $1,000,000	$248,300, plus 39 percent of the excess of such amount over $750,000.
Over $1,000,000 but not over $1,250,000	$345,800, plus 41 percent of the excess of such amount over $1,000,000.
Over $1,250,000 but not over $1,500,000	$448,300, plus 43 percent of the excess of such amount over $1,250,000.
Over $1,500,000 but not over $2,000,000	$555,800, plus 45 percent of the excess of such amount over $1,500,000.
Over $2,000,000 but not over $2,500,000	$780,800, plus 49 percent of the excess of such amount over $2,000,000.
Over $2,500,000 but not over $3,000,000	$1,025,800, plus 53 percent of the excess over $2,500,000.
Over $3,000,000	$1,290,800, plus 55 percent of the excess over $3,000,000.

2002 Tax Rates

If the amount with respect to which the tentative tax to be computed is:	The tentative tax is:
Not over $10,000	18 percent of such amount.
Over $10,000 but not over $20,000	$1,800, plus 20 percent of the excess of such amount over $10,000.
Over $20,000 but not over $40,000	$3,800, plus 22 percent of the excess of such amount over $20,000.
Over $40,000 but not over $60,000	$8,200 plus 24 percent of the excess of such amount over $40,000.
Over $60,000 but not over $80,000	$13,000, plus 26 percent of the excess of such amount over $60,000.
Over $80,000 but not over $100,000	$18,200, plus 28 percent of the excess of such amount over $80,000.
Over $100,000 but not over $150,000	$23,800, plus 30 percent of the excess of such amount over $100,000.
Over $150,000 but not over $250,000	$38,800, plus 32 percent of the excess of such amount over $150,000.
Over $250,000 but not over $500,000	$70,800, plus 34 percent of the excess of such amount over $250,000.
Over $500,000 but not over $750,000	$155,800, plus 37 percent of the excess of such amount over $500,000.
Over $750,000 but not over $1,000,000	$248,300, plus 39 percent of the excess of such amount over $750,000.
Over $1,000,000 but not over $1,250,000	$345,800, plus 41 percent of the excess of such amount over $1,000,000.
Over $1,250,000 but not over $1,500,000	$448,300, plus 43 percent of the excess of such amount over $1,250,000.
Over $1,500,000 but not over $2,000,000	$555,800, plus 45 percent of the excess of such amount over $1,500,000.
Over $2,000,000 but not over $2,500,000.	$780,800, plus 49 percent of the excess of such amount over $2,000,000.
Over $2,500,000	$1,025,800, plus 50 percent of the excess over $2,500,000.

2003 Tax Rates

If the amount with respect to which the tentative tax to be computed is:	The tentative tax is:
Not over $10,000	18 percent of such amount.
Over $10,000 but not over $20,000	$1,800, plus 20 percent of the excess of such amount over $10,000.
Over $20,000 but not over $40,000	$3,800, plus 22 percent of the excess of such amount over $20,000.
Over $40,000 but not over $60,000	$8,200, plus 24 percent of the excess of such amount over $40,000.
Over $60,000 but not over $80,000	$13,000, plus 26 percent of the excess of such amount over $60,000.
Over $80,000 but not over $100,000	$18,200, plus 28 percent of the excess of such amount over $80,000.
Over $100,000 but not over $150,000	$23,800, plus 30 percent of the excess of such amount over $100,000.
Over $150,000 but not over $250,000	$38,800, plus 32 percent of the excess of such amount over $150,000.
Over $250,000 but not over $500,000	$70,800, plus 34 percent of the excess of such amount over $250,000.
Over $500,000 but not over $750,000	$155,800, plus 37 percent of the excess of such amount over $500,000.
Over $750,000 but not over $1,000,000	$248,300, plus 39 percent of the excess of such amount over $750,000.
Over $1,000,000 but not over $1,250,000	$345,800, plus 41 percent of the excess of such amount over $1,000,000.
Over $1,250,000 but not over $1,500,000	$448,300, plus 43 percent of the excess of such amount over $1,250,000.
Over $1,500,000 but not over $2,000,000	$555,800, plus 45 percent of the excess of such amount over $1,500,000.
Over $2,000,000	$780,800, plus 49 percent of the excess of such amount over $2,000,000.

2004 Tax Rates

If the amount with respect to which the tentative tax to be computed is:

The tentative tax is:

If the amount with respect to which the tentative tax to be computed is:	The tentative tax is:
Not over $10,000	18 percent of such amount.
Over $10,000 but not over $20,000	$1,800, plus 20 percent of the excess of such amount over $10,000.
Over $20,000 but not over $40,000	$3,800, plus 22 percent of the excess of such amount over $20,000.
Over $40,000 but not over $60,000	$8,200, plus 24 percent of the excess of such amount over $40,000.
Over $60,000 but not over $80,000	$13,000, plus 26 percent of the excess of such amount over $60,000.
Over $80,000 but not over $100,000	$18,200, plus 28 percent of the excess of such amount over $80,000.
Over $100,000 but not over $150,000	$23,800, plus 30 percent of the excess of such amount over $100,000.
Over $150,000 but not over $250,000	$38,800, plus 32 percent of the excess of such amount over $150,000.
Over $250,000 but not over $500,000	$70,800, plus 34 percent of the excess of such amount over $250,000.
Over $500,000 but not over $750,000	$155,800, plus 37 percent of the excess of such amount over $500,000.
Over $750,000 but not over $1,000,000	$248,300, plus 39 percent of the excess of such amount over $750,000.
Over $1,000,000 but not over $1,250,000	$345,800, plus 41 percent of the excess of such amount over $1,000,000.
Over $1,250,000 but not over $1,500,000	$448,300, plus 43 percent of the excess of such amount over $1,250,000.
Over $1,500,000 but not over $2,000,000	$555,800, plus 45 percent of the excess of such amount over $1,500,000.
Over $2,000,000	$780,800, plus 48 percent of the excess of such amount over $2,000,000.

2005 Tax Rates

If the amount with respect to which the tentative tax to be computed is:	The tentative tax is:
Not over $10,000	18 percent of such amount.
Over $10,000 but not over $20,000	$1,800, plus 20 percent of the excess of such amount over $10,000.
Over $20,000 but not over $40,000	$3,800, plus 22 percent of the excess of such amount over $20,000.
Over $40,000 but not over $60,000	$8,200, plus 24 percent of the excess of such amount over $40,000.
Over $60,000 but not over $80,000	$13,000, plus 26 percent of the excess of such amount over $60,000.
Over $80,000 but not over $100,000	$18,200, plus 28 percent of the excess of such amount over $80,000.
Over $100,000 but not over $150,000	$23,800, plus 30 percent of the excess of such amount over $100,000.
Over $150,000 but not over $250,000	$38,800, plus 32 percent of the excess of such amount over $150,000.
Over $250,000 but not over $500,000	$70,800, plus 34 percent of the excess of such amount over $250,000.
Over $500,000 but not over $750,000	$155,800, plus 37 percent of the excess of such amount over $500,000.
Over $750,000 but not over $1,000,000	$248,300, plus 39 percent of the excess of such amount over $750,000.
Over $1,000,000 but not over $1,250,000	$345,800, plus 41 percent of the excess of such amount over $1,000,000.
Over $1,250,000 but not over $1,500,000	$448,300, plus 43 percent of the excess of such amount over $1,250,000.
Over $1,500,000 but not over $2,000,000	$555,800, plus 45 percent of the excess of such amount over $1,500,000.
Over $2,000,000	$780,800, plus 47 percent of the excess of such amount over $2,000,000.

2006 Tax Rates

If the amount with respect to which the tentative tax to be computed is:	The tentative tax is:
Not over $10,000	18 percent of such amount.
Over $10,000 but not over $20,000	$1,800, plus 20 percent of the excess of such amount over $10,000.
Over $20,000 but not over $40,000	$3,800, plus 22 percent of the excess of such amount over $20,000.
Over $40,000 but not over $60,000	$8,200, plus 24 percent of the excess of such amount over $40,000.
Over $60,000 but not over $80,000	$13,000, plus 26 percent of the excess of such amount over $60,000.
Over $80,000 but not over $100,000	$18,200, plus 28 percent of the excess of such amount over $80,000.
Over $100,000 but not over $150,000	$23,800, plus 30 percent of the excess of such amount over $100,000.
Over $150,000 but not over $250,000	$38,800, plus 32 percent of the excess of such amount over $150,000.
Over $250,000 but not over $500,000	$70,800, plus 34 percent of the excess of such amount over $250,000.
Over $500,000 but not over $750,000	$155,800, plus 37 percent of the excess of such amount over $500,000.
Over $750,000 but not over $1,000,000	$248,300, plus 39 percent of the excess of such amount over $750,000.
Over $1,000,000 but not over $1,250,000	$345,800, plus 41 percent of the excess of such amount over $1,000,000.
Over $1,250,000 but not over $1,500,000	$448,300, plus 43 percent of the excess of such amount over $1,250,000.
Over $1,500,000 but not over $2,000,000	$555,800, plus 45 percent of the excess of such amount over $1,500,000.
Over $2,000,000	$780,800, plus 46 percent of the excess of such amount over $2,000,000.

2007–2009 Tax Rates

If the amount with respect to which the tentative tax to be computed is:	The tentative tax is:
Not over $10,000	18 percent of such amount.
Over $10,000 but not over $20,000	$1,800, plus 20 percent of the excess of such amount over $10,000.
Over $20,000 but not over $40,000	$3,800, plus 22 percent of the excess of such amount over $20,000.
Over $40,000 but not over $60,000	$8,200, plus 24 percent of the excess of such amount over $40,000.
Over $60,000 but not over $80,000	$13,000, plus 26 percent of the excess of such amount over $60,000.
Over $80,000 but not over $100,000	$18,200, plus 28 percent of the excess of such amount over $80,000.
Over $100,000 but not over $150,000	$23,800, plus 30 percent of the excess of such amount over $100,000.
Over $150,000 but not over $250,000	$38,800, plus 32 percent of the excess of such amount over $150,000.
Over $250,000 but not over $500,000	$70,800, plus 34 percent of the excess of such amount over $250,000.
Over $500,000 but not over $750,000	$155,800, plus 37 percent of the excess of such amount over $500,000.
Over $750,000 but not over $1,000,000	$248,300, plus 39 percent of the excess of such amount over $750,000.
Over $1,000,000 but not over $1,250,000	$345,800, plus 41 percent of the excess of such amount over $1,000,000.
Over $1,250,000 but not over $1,500,000	$448,300, plus 43 percent of the excess of such amount over $1,250,000.
Over $1,500,000	$555,800, plus 45 percent of the excess of such amount over $1,500,000.

United States Estate (and Generation-Skipping Transfer) Tax Return

Estate of a citizen or resident of the United States (see separate instructions).
To be filed for decedents dying after December 31, 1998.
For Paperwork Reduction Act Notice, see page 1 of the separate instructions.

OMB No. 1545-0015

Part 1. — Decedent and Executor

1a Decedent's first name and middle initial (and maiden name, if any)	1b Decedent's last name	2 Decedent's Social Security No.
3a Legal residence (domicile) at time of death (county, state, and ZIP code, or foreign country)	3b Year domicile established　4 Date of birth　5 Date of death	
6a Name of executor (see page 4 of the instructions)	6b Executor's address (number and street including apartment or suite no. or rural route; city, town, or post office; state; and ZIP code)	
6c Executor's social security number (see page 4 of the instructions)		
7a Name and location of court where will was probated or estate administered		7b Case number

8 If decedent died testate, check here ▶ ☐ and attach a certified copy of the will. 　9 If Form 4768 is attached, check here ▶ ☐

10 If Schedule R-1 is attached, check here ▶ ☐

Part 2. — Tax Computation

1 Total gross estate less exclusion (from Part 5, Recapitulation, page 3, item 12)	**1**	
2 Total allowable deductions (from Part 5, Recapitulation, page 3, item 23)	**2**	
3 Taxable estate (subtract line 2 from line 1)	**3**	
4 Adjusted taxable gifts (total taxable gifts (within the meaning of section 2503) made by the decedent after December 31, 1976, other than gifts that are includible in decedent's gross estate (section 2001(b)))	**4**	
5 Add lines 3 and 4	**5**	
6 Tentative tax on the amount on line 5 from Table A on page 12 of the instructions	**6**	
7a If line 5 exceeds $10,000,000, enter the lesser of line 5 or $17,184,000. If line 5 is $10,000,000 or less, skip lines 7a and 7b and enter -0- on line 7c. . **7a**		
b Subtract $10,000,000 from line 7a **7b**		
c Enter 5% (.05) of line 7b	**7c**	
8 Total tentative tax (add lines 6 and 7c)	**8**	
9 Total gift tax payable with respect to gifts made by the decedent after December 31, 1976. Include gift taxes by the decedent's spouse for such spouse's share of split gifts (section 2513) only if the decedent was the donor of these gifts and they are includible in the decedent's gross estate (see instructions)	**9**	
10 Gross estate tax (subtract line 9 from line 8)	**10**	
11 Maximum unified credit (applicable credit amount) against estate tax **11**		
12 Adjustment to unified credit (applicable credit amount). (This adjustment may not exceed $6,000. See page 4 of the instructions.) **12**		
13 Allowable unified credit (applicable credit amount) (subtract line 12 from line 11)	**13**	
14 Subtract line 13 from line 10 (but do not enter less than zero)	**14**	
15 Credit for state death taxes. Do not enter more than line 14. Figure the credit by using the amount on line 3 less $60,000. See Table B in the instructions and attach credit evidence (see instructions).............	**15**	
16 Subtract line 15 from line 14	**16**	
17 Credit for Federal gift taxes on pre-1977 gifts (section 2012) (attach computation) **17**		
18 Credit for foreign death taxes (from Schedule(s) P). (Attach Form(s) 706-CE) .. **18**		
19 Credit for tax on prior transfers (from Schedule Q) **19**		
20 Total (add lines 17, 18, and 19)	**20**	
21 Net estate tax (subtract line 20 from line 16)	**21**	
22 Generation-skipping transfer taxes (from Schedule R, Part 2, line 10)	**22**	
23 Total transfer taxes (add lines 21 and 22)	**23**	
24 Prior payments. Explain in an attached statement **24**		
25 United States Treasury bonds redeemed in payment of estate tax **25**		
26 Total (add lines 24 and 25)	**26**	
27 Balance due (or overpayment) (subtract line 26 from line 23)	**27**	

Under penalties of perjury, I declare that I have examined this return, including accompanying schedules and statements, and to the best of my knowledge and belief, it is true, correct, and complete. Declaration of preparer other than the executor is based on all information of which preparer has any knowledge.

Signature(s) of executor(s)　　　　　　　　　　　　　　　　　　　　　　　Date

Signature of preparer other than executor　　　Address (and ZIP code)　　　Date

ISA
STF FED1288F.1

FIGURE A.1 Form 706—United States Estate (and Generation-Skipping Transfer) Tax Return and Instructions

Form 706 (Rev. 7-99)

Estate of:

Part 3 — Elections by the Executor

Please check the "Yes" or "No" box for each question. (See Instructions beginning on page 5.)		Yes	No
1 Do you elect alternate valuation?..	**1**		
2 Do you elect special use valuation?.. If "Yes," you must complete and attach Schedule A-1.	**2**	////////	///////
3 Do you elect to pay the taxes in installments as described in section 6166?............................. If "Yes," you must attach the additional information described on page 8 of the instructions.	**3**	////////	///////
4 Do you elect to postpone the part of the taxes attributable to a reversionary or remainder interest as described in section 6163?	**4**		

Part 4 — General Information (Note: *Please attach the necessary supplemental documents. You must attach the death certificate.*)
(*See instructions on page 9.*)

Authorization to receive confidential tax information under Regs. sec. 601.504(b)(2)(i); to act as the estate's representative before the IRS; and to make written or oral presentations on behalf of the estate if return prepared by an attorney, accountant, or enrolled agent for the executor:

Name of representative (print or type)	State	Address (number, street, and room or suite no., city, state, and ZIP code)

I declare that I am the ☐ attorney/ ☐ certified public accountant/ ☐ enrolled agent (you must check the applicable box) for the executor and prepared this return for the executor. I am not under suspension or disbarment from practice before the Internal Revenue Service and am qualified to practice in the state shown above.

Signature	CAF number	Date	Telephone number

1 Death certificate number and issuing authority (attach a copy of the death certificate to this return).

2 Decedent's business or occupation. If retired, check here ▶ ☐ and state decedent's former business or occupation.

3 Marital status of the decedent at time of death:
☐ Married
☐ Widow or widower — Name, SSN, and date of death of deceased spouse ▶ _____

☐ Single
☐ Legally separated
☐ Divorced — Date divorce decree became final ▶

4a Surviving spouse's name	**4b** Social security number	**4c** Amount received (see page 9 of the instructions)

5 Individuals (other than the surviving spouse), trusts, or other estates who receive benefits from the estate (do not include charitable beneficiaries shown in Schedule O) (see instructions). For Privacy Act Notice (applicable to individual beneficiaries only), see the Instructions for Form 1040.

Name of individual, trust, or estate receiving $5,000 or more	Identifying number	Relationship to decedent	Amount (see instructions)

All unascertainable beneficiaries and those who receive less than $5,000 .... ▶

Total ....

Please check the "Yes" or "No" box for each question.		Yes	No
6 Does the gross estate contain any section 2044 property (qualified terminable interest property (QTIP) from a prior gift or estate) (see page 9 of the instructions)?..			

(continued on next page)
STF FED1288F.2

Page 2

FIGURE A.1 *Continued*

292

Part 4 — General Information (continued)

Please check the "Yes" or "No" box for each question.		Yes	No
7a Have Federal gift tax returns ever been filed?			
If "Yes," please attach copies of the returns, if available, and furnish the following information:			

7b Period(s) covered	7c Internal Revenue office(s) where filed

If you answer "Yes" to any of questions 8 - 16, you must attach additional information as described in the instructions.

		Yes	No
8a	Was there any insurance on the decedent's life that is not included on the return as part of the gross estate?		
b	Did the decedent own any insurance on the life of another that is not included in the gross estate?		
9	Did the decedent at the time of death own any property as a joint tenant with right of survivorship in which (a) one or more of the other joint tenants was someone other than the decedent's spouse, and (b) less than the full value of the property is included on the return as part of the gross estate? If "Yes," you must complete and attach Schedule E		
10	Did the decedent, at the time of death, own any interest in a partnership or unincorporated business or any stock in an inactive or closely held corporation?		
11	Did the decedent make any transfer described in section 2035, 2036, 2037, or 2038 (see the instructions for Schedule G beginning on page 11 of the separate instructions)? If "Yes," you must complete and attach Schedule G		
12	Were there in existence at the time of the decedent's death:		
a	Any trusts created by the decedent during his or her lifetime?		
b	Any trusts not created by the decedent under which the decedent possessed any power, beneficial interest, or trusteeship?		
13	Did the decedent ever possess, exercise, or release any general power of appointment? If "Yes," you must complete and attach Schedule H		
14	Was the marital deduction computed under the transitional rule of Public Law 97-34, section 403(e)(3) (Economic Recovery Tax Act of 1981)?		
	If "Yes," attach a separate computation of the marital deduction, enter the amount on item 20 of the Recapitulation, and note on item 20 "computation attached."		
15	Was the decedent, immediately before death, receiving an annuity described in the "General" paragraph of the instructions for Schedule I? If "Yes," you must complete and attach Schedule I		
16	Was the decedent ever the beneficiary of a trust for which a deduction was claimed by the estate of a pre-deceased spouse under section 2056(b)(7) and which is not reported on this return? If "Yes," attach an explanation		

Part 5 — Recapitulation

Item number	Gross estate		Alternate value	Value at date of death
1	Schedule A — Real Estate	1		
2	Schedule B — Stocks and Bonds	2		
3	Schedule C — Mortgages, Notes, and Cash	3		
4	Schedule D — Insurance on the Decedent's Life (attach Form(s) 712)	4		
5	Schedule E — Jointly Owned Property (attach Form(s) 712 for life insurance)	5		
6	Schedule F — Other Miscellaneous Property (attach Form(s) 712 for life insurance)	6		
7	Schedule G — Transfers During Decedent's Life (att. Form(s) 712 for life insurance)	7		
8	Schedule H — Powers of Appointment	8		
9	Schedule I — Annuities	9		
10	Total gross estate (add items 1 through 9)	10		
11	Schedule U — Qualified Conservation Easement Exclusion	11		
12	Total gross estate less exclusion (subtract item 11 from item 10). Enter here and on line 1 of Part 2 — Tax Computation	12		

Item number	Deductions		Amount
13	Schedule J — Funeral Expenses and Expenses Incurred in Administering Property Subject to Claims	13	
14	Schedule K — Debts of the Decedent	14	
15	Schedule K — Mortgages and Liens	15	
16	Total of items 13 through 15	16	
17	Allowable amount of deductions from item 16 (see the instructions for item 17 of the Recapitulation)	17	
18	Schedule L — Net Losses During Administration	18	
19	Schedule L — Expenses Incurred in Administering Property Not Subject to Claims	19	
20	Schedule M — Bequests, etc., to Surviving Spouse	20	
21	Schedule O — Charitable, Public, and Similar Gifts and Bequests	21	
22	Schedule T — Qualified Family-Owned Business Interest Deduction	22	
23	Total allowable deductions (add items 17 through 22). Enter here and on line 2 of the Tax Computation	23	

STF FED1288F.3

FIGURE A.1 *Continued*

293

Estate of:

SCHEDULE A — Real Estate

- *For jointly owned property that must be disclosed on Schedule E, see the instructions on the reverse side of Schedule E.*
- *Real estate that is part of a sole proprietorship should be shown on Schedule F.*
- *Real estate that is included in the gross estate under section 2035, 2036, 2037, or 2038 should be shown on Schedule G.*
- *Real estate that is included in the gross estate under section 2041 should be shown on Schedule H.*
- *If you elect section 2032A valuation, you must complete Schedule A and Schedule A-1.*

Item number	Description	Alternate valuation date	Alternate value	Value at date of death
1				

Total from continuation schedules or additional sheets attached to this schedule . . . .

TOTAL. (Also enter on Part 5, Recapitulation, page 3, at item 1.) . . . .

(If more space is needed, attach the continuation schedule from the end of this package or additional sheets of the same size.)

(See the instructions.)

Schedule A — Page 4

STF FED1288F.4

___

FIGURE A.1 *Continued*

Instructions for Schedule A — Real Estate

If the total gross estate contains any real estate, you must complete Schedule A and file it with the return. On Schedule A list real estate the decedent owned or had contracted to purchase. Number each parcel in the left-hand column.

Describe the real estate in enough detail so that the IRS can easily locate it for inspection and valuation. For each parcel of real estate, report the area and, if the parcel is improved, describe the improvements. For city or town property, report the street and number, ward, subdivision, block and lot, etc. For rural property, report the township, range, landmarks, etc.

If any item of real estate is subject to a mortgage for which the decedent's estate is liable, that is, if the indebtedness may be charged against other property of the estate that is not subject to that mortgage, or if the decedent was personally liable for that mortgage, you must report the full value of the property in the value column. Enter the amount of the mortgage under "Description" on this schedule. The unpaid amount of the mortgage may be deducted on Schedule K.

If the decedent's estate is NOT liable for the amount of the mortgage, report only the value of the equity of redemption (or value of the property less the indebtedness) in the value column as part of the gross estate. Do not enter any amount less than zero. Do not deduct the amount of indebtedness on Schedule K.

Also list on Schedule A real property the decedent contracted to purchase. Report the full value of the property and not the equity in the value column. Deduct the unpaid part of the purchase price on Schedule K.

Report the value of real estate without reducing it for homestead or other exemption, or the value of dower, curtesy, or a statutory estate created instead of dower or curtesy.

Explain how the reported values were determined and attach copies of any appraisals.

Schedule A Examples

In this example, alternate valuation is not adopted; the date of death is January 1, 1999.

Item number	Description	Alternate valuation date	Alternate value	Value at date of death
1	House and lot, 1921 William Street NW, Washington, DC (lot 6, square 481). Rent of $2,700 due at end of each quarter, February 1, May 1, August 1, and November 1. Value based on appraisal, copy of which is attached			$108,000
	Rent due on item 1 for quarter ending November 1, 1998, but not collected at date of death			2,700
	Rent accrued on item 1 for November and December 1998			1,800
2	House and lot, 304 Jefferson Street, Alexandria, VA (lot 18, square 40). Rent of $600 payable monthly. Value based on appraisal, copy of which is attached			96,000
	Rent due on item 2 for December 1998, but not collected at date of death			600

In this example, alternate valuation is adopted; the date of death is January 1, 1999.

Item number	Description	Alternate valuation date	Alternate value	Value at date of death
1	House and lot, 1921 William Street NW, Washington, DC (lot 6, square 481). Rent of $2,700 due at end of each quarter, February 1, May 1, August 1, and November 1. Value based on appraisal, copy of which is attached. Not disposed of within 6 months following death	7/1/99	90,000	$108,000
	Rent due on item 1 for quarter ending November 1, 1998, but not collected until February 1, 1999.	2/1/99	2,700	2,700
	Rent accrued on item 1 for November and December 1998, collected on February 1, 1999.	2/1/99	1,800	1,800
2	House and lot, 304 Jefferson Street, Alexandria, VA (lot 18, square 40). Rent of $600 payable monthly. Value based on appraisal, copy of which is attached. Property exchanged for farm on May 1, 1999	5/1/99	90,000	96,000
	Rent due on item 2 for December 1998, but not collected until February 1, 1999.	2/1/99	600	600

Schedule A — Page 5

STF FED1288F.5

FIGURE A.1 *Continued*

Instructions for Schedule A-1. Section 2032A Valuation

The election to value certain farm and closely held business property at its special use value is made by checking "Yes" to line 2 of Part 3, Elections by the Executor, Form 706. Schedule A-1 is used to report the additional information that must be submitted to support this election. In order to make a valid election, you must complete Schedule A-1 and attach all of the required statements and appraisals.

For definitions and additional information concerning special use valuation, see section 2032A and the related regulations.

Part 1. Type of Election

Estate and GST Tax Elections. If you elect special use valuation for the estate tax, you must also elect special use valuation for the GST tax and vice versa.

You must value each specific property interest at the same value for GST tax purposes that you value it at for estate tax purposes.

Protective Election. To make the protective election described in the separate instructions for line 2 of Part 3, Elections by the Executor, you must check this box, enter the decedent's name and social security number in the spaces provided at the top of Schedule A-1, and complete line 1 and column A of lines 3 and 4 of Part 2. For purposes of the protective election, list on line 3 all of the real property that passes to the qualified heirs even though some of the property will be shown on line 2 when the additional notice of election is subsequently filed. You need not complete columns B - D of lines 3 and 4. You need not complete any other line entries on Schedule A-1. Completing Schedule A-1 as described above constitutes a Notice of Protective Election as described in Regulations section 20.2032A-8(b).

Part 2. Notice of Election

Line 10. Because the special use valuation election creates a potential tax liability for the recapture tax of section 2032A(c), you must list each person who receives an interest in the specially valued property on Schedule A-1. If there are more than eight persons who receive interests, use an additional sheet that follows the format of line 10. In the columns "Fair market value" and "Special use value," you should enter the total respective values of all the specially valued property interests received by each person.

GST Tax Savings

To compute the additional GST tax due upon disposition (or cessation of qualified use) of the property, each "skip person" (as defined in the instructions to Schedule R) who receives an interest in the specially valued property must know the total GST tax savings on all of the interests in specially valued property received. This GST tax savings is the difference between the total GST tax that was imposed on all of the interests in specially valued property received by the skip person valued at their special use value and the total GST tax that would have been imposed on the same interests received by the skip person had they been valued at their fair market value.

Because the GST tax depends on the executor's allocation of the GST exemption and the grandchild exclusion, the skip person who receives the interests is unable to compute this GST tax savings. Therefore, for each skip person who receives an interest in specially valued property, you must attach worksheets showing the total GST tax savings attributable to all of that person's interests in specially valued property.

How To Compute the GST Tax Savings. Before computing each skip person's GST tax savings, you must complete Schedules R and R-1 for the entire estate (using the special use values).

For each skip person, you must complete two Schedules R (Parts 2 and 3 only) as worksheets, one showing the interests in specially valued

property received by the skip person at their special use value and one showing the same interests at their fair market value.

If the skip person received interests in specially valued property that were shown on Schedule R-1, show these interests on the Schedule R, Parts 2 and 3 worksheets, as appropriate. Do not use Schedule R-1 as a worksheet.

Completing the Special Use Value Worksheets. On lines 2 - 4 and 6, enter -0-.

Completing the Fair Market Value Worksheets. Lines 2 and 3, fixed taxes and other charges. If valuing the interests at their fair market value (instead of special use value) causes any of these taxes and charges to increase, enter the increased amount (only) on these lines and attach an explanation of the increase. Otherwise, enter -0-.

Line 6 — GST exemption. If you completed line 10 of Schedule R, Part 1, enter on line 6 the amount shown for the skip person on the line 10 special use allocation schedule you attached to Schedule R. If you did not complete line 10 of Schedule R, Part 1, enter -0- on line 6.

Total GST Tax Savings. For each skip person, subtract the tax amount on line 10, Part 2 of the special use value worksheet from the tax amount on line 10, Part 2 of the fair market value worksheet. This difference is the skip person's total GST tax savings.

Part 3. Agreement to Special Valuation Under Section 2032A

The agreement to special valuation by persons with an interest in property is required under section 2032A(a)(1)(B) and (d)(2) and must be signed by all parties who have any interest in the property being valued based on its qualified use as of the date of the decedent's death.

An interest in property is an interest that, as of the date of the decedent's death, can be asserted under applicable local law so as to affect the disposition of the specially valued property by the estate. Any person who at the decedent's death has any such interest in the property, whether present or future, or vested or contingent, must enter into the agreement. Included are owners of remainder and executory interests; the holders of general or special powers of appointment; beneficiaries of a gift over in default of exercise of any such power; joint tenants and holders of similar undivided interests when the decedent held only a joint or undivided interest in the property or when only an undivided interest is specially valued; and trustees of trusts and representatives of other entities holding title to, or holding any interests in the property. An heir who has the power under local law to caveat (challenge) a will and thereby affect disposition of the property is not, however, considered to be a person with an interest in property under section 2032A solely by reason of that right. Likewise, creditors of an estate are not such persons solely by reason of their status as creditors.

If any person required to enter into the agreement either desires that an agent act for him or her or cannot legally bind himself or herself due to infancy or other incompetency, or due to death before the election under section 2032A is timely exercised, a representative authorized by local law to bind the person in an agreement of this nature may sign the agreement on his or her behalf.

The Internal Revenue Service will contact the agent designated in the agreement on all matters relating to continued qualification under section 2032A of the specially valued real property and on all matters relating to the special lien arising under section 6324B. It is the duty of the agent as attorney-in-fact for the parties with interests in the specially valued property to furnish the IRS with any requested information and to notify the IRS of any disposition or cessation of qualified use of any part of the property.

FIGURE A.1 *Continued*

Checklist for Section 2032A Election. *If you are going to make the special use valuation election on Schedule A-1, please use this checklist to ensure that you are providing everything necessary to make a valid election.*

To have a valid special use valuation election under section 2032A, you must file, in addition to the Federal estate tax return, **(a)** a notice of election (Schedule A-1, Part 2), and **(b)** a fully executed agreement (Schedule A-1, Part 3). You must include certain information in the notice of election. To ensure that the notice of election includes all of the information required for a valid election, use the following checklist. The checklist is for your use only. Do not file it with the return.

1. Does the notice of election include the decedent's name and social security number as they appear on the estate tax return?

2. Does the notice of election include the relevant qualified use of the property to be specially valued?

3. Does the notice of election describe the items of real property shown on the estate tax return that are to be specially valued and identify the property by the Form 706 schedule and item number?

4. Does the notice of election include the fair market value of the real property to be specially valued and also include its value based on the qualified use (determined without the adjustments provided in section 2032A(b)(3)(B))?

5. Does the notice of election include the adjusted value (as defined in section 2032A(b)(3)(B)) of **(a)** all real property that both passes from the decedent and is used in a qualified use, without regard to whether it is to be specially valued, and **(b)** all real property to be specially valued?

6. Does the notice of election include **(a)** the items of personal property shown on the estate tax return that pass from the decedent to a qualified heir and that are used in qualified use and **(b)** the total value of such personal property adjusted under section 2032A(b)(3)(B)?

7. Does the notice of election include the adjusted value of the gross estate? (See section 2032A(b)(3)(A).)

8. Does the notice of election include the method used to determine the special use value?

9. Does the notice of election include copies of written appraisals of the fair market value of the real property?

10. Does the notice of election include a statement that the decedent and/or a member of his or her family has owned all of the specially valued property for at least 5 years of the 8 years immediately preceding the date of the decedent's death?

11. Does the notice of election include a statement as to whether there were any periods during the 8-year period preceding the decedent's date of death during which the decedent or a member of his or her family did not **(a)** own the property to be specially valued, **(b)** use it in a qualified use, or **(c)** materially participate in the operation of the farm or other business? (See section 2032A(e)(6).)

12. Does the notice of election include, for each item of specially valued property, the name of every person taking an interest in that item of specially valued property and the following information about each such person: **(a)** the person's address, **(b)** the person's taxpayer identification number, **(c)** the person's relationship to the decedent, and **(d)** the value of the property interest passing to that person based on both fair market value and qualified use?

13. Does the notice of election include affidavits describing the activities constituting material participation and the identity of the material participants?

14. Does the notice of election include a legal description of each item of specially valued property?

(In the case of an election made for qualified woodlands, the information included in the notice of election must include the reason for entitlement to the woodlands election.)

Any election made under section 2032A will not be valid unless a properly executed agreement (Schedule A-1, Part 3) is filed with the estate tax return. To ensure that the agreement satisfies the requirements for a valid election, use the following checklist.

1. Has the agreement been signed by each and every qualified heir having an interest in the property being specially valued?

2. Has every qualified heir expressed consent to personal liability under section 2032A(c) in the event of an early disposition or early cessation of qualified use?

3. Is the agreement that is actually signed by the qualified heirs in a form that is binding on all of the qualified heirs having an interest in the specially valued property?

4. Does the agreement designate an agent to act for the parties to the agreement in all dealings with the IRS on matters arising under section 2032A?

5. Has the agreement been signed by the designated agent and does it give the address of the agent?

FIGURE A.1 *Continued*

Form 706 (Rev. 7-99)

Estate of:	Decedent's Social Security Number

SCHEDULE A-1 — Section 2032A Valuation

Part 1 — Type of Election (Before making an election, see the checklist on page 7.):

☐ **Protective election (Regulations section 20.2032A-8(b)).** Complete Part 2, line 1, and column A of lines 3 and 4. (See instructions.)

☐ **Regular election.** Complete all of Part 2 (including line 11, if applicable) and Part 3. (See instructions.)

Before completing Schedule A-1, see the checklist on page 7 for the information and documents that must be included to make a valid election.

The election is not valid unless the agreement (i.e., Part 3. — Agreement to Special Valuation Under Section 2032A) —

• Is signed by each and every qualified heir with an interest in the specially valued property, and

• Is attached to this return when it is filed.

Part 2 — Notice of Election (Regulations section 20.2032A-8(a)(3))

Note: *All real property entered on lines 2 and 3 must also be entered on Schedules A, E, F, G, or H, as applicable.*

1 Qualified use — check one ▶ ☐ Farm used for farming, or

▶ ☐ Trade or business other than farming

2 Real property used in a qualified use, passing to qualified heirs, and to be specially valued on this Form 706.

A Schedule and item number from Form 706	B Full value (without section 2032A(b)(3)(B) adjustment)	C Adjusted value (with section 2032A(b)(3)(B) adjustment)	D Value based on qualified use (without section 2032A(b)(3)(B) adjustment)

Totals . . . .

Attach a legal description of all property listed on line 2.

Attach copies of appraisals showing the column B values for all property listed on line 2.

3 Real property used in a qualified use, passing to qualified heirs, but not specially valued on this Form 706.

A Schedule and item number from Form 706	B Full value (without section 2032A(b)(3)(B) adjustment)	C Adjusted value (with section 2032A(b)(3)(B) adjustment)	D Value based on qualified use (without section 2032A(b)(3)(B) adjustment)

Totals . . . .

If you checked "Regular election," you must attach copies of appraisals showing the column B values for all property listed on line 3.

(continued on next page)
STF FED1288F.8

Schedule A-1 — Page 8

FIGURE A.1 *Continued*

298

4 Personal property used in a qualified use and passing to qualified heirs.

A Schedule and item number from Form 706	B Adjusted value (with section 2032A(b)(3)(B) adjustment)	A (continued) Schedule and item number from Form 706	B (continued) Adjusted value (with section 2032A(b)(3)(B) adjustment)
		"Subtotal" from Col. B, below left	

Subtotal . . . .   Total adjusted value . . . .

5 Enter the value of the total gross estate as adjusted under section 2032A(b)(3)(A). ▶

6 Attach a description of the method used to determine the special value based on qualified use.

7 Did the decedent and/or a member of his or her family own all property listed on line 2 for at least 5 of the 8 years immediately preceding the date of the decedent's death? . . . . ☐ Yes ☐ No

8 Were there any periods during the 8-year period preceding the date of the decedent's death during which the decedent or a member of his or her family:

		Yes	No
a	Did not own the property listed on line 2 above?		
b	Did not use the property listed on line 2 above in a qualified use?		
c	Did not materially participate in the operation of the farm or other business within the meaning of section 2032A(e)(6)?		

If "Yes" to any of the above, you must attach a statement listing the periods. If applicable, describe whether the exceptions of sections 2032A(b)(4) or (5) are met.

9 Attach affidavits describing the activities constituting material participation and the identity and relationship to the decedent of the material participants.

10 Persons holding interests. Enter the requested information for each party who received any interest in the specially valued property. (Each of the qualified heirs receiving an interest in the property must sign the agreement, and the agreement must be filed with this return.)

	Name	Address
A		
B		
C		
D		
E		
F		
G		
H		

	Identifying number	Relationship to decedent	Fair market value	Special use value
A				
B				
C				
D				
E				
F				
G				
H				

You must attach a computation of the GST tax savings attributable to direct skips for each person listed above who is a skip person. (See instructions.)

11 Woodlands election. — Check here ▶ ☐ if you wish to make a woodlands election as described in section 2032A(e)(13). Enter the Schedule and item numbers from Form 706 of the property for which you are making this election ▶
You must attach a statement explaining why you are entitled to make this election. The IRS may issue regulations that require more information to substantiate this election. You will be notified by the IRS if you must supply further information.

Schedule A-1 — Page 9
STF FED1288F.9

FIGURE A.1 *Continued*

Form 706 (Rev. 7-99)

Part 3 — Agreement to Special Valuation Under Section 2032A

Estate of:	Date of Death	Decedent's Social Security Number

There cannot be a valid election unless:

- The agreement is executed by each and every one of the qualified heirs, and
- The agreement is included with the estate tax return when the estate tax return is filed.

We (list all qualified heirs and other persons having an interest in the property required to sign this agreement)

_____

being all the qualified heirs and _____ ,

being all other parties having interests in the property which is qualified real property and which is valued under section 2032A of the Internal Revenue Code, do hereby approve of the election made by _____ ,

Executor/Administrator of the estate of _____ ,

pursuant to section 2032A to value said property on the basis of the qualified use to which the property is devoted and do hereby enter into this agreement pursuant to section 2032A(d).

The undersigned agree and consent to the application of subsection (c) of section 2032A of the Code with respect to all the property described on line 2 of Part 2 of Schedule A-1 of Form 706, attached to this agreement. More specifically, the undersigned heirs expressly agree and consent to personal liability under subsection (c) of 2032A for the additional estate and GST taxes imposed by that subsection with respect to their respective interests in the above-described property in the event of certain early dispositions of the property or early cessation of the qualified use of the property. It is understood that if a qualified heir disposes of any interest in qualified real property to any member of his or her family, such member may thereafter be treated as the qualified heir with respect to such interest upon filing a Form 706-A and a new agreement.

The undersigned interested parties who are not qualified heirs consent to the collection of any additional estate and GST taxes imposed under section 2032A(c) of the Code from the specially valued property.

If there is a disposition of any interest which passes, or has passed to him or her, or if there is a cessation of the qualified use of any specially valued property which passes or passed to him or her, each of the undersigned heirs agrees to file a Form 706-A, United States Additional Estate Tax Return, and pay any additional estate and GST taxes due within 6 months of the disposition or cessation.

It is understood by all interested parties that this agreement is a condition precedent to the election of special use valuation under section 2032A of the Code and must be executed by every interested party even though that person may not have received the estate (or GST) tax benefits or be in possession of such property.

Each of the undersigned understands that by making this election, a lien will be created and recorded pursuant to section 6324B of the Code on the property referred to in this agreement for the adjusted tax differences with respect to the estate as defined in section 2032A(c)(2)(C).

As the interested parties, the undersigned designate the following individual as their agent for all dealings with the Internal Revenue Service concerning the continued qualification of the specially valued property under section 2032A of the Code and on all issues regarding the special lien under section 6324B. The agent is authorized to act for the parties with respect to all dealings with the Service on matters affecting the qualified real property described earlier. This authority includes the following:

- To receive confidential information on all matters relating to continued qualification under section 2032A of the specially valued real property and on all matters relating to the special lien arising under section 6324B.
- To furnish the Internal Revenue Service with any requested information concerning the property.
- To notify the Internal Revenue Service of any disposition or cessation of qualified use of any part of the property.
- To receive, but not to endorse and collect, checks in payment of any refund of Internal Revenue taxes, penalties, or interest.
- To execute waivers (including offers of waivers) of restrictions on assessment or collection of deficiencies in tax and waivers of notice of disallowance of a claim for credit or refund.
- To execute closing agreements under section 7121.

(continued on next page)

STF FED1288F.10

FIGURE A.1 *Continued*

Form 706 (Rev. 7-99)

Part 3 — Agreement to Special Valuation Under Section 2032A *(Continued)*

Estate of:	Date of Death	Decedent's Social Security Number

● Other acts (specify) ▶ _____

By signing this agreement, the agent agrees to provide the Internal Revenue Service with any requested information concerning this property and to notify the Internal Revenue Service of any disposition or cessation of the qualified use of any part of this property.

Name of Agent	Signature	Address

The property to which this agreement relates is listed in Form 706, United States Estate (and Generation-Skipping Transfer) Tax Return, and in the Notice of Election, along with its fair market value according to section 2031 of the Code and its special use value according to section 2032A. The name, address, social security number, and interest (including the value) of each of the undersigned in this property are as set forth in the attached Notice of Election.

IN WITNESS WHEREOF, the undersigned have hereunto set their hands at _____ ,

this _____ day of _____ .

SIGNATURES OF EACH OF THE QUALIFIED HEIRS:

Signature of qualified heir	Signature of qualified heir
Signature of qualified heir	Signature of qualified heir
Signature of qualified heir	Signature of qualified heir
Signature of qualified heir	Signature of qualified heir
Signature of qualified heir	Signature of qualified heir
Signature of qualified heir	Signature of qualified heir

Signatures of other interested parties

Signatures of other interested parties

Schedule A-1 — Page 11
STF FED1288F.11

FIGURE A.1 *Continued*

301

Form 706 (Rev. 7-99)

Estate of:

SCHEDULE B — Stocks and Bonds

(For jointly owned property that must be disclosed on Schedule E, see the instructions for Schedule E.)

Item number	Description including face amount of bonds or number of shares and par value where needed for identification. Give 9-digit CUSIP number.	Unit value	Alternate valuation date	Alternate value	Value at date of death
	CUSIP number				
1					
	Total from continuation schedules (or additional sheets) attached to this schedule				
	TOTAL. (Also enter on Part 5, Recapitulation, page 3, at item 2.)				

(If more space is needed, attach the continuation schedule from the end of this package or additional sheets of the same size.)

(The instructions to Schedule B are in the separate instructions.)

Schedule B — Page 12

STF FED1288F.12

FIGURE A.1 *Continued*

Estate of:

SCHEDULE C — Mortgages, Notes, and Cash

(For jointly owned property that must be disclosed on Schedule E, see the instructions for Schedule E.)

Item number	Description	Alternate valuation date	Alternate value	Value at date of death
1				
	Total from continuation schedules (or additional sheets) attached to this schedule			
	TOTAL. (Also enter on Part 5, Recapitulation, page 3, at item 3.)			

(If more space is needed, attach the continuation schedule from the end of this package or additional sheets of the same size.)

(See the instructions.)

Schedule C — Page 13

FIGURE A.1 *Continued*

Instructions for Schedule C —
Mortgages, Notes, and Cash

Complete Schedule C and file it with your return if the total gross estate contains any:

- mortgages,
- notes, or
- cash.

List on Schedule C:

- Mortgages and notes payable **to the decedent** at the time of death.
- Cash the decedent had at the date of death.

Do not list on Schedule C:

- Mortgages and notes payable **by the decedent.** (If these are deductible, list them on Schedule K.)

List the items on Schedule C in the following order:

- mortgages,
- promissory notes,
- contracts by decedent to sell land,
- cash in possession, and
- cash in banks, savings and loan associations, and other types of financial organizations.

What to enter in the "Description" column:

For mortgages, list:

- face value,
- unpaid balance,
- date of mortgage,
- date of maturity,
- name of maker,
- property mortgaged,
- interest dates, and
- interest rate.

Example to enter in "Description" column:

"Bond and mortgage of $50,000, unpaid balance: $24,000; dated: January 1, 1981; John Doe to Richard Roe; premises: 22 Clinton Street, Newark, NJ; due: January 1, 1999; interest payable at 10% a year — January 1 and July 1."

For promissory notes, list:

- in the same way as mortgages.

For contracts by the decedent to sell land, list:

- name of purchaser,
- contract date,
- property description,
- sale price,
- initial payment,
- amounts of installment payment,
- unpaid balance of principal, and
- interest rate.

For cash in possession, list:

- such cash separately from bank deposits.

For cash in banks, savings and loan associations, and other types of financial organizations, list:

- name and address of each financial organization,
- amount in each account,
- serial or account number,
- nature of account — checking, savings, time deposit, etc., and
- unpaid interest accrued from date of last interest payment to the date of death.

Important: If you obtain statements from the financial organizations, keep them for IRS inspection.

FIGURE A.1 *Continued*

Estate of:

SCHEDULE D — Insurance on the Decedent's Life
You must list **all** policies on the life of the decedent and attach a Form 712 for each policy.

Item number	Description	Alternate valuation date	Alternate value	Value at date of death
1				

Total from continuation schedules (or additional sheets) attached to this schedule . . . .

TOTAL. (Also enter on Part 5, Recapitulation, page 3, at item 4.) . . . .

(If more space is needed, attach the continuation schedule from the end of this package or additional sheets of the same size.)

(See the instructions.)

Schedule D — Page 15

STF FED1288F.15

FIGURE A.1 *Continued*

305

Instructions for Schedule D — Insurance on the Decedent's Life

If you are required to file Form 706 and there was any insurance on the decedent's life, whether or not included in the gross estate, you must complete Schedule D and file it with the return.

Insurance you must include on Schedule D. Under section 2042 you must include in the gross estate:

- Insurance on the decedent's life receivable by or for the benefit of the estate; and
- Insurance on the decedent's life receivable by beneficiaries other than the estate, as described below.

The term "insurance" refers to life insurance of every description, including death benefits paid by fraternal beneficiary societies operating under the lodge system, and death benefits paid under no-fault automobile insurance policies if the no-fault insurer was unconditionally bound to pay the benefit in the event of the insured's death.

Insurance in favor of the estate. Include on Schedule D the full amount of the proceeds of insurance on the life of the decedent receivable by the executor or otherwise payable to or for the benefit of the estate. Insurance in favor of the estate includes insurance used to pay the estate tax, and any other taxes, debts, or charges that are enforceable against the estate. The manner in which the policy is drawn is immaterial as long as there is an obligation, legally binding on the beneficiary, to use the proceeds to pay taxes, debts, or charges. You must include the full amount even though the premiums or other consideration may have been paid by a person other than the decedent.

Insurance receivable by beneficiaries other than the estate. Include on Schedule D the proceeds of all insurance on the life of the decedent not receivable by or for the benefit of the decedent's estate if the decedent possessed at death any of the incidents of ownership, exercisable either alone or in conjunction with any person.

Incidents of ownership in a policy include:

- The right of the insured or estate to its economic benefits;
- The power to change the beneficiary;
- The power to surrender or cancel the policy;
- The power to assign the policy or to revoke an assignment;
- The power to pledge the policy for a loan;
- The power to obtain from the insurer a loan against the surrender value of the policy;
- A reversionary interest if the value of the reversionary interest was more than 5% of the value of the policy immediately before the decedent died. (An interest in an insurance policy is considered a reversionary interest if, for example, the proceeds become payable to the insured's estate or payable as the insured directs if the beneficiary dies before the insured.)

Life insurance not includible in the gross estate under section 2042 may be includible under some other section of the Code. For example, a life insurance policy could be transferred by the decedent in such a way that it would be includible in the gross estate under section 2036, 2037, or 2038. (See the instructions to Schedule G for a description of these sections.)

Completing the Schedule

You must list every policy of insurance on the life of the decedent, whether or not it is included in the gross estate.

Under "Description" list:

- Name of the insurance company and
- Number of the policy.

For every policy of life insurance listed on the schedule, you must request a statement on **Form 712,** Life Insurance Statement, from the company that issued the policy. Attach the Form 712 to the back of Schedule D.

If the policy proceeds are paid in one sum, enter the net proceeds received (from Form 712, line 24) in the value (and alternate value) columns of Schedule D. If the policy proceeds are not paid in one sum, enter the value of the proceeds as of the date of the decedent's death (from Form 712, line 25).

If part or all of the policy proceeds are not included in the gross estate, you must explain why they were not included.

Schedule D — Page 16
STF FED1268F.16

FIGURE A.1 *Continued*

Form 706 (Rev. 7-99)

Estate of:

SCHEDULE E — Jointly Owned Property
(If you elect section 2032A valuation, you must complete Schedule E and Schedule A-1.)

PART 1 — Qualified Joint Interests — Interests Held by the Decedent and His or Her Spouse as the Only Joint Tenants (Section 2040(b)(2))

Item number	Description For securities, give CUSIP number.	Alternate valuation date	Alternate value	Value at date of death

Total from continuation schedules (or additional sheets) attached to this schedule ....

			1a		

1a Totals ....

1b Amounts included in gross estate (one-half of line 1a)...................................... **1b**

PART 2 — All Other Joint Interests

2a State the name and address of each surviving co-tenant. If there are more than three surviving co-tenants, list the additional co-tenants on an attached sheet.

Name	Address (number and street, city, state, and ZIP code)
A.	
B.	
C.	

Item number	Enter letter for co-tenant	Description (including alternate valuation date if any) For securities, give CUSIP number.	Percentage includible	Includible alternate value	Includible value at date of death

Total from continuation schedules (or additional sheets) attached to this schedule ....

2b Total other joint interests..

3 Total includible joint interests (add lines 1b and 2b). Also enter on Part 5, Recapitulation, page 3, at item 5

(If more space is needed, attach the continuation schedule from the end of this package or additional sheets of the same size.)

(See the instructions.)

STF FED1288F.17

Schedule E — Page 17

FIGURE A.1 *Continued*

307

Instructions for Schedule E — Jointly Owned Property

If you are required to file Form 706, you must complete Schedule E and file it with the return if the decedent owned any joint property at the time of death, whether or not the decedent's interest is includible in the gross estate.

Enter on this schedule all property of whatever kind or character, whether real estate, personal property, or bank accounts, in which the decedent held at the time of death an interest either as a joint tenant with right to survivorship or as a tenant by the entirety.

Do not list on this schedule property that the decedent held as a tenant in common, but report the value of the interest on Schedule A if real estate, or on the appropriate schedule if personal property. Similarly, community property held by the decedent and spouse should be reported on the appropriate Schedules A through I. The decedent's interest in a partnership should not be entered on this schedule unless the partnership interest itself is jointly owned. Solely owned partnership interests should be reported on Schedule F, "Other Miscellaneous Property."

Part 1 — Qualified joint interests held by decedent and spouse. Under section 2040(b)(2), a joint interest is a qualified joint interest if the decedent and the surviving spouse held the interest as:

- Tenants by the entirety, or
- Joint tenants with right of survivorship if the decedent and the decedent's spouse are the only joint tenants.

Interests that meet either of the two requirements above should be entered in Part 1. Joint interests that do not meet either of the two requirements above should be entered in Part 2.

Under "Description," describe the property as required in the instructions for Schedules A, B, C, and F for the type of property involved. For example, jointly held stocks and bonds should be described using the rules given in the instructions to Schedule B.

Under "Alternate value" and "Value at date of death," enter the full value of the property.

Note: *You cannot claim the special treatment under section 2040(b) for property held jointly by a decedent and a surviving spouse who is not a U.S. citizen. You must report these joint interests on Part 2 of Schedule E, not Part 1.*

Part 2 — Other joint interests. All joint interests that were not entered in Part 1 must be entered in Part 2.

For each item of property, enter the appropriate letter A, B, C, etc., from line 2a to indicate the name and address of the surviving co-tenant.

Under "Description," describe the property as required in the instructions for Schedules A, B, C, and F for the type of property involved.

In the "Percentage includible" column, enter the percentage of the total value of the property that you intend to include in the gross estate.

Generally, you must include the full value of the jointly owned property in the gross estate. However, the full value should not be included if you can show that a part of the property originally belonged to the other tenant or tenants and was never received or acquired by the other tenant or tenants from the decedent for less than adequate and full consideration in money or money's worth, or unless you can show that any part of the property was acquired with consideration originally belonging to the surviving joint tenant or tenants. In this case, you may exclude from the value of the property an amount proportionate to the consideration furnished by the other tenant or tenants. Relinquishing or promising to relinquish dower, curtesy, or statutory estate created instead of dower or curtesy, or other marital rights in the decedent's property or estate is not consideration in money or money's worth. See the Schedule A instructions for the value to show for real property that is subject to a mortgage.

If the property was acquired by the decedent and another person or persons by gift, bequest, devise, or inheritance as joint tenants, and their interests are not otherwise specified by law, include only that part of the value of the property that is figured by dividing the full value of the property by the number of joint tenants.

If you believe that less than the full value of the entire property is includible in the gross estate for tax purposes, you must establish the right to include the smaller value by attaching proof of the extent, origin, and nature of the decedent's interest and the interest(s) of the decedent's co-tenant or co-tenants.

In the "Includible alternate value" and "Includible value at date of death" columns, you should enter only the values that you believe are includible in the gross estate.

FIGURE A.1 *Continued*

Estate of:

SCHEDULE F — Other Miscellaneous Property Not Reportable Under Any Other Schedule

(For jointly owned property that must be disclosed on Schedule E, see the instructions for Schedule E.)

(If you elect section 2032A valuation, you must complete Schedule F and Schedule A-1.)

		Yes	No
1	Did the decedent at the time of death own any articles of artistic or collectible value in excess of $3,000 or any collections whose artistic or collectible value combined at date of death exceeded $10,000?		
	If "Yes," submit full details on this schedule and attach appraisals.		
2	Has the decedent's estate, spouse, or any other person, received (or will receive) any bonus or award as a result of the decedent's employment or death?		
	If "Yes," submit full details on this schedule.		
3	Did the decedent at the time of death have, or have access to, a safe deposit box?		
	If "Yes," state location, and if held in joint names of decedent and another, state name and relationship of joint depositor.		
	If any of the contents of the safe deposit box are omitted from the schedules in this return, explain fully why omitted.		

Item number	Description For securities, give CUSIP number.	Alternate valuation date	Alternate value	Value at date of death
1				
	Total from continuation schedules (or additional sheets) attached to this schedule			
	TOTAL. (Also enter on Part 5, Recapitulation, page 3, at item 6.)			

(If more space is needed, attach the continuation schedule from the end of this package or additional sheets of the same size.)
(See the instructions.)

Schedule F — Page 19

FIGURE A.1 *Continued*

Instructions for Schedule F — Other Miscellaneous Property

You must complete Schedule F and file it with the return.

On Schedule F list all items that must be included in the gross estate that are not reported on any other schedule, including:

- Debts due the decedent (other than notes and mortgages included on Schedule C)
- Interests in business
- Insurance on the life of another (obtain and attach **Form 712,** Life Insurance Statement, for each policy)

Not for single premium or paid-up policies: *In certain situations, for example where the surrender value of the policy exceeds its replacement cost, the true economic value of the policy will be greater than the amount shown on line 56 of Form 712. In these situations, you should report the full economic value of the policy on Schedule F. See Rev. Rul. 78-137, 1978-1 C.B. 280 for details.*

- Section 2044 property (see **Decedent Who Was a Surviving Spouse** below)
- Claims (including the value of the decedent's interest in a claim for refund of income taxes or the amount of the refund actually received)
- Rights
- Royalties
- Leaseholds
- Judgments
- Reversionary or remainder interests
- Shares in trust funds (attach a copy of the trust instrument)
- Household goods and personal effects, including wearing apparel
- Farm products and growing crops
- Livestock
- Farm machinery
- Automobiles

If the decedent owned any interest in a partnership or unincorporated business, attach a statement of assets and liabilities for the valuation date and for the 5 years before the valuation date. Also attach statements of the net earnings for the same 5 years. You must account for goodwill in the valuation. In general, furnish the same information and follow the methods used to value close corporations. See the instructions for Schedule B.

All partnership interests should be reported on Schedule F unless the partnership interest, itself, is jointly owned. Jointly owned partnership interests should be reported on Schedule E.

If real estate is owned by the sole proprietorship, it should be reported on Schedule F and not on Schedule A. Describe the real estate with the same detail required for Schedule A.

Line 1. If the decedent owned at the date of death articles with artistic or intrinsic value (e.g., jewelry, furs, silverware, books, statuary, vases, oriental rugs, coin or stamp collections), check the "Yes" box on line 1 and provide full details. If any one article is valued at more than $3,000, or any collection of similar articles is valued at more than $10,000, attach an appraisal by an expert under oath and the required statement regarding the appraiser's qualifications (see Regulations section 20.2031-6(b)).

Decedent Who Was a Surviving Spouse

If the decedent was a surviving spouse, he or she may have received qualified terminable interest property (QTIP) from the predeceased spouse for which the marital deduction was elected either on the predeceased spouse's estate tax return or on a gift tax return, Form 709. The election was available for gifts made and decedents dying after December 31, 1981. List such property on Schedule F.

If this election was made and the surviving spouse retained his or her interest in the QTIP property at death, the full value of the QTIP property is includible in his or her estate, even though the qualifying income interest terminated at death. It is valued as of the date of the surviving spouse's death, or alternate valuation date, if applicable. Do not reduce the value by any annual exclusion that may have applied to the transfer creating the interest.

The value of such property included in the surviving spouse's gross estate is treated as passing from the surviving spouse. It therefore qualifies for the charitable and marital deductions on the surviving spouse's estate tax return if it meets the other requirements for those deductions.

For additional details, see Regulations section 20.2044-1.

FIGURE A.1 *Continued*

Estate of:

SCHEDULE G — Transfers During Decedent's Life
(If you elect section 2032A valuation, you must complete Schedule G and Schedule A-1.)

Item number	Description For securities, give CUSIP number.	Alternate valuation date	Alternate value	Value at date of death
A.	Gift tax paid by the decedent or the estate for all gifts made by the decedent or his or her spouse within 3 years before the decedent's death (section 2035(b))	X X X X X		
B.	Transfers includible under section 2035(a), 2036, 2037, or 2038:			
1				
	Total from continuation schedules (or additional sheets) attached to this schedule			
	TOTAL. (Also enter on Part 5, Recapitulation, page 3, at item 7.)			

SCHEDULE H — Powers of Appointment
(Include "5 and 5 lapsing" powers (section 2041(b)(2)) held by the decedent.)
(If you elect section 2032A valuation, you must complete Schedule H and Schedule A-1.)

Item number	Description	Alternate valuation date	Alternate value	Value at date of death
1				
	Total from continuation schedules (or additional sheets) attached to this schedule			
	TOTAL. (Also enter on Part 5, Recapitulation, page 3, at item 8.)			

(If more space is needed, attach the continuation schedule from the end of this package or additional sheets of the same size.)
(The instructions to Schedules G and H are in the separate instructions.) **Schedule G and H — Page 21**

FIGURE A.1 *Continued*

Form 706 (Rev. 7-99)

Estate of:

SCHEDULE I — Annuities

Note: *Generally, no exclusion is allowed for the estates of decedents dying after December 31, 1984 (see page 15 of the instructions.)*

A Are you excluding from the decedent's gross estate the value of a lump-sum distribution described in section 2039(f)(2)? . . . . Yes No

If "Yes," you must attach the information required by the instructions.

Item number	Description Show the entire value of the annuity before any exclusions.	Alternate valuation date	Includible alternate value	Includible value at date of death
1				
	Total from continuation schedules (or additional sheets) attached to this schedule			
	TOTAL. (Also enter on Part 5, Recapitulation, page 3, at item 9.)			

(If more space is needed, attach the continuation schedule from the end of this package or additional sheets of the same size.)

Schedule I — Page 22

(The instructions to Schedule I are in the separate instructions.)

STF FED1288F.22

FIGURE A.1 *Continued*

Estate of:

SCHEDULE J — Funeral Expenses and Expenses Incurred in Administering Property Subject to Claims

Note: *Do not list on this schedule expenses of administering property not subject to claims. For those expenses, see the instructions for Schedule L.*

If executors' commissions, attorney fees, etc., are claimed and allowed as a deduction for estate tax purposes, they are not allowable as a deduction in computing the taxable income of the estate for Federal income tax purposes. They are allowable as an income tax deduction on Form 1041 if a waiver is filed to waive the deduction on Form 706 (see the Form 1041 instructions).

Item number	Description	Expense amount	Total amount
1	**A. Funeral expenses:**		
	Total funeral expenses.................................... ▶		
	B. Administration expenses:		
	1 Executors' commissions — amount estimated/agreed upon/paid. (Strike out the words that do not apply.)		
	2 Attorney fees — amount estimated/agreed upon/paid. (Strike out the words that do not apply.)		
	3 Accountant fees — amount estimated/agreed upon/paid. (Strike out the words that do not apply.) ...		
	4 Miscellaneous expenses:	*Expense amount*	
	Total miscellaneous expenses from continuation schedules (or additional sheets) attached to this schedule...		
	Total miscellaneous expenses .... ▶		
	TOTAL. (Also enter on Part 5, Recapitulation, page 3, at item 13.) .... ▶		

(If more space is needed, attach the continuation schedule from the end of this package or additional sheets of the same size.)
(See the instructions.)   **Schedule J — Page 23**

STF FED1288F.23

FIGURE A.1 *Continued*

313

Instructions for Schedule J — Funeral Expenses and Expenses Incurred in Administering Property Subject to Claims

General. You must complete and file Schedule J if you claim a deduction on item 13 of Part 5, Recapitulation.

On Schedule J, itemize funeral expenses and expenses incurred in administering property subject to claims. List the names and addresses of persons to whom the expenses are payable and describe the nature of the expense. **Do not list expenses incurred in administering property not subject to claims on this schedule. List them on Schedule L instead.**

The deduction is limited to the amount paid for these expenses that is allowable under local law but may not exceed:

1. The value of property subject to claims included in the gross estate, plus

2. The amount paid out of property included in the gross estate but not subject to claims. This amount must actually be paid by the due date of the estate tax return.

The applicable local law under which the estate is being administered determines which property is and is not subject to claims. If under local law a particular property interest included in the gross estate would bear the burden for the payment of the expenses, then the property is considered property subject to claims.

Unlike certain claims against the estate for debts of the decedent (see the instructions for Schedule K in the separate instructions), you cannot deduct expenses incurred in administering property subject to claims on both the estate tax return and the estate's income tax return. If you choose to deduct them on the estate tax return, you cannot deduct them on a Form 1041 filed for the estate. Funeral expenses are only deductible on the estate tax return.

Funeral Expenses. Itemize funeral expenses on line A. Deduct from the expenses any amounts that were reimbursed, such as death benefits payable by the Social Security Administration and the Veterans Administration.

Executors' Commissions. When you file the return, you may deduct commissions that have actually been paid to you or that you expect will be paid. You may not deduct commissions if none will be collected. If the amount of the commissions has not been fixed by decree of the proper court, the deduction will be allowed on the final examination of the return, provided that:

- The District Director is reasonably satisfied that the commissions claimed will be paid;

- The amount entered as a deduction is within the amount allowable by the laws of the jurisdiction where the estate is being administered;

- It is in accordance with the usually accepted practice in that jurisdiction for estates of similar size and character.

If you have not been paid the commissions claimed at the time of the final examination of the return, you must support the amount you deducted with an affidavit or statement signed under the penalties of perjury that the amount has been agreed upon and will be paid.

You may not deduct a bequest or devise made to you instead of commissions. If, however, the decedent fixed by will the compensation payable to you for services to be rendered in the administration of the estate, you may deduct this amount to the extent it is not more than the compensation allowable by the local law or practice.

Do not deduct on this schedule amounts paid as trustees' commissions whether received by you acting in the capacity of a trustee or by a separate trustee. If such amounts were paid in administering property not subject to claims, deduct them on Schedule L.

Note: *Executors' commissions are taxable income to the executors. Therefore, be sure to include them as income on your individual income tax return.*

Attorney Fees. Enter the amount of attorney fees that have actually been paid or that you reasonably expect to be paid. If on the final examination of the return the fees claimed have not been awarded by the proper court and paid, the deduction will be allowed provided the District Director is reasonably satisfied that the amount claimed will be paid and that it does not exceed a reasonable payment for the services performed, taking into account the size and character of the estate and the local law and practice. If the fees claimed have not been paid at the time of final examination of the return, the amount deducted must be supported by an affidavit, or statement signed under the penalties of perjury, by the executor or the attorney stating that the amount has been agreed upon and will be paid.

Do not deduct attorney fees incidental to litigation incurred by the beneficiaries. These expenses are charged against the beneficiaries personally and are not administration expenses authorized by the Code.

Interest Expense. Interest expenses incurred after the decedent's death are generally allowed as a deduction if they are reasonable, necessary to the administration of the estate, and allowable under local law.

Interest incurred as the result of a Federal estate tax deficiency is a deductible administrative expense. Penalties are not deductible even if they are allowable under local law.

Note: *If you elect to pay the tax in installments under section 6166, you may not deduct the interest payable on the installments.*

Miscellaneous Expenses. Miscellaneous administration expenses necessarily incurred in preserving and distributing the estate are deductible. These expenses include appraiser's and accountant's fees, certain court costs, and costs of storing or maintaining assets of the estate.

The expenses of selling assets are deductible only if the sale is necessary to pay the decedent's debts, the expenses of administration, or taxes, or to preserve the estate or carry out distribution.

FIGURE A.1 *Continued*

314

Estate of:

SCHEDULE K — Debts of the Decedent, and Mortgages and Liens

Item number	Debts of the Decedent — Creditor and nature of claim, and allowable death taxes	Amount unpaid to date	Amount in contest	Amount claimed as a deduction
1				

Total from continuation schedules (or additional sheets) attached to this schedule . . . .

TOTAL. (Also enter on Part 5, Recapitulation, page 3, at item 14.) . . . .

Item number	Mortgages and Liens — Description	Amount
1		

Total from continuation schedules (or additional sheets) attached to this schedule . . . .

TOTAL. (Also enter on Part 5, Recapitulation, page 3, at item 15.) . . . .

(If more space is needed, attach the continuation schedule from the end of this package or additional sheets of the same size.)
(The instructions to Schedule K are in the separate instructions.)

Schedule K — Page 25

STF FED1288F.25

FIGURE A.1 *Continued*

315

Estate of:

SCHEDULE L — Net Losses During Administration and
Expenses Incurred in Administering Property Not Subject to Claims

Item number	Net losses during administration (Note: *Do not deduct losses claimed on a Federal income tax return.*)	Amount
1		

Total from continuation schedules (or additional sheets) attached to this schedule . . . .

TOTAL. (Also enter on Part 5, Recapitulation, page 3, at item 18.) . . . .

Item number	Expenses incurred in administering property not subject to claims (indicate whether estimated, agreed upon, or paid.)	Amount
1		

Total from continuation schedules (or additional sheets) attached to this schedule . . . .

TOTAL. (Also enter on Part 5, Recapitulation, page 3, at item 19.) . . . .

(If more space is needed, attach the continuation schedule from the end of this package or additional sheets of the same size.)
Schedule L — Page 26 (The instructions to Schedule L are in the separate instructions.)
STF FED1288F.26

___

FIGURE A.1 *Continued*

316

Estate of:

SCHEDULE M — Bequests, etc., to Surviving Spouse

Election To Deduct Qualified Terminable Interest Property Under Section 2056(b)(7). If a trust (or other property) meets the requirements to qualified terminable interest property under section 2056(b)(7), and

    a. The trust or other property is listed on Schedule M, and

    b. The value of the trust (or other property) is entered in whole or in part as a deduction on Schedule M,

then unless the executor specifically identifies the trust (all or a fractional portion or percentage) or other property to be excluded from the election, the executor shall be deemed to have made an election to have such trust (or other property) treated as qualified terminable interest property under section 2056(b)(7).

    If less than the entire value of the trust (or other property) that the executor has included in the gross estate is entered as a deduction on Schedule M, the executor shall be considered to have made an election only as to a fraction of the trust (or other property). The numerator of this fraction is equal to the amount of the trust (or other property) deducted on Schedule M. The denominator is equal to the total value of the trust (or other property).

Election To Deduct Qualified Domestic Trust Property Under Section 2056A. If a trust meets the requirements of a qualified domestic trust under section 2056A(a) and this return is filed no later than 1 year after the time prescribed by law (including extensions) for filing the return, and

    a. The entire value of a trust or trust property is listed on Schedule M, and

    b. The entire value of the trust or trust property is entered as a deduction on Schedule M,

then unless the executor specifically identifies the trust to be excluded from the election, the executor shall be deemed to have made an election to have the entire trust treated as qualified domestic trust property.

			Yes	No
1	Did any property pass to the surviving spouse as a result of a qualified disclaimer?	**1**		
	If "Yes," attach a copy of the written disclaimer required by section 2518(b).			
2a	In what country was the surviving spouse born? _____			
b	What is the surviving spouse's date of birth? _____			
c	Is the surviving spouse a U.S. citizen?	**2c**		
d	If the surviving spouse is a naturalized citizen, when did the surviving spouse acquire citizenship? _____			
e	If the surviving spouse is not a U.S. citizen, of what country is the surviving spouse a citizen? _____			
3	**Election Out of QTIP Treatment of Annuities** — Do you elect under section 2056(b)(C)(ii) **not** to treat as qualified terminable interest property any joint and survivor annuities that are included in the gross estate and would otherwise be treated as qualified terminable interest property under section 2056(b)(7)(C)? (see instructions)	**3**		

Item number	Description of property interests passing to surviving spouse	Amount
1		
	Total from continuation schedules (or additional sheets) attached to this schedule	
4	Total amount of property interests listed on Schedule M **4**	

5a	Federal estate taxes payable out of property interests listed on Schedule M	**5a**	
b	Other death taxes payable out of property interests listed on Schedule M	**5b**	
c	Federal and state GST taxes payable out of property interests listed on Schedule M .	**5c**	
d	Add items 5a, b, and c	**5d**	
6	Net amount of property interests listed on Schedule M (subtract 5d from 4). Also enter on Part 5, Recapitulation, page 3, at item 20	**6**	

(If more space is needed, attach the continuation schedule from the end of this package or additional sheets of the same size.) (See the instructions.)

Schedule M — Page 27

FIGURE A.1 *Continued*

317

Examples of Listing of Property Interests on Schedule M

Item number	Description of property interests passing to surviving spouse	Amount
1	One-half the value of a house and lot, 256 South West Street, held by decedent and surviving spouse as joint tenants with right of survivorship under deed dated July 15, 1957 (Schedule E, Part I, item 1)	$132,500
2	Proceeds of Gibraltar Life Insurance Company policy No. 104729, payable in one sum to surviving spouse (Schedule D, item 3)...	200,000
3	Cash bequest under Paragraph Six of will	100,000

Instructions for Schedule M — Bequests, etc., to Surviving Spouse (Marital Deduction)

General

You must complete Schedule M and file it with the return if you claim a deduction on item 20 of Part 5, Recapitulation.

The marital deduction is authorized by section 2056 for certain property interests that pass from the decedent to the surviving spouse. You may claim the deduction only for property interests that are included in the decedent's gross estate (Schedules A through I).

Note: *The marital deduction is generally not allowed if the surviving spouse is not a U.S. citizen. The marital deduction is allowed for property passing to such a surviving spouse in a "qualified domestic trust" or if such property is transferred or irrevocably assigned to such a trust before the estate tax return is filed. The executor must elect qualified domestic trust status on this return. See the instructions that follow, on pages 29 - 30, for details on the election.*

Property Interests That You May List on Schedule M

Generally, you may list on Schedule M all property interests that pass from the decedent to the surviving spouse and are included in the gross estate. However, you should not list any "Nondeductible terminable interests" (described below) on Schedule M unless you are making a QTIP election. The property for which you make this election must be included on Schedule M. See "Qualified terminable interest property" on the following page.

For the rules on common disaster and survival for a limited period, see section 2056(b)(3).

You may list on Schedule M only those interests that the surviving spouse takes:

1. As the decedent's legatee, devisee, heir, or donee;

2. As the decedent's surviving tenant by the entirety or joint tenant;

3. As an appointee under the decedent's exercise of a power or as a taker in default at the decedent's nonexercise of a power;

4. As a beneficiary of insurance on the decedent's life;

5. As the surviving spouse taking under dower or curtesy (or similar statutory interest); and

6. As a transferee of a transfer made by the decedent at any time.

Property Interests That You May Not List on Schedule M

You should not list on Schedule M:

1. The value of any property that does not pass from the decedent to the surviving spouse;

2. Property interests that are not included in the decedent's gross estate;

3. The full value of a property interest for which a deduction was claimed on Schedules J through L. The value of the property interest should be reduced by the deductions claimed with respect to it;

4. The full value of a property interest that passes to the surviving spouse subject to a mortgage or other encumbrance or an obligation of the surviving spouse. Include on Schedule M only the net value of the interest after reducing it by the amount of the mortgage or other debt;

5. Nondeductible terminable interests (described below); and

6. Any property interest disclaimed by the surviving spouse.

Terminable Interests

Certain interests in property passing from a decedent to a surviving spouse are referred to as *terminable interests*. These are interests that will terminate or fail after the passage of time, or on the occurrence or nonoccurrence of some contingency. Examples are: life estates, annuities, estates for terms of years, and patents.

The ownership of a bond, note or other contractual obligation, which when discharged would not have the effect of an annuity for life or for a term, is not considered a terminable interest.

Nondeductible terminable interests. A terminable interest is *nondeductible*, and should not be entered on Schedule M (unless you are making a QTIP election) if:

1. Another interest in the same property passed from the decedent to some other person for less than adequate and full consideration in money or money's worth; and

2. By reason of its passing, the other person or that person's heirs may enjoy part of the property after the termination of the surviving spouse's interest.

This rule applies even though the interest that passes from the decedent to a person other than the surviving spouse is not included in the gross estate, and regardless of when the interest passes. The rule also applies regardless of whether the surviving spouse's interest and the other person's interest pass from the decedent at the same time.

Property interests that are considered to pass to a person other than the surviving spouse are any property interest that: (a) passes under a decedent's will or intestacy; (b) was transferred by a decedent during life; or (c) is held by or passed on to any person as a decedent's joint tenant, as appointee under a decedent's exercise of a power, as taker in default at a decedent's release or nonexercise of a power, or as a beneficiary of insurance on the decedent's life.

For example, a decedent devised real property to his wife for life, with remainder to his children. The life interest that passed to the wife does not qualify for the marital deduction because it will terminate at her death and the children will thereafter possess or enjoy the property.

However, if the decedent purchased a joint and survivor annuity for himself and his wife who survived him, the value of the survivor's annuity, to the extent that it is included in the gross estate, qualifies for the marital deduction because even though the interest will terminate on the wife's death, no one else will possess or enjoy any part of the property.

The marital deduction is not allowed for an interest that the decedent directed the executor or a trustee to convert, after death, into a terminable interest for the surviving spouse. The marital deduction is not allowed for such an interest even if there was no interest

FIGURE A.1 *Continued*

in the property passing to another person and even if the terminable interest would otherwise have been deductible under the exceptions described below for life estate and life insurance and annuity payments with powers of appointment. For more information, see Regulations sections 20.2056(b)-1(f) and 20.2056(b)-1(g), Example (7).

If any property interest passing from the decedent to the surviving spouse may be paid or otherwise satisfied out of any of a group of assets, the value of the property interest is, for the entry on Schedule M, reduced by the value of any asset or assets that, if passing from the decedent to the surviving spouse, would be nondeductible terminable interests. Examples of property interests that may be paid or otherwise satisfied out of any of a group of assets are a bequest of the residue of the decedent's estate, or of a share of the residue, and a cash legacy payable out of the general estate.

Example: A decedent bequeathed $100,000 to the surviving spouse. The general estate includes a term for years (valued at $10,000 in determining the value of the gross estate) in an office building, which interest was retained by the decedent under a deed of the building by gift to a son. Accordingly, the value of the specific bequest entered on Schedule M is $90,000.

Life Estate With Power of Appointment in the Surviving Spouse. A property interest, whether or not in trust, will be treated as passing to the surviving spouse, and will not be treated as a nondeductible terminable interest if: **(a)** the surviving spouse is entitled for life to all of the income from the entire interest; **(b)** the income is payable annually or at more frequent intervals; **(c)** the surviving spouse has the power, exercisable in favor of the surviving spouse or the estate of the surviving spouse, to appoint the entire interest; **(d)** the power is exercisable by the surviving spouse alone and (whether exercisable by will or during life) is exercisable by the surviving spouse in all events; and **(e)** no part of the entire interest is subject to a power in any other person to appoint any part to any person other than the surviving spouse (or the surviving spouse's legal representative or relative if the surviving spouse is disabled. See Rev. Rul. 85-35, 1985-1 C.B. 328). If these five conditions are satisfied only for a specific portion of the entire interest, see the section 2056(b) regulations to determine the amount of the marital deduction.

Life Insurance, Endowment, or Annuity Payments, With Power of Appointment in Surviving Spouse. A property interest consisting of the entire proceeds under a life insurance, endowment, or annuity contract is treated as passing from the decedent to the surviving spouse, and will not be treated as a nondeductible terminable interest if: **(a)** the surviving spouse is entitled to receive the proceeds in installments, or is entitled to interest on them, with all amounts payable during the life of the spouse, payable only to the surviving spouse; **(b)** the installment or interest payments are payable annually, or more frequently, beginning not later than 13 months after the decedent's death; **(c)** the surviving spouse has the power, exercisable in favor of the surviving spouse or of the estate of the surviving spouse, to appoint all amounts payable under the contract; **(d)** the power is exercisable by the surviving spouse alone and (whether exercisable by will or during life) is exercisable by the surviving spouse in all events; and **(e)** no part of the amount payable under the contract is subject to a power in any other person to appoint any part to any person other than the surviving spouse. If these five conditions are satisfied only for a specific portion of the proceeds, see the section 2056(b) regulations to determine the amount of the marital deduction.

Charitable Remainder Trusts. An interest in a charitable remainder trust will not be treated as a nondeductible terminable interest if:

1. The interest in the trust passes from the decedent to the surviving spouse; and

2. The surviving spouse is the only beneficiary of the trust other than charitable organizations described in section 170(c).

A "charitable remainder trust" is either a charitable remainder annuity trust or a charitable remainder unitrust. (See section 664 for descriptions of these trusts.)

Election To Deduct Qualified Terminable Interests (QTIP)

You may elect to claim a marital deduction for qualified terminable interest property or property interests. You make the QTIP election simply by listing the qualified terminable interest property on Schedule M and deducting its value. You are presumed to have made the QTIP election if you list the property and deduct its value on Schedule M. If you make this election, the surviving spouse's gross estate will include the value of the "qualified terminable interest property." See the instructions for line 6 of General Information for more details. **The election is irrevocable.**

If you file Form 706 in which you do not make this election, you may not file an amended return to make the election unless you file the amended return on or

before the due date for filing the original Form 706.

The effect of the election is that the property (interest) will be treated as passing to the surviving spouse and will not be treated as a nondeductible terminable interest. All of the other marital deduction requirements must still be satisfied before you may make this election. For example, you may not make this election for property or property interests that are not included in the decedent's gross estate.

Qualified terminable interest property is property **(a)** that passes from the decedent, and **(b)** in which the surviving spouse has a qualifying income interest for life.

The surviving spouse has a *qualifying income interest for life* if the surviving spouse is entitled to all of the income from the property payable annually or at more frequent intervals, or has a usufruct interest for life in the property, and during the surviving spouse's lifetime no person has a power to appoint any part of the property to any person other than the surviving spouse. An annuity is treated as an income interest regardless of whether the property from which the annuity is payable can be separately identified.

Amendments to Regulations sections 20.2044-1, 20.2056(b)-7 and 20.2056(b)-10 clarify that an interest in property is eligible for QTIP treatment if the income interest is contingent upon the executor's election even if that portion of the property for which no election is made will pass to or for the benefit of beneficiaries other than the surviving spouse.

The QTIP election may be made for all or any part of qualified terminable interest property. A partial election must relate to a fractional or percentile share of the property so that the elective part will reflect its proportionate share of the increase or decline in the whole of the property when applying sections 2044 or 2519. Thus, if the interest of the surviving spouse in a trust (or other property in which the spouse has a qualified life estate) is qualified terminable interest property, you may make an election for a part of the trust (or other property) only if the election relates to a defined fraction or percentage of the entire trust (or other property). The fraction or percentage may be defined by means of a formula.

Qualified Domestic Trust Election (QDOT)

The marital deduction is allowed for transfers to a surviving spouse who is not a U.S. citizen only if the property passes to the surviving spouse in a "qualified domestic trust" (QDOT) or if

Page 29

FIGURE A.1 *Continued*

such property is transferred or irrevocably assigned to a QDOT before the decedent's estate tax return is filed.

A QDOT is any trust:

1. That requires at least one trustee to be either an individual who is a citizen of the United States or a domestic corporation;

2. That requires that no distribution of corpus from the trust can be made unless such a trustee has the right to withhold from the distribution the tax imposed on the QDOT;

3. That meets the requirements of any applicable regulations; and

4. For which the executor has made an election on the estate tax return of the decedent.

Note: *For trusts created by an instrument executed before November 5, 1990, paragraphs 1 and 2 above will be treated as met if the trust instrument requires that all trustees be individuals who are citizens of the United States or domestic corporations.*

You make the QDOT election simply by listing the qualified domestic trust or the **entire value** of the trust property on Schedule M and deducting its value. You are presumed to have made the QDOT election if you list the trust or trust property and deduct its value on Schedule M. **Once made, the election is irrevocable.**

If an election is made to deduct qualified domestic trust property under section 2056A(d), the following information should be provided for each qualified domestic trust on an attachment to this schedule:

1. The name and address of every trustee;

2. A description of each transfer passing from the decedent that is the source of the property to be placed in trust; and

3. The employer identification number (EIN) for the trust.

The election must be made for an entire QDOT trust. In listing a trust for which you are making a QDOT election, unless you specifically identify the trust as not subject to the election, the election will be considered made for the entire trust.

The determination of whether a trust qualifies as a QDOT will be made as of the date the decedent's Form 706 is filed. If, however, judicial proceedings are

brought before the Form 706's due date (including extensions) to have the trust revised to meet the QDOT requirements, then the determination will not be made until the court-ordered changes to the trust are made.

Line 1

If property passes to the surviving spouse as the result of a qualified disclaimer, check "Yes" and attach a copy of the written disclaimer required by section 2518(b).

Line 3

Section 2056(b)(7) creates an automatic QTIP election for certain joint and survivor annuities that are includible in the estate under section 2039. To qualify, only the surviving spouse can have the right to receive payments before the death of the surviving spouse.

The executor can elect out of QTIP treatment, however, by checking the "Yes" box on line 3. Once made, the election is irrevocable. If there is more than one such joint and survivor annuity, you are not required to make the election for all of them.

If you make the election out of QTIP treatment by checking "Yes" on line 3, you cannot deduct the amount of the annuity on Schedule M. If you do not make the election out, you must list the joint and survivor annuities on Schedule M.

Listing Property Interests on Schedule M

List each property interest included in the gross estate that passes from the decedent to the surviving spouse and for which a marital deduction is claimed. This includes otherwise nondeductible terminable interest property for which you are making a QTIP election. Number each item in sequence and describe each item in detail. Describe the instrument (including any clause or paragraph number) or provision of law under which each item passed to the surviving spouse. If possible, show where each item appears (number and schedule) on Schedules A through I.

In listing otherwise nondeductible property for which you are making a QTIP election, unless you specifically identify a fractional portion of the trust or other property as not subject to the election, the election will be considered made for all of the trust or other property.

Enter the value of each interest before taking into account the Federal estate tax or any other death tax. The valuation dates used in determining the value of the gross estate apply also on Schedule M.

If Schedule M includes a bequest of the residue or a part of the residue of the decedent's estate, attach a copy of the computation showing how the value of the residue was determined. Include a statement showing:

● The value of all property that is included in the decedent's gross estate (Schedules A through I) but is not a part of the decedent's probate estate, such as lifetime transfers, jointly owned property that passed to the survivor on decedent's death, and the insurance payable to specific beneficiaries.

● The values of all specific and general legacies or devises, with reference to the applicable clause or paragraph of the decedent's will or codicil. (If legacies are made to each member of a class, for example, $1,000 to each of decedent's employees, only the number in each class and the total value of property received by them need be furnished.)

● The date of birth of all persons, the length of whose lives may affect the value of the residuary interest passing to the surviving spouse.

● Any other important information such as that relating to any claim to any part of the estate not arising under the will.

Lines 5a, b, and c. The total of the values listed on Schedule M must be reduced by the amount of the Federal estate tax, the Federal GST tax, and the amount of state or other death and GST taxes paid out of the property interest involved. If you enter an amount for state or other death or GST taxes on lines 5b or 5c, identify the taxes and attach your computation of them.

Attachments. If you list property interests passing by the decedent's will on Schedule M, attach a certified copy of the order admitting the will to probate. If, when you file the return, the court of probate jurisdiction has entered any decree interpreting the will or any of its provisions affecting any of the interests listed on Schedule M, or has entered any order of distribution, attach a copy of the decree or order. In addition, the District Director may request other evidence to support the marital deduction claimed.

FIGURE A.1 *Continued*

Estate of:

SCHEDULE O — Charitable, Public, and Similar Gifts and Bequests

	Yes	No
1a If the transfer was made by will, has any action been instituted to have interpreted or to contest the will or any of its provisions affecting the charitable deductions claimed in this schedule? . . . . If "Yes," full details must be submitted with this schedule.		
b According to the information and belief of the person or persons filing this return, is any such action planned? . . . . . If "Yes," full details must be submitted with this schedule.		
2 Did any property pass to charity as the result of a qualified disclaimer? . . . . If "Yes," attach a copy of the written disclaimer required by section 2518(b).		

Item number	Name and address of beneficiary	Character of institution	Amount
1			

Total from continuation schedules (or additional sheets) attached to this schedule . . . .

3 Total.	**3**	
4a Federal estate tax payable out of property interests listed above	**4a**	
b Other death taxes payable out of property interests listed above	**4b**	
c Federal and state GST taxes payable out of property interests listed above . .	**4c**	
d Add items 4a, b, and c	**4d**	
5 Net value of property interests listed above (subtract 4d from 3). Also enter on Part 5, Recapitulation, page 3, at item 21	**5**	

(If more space is needed, attach the continuation schedule from the end of this package or additional sheets of the same size.)
(The instructions to Schedule O are in the separate instructions.)

Schedule O — Page 31

FIGURE A.1 *Continued*

Form 706 (Rev. 7-99)

Estate of:

SCHEDULE P — Credit for Foreign Death Taxes

List all foreign countries to which death taxes have been paid and for which a credit is claimed on this return.

If a credit is claimed for death taxes paid to more than one foreign country, compute the credit for taxes paid to one country on this sheet and attach a separate copy of Schedule P for each of the other countries.

The credit computed on this sheet is for the_____
(Name of death tax or taxes)

_____ imposed in _____
(Name of country)

Credit is computed under the _____
(Insert title of treaty or "statute")

Citizenship (nationality) of decedent at time of death

(All amounts and values must be entered in United States money.)

1 Total of estate, inheritance, legacy, and succession taxes imposed in the country named above attributable to property situated in that country, subjected to these taxes, and included in the gross estate (as defined by statute)	**1**
2 Value of the gross estate (adjusted, if necessary, according to the instructions for item 2)	**2**
3 Value of property situated in that country, subjected to death taxes imposed in that country, and included in the gross estate (adjusted, if necessary, according to the instructions for item 3)	**3**
4 Tax imposed by section 2001 reduced by the total credits claimed under sections 2010, 2011, and 2012 (see instructions) .	**4**
5 Amount of Federal estate tax attributable to property specified at item 3. (Divide item 3 by item 2 and multiply the result by item 4.)	**5**
6 Credit for death taxes imposed in the country named above (the smaller of item 1 or item 5). Also enter on line 18 of Part 2, Tax Computation	**6**

SCHEDULE Q — Credit for Tax on Prior Transfers

Part 1 — Transferor Information

	Name of transferor	Social security number	IRS office where estate tax return was filed	Date of death
A				
B				
C				

Check here ▶ ☐ if section 2013(f) (special valuation of farm, etc., real property) adjustments to the computation of the credit were made (see page 18 of the instructions).

Part 2 — Computation of Credit (see instructions beginning on page 18)

Item	Transferor			Total A, B, & C
	A	B	C	
1 Transferee's tax as apportioned (from worksheet, (line 7 ÷ line 8) × line 35 for each column)				
2 Transferor's tax (from each column of worksheet, line 20)				
3 Maximum amount before percentage requirement (for each column, enter amount from line 1 or 2, whichever is smaller)				
4 Percentage allowed (each column) (see instructions)	%	%	%	
5 Credit allowable (line 3 × line 4 for each column) . .				
6 TOTAL credit allowable (add columns A, B, and C of line 5). Enter here and on line 19 of Part 2, Tax Computation				

Schedules P and Q — Page 32
STF FED1288F.32

(The instructions to Schedules P and Q are in the separate instructions.)

FIGURE A.1 *Continued*

SCHEDULE R — Generation-Skipping Transfer Tax

Note: *To avoid application of the deemed allocation rules, Form 706 and Schedule R should be filed to allocate the GST exemption to trusts that may later have taxable terminations or distributions under section 2612 even if the form is not required to be filed to report estate or GST tax.*

*The GST tax is imposed on taxable transfers of interests in property located **outside the United States** as well as property located inside the United States.*

See instructions beginning on page 19.

Part 1 — GST Exemption Reconciliation (Section 2631) and Section 2652(a)(3) (Special QTIP) Election

You no longer need to check a box to make a section 2652(a)(3) (special QTIP) election. If you list qualifying property in Part 1, line 9, below, you will be considered to have made this election. See page 21 of the separate instructions for details.

1	Maximum allowable GST exemption...	1
2	Total GST exemption allocated by the decedent against decedent's lifetime transfers	2
3	Total GST exemption allocated by the executor, using Form 709, against decedent's lifetime transfers	3
4	GST exemption allocated on line 6 of Schedule R, Part 2	4
5	GST exemption allocated on line 6 of Schedule R, Part 3	5
6	Total GST exemption allocated on line 4 of Schedule(s) R-1	6
7	Total GST exemption allocated to intervivos transfers and direct skips (add lines 2 - 6).........	7
8	GST exemption available to allocate to trusts and section 2032A interests (subtract line 7 from line 1)	8
9	Allocation of GST exemption to trusts (as defined for GST tax purposes):	

A Name of trust	B Trust's EIN (if any)	C GST exemption allocated on lines 2 - 6, above (see instructions)	D Additional GST exemption allocated (see instructions)	E Trust's inclusion ratio (optional — see instructions)

9D Total. May not exceed line 8, above .... | **9D** | |

10 GST exemption available to allocate to section 2032A interests received by individual beneficiaries (subtract line 9D from line 8). You must attach special use allocation schedule (see instructions) .. | **10** |

(The instructions to Schedule R are in the separate instructions.)

Schedule R — Page 33

FIGURE A.1 *Continued*

Estate of:

Part 2 — Direct Skips Where the Property Interests Transferred Bear the GST Tax on the Direct Skips

Name of skip person	Description of property interest transferred	Estate tax value

1	Total estate tax values of all property interests listed above	1	
2	Estate taxes, state death taxes, and other charges borne by the property interests listed above	2	
3	GST taxes borne by the property interests listed above but imposed on direct skips other than those shown on this Part 2 (see instructions)	3	
4	Total fixed taxes and other charges (add lines 2 and 3)	4	
5	Total tentative maximum direct skips (subtract line 4 from line 1)	5	
6	GST exemption allocated.	6	
7	Subtract line 6 from line 5	7	
8	GST tax due (divide line 7 by 2.818182)	8	
9	Enter the amount from line 8 of Schedule R, Part 3	9	
10	Total GST taxes payable by the estate (add lines 8 and 9). Enter here and on line 22 of Part 2 — Tax Computation, on page 1	10	

Schedule R — Page 34
STF FED1288F.34

FIGURE A.1 *Continued*

Estate of:

Part 3 — Direct Skips Where the Property Interests Transferred Do Not Bear the GST
Tax on the Direct Skips

Name of skip person	Description of property interest transferred	Estate tax value

1 Total estate tax values of all property interests listed above	1	
2 Estate taxes, state death taxes, and other charges borne by the property interests listed above	2	
3 GST taxes borne by the property interests listed above but imposed on direct skips other than those shown on this Part 3 (see instructions)	3	
4 Total fixed taxes and other charges (add lines 2 and 3)	4	
5 Total tentative maximum direct skips (subtract line 4 from line 1)	5	
6 GST exemption allocated	6	
7 Subtract line 6 from line 5	7	
8 GST tax due (multiply line 7 by .55). Enter here and on Schedule R, Part 2, line 9	8	

Schedule R — Page 35

FIGURE A.1 *Continued*

Generation-Skipping Transfer Tax

Direct Skips From a Trust

Payment Voucher

OMB No. 1545-0015

Executor: File one copy with Form 706 and send two copies to the fiduciary. Do not pay the tax shown. See the separate instructions.
Fiduciary: See instructions on the following page. Pay the tax shown on line 6.

Name of trust		Trust's EIN
Name and title of fiduciary	Name of decedent	
Address of fiduciary (number and street)	Decedent's SSN	Service Center where Form 706 was filed
City, state, and ZIP code	Name of executor	
Address of executor (number and street)	City, state, and ZIP code	
Date of decedent's death	Filing due date of Schedule R, Form 706 (with extensions)	

Part 1 — Computation of the GST Tax on the Direct Skip

Description of property interests subject to the direct skip	Estate tax value

1	Total estate tax value of all property interests listed above	1	
2	Estate taxes, state death taxes, and other charges borne by the property interest listed above	2	
3	Tentative maximum direct skip from trust (subtract line 2 from line 1)	3	
4	GST exemption allocated.	4	
5	Subtract line 4 from line 3	5	
6	**GST tax due from fiduciary (divide line 5 by 2.818182) (See instructions if property will not bear the GST tax.)**	6	

Under penalties of perjury, I declare that I have examined this return, including accompanying schedules and statements, and to the best of my knowledge and belief, it is true, correct, and complete.

Signature(s) of executor(s)	Date
	Date
Signature of fiduciary or officer representing fiduciary	Date

Schedule R-1 (Form 706) — Page 36

STF FED1288F.36

FIGURE A.1 *Continued*

326

Instructions for the Trustee

Introduction   Schedule R-1 (Form 706) serves as a payment voucher for the Generation-Skipping Transfer (GST) tax imposed on a direct skip from a trust, which you, the trustee of the trust, must pay. The executor completes the Schedule R-1 (Form 706) and gives you 2 copies. File one copy and keep one for your records.

How to pay   You can pay by check or money order.
- Make it payable to the "United States Treasury."
- Make the check or money order for the amount on line 6 of Schedule R-1.
- Write "GST Tax" and the trust's EIN on the check or money order.

Signature   You must sign the Schedule R-1 in the space provided.

What to mail   Mail your check or money order and the copy of Schedule R-1 that you signed.

Where to mail   Mail to the Service Center shown on Schedule R-1.

When to pay   The GST tax is due and payable 9 months after the decedent's date of death (shown on the Schedule R-1). You will owe interest on any GST tax not paid by that date.

Automatic extension   You have an automatic extension of time to file Schedule R-1 and pay the GST tax. The automatic extension allows you to file and pay by 2 months after the due date (with extensions) for filing the decedent's Schedule R (shown on the Schedule R-1).

If you pay the GST tax under the automatic extension, you will be charged interest (but no penalties).

Additional information   For more information, see Code section 2603(a)(2) and the instructions for Form 706, United States Estate (and Generation-Skipping Transfer) Tax Return.

Schedule R-1 (Form 706) — Page 37

FIGURE A.1 *Continued*

Estate of:

SCHEDULE T — Qualified Family-Owned Business Interest Deduction

For details on the deduction, including trades and businesses that do not qualify, see page 22 of the separate Instructions for Form 706.

Part 1 — Election

Note: *The executor is deemed to have made the election under section 2057 if he or she files Schedule T and deducts any qualifying business interests from the gross estate.*

Part 2 — General Qualifications

1 Did the decedent and/or a member of the decedent's family own the business interests listed on line 5 of this schedule for at least 5 of the 8 years immediately preceding the date of the decedent's death?. . . . . ☐ Yes ☐ No

2 Were there any periods during the 8-year period preceding the date of the decedent's death during which the decedent or a member of his or her family:

		Yes	No
a	Did not own the business interests listed on this schedule?		
b	Did not materially participate, within the meaning of section 2032A(e)(6), in the operation of the business to which such interests relate?		

If "Yes" to either of the above, you must attach a statement listing the periods. If applicable, describe whether the exceptions of sections 2032A(b)(4) or (5) are met.

Attach affidavits describing the activities constituting material participation and the identity and relationship to the decedent of the material participants.

3 Check the applicable box(es). The qualified family-owned business interest(s) is:

☐ An interest as a proprietor in a trade or business carried on as a proprietorship.

☐ An interest in an entity, at least 50% of which is owned (directly or indirectly) by the decedent and members of the decedent's family.

☐ An interest in an entity, at least 70% of which is owned (directly or indirectly) by members of 2 families and at least 30% of which is owned (directly or indirectly) by the decedent and members of the decedent's family.

☐ An interest in an entity, at least 90% of which is owned (directly or indirectly) by members of 3 families and at least 30% of which is owned (directly or indirectly) by the decedent and members of the decedent's family.

4 Persons holding interests. Enter the requested information for each party who received any interest in the family-owned business. If any qualified heir is not a U.S. citizen, see the line 4 instructions beginning on page 23 of the separate instructions.

(Each of the qualified heirs receiving an interest in the business must sign the agreement that begins on the following page 40, and the agreement must be filed with this return.)

	Name	Address
A		
B		
C		
D		
E		
F		
G		
H		

	Identifying number	Relationship to decedent	Value of interest
A			
B			
C			
D			
E			
F			
G			
H			

Schedule T (Form 706) — Page 38

STF FED1288F.38

FIGURE A.1 *Continued*

Part 3 — Adjusted Value of Qualified Family-Owned Business Interests

5 Qualified family-owned business interests reported on this return:

Note: *All property listed on line 5 must also be entered on Schedules A, B, C, E, F, G, or H, as applicable.*

A Schedule and item number from Form 706	B Description of business interest and principal place of business	C Reported value

6	Total reported value	**6**	
7	Amount of claims or mortgages deductible under section 2053(a)(3) or (4) (see separate instructions)	**7**	
8a	Enter the amount of any indebtedness on qualified residence of the decedent (see separate instructions) **8a**		
b	Enter the amount of any indebtedness used for educational or medical expenses (see separate instructions) . **8b**		
c	Enter the amount of any indebtedness other than that listed on line 8a or 8b, but do not enter more than $10,000 (see separate instructions) **8c**		
d	Total (add lines 8a through 8c) **8d**		
9	Subtract line 8d from line 7	**9**	
10	Adjusted value of qualified family-owned business interests (subtract line 9 from line 6)	**10**	

Part 4 — Qualifying Estate

11	Includible gifts of qualified family-owned business interests (see separate instructions):		
a	Amount of gifts taken into account under section 2001(b)(1)(B) **11a**		
b	Amount of such gifts excluded under section 2503(b) **11b**		
c	Add lines 11a and 11b	**11c**	
12	Add lines 10 and 11c	**12**	
13	Adjusted gross estate (see separate instructions):		
a	Amount of gross estate **13a**		
b	Enter the amount from line 7 . . . . **13b**		
c	Subtract line 13b from line 13a **13c**		
d	Enter the amount from line 11c **13d**		
e	Enter the amount of transfers, if any, to the decedent's spouse (see inst.) . . **13e**		
f	Enter the amount of other gifts (see inst.) **13f**		
g	Add the amounts on lines 13d, 13e, and 13f **13g**		
h	Enter any amounts from line 13g that are otherwise includible in the gross estate **13h**		
i	Subtract line 13h from line 13g . . . . **13 i**		
j	Adjusted gross estate (add lines 13c and 13i)	**13 j**	
14	Enter one-half of the amount on line 13j	**14**	
	Note: *If line 12 does not exceed line 14, stop here; the estate does not qualify for the deduction.* *Otherwise, complete line 15.*		
15	Net value of qualified family-owned business interests you elect to deduct (line 10 reduced by any marital or other deductions) — **DO NOT** enter more than $675,000 — (see instructions) (attach schedule) — enter here and on Part 5, Recapitulation, page 3, at item 22.	**15**	

Schedule T — Page 39

STF FED1288F.39

FIGURE A.1 *Continued*

329

Form 706 (Rev. 7-99)

Part 5 — Agreement to Family-Owned Business Interest Deduction Under Section 2057

Estate of:	Date of Death	Decedent's Social Security Number

There cannot be a valid election unless:

• The agreement is executed by each and every one of the qualified heirs, and

• The agreement is included with the estate tax return when the estate tax return is filed.

We (list all qualified heirs and other persons having an interest in the business required to sign this agreement)

_____

_____ ,

being all the qualified heirs and _____

_____ ,

being all other parties having interests in the business(es) which are deducted under section 2057 of the Internal Revenue Code, do hereby approve of the election made by _____ ,

Executor/Administrator of the estate of _____ ,

pursuant to section 2057 to deduct said interests from the gross estate and do hereby enter into this agreement pursuant to section 2057(h).

The undersigned agree and consent to the application of subsection (f) of section 2057 of the Code with respect to all the qualified family-owned business interests deducted on Schedule T of Form 706, attached to this agreement. More specifically, the undersigned heirs expressly agree and consent to personal liability under subsection (c) of 2032A (as made applicable by section 2057(i)(3)(F) of the Code) for the additional estate tax imposed by that subsection with respect to their respective interests in the above-described business interests in the event of certain early dispositions of the interests or the occurrence of any of the disqualifying acts described in section 2057(f)(1) of the Code. It is understood that if a qualified heir disposes of any deducted interest to any member of his or her family, such member may thereafter be treated as the qualified heir with respect to such interest upon filing a new agreement and any other form required by the Internal Revenue Service.

The undersigned interested parties who are not qualified heirs consent to the collection of any additional estate tax imposed under section 2057(f) of the Code from the deducted interests.

If there is a disposition of any interest which passes or has passed to him or her, each of the undersigned heirs agrees to file the appropriate form and pay any additional estate tax due within 6 months of the disposition or other disqualifying act.

It is understood by all interested parties that this agreement is a condition precedent to the election of the qualified family-owned business deduction under section 2057 of the Code and must be executed by every interested party even though that person may not have received the estate tax benefits or be in possession of such property.

Each of the undersigned understands that by making this election, a lien will be created and recorded pursuant to section 6324B of the Code on the interests referred to in this agreement for the applicable percentage of the adjusted tax differences with respect to the estate as defined in section 2057(f)(2)(C).

As the interested parties, the undersigned designate the following individual as their agent for all dealings with the Internal Revenue Service concerning the continued qualification of the deducted property under section 2057 of the Code and on all issues regarding the special lien under section 6324B. The agent is authorized to act for the parties with respect to all dealings with the Service on matters affecting the qualified interests described earlier. This authority includes the following:

• To receive confidential information on all matters relating to continued qualification under section 2057 of the deducted interests and on all matters relating to the special lien arising under section 6324B.

• To furnish the Service with any requested information concerning the interests.

• To notify the Service of any disposition or other disqualifying events specified in section 2057(f)(1) of the Code.

• To receive, but not to endorse and collect, checks in payment of any refund of Internal Revenue taxes, penalties, or interest.

• To execute waivers (including offers of waivers) of restrictions on assessment or collection of deficiencies in tax and waivers of notice of disallowance of a claim for credit or refund.

• To execute closing agreements under section 7121.

(continued on next page)

Schedule T, Part 5 — Page 40
STF FED1288F.40

FIGURE A.1 *Continued*

330

Part 5 — Agreement to Family-Owned Business Interest Deduction Under Section 2057 (continued)

Estate of:	Date of Death	Decedent's Social Security Number

● Other acts (specify) ▶ _____

By signing this agreement, the agent agrees to provide the Internal Revenue Service with any requested information concerning the qualified business interests and to notify the Internal Revenue Service of any disposition or other disqualifying events with regard to said interests.

Name of Agent	Signature	Address

The interests to which this agreement relates are listed in Form 706, United States Estate (and Generation-Skipping Transfer) Tax Return, along with their fair market value according to section 2031 (or, if applicable, section 2032A) of the Code. The name, address, social security number, and interest (including the value) of each of the undersigned in this business(es) are as set forth in the attached Schedule T.

IN WITNESS WHEREOF, the undersigned have hereunto set their hands at _____ ,

this _____ day of _____ .

SIGNATURES OF EACH OF THE QUALIFIED HEIRS:

Signature of qualified heir	Signature of qualified heir
Signature of qualified heir	Signature of qualified heir
Signature of qualified heir	Signature of qualified heir
Signature of qualified heir	Signature of qualified heir
Signature of qualified heir	Signature of qualified heir
Signature of qualified heir	Signature of qualified heir

Signature(s) of other interested parties

Signature(s) of other interested parties

STF FED1288F.41

FIGURE A.1 *Continued*

Form 706 (Rev. 7-99)

Estate of:

SCHEDULE U — Qualified Conservation Easement Exclusion

Part 1 — Election

Note: *The executor is deemed to have made the election under section 2031(c)(6) if he or she files Schedule U and excludes any qualifying conservation easements from the gross estate.*

Part 2 — General Qualifications

1 Describe the land subject to the qualified conservation easement (see separate instructions) _____

2 Did the decedent or a member of the decedent's family own the land described above during the 3-year period
ending on the date of the decedent's death? . . . . ☐ Yes ☐ No
3 The land described above is located (check whichever applies) (see separate instructions)
   ☐ In or within 25 miles of an area which, on the date of the decedent's death, is a metropolitan area.
   ☐ In or within 25 miles of an area which, on the date of the decedent's death, is a national park or wilderness area.
   ☐ In or within 10 miles of an area which, on the date of the decedent's death, is an Urban National Forest.
4 Describe the conservation easement with regard to which the exclusion is being claimed (see separate instructions).
_____

Part 3 — Computation of Exclusion

5 Estate tax value of the land subject to the qualified conservation easement (see separate instructions).	**5**	
6 Date of death value of any easements granted prior to decedent's death and included on line 11 below (see instructions)	**6**	
7 Add lines 5 and 6.	**7**	
8 Value of retained development rights on the land (see instructions) . .	**8**	
9 Subtract line 8 from line 7	**9**	
10 Multiply line 9 by 30% (.30)	**10**	
11 Value of qualified conservation easement for which the exclusion is being claimed (see instructions).	**11**	
Note: *If line 11 is less than line 10, continue with line 12. If line 11 is equal to or more than line 10, skip lines 12 through 14, enter ".40" on line 15, and complete the schedule.*		
12 Divide line 11 by line 9. Figure to 3 decimal places (e.g., .123).	**12**	
If line 12 is equal to or less than .100, stop here; the estate does not qualify for the conservation easement exclusion.		
13 Subtract line 12 from .300. Enter the answer in hundredths by rounding any thousandths up to the next higher hundredth (i.e., .030 = .03; but .031 = .04).	**13**	
14 Multiply line 13 by 2	**14**	
15 Subtract line 14 from .40	**15**	
16 Deduction under section 2055(f) for the conservation easement (see separate instructions)	**16**	
17 Amount of indebtedness on the land (see separate instructions)	**17**	
18 Total reductions in value (add lines 8, 16, and 17)	**18**	
19 Net value of land (subtract line 18 from line 5)	**19**	
20 Multiply line 19 by line 15	**20**	
21 Enter the smaller of line 20 or the exclusion limitation (see instructions). Also enter this amount on item 11, Part 5, Recapitulation, Page 3	**21**	

Schedule U — Page 42
STF FED1288F.42

FIGURE A.1 *Continued*

332

Estate of:

CONTINUATION SCHEDULE

Continuation of Schedule _____
(Enter letter of schedule you are continuing.)

Item number	Description For securities, give CUSIP number.	Unit value (Sch. B, E, or G only)	Alternate valuation date	Alternate value	Value at date of death or amount deductible

TOTAL. (Carry forward to main schedule.) . . . .

See the instructions.

Continuation Schedule — Page 43

STF FED1288F.43

FIGURE A.1 *Continued*

Instructions for Continuation Schedule

When you need to list more assets or deductions than you have room for on one of the main schedules, use the Continuation Schedule on page 43. If provides a uniform format for listing additional assets from Schedules A through I and additional deductions from Schedules J, K, L, M, and O.

Please keep the following points in mind:

● Use a separate Continuation Schedule for each main schedule you are continuing. Do not combine assets or deductions from different schedules on one Continuation Schedule.

● Make copies of the blank schedule before completing it if you expect to need more than one.

● Use as many Continuation Schedules as needed to list all the assets or deductions.

● Enter the letter of the schedule you are continuing in the space at the top of the Continuation Schedule.

● Use the *Unit value* column only if continuing Schedule B, E, or G. For all other schedules, use this space to continue the description.

● Carry the total from the Continuation Schedules forward to the appropriate line on the main schedule.

If continuing	Report	Where on Continuation Schedule
Schedule E, Pt. 2	*Percentage includible*	*Alternate valuation date*
Schedule K	*Amount unpaid to date*	*Alternate valuation date*
Schedule K	*Amount in contest*	*Alternate value*
Schedules J, L, M	*Description of deduction continuation*	*Alternate valuation date* and *Alternate value*
Schedule O	*Character of institution*	*Alternate valuation date* and *Alternate value*
Schedule O	*Amount of each deduction*	*Amount deductible*

FIGURE A.1 *Continued*

334

Instructions for Form 706

(Revised July 1999)
United States Estate (and Generation-Skipping Transfer) Tax Return
(For decedents dying after December 31, 1998).
Section references are to the Internal Revenue Code unless otherwise noted.

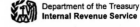

Department of the Treasury
Internal Revenue Service

Paperwork Reduction Act Notice. We ask for the information on this form to carry out the Internal Revenue laws of the United States. You are required to give us the information. We need it to ensure that you are complying with these laws and to allow us to figure and collect the right amount of tax.

You are not required to provide the information requested on a form that is subject to the Paperwork Reduction Act unless the form displays a valid OMB control number. Books or records relating to a form or its instructions must be retained as long as their contents may become material in the administration of any Internal Revenue law. Generally, tax returns and return information are confidential as required by section 6103.

The time needed to complete and file this form and related schedules will vary depending on individual circumstances. The estimated average times are:

Form	Recordkeeping	Learning about the law or the form	Preparing the form	Copying, assembling, and sending the form to the IRS
706	2 hr., 11 min.	1 hr., 25 min.	3 hr., 35 min.	49 min.
Sch. A	20 min.	16 min.	10 min.	20 min.
A-1	46 min.	25 min.	59 min.	49 min.
B	20 min.	16 min.	20 min.	20 min.
C	13 min.	2 min.	8 min.	8 min.
D	7 min.	6 min.	8 min.	20 min.
E	40 min.	7 min.	24 min.	20 min.
F	33 min.	8 min.	21 min.	20 min.
G	26 min.	23 min.	11 min.	14 min.
H	26 min.	7 min.	10 min.	14 min.
I	26 min.	27 min.	11 min.	20 min.
J	26 min.	7 min.	16 min.	20 min.
K	26 min.	10 min.	10 min.	20 min.
L	13 min.	5 min.	10 min.	20 min.
M	13 min.	31 min.	24 min.	20 min.
O	20 min.	11 min.	18 min.	17 min.
P	7 min.	14 min.	18 min.	14 min.
Q	7 min.	10 min.	11 min.	14 min.
Q Wksheet	7 min.	10 min.	10 min.	20 min.
R	20 min.	34 min.	1 hr., 2 min.	49 min.
R-1	7 min.	29 min.	24 min.	20 min.
T	1 hr., 12 min.	27 min.	1 hr., 14 min.	1 hr., 3 min.
U	20 min.	3 min.	29 min.	20 min.
Cont. Sch.	20 min.	3 min.	7 min.	20 min.

If you have comments concerning the accuracy of these time estimates or suggestions for making this form simpler, we would be happy to hear from you. You can write to the Tax Forms Committee, Western Area Distribution Center, Rancho Cordova, CA 95743-0001. DO NOT send the tax form to this address. Instead, see **Where To File** on page 2.

After	For Decedents Dying and	Before	Use Revision of Form 706 Dated
....		January 1, 1982	November 1981
December 31, 1981		October 23, 1986	November 1987
December 31, 1989		October 9, 1990	October 1988
October 8, 1990		January 1, 1998	April 1997
December 31, 1997		January 1, 1999	July 1998
December 31, 1998		....	July 1999

Contents

*For Schedules A, A-1, C, D, E, F, J, and M, see instructions in the Form 706 itself.

General Instructions

Changes To Note

• See the Instructions for Part 2. Tax Computation, line 11, for unified credit (applicable credit amounts) and applicable exclusion amounts for years 1987 through 2006 and after.

• Various dollar amounts and limitations relevant to Form 706 are now indexed for inflation. For decedents dying in 1999, the following amounts have increased:

  • the ceiling on special use valuation is $760,000;

  • the generation-skipping transfer tax exemption is $1,010,000; and

  • the amount used in computing the 2% portion of estate tax payable in installments is $1,010,000.

The IRS will publish amounts for future years in an annual revenue procedure.

STF FED1288L1

FIGURE A.1 *Continued*

335

- See the instructions for Schedule U on page 23 for the table showing the exclusion limitation for the qualified conservation easement exclusion for the years 1999 through 2002 or thereafter.

A. Purpose of Form

The executor of a decedent's estate uses Form 706 to figure the estate tax imposed by Chapter 11 of the Internal Revenue Code. This tax is levied on the entire taxable estate, not just on the share received by a particular beneficiary. Form 706 is also used to compute the generation-skipping transfer (GST) tax imposed by Chapter 13 on direct skips (transfers to skip persons of interests in property included in the decedent's gross estate).

B. Which Estates Must File

For decedents dying in 1999, Form 706 must be filed by the executor for the estate of every U.S. citizen or resident whose gross estate, plus adjusted taxable gifts and specific exemption, is more than $650,000 in 1999.

To determine whether you must file a return for the estate, add:

1. The adjusted taxable gifts (under section 2001(b)) made by the decedent after December 31, 1976;

2. The total specific exemption allowed under section 2521 (as in effect before its repeal by the Tax Reform Act of 1976) for gifts made by the decedent after September 8, 1976; and

3. The decedent's gross estate valued at the date of death.

For dates of death after 1999, the executor must file Form 706 for any estate in which the sum of these items exceeds the applicable exclusion amount for that year. See the table for line 11 on page 4 for the applicable exclusion amounts.

Gross Estate
The gross estate includes all property in which the decedent had an interest (including real property outside the United States). It also includes:

- Certain transfers made during the decedent's life without an adequate and full consideration in money or money's worth;
- Annuities;
- The includible portion of joint estates with right of survivorship (see the instructions on the back of Schedule E);
- The includible portion of tenancies by the entirety (see the instructions on the back of Schedule E);
- Certain life insurance proceeds (even though payable to beneficiaries other than the estate) (see the instructions on the back of Schedule D);
- Property over which the decedent possessed a general power of appointment;
- Dower or curtesy (or statutory estate) of the surviving spouse;
- Community property to the extent of the decedent's interest as defined by applicable law.

For more specific information, see the instructions for Schedules A through I.

U. S. Citizens or Residents; Nonresident Noncitizens
File Form 706 for the estates of decedents who were either U.S. citizens or U.S. residents at the time of death. For estate tax purposes, a resident is someone who had a domicile in the United States at the time of death. A person acquires a domicile by living in a place for even a brief period of time, as long as the person had no intention of moving from that place.

File Form 706-NA, United States Estate (and Generation-Skipping Transfer) Tax Return, Estate of nonresident not a citizen of the United States, for the estates of nonresident alien decedents (decedents who were neither U.S. citizens nor residents at the time of death).

Residents of U. S. Possessions
All references to citizens of the United States are subject to the provisions of sections 2208 and 2209, relating to decedents who were U.S. citizens and residents of a U.S. possession on the date of death. If such a decedent became a U.S. citizen only because of his or her connection with a possession, then the decedent is considered a nonresident alien decedent for estate tax purposes, and you should file Form 706-NA. If such a decedent became a U.S. citizen wholly independently of his or her connection with a possession, then the decedent is considered a U.S. citizen for estate tax purposes, and you should file Form 706.

C. Executor

The term "executor" means the executor, personal representative, or administrator of the decedent's estate. If none of these is appointed, qualified, and acting in the United States, every person in actual or constructive possession of any property of the decedent is considered an executor and must file a return.

D. When To File

You must file Form 706 to report estate and/or generation-skipping transfer tax within 9 months after the date of the decedent's death unless you receive an extension of time to file. Use **Form 4768**, Application for Extension of Time To File a Return and/or Pay U.S. Estate (and Generation-Skipping Transfer) Taxes, to apply for an extension of time to file. If you received an extension, attach a copy of it to Form 706.

Private delivery services. You can use certain private delivery services designated by the IRS to meet the "timely mailing as timely filing/paying" rule for tax returns and payments. The most recent list of designated private delivery services was published by the IRS in September 1998. The list includes only the following:

- Airborne Express (Airborne): Overnight Air Express Service, Next Afternoon Service, Second Day Service.
- DHL Worldwide Express (DHL): DHL "Same Day" Service, DHL USA Overnight.
- Federal Express (FedEx): FedEx Priority Overnight, FedEx Standard Overnight, FedEx 2Day.
- United Parcel Service (UPS): UPS Next Day Air, UPS Next Day Air Saver, UPS 2nd Day Air, UPS 2nd Day Air A.M.

The private delivery service can tell you how to get written proof of the mailing date.

E. Where To File

Unless the return is hand carried to the office of the District Director, please mail it to the Internal Revenue Service Center indicated below for the state where the **decedent was domiciled** at the time of death. If you are filing a return for the estate of a nonresident U.S. citizen, mail it to the Internal Revenue Service Center, Philadelphia, PA 19255, USA.

New Jersey, New York (New York City and counties of Nassau, Rockland, Suffolk, and Westchester)	Holtsville, NY 00501
New York (all other counties), Connecticut, Maine, Massachusetts, New Hampshire, Rhode Island, Vermont	Andover, MA 05501
Delaware, District of Columbia, Maryland, Pennsylvania, Virginia	Philadelphia, PA 19255
Indiana, Kentucky, Michigan, Ohio, West Virginia	Cincinnati, OH 45999
Kansas, New Mexico, Oklahoma, Texas	Austin, TX 73301
Alaska, Arizona, California (counties of Alpine, Amador, Butte, Calaveras, Colusa, Contra Costa, Del Norte, El Dorado, Glenn, Humboldt, Lake, Lassen, Marin, Mendocino, Modoc, Napa, Nevada, Placer, Plumas, Sacramento, San Joaquin, Shasta, Sierra, Siskiyou, Solano, Sonoma, Sutter, Tehama, Trinity, Yolo, and Yuba), Colorado, Idaho, Montana, Nebraska, Nevada, North Dakota, Oregon, South Dakota, Utah, Washington, Wyoming	Ogden, UT 84201
California (all other counties), Hawaii	Fresno, CA 93888
Alabama, Arkansas, Louisiana, Mississippi, North Carolina, Tennessee	Memphis, TN 37501
Florida, Georgia, South Carolina	Atlanta, GA 39901
Illinois, Iowa, Minnesota, Missouri, Wisconsin	Kansas City, MO 64999

F. Paying the Tax

The estate and GST taxes are due within 9 months after the date of the decedent's death unless an extension of time for payment has been granted, or unless you have properly elected under section 6166 to pay in installments, or under section 6163 to postpone the part of the tax attributable to a reversionary or remainder interest. These elections are made by checking lines 3 and 4 (respectively) of Part 3, Elections by the Executor, and attaching the required statements.

If the tax paid with the return is different from the balance due as figured on the return, explain the difference in an attached statement. If you have made prior payments to IRS or redeemed certain marketable United States Treasury bonds to pay the estate tax (see the last paragraph of the instructions to Schedule B), attach a statement to Form 706 including these facts. If an extension of time to pay has been granted, attach a copy of the approved Form 4768 to Form 706.

Paying by check. Make the check payable to the United States Treasury. Please write the decedent's name, social security number, and "Form 706" on the check to assist us in posting it to the proper account.

G. Signature and Verification

If there is more than one executor, all listed executors must verify and sign the return. All executors are responsible for the return as filed and are liable for penalties provided for erroneous or false returns.

FIGURE A.1 *Continued*

If two or more persons are liable for filing the return, they should all join together in filing one complete return. However, if they are unable to join in making one complete return, each is required to file a return disclosing all the information the person has in the case, including the name of every person holding an interest in the property and a full description of the property. If the appointed, qualified, and acting executor is unable to make a complete return, then every person holding an interest in the property must, on notice from the IRS, make a return regarding that interest.

The executor who files the return must, in every case, sign the declaration on page 1 under penalties of perjury. If the return is prepared by someone other than the person who is filing the return, the preparer must also sign at the bottom of page 1.

H. Amending Form 706

If you find that you must change something on a return that has already been filed, you should file another Form 706 and write "Supplemental Information" across the top of page 1 of the form. If you have already been notified that the return has been selected for examination, you should provide the additional information directly to the office conducting the examination.

I. Supplemental Documents

You must attach the death certificate to the return.

If the decedent was a citizen or resident and died testate, attach a certified copy of the will to the return. If you cannot obtain a certified copy, attach a copy of the will and an explanation of why it is not certified. Other supplemental documents may be required as explained below. Examples include Forms 712, 709, 709-A, and 706-CE, trust and power of appointment instruments, death certificate, and state certification of payment of death taxes. If you do not file these documents with the return, the processing of the return will be delayed.

If the decedent was a U.S. citizen but not a resident of the United States, you must attach the following documents to the return:

1. A copy of the inventory of property and the schedule of liabilities, claims against the estate, and expenses of administration filed with the foreign court of probate jurisdiction, certified by a proper official of the court;

2. A copy of the return filed under the foreign inheritance, estate, legacy, succession tax, or other death tax act, certified by a proper official of the foreign tax department, if the estate is subject to such a foreign tax; and

3. If the decedent died testate, a certified copy of the will.

J. Rounding Off to Whole Dollars

You may show the money items on the return and accompanying schedules as whole-dollar amounts. To do so, drop any amount less than 50 cents and increase any amount from 50 cents through 99 cents to the next higher dollar.

K. Penalties

Late filing and late payment. Section 6651 provides for penalties for both late filing and for late payment unless there is reasonable cause for the delay. The law also provides for penalties for willful attempts to evade payment of tax. The late filing penalty will not be imposed if the taxpayer can show that the failure to file a timely return is due to reasonable cause. Executors filing late (after the due date, including extensions) should attach an explanation to the return to show reasonable cause.

Valuation understatement. Section 6662 provides a 20% penalty for the underpayment of estate tax of $5,000 or more when the underpayment is attributable to valuation understatements. A valuation understatement occurs when the value of property reported on Form 706 is 50% or less of the actual value of the property.

This penalty increases to 40% if there is a **gross** valuation understatement. A gross valuation understatement occurs if any property on the return is valued at 25% or less of the value determined to be correct.

These penalties also apply to late filing, late payment, and underpayment of GST taxes.

L. Obtaining Forms and Publications To File or Use

Personal computer. Access the IRS's Internet web site at www.irs.gov to do the following:

- Download forms, instructions, and publications.
- Search publications on-line by topic or keyword.

You can also reach us using:

- Telnet at iris.irs.ustreas.gov
- File transfer protocol at ftp.irs.ustreas.gov
- Direct dial (by modem) 703-321-8020. CD-ROM. Order Pub. 1796, Federal Tax Products on CD-ROM, and get:
- Current year forms, instructions, and publications, and
- Prior year forms and instructions.

Buy the CD-ROM on the Internet at www.irs.ustreas.gov/cdorders from the National Technical Information Service (NTIS), or call 1-877-CDFORMS (1-877-233-6767) toll-free to buy the CD-ROM. (Prices may differ at each of these locations.)

By phone and in person. You can order forms and publications 24 hours a day, 7 days a week, by calling 1-800-TAX-FORM (1-800-829-3676). You can also get most forms and publications at your local IRS office.

Forms and Publications to file or use.
- **Forms:** The title for forms to file or use are given within these instructions.
- **Publications:**

    Publication 910. Guide to Free Tax Services
    Publication 559. Survivors, Executors, and Administrators

Specific Instructions

- You must file the first three pages of Form 706 and all required schedules.
- File Schedules A through I, as appropriate, to support the entries in items 1 through 9 of the Recapitulation.

IF . . .	THEN . . .
you enter zero on any item of the Recapitulation,	you need not file the schedule (except for Schedule F) referred to on that item.
you claim an exclusion on item 11,	complete and attach Schedule U.
you claim any deductions on items 13 through 23 of the Recapitulation,	complete and attach the appropriate schedules to support the claimed deductions.
you claim the credits for foreign death taxes or tax on prior transfers,	complete and attach Schedule P or Q.
there is not enough space on a schedule to list all the items,	attach a Continuation Schedule (or additional sheets of the same size) to the back of the schedule; (see the end of the Form 706 package for the Continuation Schedule). photocopy the blank schedule before completing it, if you will need more than one copy.

- Form 706 has 44 numbered pages. The pages are perforated so that you can remove them for copying and filing.
- When you complete the return, staple all the required pages together in the proper order.
- Number the items you list on each schedule, beginning with the number 1 each time.
- Total the items listed on the schedule and its attachments, Continuation Schedules, etc.
- Enter the total of all attachments, Continuation Schedules, etc., at the bottom of the printed schedule, but do not carry the totals forward from one schedule to the next.
- Enter the total, or totals, for each schedule on the Recapitulation, page 3, Form 706
- Do not complete the "Alternate valuation date" or "Alternate value" columns of any schedule unless you elected alternate valuation on line 1 of Part 3, Elections by the Executor.

FIGURE A.1 *Continued*

Instructions for Part 1. Decedent and Executor (Page 1 of Form 706)

Line 2

Enter the social security number assigned specifically to the decedent. You cannot use the social security number assigned to the decedent's spouse. If the decedent did not have a social security number, the executor should obtain one for the decedent by filing **Form SS-5**, Application for Social Security Card, with a local Social Security Administration office.

Line 6a — Name of Executor

If there is more than one executor, enter the name of the executor to be contacted by the IRS. List the other executors' names, addresses, and SSNs (if applicable) on an attached sheet.

Line 6b — Executor's Address

Use **Form 8822**, Change of Address, to report a change of the executor's address.

Line 6c — Executor's Social Security Number

Only individual executors should complete this line. If there is more than one individual executor, all should list their social security numbers on an attached sheet.

Instructions for Part 2. Tax Computation (Page 1 of Form 706)

In general, the estate tax is figured by applying the unified rates shown in **Table A**, on page 12, to the total of transfers both during life and at death, and then subtracting the gift taxes. **You must complete the Tax Computation.**

Line 1

If you elected alternate valuation on line 1, Part 3, Elections by the Executor, enter the amount you entered in the "Alternate value" column of item 12 of Part 5, Recapitulation. Otherwise, enter the amount from the "Value at date of death" column.

Lines 4 and 9

Three worksheets are provided to help you compute the entries for these lines. You need not file these worksheets with your return but should keep them for your records. **Worksheet TG — Taxable Gifts Reconciliation**, on page 5, allows you to reconcile the decedent's lifetime taxable gifts to compute totals that will be used for the line 4 and line 9 worksheets.

You must get all of the decedent's gift tax returns (Form 709, United States Gift (and Generation-Skipping Transfer) Tax Return) before you complete Worksheet TG. The amounts you will enter on Worksheet TG can usually be derived from these returns as filed. However, if any of the returns were audited by the IRS, you should use the amounts that were finally determined as a result of the audits.

In addition, you must include in column b of Worksheet TG any gifts in excess of the annual exclusion made by the decedent (or on behalf of the decedent under a power of attorney) but for which no Forms 709 were filed. You must make a reasonable inquiry as to the existence of any such gifts. The annual exclusion for 1977 through 1981 was $3,000 per donee per year and $10,000 for years after 1981.

For tax years beginning *after* 1998 the annual $10,000 exclusion for gifts is indexed for inflation. For calendar year 1999, the annual exclusion for gifts remained at $10,000, however. See Rev. Proc. 98-61, 1998-52 I.R.B. 23.

Note: *In figuring the line 9 amount, do not include any tax paid or payable on gifts made before 1977. The line 9 amount is a hypothetical figure based only on gifts made after 1976 and used to calculate the estate tax.*

Special treatment of split gifts. These special rules apply only if:

1. The decedent's spouse predeceased the decedent;

2. The decedent's spouse made gifts that were "split" with the decedent under the rules of section 2513;

3. The decedent was the "consenting spouse" for those split gifts, as that term is used on Form 709; and

4. The split gifts were included in the decedent's spouse's gross estate under section 2035.

If all four conditions above are met, *do not include* these gifts on line 4 of the Tax Computation and *do not include* the gift taxes payable on these gifts on line 9 of the Tax Computation. These adjustments are incorporated into the worksheets.

Line 7

Lines 7a - c are used to calculate the phaseout of the graduated rates. The phaseout applies only to estates in which the amount the tentative tax is computed on exceeds $10 million.

Line 11 — Unified Credit (applicable credit amount)

The Taxpayer Relief Act of 1997 replaced the *unified credit amount* with an *applicable credit amount*, effective for the estates of decedents dying, and gifts made, after December 31, 1997. The applicable credit amount will increase as shown in the table below until 2006, when $1 million will be exempted from transfer tax. The amount of the credit cannot exceed the amount of estate tax imposed.

The unified credit and exemption equivalent *(applicable exclusion amount)* for 1987 and later are as follows:

Year	Applicable credit amounts	Applicable exclusion amount
1987 through 1997	$192,800	$ 600,000
1998	202,050	625,000
1999	211,300	650,000
2000 and 2001 .	220,550	675,000
2002 and 2003 .	229,800	700,000
2004	287,300	850,000
2005	326,300	950,000
2006 and after . . .	345,800	1,000,000

Important: *If the estate is claiming a qualified family-owned business interest deduction, see Coordination with unified credit on page 22 before completing line 11.*

Line 12 — Adjustment to Unified credit (applicable credit amount)

If the decedent made gifts (including gifts made by the decedent's spouse and treated as made by the decedent by reason of gift splitting) after September 8, 1976, and before January 1, 1977, for which the

decedent claimed a specific exemption, the unified credit (applicable credit amount) on this estate tax return must be reduced. The reduction is figured by entering 20% of the specific exemption claimed for these gifts.

Note: *(The specific exemption was allowed by section 2521 for gifts made before January 1, 1977.)*

If the decedent did not make any gifts between September 8, 1976, and January 1, 1977, or if the decedent made gifts during that period but did not claim the specific exemption, enter zero.

Line 15 — Credit for state death taxes

You may take a credit on line 15 for estate, inheritance, legacy, or succession taxes paid as the result of the decedent's death to any state or the District of Columbia. However, see section 2053(d) and the related regulations for exceptions and limits if you elected to deduct the taxes from the value of the gross estate.

If you make a section 6166 election, to pay the Federal estate tax in installments and make a similar election to pay the state death tax in installments, see Rev. Rul. 86-38, 1986-1 C.B. 296, for the method of computing the credit allowed with this Form 706.

If you have elected to extend the time to pay the tax on a reversionary or remainder interest, you may take a credit against that portion of the Federal estate tax for state death taxes attributable to the reversionary or remainder interest. The state death taxes must be paid and claimed before the expiration of the extended time for paying the estate tax.

The credit may not be more than the amount figured by using **Table B**, on page 12, based on the value of the adjusted taxable estate. The adjusted taxable estate is the amount of the Federal taxable estate (line 3 of the Tax Computation) reduced by $60,000. You may claim an anticipated amount of credit and figure the Federal estate tax on the return before the state death taxes have been paid. However, the credit cannot be finally allowed unless you pay the state death taxes and claim the credit within 4 years after the return is filed (or later as provided by the Code if a petition is filed with the Tax Court of the United States, or if you have an extension of time to pay) and submit evidence that the tax has been paid. If you claim the credit for any state death tax that is later recovered, see Regulations section 20.2016-1 for the notice you are required to give the IRS within 30 days.

If you transfer property other than cash to the state in payment of state inheritance taxes, the amount you may claim as a credit is the lesser of the state inheritance tax liability discharged or the fair market value of the property on the date of the transfer.

For more details, see Rev. Rul. 86-117, 1986-2 C.B. 157.

You should send the following evidence to the IRS:

1. Certificate of the proper officer of the taxing state, or the District of Columbia, showing the:

a. total amount of tax imposed (before adding interest and penalties and before allowing discount);

b. amount of discount allowed;

c. amount of penalties and interest imposed or charged;

d. total amount actually paid in cash; and

e. date of payment.

2. Any additional proof the IRS specifically requests.

You should file the evidence requested above with the return if possible. Otherwise, send it as soon after you file the return as possible.

FIGURE A.1 *Continued*

Worksheet TG — Taxable Gifts Reconciliation
(To be used for lines 4 and 9 of the Tax Computation)

	a. Calendar year or calendar quarter	b. Total taxable gifts for period (see Note)	Note: For the definition of a taxable gift see section 2503. Ignore the old specific exemption. Follow Form 709. That is, include only the decedent's one-half of split gifts, whether the gifts were made by the decedent or the decedent's spouse. In addition to gifts reported on Form 709, you must include any taxable gifts in excess of the annual exclusion that were not reported on Form 709.			
			c. Taxable amount included in col. b for gifts included in the gross estate	d. Taxable amount included in col. b for gifts that qualify for "special treatment of split gifts" described above	e. Gift tax paid by decedent on gifts in col. d	f. Gift tax paid by decedent's spouse on gifts in col. c
Gifts made after June 6, 1932, and before 1977 1. Total taxable gifts made before 1977						
Gifts made after 1976						
2. Totals for gifts made after 1976						

Line 4 Worksheet — Adjusted Taxable Gifts Made After 1976

1. Taxable gifts made after 1976. Enter the amount from line 2, column b, Worksheet TG **1**
2. Taxable gifts made after 1976 reportable on Schedule G. Enter the amount from line 2, column c, Worksheet TG **2**
3. Taxable gifts made after 1976 that qualify for "special treatment." Enter the amount from line 2, column d, Worksheet TG **3**
4. Add lines 2 and 3 . . . . **4**
5. Adjusted taxable gifts. Subtract line 4 from line 1. Enter here and on line 4 of the Tax Computation of Form 706 . . . . **5**

Line 17 — Credit for Federal Gift Taxes

You may take a credit for Federal gift taxes imposed by Chapter 12 of the Code, and the corresponding provisions of prior laws, on certain transfers the decedent made before January 1, 1977, that are included in the gross estate. The credit cannot be more than the amount figured by the following formula:

$$\frac{\text{Gross estate tax minus (the sum of the state death taxes and unified credit)}}{\text{Value of gross estate minus (the sum of the deductions for charitable, public, and similar gifts and bequests and marital deduction)}} \times \text{Value of included gift}$$

For more information, see the regulations under section 2012. This computation may be made using Form 4808, Computation of Credit for Gift Tax. Attach a copy of a completed Form 4808 or the computation of the credit. Also attach all available copies of Forms 709 filed by the decedent to help verify the amounts entered on lines 4, 9, and 17.

Line 25 — United States Treasury Bonds

You may not use these bonds to pay the GST tax.

Instructions for Part 3. Elections by the Executor (Page 2 of Form 706)

Line 1 — Alternate Valuation

Unless you elect at the time you file the return to adopt alternate valuation as authorized by section 2032, you must value all property included in the gross estate on the date of the decedent's death. Alternate valuation cannot be applied to only a part of the property.

You may elect special use valuation (line 2) in addition to alternate valuation.

You may not elect alternate valuation unless the election will decrease both the value of the gross estate and the total net estate and GST taxes due after application of all allowable credits.

You elect alternate valuation by checking "Yes" on line 1 and filing Form 706. Once made, the election may not be revoked. The election may be made on a late filed Form 706 provided it is not filed later than 1 year after the due date (including extensions).

If you elect alternate valuation, value the property that is included in the gross estate as of the applicable dates as follows:

1. Any property distributed, sold, exchanged, or otherwise disposed of or separated or passed from the gross estate by any method within 6 months after the decedent's death is valued on the date of distribution, sale, exchange, or other disposition, whichever occurs first. Value this property on the date it ceases to form a part of the gross estate; i.e., on the date the title passes as the result of its sale, exchange, or other disposition.

2. Any property not distributed, sold, exchanged, or otherwise disposed of within the 6-month period is valued on the date 6 months after the date of the decedent's death.

3. Any property, interest, or estate that is "affected by mere lapse of time" is valued as of the date of decedent's death or on the date of its distribution, sale, exchange, or other disposition, whichever occurs first. However, you may change the date of death value to account for any change in value that is not due to a "mere lapse of time" on the date of its distribution, sale, exchange, or other disposition.

The property included in the alternate valuation and valued as of 6 months after the date of the decedent's death, or as of some intermediate date (as described above) is the property included in the gross estate on the date of the decedent's death. Therefore, you must first determine what property constituted the gross estate at the date of the decedent's death.

Interest. Interest accrued to the date of the decedent's death on bonds, notes, and other interest-bearing obligations is property of the estate on the date of death and is included in the alternate valuation.

Rent. Rent accrued to the date of the decedent's death on leased real or personal property is property of the gross estate on the date of death and is included in the alternate valuation.

Dividends. Outstanding dividends that were declared to stockholders of record on or before the date of the decedent's death are considered property of the gross estate on the date of death, and are included in the alternate valuation. Ordinary dividends declared to stockholders after the date of the decedent's death are not property of the gross estate on the date of death and are not included in the alternate valuation. However, if dividends are declared to stockholders of record after the date of the decedent's death so that the shares of stock at the later valuation date do not reasonably represent the same property at the date of the decedent's death, include those dividends (except dividends paid from earnings of the corporation after the date of the decedent's death) in the alternate valuation.

FIGURE A.1 *Continued*

Line 9 Worksheet — Gift Tax on Gifts Made After 1976

a. Calendar year or calendar quarter Total pre-1977 taxable gifts. Enter the amount from line 1, Worksheet TG	b. Total taxable gifts for prior periods (from Form 709, Tax Computation, line 2)	c. Taxable gifts for this period (from Form 709, Tax Computation, line 1) (see below)	d. Tax payable using Table A (on page 12) (see below)	e. Unused unified credit (applicable credit amount) for this period (see below)	f. Tax payable for this period (subtract col. e from col. d)

1. Total gift taxes payable on gifts made after 1976 (combine the amounts in column f) .... **1** ___
2. Gift taxes paid by the decedent on gifts that qualify for "special treatment." Enter the amount from line 2, column e, Worksheet TG on page 5 .... **2** ___
3. Subtract line 2 from line 1 .... **3** ___
4. Gift tax paid by decedent's spouse on split gifts included on Schedule G. Enter the amount from line 2, column f, Worksheet TG on page 5 .... **4** ___
5. Add lines 3 and 4. Enter here and on line 9 of the Tax Computation of Form 706 .... **5** ___

Columns b and c — In addition to gifts reported on Form 709, you must include in these columns any taxable gifts in excess of the annual exclusion that were not reported on Form 709.

Column d — To figure the "tax payable" for this column, you must use Table A in these instructions, as it applies to the year of the decedent's death rather than to the year the gifts were actually made. To compute the entry for col. d, you should figure the "tax payable" on the amount in col. b and subtract it from the "tax payable" on the amounts in cols. b and c added together. Enter the difference in col. d.

"Tax payable" as used here is an hypothetical amount and does not necessarily reflect tax actually paid. Figure "tax payable" only on gifts made after 1976. Do not include any tax paid or payable on gifts made before 1977. Pre-1977 gifts are listed only to exclude them from the calculation.

If the amount in columns b and c combined exceeds $10 million for any given calendar year, then you must calculate the tax in column d for that year using the Form 709 revision in effect for the year of the decedent's death.

To calculate the tax, enter the amount for the appropriate year from column c of the worksheet on line 1 of the Tax Computation of the Form 709. Enter the amount from column b on line 2 of the Tax Computation. Complete the Tax Computation through the tax due before any reduction for the unified credit (applicable credit amount) and enter that amount in column d, above.

Column e — To figure the unused unified credit, (applicable credit amount), use the unified credit (applicable credit amount) in effect for the year the gift was made. This amount should be on line 12 of the Tax Computation of the Form 709 filed for the gift.

As part of each Schedule A through I, you must show:

1. what property is included in the gross estate on the date of the decedent's death;

2. what property was distributed, sold, exchanged, or otherwise disposed of within the 6-month period after the decedent's death, and the dates of these distributions, etc. (These two items should be entered in the "Description" column of each schedule. Briefly explain the status or disposition governing the alternate valuation date, such as: "Not disposed of within 6 months following death," "Distributed," "Sold," "Bond paid on maturity," etc. In this same column, describe each item of principal and includible income);

3. the date of death value, entered in the appropriate value column with items of principal and includible value shown separately; and

4. the alternate value, entered in the appropriate value column with items of principal and includible income shown separately. (In the case of any interest or estate, the value of which is affected by lapse of time, such as patents, leaseholds, estates for the life of another, or remainder interests, the value shown under the heading "Alternate value" must be the adjusted value; i.e., the value as of the date of death with an adjustment reflecting any difference in its value as of the later date not due to lapse of time.)

Distributions, sales, exchanges, and other dispositions of the property within the 6-month period after the decedent's death must be supported by evidence. If the court issued an order of distribution during that period, you must submit a certified copy of the order as part of the evidence. The District Director may require you to submit additional evidence if necessary.

If the alternate valuation method is used, the values of life estates, remainders, and similar interests are figured using the age of the recipient on the date of the decedent's death and the value of the property on the alternate valuation date.

Line 2 — Special Use Valuation of Section 2032A

In general. Under section 2032A, you may elect to value certain farm and closely held business real property at its farm or business use value rather than its fair market value. You may elect both special use valuation and alternate valuation.

To elect this valuation you must check "Yes" on line 2 and complete and attach Schedule A-1 and its required additional statements. You must file **Schedule A-1 and its required attachments with Form 706 for this election to be valid.** You may make the election on a late filed return so long as it is the first return filed.

The total value of the property valued under section 2032A may not be decreased from FMV by more than $760,000 for decedents dying in 1999 (subject to inflation in later years).

Real property may qualify for the section 2032A election if:

1. The decedent was a U.S. citizen or resident at the time of death;

2. The real property is located in the United States;

3. At the decedent's death the real property was used by the decedent or a family member for farming or in a trade or business, or was rented for such use by either the surviving spouse or a lineal descendant of the decedent to a family member of the decedent;

4. The real property was acquired from or passed from the decedent to a qualified heir of the decedent;

5. The real property was owned and used in a qualified manner by the decedent or a member of the

decedent's family during 5 of the 8 years before the decedent's death;

6. There was material participation by the decedent or a member of the decedent's family during 5 of the 8 years before the decedent's death; and

7. The qualified property meets the following percentage requirements:

a. At least 50% of the adjusted value of the gross estate must consist of the adjusted value of real or personal property that was being used as a farm or in a closely held business and that was acquired from, or passed from, the decedent to a qualified heir of the decedent, and

b. At least 25% of the adjusted value of the gross estate must consist of the adjusted value of qualified farm or closely held business real property.

For this purpose, adjusted value is the value of property determined without regard to its special-use value. The value is reduced for unpaid mortgages on the property or any indebtedness against the property, if the full value of the property in the property (not reduced by such mortgage or indebtedness) is included in the value of the gross estate. The adjusted value of the qualified real and personal property used in different businesses may be combined to meet the 50% and 25% requirements.

Qualified Real Property

Qualified use. The term qualified use means the use of the property as a farm for farming purposes or the use of property in a trade or business other than farming. Trade or business applies only to the active conduct of a business. It does not apply to passive investment activities or the mere passive rental of property to a person other than a member of the decedent's family. Also, no trade or

Part Instructions
STF FED1288L6

Page 6

FIGURE A.1 Continued

340

business is present in the case of activities not engaged in for profit.

Ownership. To qualify as special-use property, the decedent or a member of the decedent's family must have owned and used the property in a qualified use for 5 of the last 8 years before the decedent's death. Ownership may be direct or indirect through a corporation, a partnership, or a trust.

If the ownership is indirect, the business must qualify as a closely held business under section 6166. The ownership, when combined with periods of direct ownership, must meet the requirements of section 6166 on the date of the decedent's death and for a period of time that equals at least 5 of the 8 years preceding death.

If the property was leased by the decedent to a closely held business, it qualifies as long as the business entity to which it was rented was a closely held business with respect to the decedent on the date of the decedent's death and for sufficient time to meet the "5 in 8 years" test explained above.

Structures and other real property improvements. Qualified real property includes residential buildings and other structures and real property improvements regularly occupied or used by the owner or lessee) to operate the farm or business. A farm residence which the decedent had occupied is considered to have been occupied for the purpose of operating the farm even when a family member and not the decedent was the person materially participating in the operation of the farm.

Qualified real property also includes roads, buildings, and other structures and improvements functionally related to the qualified use.

Elements of value such as mineral rights that are not related to the farm or business use are not eligible for special-use valuation.

Property acquired from the decedent. Property is considered to have been acquired from or to have passed from the decedent if one of the following applies:

• The property is considered to have been acquired from or to have passed from the decedent under section 1014(b) (relating to basis of property acquired from a decedent).

• The property is acquired by any person from the estate.

• The property is acquired by any person from a trust, to the extent the property is includible in the gross estate.

Qualified heir. A person is a qualified heir of property if he or she is a member of the decedent's family and acquired or received the property from the decedent. If a qualified heir disposes of any interest in qualified property to any member of his or her family, that person will then be treated as the qualified heir with respect to that interest.

The term **member of the family** includes only:

1. An ancestor (parent, grandparent, etc.) of the individual;

2. The spouse of the individual;

3. The lineal descendant (child, stepchild, grandchild, etc.) of the individual, the individual's spouse, or a parent of the individual; or

4. The spouse, widow, or widower of any lineal descendant described above. A legally adopted child of an individual is treated as a child of that individual by blood.

Material Participation

To elect special-use valuation, either the decedent or a member of his or her family must have materially participated in the operation of the farm or other business for at least 5 of the 8 years ending on the date of the decedent's death. The existence of material participation is a factual determination, but passively collecting rents, salaries, draws, dividends, or other income from the farm or other business does not constitute material participation. Neither does merely advancing capital and reviewing a crop plan and financial reports each season or business year.

In determining whether the required participation has occurred, disregard brief periods (e.g., 30 days or less) during which there was no material participation, as long as such periods were both preceded and followed by substantial periods (more than 120 days) during which there was uninterrupted material participation.

Retirement or disability. If, on the date of death, the time period for material participation could not be met because the decedent had retired or was disabled, a substitute period may apply. The decedent must have retired on Social Security or been disabled for a continuous period ending with death. A person is disabled for this purpose if he or she was mentally or physically unable to materially participate in the operation of the farm or other business.

The substitute time period for material participation for these decedents is a period totaling at least 5 years out of the 8-year period that ended on the earlier of (1) the date the decedent began receiving social security benefits, or (2) the date the decedent became disabled.

Surviving spouse. A surviving spouse who received qualified real property from the predeceased spouse is considered to have materially participated if he or she was engaged in the active management of the farm or other business. If the surviving spouse died within 8 years of the first spouse's death, you may add the period of material participation of the predeceased spouse to the period of active management by the surviving spouse to determine if the surviving spouse's estate qualifies for special-use valuation. To qualify for this, the property must have been eligible for special-use valuation in the predeceased spouse's estate, though it does not have to have been elected by that estate.

For additional details regarding material participation, see Regulations section 20.2032A-3(e).

Valuation Methods

The primary method of valuing special-use value property that is used for farming purposes is the annual gross cash rental method. If comparable gross cash rentals are not available, you can substitute comparable average annual net share rentals. If neither of these are available, or if you so elect, you can use the method for valuing real property in a closely held business.

Average annual gross cash rental. Generally, the special-use value of property that is used for farming purposes is determined as follows:

1. Subtract the average annual state and local real estate taxes on actual tracts of comparable real property from the average annual gross cash rental for that same comparable property, and

2. Divide the result in 1 by the average annual effective interest rate charged for all new Federal Land Bank loans.

The computation of each average annual amount is based on the 5 most recent calendar years ending before the date of the decedent's death.

Gross cash rental. Generally, gross cash rental is the total amount of cash received in a calendar year for the use of actual tracts of comparable farm real property in the same locality as the property being specially valued. You may not use rents that are paid wholly or partly in kind, and the amount of rent may not be based on production. The rental must have resulted from an arm's-length transaction. Also, the amount of rent is not reduced by the amount of any expenses or liabilities associated with the farm operation or the lease.

Comparable property. Comparable property must be situated in the same locality as the specially valued property as determined by generally accepted real property valuation rules. The determination of comparability is based on all the facts and circumstances. It is often necessary to value land in segments where there are different uses or land characteristics included in the specially valued land. The following list contains some of the factors considered in determining comparability.

• Similarity of soil.

• Whether the crops grown would deplete the soil in a similar manner.

• Types of soil conservation techniques that have been practiced on the 2 properties.

• Whether the 2 properties are subject to flooding.

• Slope of the land.

• For livestock operations, the carrying capacity of the land.

• For timbered land, whether the timber is comparable.

• Whether the property as a whole is unified or segmented; if segmented, the availability of the means necessary for movement among the different sections.

• Number, types, and conditions of all buildings and other fixed improvements located on the properties and their location as it affects efficient management, use, and value of the property.

• Availability and type of transportation facilities in terms of costs and of proximity of the properties to local markets.

You must specifically identify on the return the property being used as comparable property. Use the type of descriptions used to list real property on Schedule A.

Effective interest rate. To get the effective annual interest in effect for the year of death and the area in which the property is located, contact your IRS District Director.

Net share rental. You may use average annual net share rental from comparable land only if there is no comparable land from which average annual gross cash rental can be determined. Net share rental is the difference between the gross value of produce received by the lessor from the comparable land and the cash operating expenses (other than real estate taxes) of growing the produce that, under the lease, are paid by the lessor. The production of the produce must be the business purpose of the farming operation. For this purpose, produce includes livestock.

The gross value of the produce is generally the gross amount received if the produce was disposed of in an arm's-length transaction within the period established by the Department of Agriculture for its price support program. Otherwise, the value is the weighted average price for which the produce sold on the closest national or regional commodities market. The value is figured for the date or dates on which the lessor received (or constructively received) the produce.

FIGURE A.1 *Continued*

Valuing a real property interest in closely held business. Use this method to determine the special-use valuation for qualifying real property used in a trade or business other than farming. You may also use this method for qualifying farm property if there is no comparable land or if you elect to use it. Under this method, the following factors are considered:

• The capitalization of income that the property can be expected to yield for farming or for closely held business purposes over a reasonable period of time with prudent management and traditional cropping patterns for the area, taking into account soil capacity, terrain configuration, and similar factors.

• The capitalization of the fair rental value of the land for farming or for closely held business purposes.

• The assessed land values in a state that provides a differential or use value assessment law for farmland or closely held business.

• Comparable sales of other farm or closely held business land in the same geographical area far enough removed from a metropolitan or resort area so that nonagricultural use is not a significant factor in the sales price.

• Any other factor that fairly values the farm or closely held business value of the property.

Making the Election

Include the words "section 2032A valuation" in the "Description" column of any Form 706 schedule if section 2032A property is included in the decedent's gross estate.

An election under section 2032A need not include all the property in an estate that is eligible for special use valuation, but sufficient property to satisfy the threshold requirements of section 2032A(b)(1)(B) must be specially valued under the election.

If joint or undivided interests (e.g., interests as joint tenants or tenants in common) in the same property are received from a decedent by qualified heirs, an election with respect to one heir's joint or undivided interest need not include any other heir's interest in the same property if the electing heir's interest plus other property to be specially valued satisfies the requirements of section 2032A(b)(1)(B).

If successive interests (e.g., life estates and remainder interests) are created by a decedent in otherwise qualified property, an election under section 2032A is available only with respect to that property (or part) in which qualified heirs of the decedent receive all of the successive interests, and such an election must include the interests of all of those heirs.

For example, if a surviving spouse receives a life estate in otherwise qualified property and the spouse's brother receives a remainder interest in fee, no part of the property may be valued pursuant to an election under section 2032A.

Where successive interests in specially valued property are created, remainder interests are treated as being received by qualified heirs only if the remainder interests are not contingent on surviving a nonfamily member or are not subject to divestment in favor of a nonfamily member.

Protective Election

You may make a protective election to specially value qualified real property. Under this election, whether or not you may ultimately use special valuation depends upon values as finally determined (or agreed to following examination of the return) meeting the requirements of section 2032A.

To make a protective election, check "Yes" to line 2 and complete Schedule A-1 according to its instructions for "Protective Election."

If you make a protective election, you should complete this Form 706 by valuing all property at its fair market value. Do not use special use valuation. Usually, this will result in higher estate and GST tax liabilities than will be ultimately determined if special use valuation is allowed. **The protective election does not extend the time to pay the taxes shown on the return.** If you wish to extend the time to pay the taxes, you should file Form 4768 in adequate time *before* the return due date.

If it is found that the estate qualifies for special use valuation based on the values as finally determined (or agreed to following examination of the return), you must file an amended Form 706 (with a complete section 2032A election) within 60 days after the date of this determination. Complete the amended return using special use values under the rules of section 2032A, and complete Schedule A-1 and attach *all* of the required statements.

Additional information

For definitions and additional information, see section 2032A and the related regulations.

Line 3 — Installment Payments

If the gross estate includes an interest in a closely held business, you may be able to elect to pay part of the estate tax in installments.

The maximum amount that can be paid in installments is that part of the estate tax that is attributable to the closely held business. In general, that amount is the amount of tax that bears the same ratio to the total estate tax that the value of the closely held business included in the gross estate bears to the total gross estate.

Percentage requirements. To qualify for installment payments, the value of the interest in the closely held business that is included in the gross estate must be more than 35% of the adjusted gross estate (the gross estate less expenses, indebtedness, taxes, and losses).

Interests in two or more closely held businesses are treated as an interest in a single business if at least 20% of the total value of each business is included in the gross estate. For this purpose, include any interest held by the surviving spouse that represents the surviving spouse's interest in a business held jointly with the decedent as community property or as joint tenants, tenants by the entirety, or tenants in common.

Value. The value used for meeting the percentage requirements is the same value used for determining the gross estate. Therefore, if the estate is valued under alternate valuation or special use valuation, you must use those values to meet the percentage requirements.

Transfers before death. Generally, gifts made before death are not included in the gross estate. However, the estate must meet the 35% requirement by both including and excluding in the gross estate any gifts made by the decedent within 3 years of death.

Passive assets. In determining the value of a closely held business and whether the 35% requirement is met, do not include the value of any passive assets held by the business. A passive asset is any asset not used in carrying on a trade or business. Stock in another corporation is a passive asset unless the stock is treated as held by the decedent because of the election to treat holding company stock as business company stock, as discussed below.

If a corporation owns at least 20% in value of the voting stock of another corporation, or the other corporation had no more than 15 shareholders and at least 80% of the value of the assets of each corporation is attributable to assets used in carrying on a trade or

business, then these corporations will be treated as a single corporation, and the stock will not be treated as a passive asset. Stock held in the other corporation is not taken into account in determining the 80% requirement.

Interest in closely held business. For purposes of the installment payment election, an interest in a closely held business means:

• Ownership of a trade or business carried on as a proprietorship.

• An interest as a partner in a partnership carrying on a trade or business if 20% or more of the total capital interest was included in the gross estate of the decedent or the partnership had no more than 15 partners.

• Stock in a corporation carrying on a trade or business if 20% or more in value of the voting stock of the corporation is included in the gross estate of the decedent or the corporation had no more than 15 shareholders.

The partnership or corporation must be carrying on a trade or business at the time of the decedent's death.

In determining the number of partners or shareholders, a partnership or stock interest is treated as owned by one partner or shareholder if it is community property or held by a husband and wife as joint tenants, tenants in common, or as tenants by the entirety.

Property owned directly or indirectly by or for a corporation, partnership, estate, or trust is treated as owned proportionately by or for its shareholders, partners, or beneficiaries. For trusts, only beneficiaries with current interests are considered.

The interest in a closely held farm business includes the interest in the residential buildings and related improvements occupied regularly by the owners, lessees, and employees operating the farm.

Holding company stock. The executor may elect to treat as business company stock the portion of any holding company stock that represents direct ownership (or indirect ownership through one or more other holding companies) in a business company. A *holding company* is a corporation holding stock in another corporation. A *business company* is a corporation carrying on a trade or business.

This election applies only to stock that is not readily tradable. For purposes of the 20% voting stock requirement, stock is treated as owning stock to the extent the holding company owns voting stock in the business company.

If the executor makes this election, the first installment payment is due when the estate tax return is filed. The 5-year deferral for payment of the tax, as discussed below under Time for payment, does not apply. In addition, the 2% interest rate, discussed below under Interest computation, will not apply.

Time for payment. Under the installment method, the executor may elect to *defer* payment of the qualified estate tax, but not interest, for up to 5 years from the original payment due date. After the first installment of tax is paid, you must pay the remaining installments annually by the date 1 year after the due date of the preceding installment. There can be no more than 10 installment payments.

Interest on the unpaid portion of the tax is not deferred and must be paid annually. Interest must be paid at the same time and as and as a part of each installment payment of the tax.

For information on the acceleration of payment when an interest in the closely held business is disposed of, see section 6166(g).

Interest computation. A special interest rate applies to installment payments. For decedent's dying in 1999, the interest rate is 2% on the lesser of:

FIGURE A.1 *Continued*

- $416,500 (subject to inflation, see below) OR
- The amount of the estate tax that is attributable to the closely held business and that is payable in installments.

2% portion. The 2% portion is an amount equal to the amount of the tentative estate tax on ($1,000,000 + the applicable exclusion amount in effect) minus the applicable credit amount in effect. However, if the amount of estate tax extended under section 6166 is less than the amount computed above, the 2% portion is the lesser amount.

Inflation adjustment. The $1,000,000 amount used to calculate the 2% portion is indexed for inflation for the estates of decedents dying in a calendar year after 1998. For an estate of a decedent dying in calendar year 1999, the dollar amount used to determine the "2% portion" of the estate tax payable in installments under section 6166 is $1,010,000. See Rev. Proc. 98-61.

Interest on the portion of the tax in excess of the 2% portion is figured at 45% of the annual rate of interest on underpayments. This rate is based on the Federal short-term rate and is announced quarterly by the IRS in the Internal Revenue Bulletin.

If you elect installment payments and the estate tax due is more than the maximum amount to which the 2% interest rate applies, each installment payment is deemed to comprise both tax subject to the 2% interest rate and tax subject to 45% of the regular underpayment rate. The amount of each installment that is subject to the 2% rate is the same as the percentage of total tax payable in installments that is subject to the 2% rate.

Important: The interest paid on installment payments is not deductible as an administrative expense of the estate.

Making the election. If you check this line to make a protective election, you should attach a notice of protective election as described in Regulations section 20.6166-1(d). If you check this line to make a final election, you should attach the notice of election described in Regulations section 20.6166-1(b).

In computing the adjusted gross estate under section 6166(b)(6) to determine whether an election may be made under section 6166, the net amount of any real estate in a closely held business must be used.

You may also elect to pay GST taxes in installments. See section 6166(i).

Line 4 — Reversionary or Remainder Interests

For details of this election, see section 6163 and the related regulations.

Instructions for Part 4. General Information (Pages 2 and 3 of Form 706)

Authorization

- Completing the authorization on page 2 of Form 706 will authorize one attorney, accountant, or enrolled agent to represent the estate and receive confidential

tax information, but will not authorize the representative to enter into closing agreements for the estate.

- If you wish to represent the estate, you must complete and sign the authorization.
- If you wish to authorize persons other than attorneys, accountants, and enrolled agents, or if you wish to authorize more than one person, to receive confidential information or represent the estate, you must complete and attach Form 2848, Power of Attorney and Declaration of Representative.
- You must also complete and attach Form 2848 if you wish to authorize someone to enter into closing agreements for the estate.
- If you wish only to authorize someone to inspect and/or receive confidential tax information (but not to represent you before the IRS), complete and file Form 8821, Tax Information Authorization.

Line 4

Complete line 4 whether or not there is a surviving spouse and whether or not the surviving spouse received any benefits from the estate. If there was no surviving spouse on the date of decedent's death, enter "None" in line 4a and leave lines 4b and 4c blank. The value entered in line 4c need not be exact. See the instructions for "Amount" under line 5, below.

Line 5

Name. Enter the name of each individual, trust, or estate who received (or will receive) benefits of $5,000 or more from the estate directly as an heir, next-of-kin, devisee, or legatee; or indirectly (for example, as beneficiary of an annuity or insurance policy, shareholder of a corporation, or partner of a partnership that is an heir, etc.).

Identifying number. Enter the SSN of each individual beneficiary listed. If the number is unknown, or the individual has no number, please indicate "unknown" or "none." For trusts and other estates, enter the EIN.

Relationship. For each individual beneficiary enter the relationship (if known) to the decedent by reason of blood, marriage, or adoption. For trust or estate beneficiaries, indicate TRUST or ESTATE.

Amount. Enter the amount actually distributed (or to be distributed) to each beneficiary including transfers during the decedent's life from Schedule G required to be included in the gross estate. The value to be entered need not be exact. A reasonable estimate is sufficient. For example, where precise values cannot readily be determined, as with certain future interests, a reasonable approximation should be entered. The total of these distributions should approximate the amount of gross estate reduced by funeral and administrative expenses, debts and mortgages, bequests to surviving spouse, charitable bequests, and any Federal and state estate and GST taxes paid (or payable) relating to the benefits received by the beneficiaries listed on lines 4 and 5.

All distributions of less than $5,000 to specific beneficiaries may be included with distributions to unascertainable beneficiaries on the line provided.

Line 6 — Section 2044 Property

If you answered "Yes," these assets must be shown on Schedule F.

Section 2044 property is property for which a previous section 2056(b)(7) election (QTIP election) has been made, or for which a similar gift tax election (section 2523) has been made. For more information, see the instructions on the back of Schedule F.

Line 8 — Insurance Not Included in the Gross Estate

If you checked "Yes" for either 8a or 8b, you must complete and attach Schedule D and attach a Form 712, Life Insurance Statement, for each policy and an explanation of why the policy or its proceeds are not includible in the gross estate.

Line 10 — Partnership Interests and Stock in Close Corporations

If you answered "Yes" to line 10, you must include full details for partnership and unincorporated businesses on Schedule F (Schedule E if the partnership interest is jointly owned). You must include full details for the stock of inactive or close corporations on Schedule B.

Value these interests using the rules of Regulations section 20.2031-2 (stocks) or 20.2031-3 (other business interests).

A "close corporation" is a corporation whose shares are owned by a limited number of shareholders. Often, one family holds the entire stock issue. As a result, little, if any, trading of the stock takes place. There is, therefore, no established market for the stock, and those sales that do occur are at irregular intervals and seldom reflect all the elements of a representative transaction as defined by the term "fair market value" (FMV).

Line 12 — Trusts

If you answered "Yes" to either 12a or 12b, you must attach a copy of the trust instrument for each trust.

You must complete Schedule G if you answered "Yes" to 12a and Schedule F if you answered "Yes" to 12b.

Line 14 — Transitional Marital Deduction Computation

Check "Yes" if property passes to the surviving spouse under a maximum marital deduction formula provision that meets the requirements of section 403(e)(3) of the Economic Recovery Tax Act of 1981 (P.L. 97-34; 95 Stat. 305).

If you check "Yes" to line 14, compute the marital deduction under the rules that were in effect before the Economic Recovery Tax Act of 1981.

For a format for this computation, you should obtain the November 1981 revision of Form 706 and its instructions. The computation is items 19 through 26 of the Recapitulation. You should also apply the rules of Rev. Rul. 80-148, 1980-1 C.B. 207, if there is property that passes to the surviving spouse outside of the maximum marital deduction formula provision.

FIGURE A.1 *Continued*

Instructions for Part 5. Recapitulation (Page 3 of Form 706)

Gross Estate

Items 1 through 10 — You must make an entry in each of Items 1 through 9.

If the gross estate does not contain any assets of the type specified by a given item, enter zero for that item. Entering zero for any of items 1 through 9 is a statement by the executor, made under penalties of perjury, that the gross estate does not contain any includible assets covered by that item.

Do not enter any amounts in the "Alternate value" column unless you elected alternate valuation on line 1 of Elections by the Executor on page 2 of the Form 706.

Which schedules to attach for Items 1 through 9. You must attach —

• Schedule F to the return and answer its questions even if you report no assets on it.

• Schedules A, B, and C if the gross estate includes any Real Estate; Stocks and Bonds; or Mortgages, Notes, and Cash, respectively.

• Schedule D if the gross estate includes any Life Insurance or if you answered "Yes" to question 8a of Part 4, General Information.

• Schedule E if the gross estate contains any Jointly Owned Property or if you answered "Yes" to question 9 of Part 4.

• Schedule G if the decedent made any of the lifetime transfers to be listed on that schedule or if you answered "Yes" to question 11 or 12a of Part 4.

• Schedule H if you answered "Yes" to question 13 of Part 4.

• Schedule I if you answered "Yes" to question 15 of Part 4.

Exclusion

Item 11 — Conservation easement exclusion.

You must complete and attach Schedule U (along with any required attachments) to claim the exclusion on this line.

Deductions

Items 13 through 22 — You must attach the appropriate schedules for the deductions you claim.

Item 17— If item 16 is less than or equal to the value (at the time of the decedent's death) of the property subject to claims, enter the amount from item 16 on item 17.

If the amount on item 16 is more than the value of the property subject to claims, enter the greater of (a) the value of the property subject to claims, or (b) the amount actually paid at the time the return is filed.

In no event should you enter more on item 17 than the amount on item 16. See section 2053 and the related regulations for more information.

FIGURE A.1 *Continued*

344

Instructions for Schedule A. Real Estate

See the reverse side of Schedule A on Form 706.

Schedule A-1. Section 2032A Valuation

See Schedule A-1 on Form 706.

Instructions for Schedule B. Stocks and Bonds

General

If the total gross estate contains any stocks or bonds, you must complete Schedule B and file it with the return.

On Schedule B list the stocks and bonds included in the decedent's gross estate. Number each item in the left-hand column. Bonds that are exempt from Federal income tax are not exempt from estate tax unless specifically exempted by an estate tax provision of the Code. Therefore, you should list these bonds on Schedule B.

Public housing bonds includible in the gross estate must be included at their full value.

If you paid any estate, inheritance, legacy, or succession tax to a foreign country on any stocks or bonds included in this schedule, group those stocks and bonds together and label them "Subjected to Foreign Death Taxes."

List interest and dividends on each stock or bond separately. Indicate as a separate item dividends that have not been collected at death, but which are payable to the decedent or the estate because the decedent was a stockholder of record on the date of death. However, if the stock is being traded on an exchange and is selling ex-dividend on the date of the decedent's death, do not include the amount of the dividend as a separate item. Instead, add it to the ex-dividend quotation in determining the fair market value of the stock on the date of the decedent's death. Dividends declared on shares of stock before the death of the decedent but payable to stockholders of record on a date after the decedent's death are not includible in the gross estate for Federal estate tax purposes.

Description

Stocks. For stocks indicate:
- Number of shares
- Whether common or preferred
- Issue
- Par value where needed for identification
- Price per share
- Exact name of corporation
- Principal exchange upon which sold, if listed on an exchange
- Nine-digit CUSIP number

Bonds. For bonds indicate:
- Quantity and denomination
- Name of obligor
- Date of maturity
- Interest rate
- Interest due date
- Principal exchange, if listed on an exchange
- Nine-digit CUSIP number

If the stock or bond is unlisted, show the company's principal business office.

The CUSIP (Committee on Uniform Security Identification Procedure) number is a nine-digit number that is assigned to all stocks and bonds traded on major exchanges and many unlisted securities. Usually, the CUSIP number is printed on the face of the stock certificate. If the CUSIP number is not printed on the certificate, it may be obtained through the company's transfer agent.

Valuation

List the fair market value (FMV) of the stocks or bonds. The FMV of a stock or bond (whether listed or unlisted) is the mean between the highest and lowest selling prices quoted on the valuation date. If only the closing selling prices are available, then the FMV is the mean between the quoted closing selling price on the valuation date and on the trading day before the valuation date.

To figure the FMV if there were no sales on the valuation date:

1. Find the mean between the highest and lowest selling prices on the nearest trading date before and the nearest trading date after the valuation date. Both trading dates must be reasonably close to the valuation date.

2. Prorate the difference between the mean prices to the valuation date.

3. Add or subtract (whichever applies) the prorated part of the difference to or from the mean price figured for the nearest trading date before the valuation date.

If no actual sales were made reasonably close to the valuation date, make the same computation using the mean between the bona fide bid and asked prices instead of sales prices. If actual sales prices or bona fide bid and asked prices are available within a reasonable period of time before the valuation date but not after the valuation date, or vice versa, use the mean between the highest and lowest sales prices or bid and asked prices as the FMV.

For example, assume that sales of stock nearest the valuation date (June 15) occurred 2 trading days before (June 13) and 3 trading days after (June 18). On those days the mean sale prices per share were $10 and $15, respectively. Therefore, the price of $12 is considered the FMV of a share of stock on the valuation date. If, however, on June 13 and 18, the mean sale prices per share were $15 and $10, respectively, the FMV of a share of stock on the valuation date is $13.

If only closing prices for bonds are available, see Regulations section 20.2031-2(b).

Apply the rules in the section 2031 regulations to determine the value of inactive stock and stock in close corporations. Send with the schedule complete financial and other data used to determine value, including balance sheets (particularly the one nearest to the valuation date) and statements of the net earnings or operating results and dividends paid for each of the 5 years immediately before the valuation date.

Securities reported as of no value, nominal value, or obsolete should be listed last. Include the address of the company and the state and date of the incorporation. Attach copies of correspondence or statements used to determine the "no value."

If the security was listed on more than one stock exchange, use either the records of the exchange where the security is principally traded or the composite listing of combined exchanges, if available, in a publication of general circulation. In valuing listed stocks and bonds, you should carefully check accurate records to obtain values for the applicable valuation date.

If you get quotations from brokers, or evidence of the sale of securities from the officers of the issuing companies, attach to the schedule copies of the letters furnishing these quotations or evidence of sale.

See Rev. Rul. 69-489, 1969-2 C.B. 172, for the special valuation rules for certain marketable U.S. Treasury Bonds (issued before March 4, 1971). These bonds, commonly called "flower bonds," may be redeemed at par plus accrued interest in payment of the tax at any Federal Reserve bank, the office of the Treasurer of the United States, or the Bureau of the Public Debt, as explained in Rev. Proc. 69-18, 1969-2 C.B. 300.

Instructions for Schedule C. Mortgages, Notes, and Cash

See the reverse side of Schedule C on Form 706.

Instructions for Schedule D. Insurance on the Decedent's Life

See the reverse side of Schedule D on Form 706.

Instructions for Schedule E. Jointly Owned Property

See the reverse side of Schedule E on Form 706.

Instructions for Schedule F. Other Miscellaneous Property

See the reverse side of Schedule F on Form 706.

Instructions for Schedule G. Transfers During Decedent's Life

Complete Schedule G and file it with the return if the decedent made any of the transfers described in 1 through 5 below, or if you answered "Yes" on line 11 or 12a of Part 4, General Information.

Report the following types of transfers on this schedule.

Beginning with the estates of decedents dying after August 5, 1997:

IF ...	AND ...	THEN ...
the decedent made a transfer from a trust,	at the time of the transfer, the transfer was from a portion of the trust that was owned by the grantor under section 676 (other than by reason of section 672(e)) by reason of a power in the grantor,	for purposes of sections 2035 and 2038, treat the transfer as made directly by the decedent. Any such transfer within the annual gift tax exclusion is not includible in the gross estate.

1. **Certain gift taxes (section 2035(b)).** Enter at item A of the Schedule the total value of the gift taxes that were paid by the decedent or the estate on gifts made by the decedent or the decedent's spouse within 3 years before death.

The date of the gift, not the date of payment of the gift tax, determines whether a gift tax paid is included in the gross estate under this rule. Therefore, you should carefully examine the Forms 709 filed by the decedent and the decedent's spouse to determine what part of the total gift taxes reported on them was attributable to gifts made within 3 years before death.

FIGURE A.1 *Continued*

345

Column A	Column B	Column C	Column D
Taxable amount over	Taxable amount not over	Tax on amount in column A	Rate of tax on excess over amount in column A
			(Percent)
0	$ 10,000	0	18
$ 10,000	20,000	$ 1,800	20
20,000	40,000	3,800	22
40,000	60,000	8,200	24
60,000	80,000	13,000	26
80,000	100,000	18,200	28
100,000	150,000	23,800	30
150,000	250,000	38,800	32
250,000	500,000	70,800	34
500,000	750,000	155,800	37
750,000	1,000,000	248,300	39
1,000,000	1,250,000	345,800	41
1,250,000	1,500,000	448,300	43
1,500,000	2,000,000	555,800	45
2,000,000	2,500,000	780,800	49
2,500,000	3,000,000	1,025,800	53
3,000,000	– – – –	1,290,800	55

Table B Worksheet

Federal Adjusted Taxable Estate

1 Federal taxable estate (from Tax Computation, Form 706, line 3) $ _____

2 Adjustment 60,000

3 Federal adjusted taxable estate. Subtract line 2 from line 1. Use this amount to compute maximum credit for state death taxes in **Table B**. _____

Table B

Computation of Maximum Credit for State Death Taxes

(Based on Federal adjusted taxable estate computed using the worksheet above.)

(1) Adjusted taxable estate equal to or more than -	(2) Adjusted taxable estate less than -	(3) Credit on amount in column (1)	(4) Rate of credit on excess over amount in column (1)	(1) Adjusted taxable estate equal to or more than -	(2) Adjusted taxable estate less than -	(3) Credit on amount in column (1)	(4) Rate of credit on excess over amount in column (1)
			(Percent)				(Percent)
0	$ 40,000	0	None	2,040,000	2,540,000	106,800	8.0
$ 40,000	90,000	0	0.8	2,540,000	3,040,000	146,800	8.8
90,000	140,000	$ 400	1.6	3,040,000	3,540,000	190,800	9.6
140,000	240,000	1,200	2.4	3,540,000	4,040,000	238,800	10.4
240,000	440,000	3,600	3.2	4,040,000	5,040,000	290,800	11.2
440,000	640,000	10,000	4.0	5,040,000	6,040,000	402,800	12.0
640,000	840,000	18,000	4.8	6,040,000	7,040,000	522,800	12.8
840,000	1,040,000	27,600	5.6	7,040,000	8,040,000	650,800	13.6
1,040,000	1,540,000	38,800	6.4	8,040,000	9,040,000	786,800	14.4
1,540,000	2,040,000	70,800	7.2	9,040,000	10,040,000	930,800	15.2
				10,040,000	– – – –	1,082,800	16.0

Examples showing use of Schedule B

Example where the alternate valuation is not adopted; date of death, January 1, 1999

Item number	Description including face amount of bonds or number of shares and par value where needed for identification. Give CUSIP number.	Unit value	Alternate valuation date	Alternate value	Value at date of death
1	$60,000 - Arkansas Railroad Co. first mortgage 4%, 20-year bonds, due 2001. Interest payable quarterly on Feb. 1, May 1, Aug. 1 and Nov. 1; N.Y. Exchange, CUSIP No. XXXXXXXXX...............	100	– – – –	$ – – – –	$ 60,000
	Interest coupons attached to bonds, item 1, due and payable on Nov. 1, 1998, but not cashed at date of death	– – – –	– – – –	– – – –	600
	Interest accrued on item 1, from Nov. 1, 1998, to Jan. 1, 1999.....	– – – –	– – – –	– – – –	400
2	500 shares Public Service Corp., common; N.Y. Exchange, CUSIP No. XXXXXXXXX	110	– – – –	– – – –	55,000
	Dividend on item 2 of $2 per share declared Dec. 10, 1998, payable on Jan. 10, 1999, to holders of record on Dec. 30, 1998	– – – –	– – – –	– – – –	1,000

Instructions for Schedules
STF FED1288L12

FIGURE A.1 *Continued*

Item number	Description including face amount of bonds or number of shares and par value where needed for identification. Give CUSIP number.	Unit value	Alternate valuation date	Alternate value	Value at date of death
1	$60,000 - Arkansas Railroad Co. first mortgage 4%, 20-year bonds, due 2001. Interest payable quarterly on Feb. 1, May 1, Aug. 1 and Nov. 1; N.Y. Exchange, CUSIP No. XXXXXXXXX	100	- - - - - -	$_ _ _ _ _ _	$ 60,000
	$30,000 of item 1 distributed to legatees on Apr. 1, 1999	99	4/1/99	29,700	- - - - - -
	$30,000 of item 1 sold by executor on May 2, 1999	98	5/2/99	29,400	- - - - - -
	Interest coupons attached to bonds, item 1, due and payable on Nov. 1, 1998, but not cashed at date of death. Cashed by executor on Feb. 1, 1999	- - - - - -	2/1/99	600	600
	Interest accrued on item 1, from Nov. 1, 1998, to Jan. 1, 1999. Cashed by executor on Feb. 1, 1999	- - - - - -	2/1/99	400	400
2	500 shares of Public Service Corp., common; N.Y. Exchange, CUSIP No. XXXXXXXXX	110	- - - - - -	- - - - - -	55,000
	Not disposed of within 6 months following death	90	7/1/99	45,000	- - - - - -
	Dividend on item 2 of $2 per share declared Dec. 10, 1998, and paid on Jan. 10, 1999, to holders of record on Dec. 30, 1998	- - - - - -	1/10/99	1,000	1,000

(Continued from page 11)

For example, if the decedent died on July 10, 1999, you should examine gift tax returns for 1999, 1998, 1997, and 1996. However, the gift taxes on the 1996 return that are attributable to gifts made before July 10, 1996, are not included in the gross estate.

Attach an explanation of how you computed the includible gift taxes if you do not include in the gross estate the entire gift taxes shown on any Form 709 filed for gifts made within 3 years of death. Also attach copies of any pertinent gift tax returns filed by the decedent's spouse for gifts made within 3 years of death.

2. Other transfers within 3 years before death (section 2035(a)). These transfers include *only* the following:

• Any transfer by the decedent with respect to a life insurance policy within 3 years before death.

• Any transfer within 3 years before death of a retained section 2036 life estate, section 2037 reversionary interest, or section 2038 power to revoke, etc., if the property subject to the life estate, interest, or power would have been included in the gross estate had the decedent continued to possess the life estate, interest, or power until death.

These transfers are reported on Schedule G regardless of whether a gift tax return was required to be filed for them when they were made. However, the amount includible and the information required to be shown for the transfers are determined:

• For insurance on the life of the decedent using the instructions to Schedule D. (Attach Forms 712.)

• For insurance on the life of another using the instructions to Schedule F. (Attach Forms 712.)

• For sections 2036, 2037, and 2038 transfers, using paragraphs 3, 4, and 5 of these instructions.

3. Transfers with retained life estate (section 2036). These are transfers by the decedent in which the decedent retained an interest in the transferred property. The transfer can be in trust or otherwise, but excludes bona fide sales for adequate and full consideration.

Interests or rights. Section 2036 applies to the following retained interests or rights:

• The right to income from the transferred property.

• The right to the possession or enjoyment of the property.

• The right, either alone or with any person, to designate the persons who shall receive the income from, or possess or enjoy, the property.

Retained voting rights. Transfers with a retained life estate also include transfers of stock in a "controlled corporation" after June 22, 1976, if the decedent retained or acquired voting rights in the stock. If the decedent retained direct or indirect voting rights in a controlled corporation, the decedent is considered to have retained enjoyment of the transferred property. A corporation is a "controlled corporation" if the decedent owned (actually or constructively) or had the right (either alone or with any other person) to vote at least 20% of the total combined voting power of all classes of stock. See section 2036(b). If these voting rights ceased or were relinquished within 3 years before the decedent's death, the corporate interests are included in the gross estate as if the decedent had actually retained the voting rights until death.

The amount includible in the gross estate is the value of the transferred property at the time of the decedent's death. If the decedent kept or reserved an interest or right to only a part of the transferred property, the amount includible in the gross estate is a corresponding part of the entire value of the property.

A retained life estate does not have to be legally enforceable. What matters is that a substantial economic benefit was retained. For example, if a mother transferred title to her home to her daughter but with the informal understanding that she was to continue living there until her death, the value of the home would be includible in the mother's estate even if the agreement would not have been legally enforceable.

4. Transfers taking effect at death (section 2037). A transfer that takes effect at the decedent's death is one under which possession or enjoyment can be obtained only by surviving the decedent. A transfer is not treated as one that takes effect at the decedent's death unless the decedent retained a reversionary interest (defined below) in the property that immediately before the decedent's death had a value of more than 5% of the value of the transferred property. If the transfer was made before October 8, 1949, the reversionary interest must have arisen by the express terms of the instrument of transfer.

A *reversionary interest* is generally any right under which the transferred property will or may be returned to the decedent or the decedent's estate. It also includes the possibility that the transferred property may become subject to a power of disposition by the decedent. It does not matter if the right arises by the express terms of the instrument of transfer or by operation of law. For this purpose, reversionary interest does not include the possibility the income alone from the property may return to the decedent or become subject to the decedent's power of disposition.

5. Revocable transfers (section 2038). The gross estate includes the value of transferred property in which the enjoyment of the transferred property was subject at decedent's death to any change through the exercise of a power to alter, amend, revoke, or terminate. A decedent's power to change the beneficiaries and to hasten or increase any beneficiary's enjoyment of the property are examples of this.

It does not matter whether the power was reserved at the time of the transfer, whether it arose by operation of law, or was later created or conferred. The rule applies regardless of the source from which the power was acquired, and regardless of whether the power was exercisable by the decedent alone or with any person (and regardless of whether that person had a substantial adverse interest in the transferred property).

The capacity in which the decedent could use a power has no bearing. If the decedent gave property in trust and was the trustee with the power to revoke the trust, the property would be included in his or her gross estate. For transfers or additions to an irrevocable trust after October 28, 1979, the transferred property is includible if the decedent reserved the power to remove the trustee at will and appoint another trustee.

If the decedent relinquished within 3 years before death any of the includible powers described above, figure the gross estate as if the decedent had actually retained the powers until death.

Only the part of the transferred property that is subject to the decedent's power is included in the gross estate.

For more detailed information on which transfers are includible in the gross estate, see the Estate Tax Regulations.

FIGURE A.1 *Continued*

347

Special Valuation Rules for Certain Lifetime Transfers

Code sections 2701-2704 provide rules for valuing certain transfers to family members.

Section 2701 deals with the transfer of an interest in a corporation or partnership while retaining certain distribution rights, or a liquidation, put, call, or conversion right.

Section 2702 deals with the transfer of an interest in a trust while retaining other than a qualified interest. In general, a qualified interest is a right to receive certain distributions from the trust at least annually, or a noncontingent remainder interest if all of the other interests in the trust are distribution rights specified in section 2702.

Section 2703 provides rules for the valuation of property transferred to a family member but subject to an option, agreement, or other right to acquire or use the property at less than FMV. It also applies to transfers subject to restrictions on the right to sell or use the property.

Finally, section 2704 provides that in certain cases the lapse of a voting or liquidation right in a family-owned corporation or partnership will result in a deemed transfer.

These rules have potential consequences for the valuation of property in an estate. If the decedent (or any member of his or her family) was involved in any such transactions, see Code sections 2701 through 2704 and the related regulations for additional details.

How To Complete Schedule G

All transfers (other than outright transfers not in trust and bona fide sales) made by the decedent at any time during life must be reported on the Schedule regardless of whether you believe the transfers are subject to tax. If the decedent made any transfers not described in the instructions above, the transfers should not be shown on Schedule G. Instead, attach a statement describing these transfers: list the date of the transfer, the amount or value of the transferred property, and the type of transfer.

Complete the schedule for each transfer that is included in the gross estate under sections 2035(a), 2036, 2037, and 2038 as described in the Instructions for Schedule G above.

In the "Item number" column, number each transfer consecutively beginning with 1. In the "Description" column, list the name of the transferee, the date of the transfer, and give a complete description of the property. Transfers included in the gross estate should be valued on the date of the decedent's death or, if alternate valuation is adopted, according to section 2032.

If only part of the property transferred meets the terms of section 2035(a), 2036, 2037, or 2038, then only a corresponding part of the value of the property should be included in the value of the gross estate. If the transferee makes additions or improvements to the property, the increased value of the property at the valuation date should not be included on Schedule G. However, if only a part of the value of the property is included, enter the value of the whole under the column headed "Description" and explain what part was included.

Attachments. If a transfer, by trust or otherwise, was made by a written instrument, attach a copy of the instrument to the Schedule. If of public record, the copy should be certified; if not of record, the copy should be verified.

Instructions for Schedule H. Powers of Appointment

Complete Schedule H and file it with the return if you answered "Yes" to line 13 of Part 4, General Information.

On Schedule H, include in the gross estate:

1. The value of property for which the decedent possessed a general power of appointment (defined below) on the date of his or her death; and

2. The value of property for which the decedent possessed a general power of appointment that he or she exercised or released before death by disposing of it in such a way that if it were a transfer of property owned by the decedent, the property would be includible in the decedent's gross estate as a transfer with a retained life estate, a transfer taking effect at death, or a revocable transfer.

With the above exceptions, property subject to a power of appointment is not includible in the gross estate if the decedent released the power completely and the decedent held no interest in or control over the property.

If the failure to exercise a general power of appointment results in a lapse of the power, the lapse is treated as a release only to the extent that the value of the property that could have been appointed by the exercise of the lapsed power is more than the greater of $5,000 or 5% of the total value, at the time of the lapse, of the assets out of which, or the proceeds of which, the exercise of the lapsed power could have been satisfied.

Powers of Appointment

A power of appointment determines who will own or enjoy the property subject to the power and when they will own or enjoy it. The power must be created by someone other than the decedent. It does not include a power created or held on property transferred by the decedent.

A power of appointment includes all powers which are in substance and effect powers of appointment regardless of how they are identified and regardless of local property laws. For example, if a settlor transfers property in trust for the life of his wife, with a power in the wife to appropriate or consume the principal of the trust, the wife has a power of appointment.

Some powers do not in themselves constitute a power of appointment. For example, a power to amend only administrative provisions of a trust that cannot substantially affect the beneficial enjoyment of the trust property or income is not a power of appointment. A power to manage, invest, or control assets, or to allocate receipts and disbursements, when exercised only in a fiduciary capacity, is not a power of appointment.

General power of appointment. A general power of appointment is a power that is exercisable in favor of the decedent, the decedent's estate, the decedent's creditors, or the creditors of the decedent's estate, **except:**

1. A power to consume, invade, or appropriate property for the benefit of the decedent that is limited by an ascertainable standard relating to health, education, support, or maintenance of the decedent.

2. A power exercisable by the decedent only in conjunction with —

   a. the creator of the power, or

   b. a person who has a substantial interest in the property subject to the power, which is adverse to the exercise of the power in favor of the decedent.

A part of a power is considered a general power of appointment if the power:

1. May only be exercised by the decedent in conjunction with another person; and

2. Is also exercisable in favor of the other person (in addition to being exercisable in favor of the decedent, the decedent's creditors, the decedent's estate, or the creditors of the decedent's estate).

The part to include in the gross estate as a general power of appointment is figured by dividing the value of the property by the number of persons (including the decedent) in favor of whom the power is exercisable.

Date power was created. Generally, a power of appointment created by will is considered created on the date of the testator's death.

A power of appointment created by an inter vivos instrument is considered created on the date the instrument takes effect. If the holder of a power exercises it by creating a second power, the second power is considered as created at the time of the exercise of the first.

Attachments

If the decedent ever possessed a power of appointment, attach a certified or verified copy of the instrument granting the power and a certified or verified copy of any instrument by which the power was exercised or released. You must file these copies even if you contend that the power was not a general power of appointment, and that the property is not otherwise includible in the gross estate.

Instructions for Schedule I. Annuities

You must complete Schedule I and file it with the return if you answered "Yes" to question 15 of Part 4, General Information.

Enter on Schedule I every annuity that meets all of the conditions under **General**, below, and every annuity described in paragraphs a - h of **Annuities Under Approved Plans**, even if the annuities are wholly or partially excluded from the gross estate.

See the instructions for line 3 of Schedule M for a discussion regarding the QTIP treatment of certain joint and survivor annuities.

General

In general, you must include in the gross estate all or part of the value of any annuity that meets the following requirements:

• It is receivable by a beneficiary following the death of the decedent and by reason of surviving the decedent;

• The annuity is under a contract or agreement entered into after March 3, 1931;

• The annuity was payable to the decedent (or the decedent possessed the right to receive the annuity) either alone or in conjunction with another, for the decedent's life or for any period not ascertainable without reference to the decedent's death or for any period that did not in fact end before the decedent's death;

• The contract or agreement is not a policy of insurance on the life of the decedent.

These rules apply to all types of annuities, including pension plans, individual retirement arrangements, and purchased commercial annuities.

An annuity contract that provides periodic payments to a person for life and ceases at the person's death is not includible in the gross estate. Social Security benefits are not includible in the gross estate even if the surviving spouse receives benefits.

An annuity or other payment that is not includible in the decedent's or the survivor's gross estate as an annuity may still be includible under some other applicable

FIGURE A.1 *Continued*

provision of the law. For example, see **Powers of Appointment** above.

If the decedent retired before January 1, 1985, see **Annuities Under Approved Plans** below for rules that allow the exclusion of part or all of certain annuities.

Part Includible

If the decedent contributed only part of the purchase price of the contract or agreement, include in the gross estate only that part of the value of the annuity receivable by the surviving beneficiary that the decedent's contribution to the purchase price of the annuity or agreement bears to the total purchase price.

For example, if the value of the survivor's annuity was $20,000 and the decedent had contributed three-fourths of the purchase price of the contract, the amount includible is $15,000 (¾ × $20,000).

Except as provided under **Annuities Under Approved Plans**, contributions made by the decedent's employer to the purchase price of the contract or agreement are considered made by the decedent if they were made by the employer because of the decedent's employment. For more information, see section 2039.

Definitions

Annuity. The term "annuity" includes one or more payments extending over any period of time. The payments may be equal or unequal, conditional or unconditional, periodic or sporadic.

Examples. The following are examples of contracts (but not necessarily the only forms of contracts) for annuities that must be included in the gross estate.

1. A contract under which the decedent immediately before death was receiving or was entitled to receive, for the duration of life, an annuity with payments to continue after death to a designated beneficiary, if surviving the decedent.

2. A contract under which the decedent immediately before death was receiving or was entitled to receive, together with another person, an annuity payable to the decedent and the other person for their joint lives, with payments to continue to the survivor following the death of either.

3. A contract or agreement entered into by the decedent and employer under which the decedent immediately before death and following retirement was receiving, or was entitled to receive, an annuity payable to the decedent for life and after the decedent's death to a designated beneficiary, whether the payments after the decedent's death are fixed by the contract or subject to an option or election exercised or exercisable by the decedent. However, see **Annuities Under Approved Plans**, below.

4. A contract or agreement entered into by the decedent and the decedent's employer under which at the decedent's death, before retirement, or before the expiration of a stated period of time, an annuity was payable to a designated beneficiary, if surviving the decedent. However, see **Annuities Under Approved Plans**, below.

5. A contract or agreement under which the decedent immediately before death was receiving, or was entitled to receive, an annuity for a stated period of time, with the annuity to continue to a designated beneficiary, surviving the decedent, upon the decedent's death and before the expiration of that period of time.

6. An annuity contract or other arrangement providing for a series of substantially equal periodic payments to be made to a beneficiary for life or over a period of at least 36 months after the date of the

decedent's death under an individual retirement account, annuity, or bond as described in section 2039(e) (before its repeal by P.L. 98-369).

Payable to the decedent. An annuity or other payment was payable to the decedent if, at the time of death, the decedent was in fact receiving an annuity or other payment, with or without an enforceable right to have the payments continued.

Right to receive an annuity. The decedent had the right to receive an annuity or other payment if, immediately before death, the decedent had an enforceable right to receive payments at some time in the future, whether or not at the time of death the decedent had a present right to receive payments.

Annuities Under Approved Plans

The following rules relate to whether part or all of an otherwise includible annuity may be excluded. These rules have been repealed and apply only if the decedent either:

1. On December 31, 1984, was both a participant in the plan and in pay status (i.e., had received at least one benefit payment on or before December 31, 1984), and had irrevocably elected the form of the benefit before July 18, 1984; or

2. Had separated from service before January 1, 1985, and did not change the form of benefit before death.

The amount excluded cannot exceed $100,000 unless either of the following conditions is met:

1. On December 31, 1982, the decedent was both a participant in the plan and in pay status (i.e., had received at least one benefit payment on or before December 31, 1982), and the decedent irrevocably elected the form of the benefit before January 1, 1983; or

2. The decedent separated from service before January 1, 1983, and did not change the form of benefit before death.

Approved Plans

Approved plans may be separated into two categories:

- Pension, profit-sharing, stock bonus, and other similar plans, and

- Individual retirement arrangements (IRAs), and retirement bonds

Different exclusion rules apply to the two categories of plans.

Pension, etc., plans. The following plans are approved plans for the exclusion rules:

a. An employees' trust (or under a contract purchased by an employees' trust) forming part of a pension, stock bonus, or profit-sharing plan that met all the requirements of section 401(a), either at the time of the decedent's separation from employment (whether by death or otherwise) or at the time of the termination of the plan (if earlier).

b. A retirement annuity contract purchased by the employer (but not by an employees' trust) under a plan that, at the time of the decedent's separation from employment (by death or otherwise), or at the time of the termination of the plan (if earlier), was a plan described in section 403(a).

c. A retirement annuity contract purchased for an employee by an employer that is an organization referred to in section 170(b)(1)(A)(ii) or (vi), or that is a religious organization (other than a trust), and that is exempt from tax under section 501(a).

d. Chapter 73 of Title 10 of the United States Code.

e. A bond purchase plan described in section 405 (before its repeal by P.L. 98-369, effective for obligations issued after December 31, 1983.)

Exclusion rules for pension, etc., plans. If an annuity under an "approved plan" described in a - e above is receivable by a beneficiary other than the executor and the decedent made no contributions under the plan toward the cost, no part of the value of the annuity, subject to the $100,000 limitation (if applicable), is includible in the gross estate.

If the decedent made a contribution under a plan described in a - e above toward the cost, include in the gross estate on this schedule that proportion of the value of the annuity which the amount of the decedent's contribution under the plan bears to the total amount of all contributions under the plan. The remaining value of the annuity is excludable from the gross estate subject to the $100,000 limitation (if applicable). For the rules to determine whether the decedent made contributions to the plan, see Regulations section 20.2039.

IRAs and retirement bonds. The following plans are approved plans for the exclusion rules:

f. An individual retirement account described in section 408(a);

g. An individual retirement annuity described in section 408(b);

h. A retirement bond described in section 409(a) (before its repeal by P.L. 98-369).

Exclusion rules for IRAs and retirement bonds. These plans are approved plans only if they provide for a series of substantially equal periodic payments made to a beneficiary for life, or over a period of at least 36 months after the date of the decedent's death.

Subject to the $100,000 limitation, if applicable, if an annuity under a "plan" described in f - h above is receivable by a beneficiary other than the executor, the entire value of the annuity is excludable from the gross estate even if the decedent made a contribution under the plan.

However, if any payment to or for an account or annuity described in paragraph f, g, or h above was not allowable as an income tax deduction under section 219 (and was not a rollover contribution as described in section 2039(e) before its repeal by P.L. 98-369), include in the gross estate on this schedule that proportion of the value of the annuity which the amount not allowable as a deduction under section 219 and not a rollover contribution bears to the total amount paid to or for such account or annuity. For more information, see Regulations section 20.2039-5.

Rules applicable to all approved plans. The following rules apply to all approved plans described in paragraphs a - h above.

If any part of an annuity under a "plan" described in a - h above is receivable by the executor, it is generally includible in the gross estate on this schedule to the extent that it is receivable by the executor in that capacity. In general, the annuity is receivable by the executor if it is to be paid to the executor or if there is an agreement (expressed or implied) that it will be applied by the beneficiary for the benefit of the estate (such as in discharge of the estate's liability for death taxes or debts of the decedent, etc.) or that its distribution will be governed to any extent by the terms of the decedent's will or the laws of descent and distribution.

If data available to you does not indicate whether the plan satisfies the requirements of section 401(a), 403(a), 408(a), 408(b), or 409(a), you may obtain that information from the District Director of Internal Revenue for the

FIGURE A.1 *Continued*

district where the employer's principal place of business is located.

Line A — Lump Sum Distribution Election

The election pertaining to the lump sum distribution from qualified plans (approved plans) excludes from the gross estate all or part of the lump sum distribution that would otherwise be includible. When the recipient makes the election to take a lump sum distribution and include it in his or her income tax, the amount excluded from the gross estate is the portion attributable to the employer contributions. The portion, if any, attributable to the employee-decedent's contributions is always includible. The actual election is made by the recipient of the distribution by taking the lump sum distribution and by treating it as taxable on his or her income tax return as described in Regulations section 20.2039-4(d). The election is irrevocable. However, you may not compute the gross estate in accordance with this election unless you check "Yes" to line A and attach the name, address, and identifying number of the recipients of the lump sum distributions. See Regulations section 20.2039-4.

How To Complete Schedule I

In describing an annuity, give the name and address of the grantor of the annuity. Specify if the annuity is under an approved plan.

IF . . .	THEN . . .
the annuity is under an approved plan,	state the ratio of the decedent's contribution to the total purchase price of the annuity.
the decedent was employed at the time of death and an annuity as described in Definitions, Annuity, Example 4, on page 15, became payable to any beneficiary because the beneficiary survived the decedent,	state the ratio of the decedent's contribution to the total purchase price of the annuity.
an annuity under an individual retirement account or annuity became payable to any beneficiary because that beneficiary survived the decedent and is payable to the beneficiary for life or for at least 36 months following the decedent's death,	state the ratio of the amount paid for the individual retirement account or annuity that was not allowable as an income tax deduction under section 219 (other than a rollover contribution) to the total amount paid for the account or annuity.
the annuity is payable out of a trust or other fund,	the description should be sufficiently complete to fully identify it.
the annuity is payable for a term of years,	include the duration of the term and the date on which it began.
the annuity is payable for the life of a person other than the decedent,	include the date of birth of that person.
the annuity is wholly or partially excluded from the gross estate,	enter the amount excluded under "Description" and explain how you computed the exclusion.

Instructions for Schedule J. Funeral Expenses and Expenses Incurred in Administering Property Subject to Claims

See the reverse side of Schedule J on Form 706.

Instructions for Schedule K. Debts of the Decedent and Mortgages and Liens

You must complete and attach Schedule K if you claimed deductions on either item 14 or item 15 of Part 5, Recapitulation.

Income vs. estate tax deduction. Taxes, interest, and business expenses accrued at the date of the decedent's death are deductible both on Schedule K and as deductions in respect of the decedent on the income tax return of the estate.

If you choose to deduct medical expenses of the decedent only on the estate tax return, they are fully deductible as claims against the estate. If, however, they are claimed on the decedent's final income tax return under section 213(c), they may not also be claimed on the estate tax return. In this case, you also may not deduct on the estate tax return any amounts that were not deductible on the income tax return because of the percentage limitations.

Debts of the Decedent

List under "Debts of the Decedent" only valid debts the decedent owed at the time of death. List any indebtedness secured by a mortgage or other lien on property of the gross estate under the heading "Mortgages and Liens." If the amount of the debt is disputed or the subject of litigation, deduct only the amount the estate concedes to be a valid claim. Enter the amount in contest in the column provided.

Generally, if the claim against the estate is based on a promise or agreement, the deduction is limited to the extent that the liability was contracted bona fide and for an adequate and full consideration in money or money's worth. However, any enforceable claim based on a promise or agreement of the decedent to make a contribution or gift (such as a pledge or a subscription) to or for the use of a charitable, public, religious, etc., organization is deductible to the extent that the deduction would be allowed as a bequest under the statute that applies.

Certain claims of a former spouse against the estate based on the relinquishment of marital rights are deductible on Schedule K. For these claims to be deductible, all of the following conditions must be met:
• The decedent and the decedent's spouse must have entered into a written agreement relative to their marital and property rights.
• The decedent and the spouse must have been divorced before the decedent's death and the divorce must have occurred within the 3-year period beginning on the date 1 year before the agreement was entered into. It is not required that the agreement be approved by the divorce decree.
• The property or interest transferred under the agreement must be transferred to the decedent's spouse in settlement of the spouse's marital rights.

You may not deduct a claim made against the estate by a remainderman relating to section 2044 property. Section 2044 property is described in the instructions to line 6 of Part 4, General Information.

Include in this schedule notes unsecured by mortgage or other lien and give full details, including name of payee, face and unpaid balance, date and term of note, interest rate, and date to which interest was paid before death. Include the exact nature of the claim as well as the name of the creditor. If the claim is for services performed over a period of time, state the period covered by the claim. Example: Edison Electric Illuminating Co., for electric service during December 1998, $150.

If the amount of the claim is the unpaid balance due on a contract for the purchase of any property included in the gross estate, indicate the schedule and item number where you reported the property. If the claim represents a joint and separate liability, give full facts and explain the financial responsibility of the co-obligor.

Property and income taxes. The deduction for property taxes is limited to the taxes accrued before the date of the decedent's death. Federal taxes on income received during the decedent's lifetime are deductible, but taxes on income received after death are not deductible.

Keep all vouchers or original records for inspection by the IRS.

Allowable death taxes. If you elect to take a deduction under section 2053(d) rather than a credit under section 2011 or section 2014, the deduction is subject to the limitations described in section 2053(d) and its regulations. If you have difficulty figuring the deduction, you may request a computation of it. Send your request within a reasonable amount of time before the due date of the return to the Commissioner of Internal Revenue, Washington, DC 20224. Attach to your request a copy of the will and relevant documents, a statement showing the distribution of the estate under the decedent's will, and a computation of the state or foreign death tax showing the amount payable by charity.

Mortgages and Liens

List under "Mortgages and Liens" only obligations secured by mortgages or other liens on property that you included in the gross estate at its full value or at a value that was undiminished by the amount of the mortgage or lien. If the debt is enforceable against other property of the estate not subject to the mortgage or lien, or if the decedent was personally liable for the debt, you must include the full value of the property subject to the mortgage or lien in the gross estate under the appropriate schedule and may deduct the mortgage or lien on the property on this schedule.

However, if the decedent's estate is not liable, include in the gross estate only the value of the equity of redemption (or the value of the property less the amount of the debt), and do not deduct any portion of the indebtedness on this schedule.

Notes and other obligations secured by the deposit of collateral, such as stocks, bonds, etc., also should be listed under "Mortgages and Liens."

Description

Include under the "Description" column the particular schedule and item number where the property subject to the mortgage or lien is reported in the gross estate.

· Include the name and address of the mortgagee, payee, or obligee, and the date and term of the mortgage, note, or other agreement by which the debt was established. Also include the face amount, the unpaid balance, the rate of interest, and date to which the interest was paid before the decedent's death.

FIGURE A.1 *Continued*

Instructions for Schedule L. Net Losses During Administration and Expenses Incurred in Administering Property Not Subject to Claims

You must complete Schedule L and file it with the return if you claim deductions on either item 18 or item 19 of Part 5, Recapitulation.

Net Losses During Administration

You may deduct only those losses from thefts, fires, storms, shipwrecks, or other casualties that occurred during the settlement of the estate. You may deduct only the amount not reimbursed by insurance or otherwise.

Describe in detail the loss sustained and the cause. If you received insurance or other compensation for the loss, state the amount collected. Identify the property for which you are claiming the loss by indicating the particular schedule and item number where the property is included in the gross estate.

If you elect alternate valuation, do not deduct the amount by which you reduced the value of an item to include it in the gross estate.

Do not deduct losses claimed as a deduction on a Federal income tax return or depreciation in the value of securities or other property.

Expenses Incurred in Administering Property Not Subject to Claims

You may deduct expenses incurred in administering property that is included in the gross estate but that is not subject to claims. You may only deduct these expenses if they were paid before the section 6501 period of limitations for assessment expired.

The expenses deductible on this schedule are usually expenses incurred in the administration of a trust established by the decedent before death. They may also be incurred in the collection of other assets or the transfer or clearance of title to other property included in the decedent's gross estate for estate tax purposes, but not included in the decedent's probate estate.

The expenses deductible on this schedule are limited to those that are the result of settling the decedent's interest in the property or of vesting good title to the property in the beneficiaries. Expenses incurred on behalf of the transferees (except those described above) are not deductible. Examples of deductible and nondeductible expenses are provided in Regulations section 20.2053-8.

List the names and addresses of the persons to whom each expense was payable and the nature of the expense. Identify the property for which the expense was incurred by indicating the schedule and item number where the property is included in the gross estate. If you do not know the exact amount of the expense, you may deduct an estimate, provided that the amount may be verified with reasonable certainty and will be paid before the period of limitations for assessment (referred to above) expires. Keep all vouchers and receipts for inspection by the Internal Revenue Service.

Instructions for Schedule M. Bequests, etc., to Surviving Spouse (Marital Deduction)

See the Form 706 itself for these instructions.

Instructions for Schedule O. Charitable, Public, and Similar Gifts and Bequests

General

You must complete Schedule O and file it with the return if you claim a deduction on item 21 of the Recapitulation.

You can claim the charitable deduction allowed under section 2055 for the value of property in the decedent's gross estate that was transferred by the decedent during life or by will to or for the use of any of the following:

- The United States, a state, a political subdivision of a state, or the District of Columbia, for exclusively public purposes;

- Any corporation or association organized and operated exclusively for religious, charitable, scientific, literary, or educational purposes, including the encouragement of art, or to foster national or international amateur sports competition (but only if none of its activities involve providing athletic facilities or equipment, unless the organization is a qualified amateur sports organization) and the prevention of cruelty to children and animals, as long as no part of the net earnings benefits any private individual and no substantial activity is undertaken to carry on propaganda, or otherwise attempt to influence legislation or participate in any political campaign on behalf of any candidate for public office;

- A trustee or a fraternal society, order or association operating under the lodge system, if the transferred property is to be used exclusively for religious, charitable, scientific, literary, or educational purposes, or for the prevention of cruelty to children or animals, and no substantial activity is undertaken to carry on propaganda or otherwise attempt to influence legislation, or participate in any political campaign on behalf of any candidate for public office;

- Any veterans organization incorporated by an Act of Congress or any of its departments, local chapters, or posts, for which none of the net earnings benefits any private individual; or

- A foreign government or its political subdivision when the use of such property is limited exclusively to charitable purposes.

For this purpose, certain Indian tribal governments are treated as states and transfers to them qualify as deductible charitable contributions. See Rev. Proc. 83-87, 1983-2 C.B. 606, as modified and supplemented by subsequent Revenue Procedures, for a list of qualifying Indian tribal governments.

You may also claim a charitable contribution deduction for a qualifying conservation easement granted after the decedent's death under the provisions of section 2031(c)(9).

The charitable deduction is allowed for amounts that are transferred to charitable organizations as a result of either a qualified disclaimer (see Line 2, Qualified Disclaimer, below) or the complete termination of a power to consume, invade, or appropriate property for the benefit of an individual. It does not matter whether termination occurs because of the death of the individual or in any other way. The

termination must occur within the period of time (including extensions) for filing the decedent's estate tax return and before the power has been exercised.

The deduction is limited to the amount actually available for charitable uses. Therefore, if under the terms of a will or the provisions of local law, or for any other reason, the Federal estate tax, the Federal GST tax, or any other estate, GST, succession, legacy, or inheritance tax is payable in whole or in part out of any bequest, legacy, or devise that would otherwise be allowed as a charitable deduction, the amount you may deduct is the amount of the bequest, legacy, or devise reduced by the total amount of the taxes.

If you elected to make installment payments of the estate tax, and the interest is payable out of property transferred to charity, you must reduce the charitable deduction by an estimate of the maximum amount of interest that will be paid on the deferred tax.

For split-interest trusts (or pooled income funds) enter in the "Amount" column the amount treated as passing to the charity. Do not enter the entire amount that passes to the trust (fund).

If you are deducting the value of the residue or a part of the residue passing to charity under the decedent's will, attach a copy of the computation showing how you determined the value, including any reduction for the taxes described above.

Also include:

1. A statement that shows the values of all specific and general legacies or devises for both charitable and noncharitable uses. For each legacy or devise, indicate the paragraph or section of the decedent's will or codicil that applies. (If legacies are made to each member of a class (e.g., $1,000 to each of the decedent's employees), show only the number of each class and the total value of property they received.)

2. The date of birth of all life tenants or annuitants, the length of whose lives may affect the value of the interest passing to charity under the decedent's will.

3. A statement showing the value of all property that is included in the decedent's gross estate but does not pass under the will, such as transfers, jointly owned property that passed to the survivor on decedent's death, and insurance payable to specific beneficiaries.

4. Any other important information such as that relating to any claim, not arising under the will, to any part of the estate (e.g., a spouse claiming dower or curtesy, or similar rights).

Line 2 — Qualified Disclaimer

The charitable deduction is allowed for amounts that are transferred to charitable organizations as a result of a qualified disclaimer. To be a qualified disclaimer, a refusal to accept an interest in property must meet the conditions of section 2518. These are explained in Regulations sections 25.2518-1 through 25.2518-3. If property passes to a charitable beneficiary as the result of a qualified disclaimer, check the "Yes" box on line 2 and attach a copy of the written disclaimer required by section 2518(b).

Attachments

If the charitable transfer was made by will, attach a certified copy of the order admitting the will to probate, in addition to the copy of the will. If the charitable transfer was made by any other written instrument, attach a copy. If the instrument is of record, the copy should be certified; if not, the copy should be verified.

Value

The valuation dates used in determining the value of the gross estate apply also on Schedule O.

FIGURE A.1 *Continued*

351

Instructions for Schedule P. Credit for Foreign Death Taxes

General

If you claim a credit on line 18 of Part 2, Tax Computation, you must complete Schedule P and file it with the return. You must attach Form(s) 706-CE, Certificate of Payment of Foreign Death Tax, to support any credit you claim.

If the foreign government refuses to certify Form 706-CE, you must file it directly with the District Director as instructed on the Form 706-CE. See Form 706-CE for instructions on how to complete the form and for a description of the items that must be attached to the form when the foreign government refuses to certify it.

The credit for foreign death taxes is allowable only if the decedent was a citizen or resident of the United States. However, see section 2053(d) and the related regulations for exceptions and limitations if the executor has elected, in certain cases, to deduct these taxes from the value of the gross estate. For a resident, not a citizen, who was a citizen or subject of a foreign country for which the President has issued a proclamation under section 2014(h), the credit is allowable only if the country of which the decedent was a national allows a similar credit to decedents who were U.S. citizens residing in that country.

The credit is authorized either by statute or by treaty. If a credit is authorized by a treaty, whichever of the following is the most beneficial to the estate is allowed: (a) the credit computed under the treaty; (b) the credit computed under the statute; or (c) the credit computed under the treaty, plus the credit computed under the statute for death taxes paid to each political subdivision or possession of the treaty country that are not directly or indirectly creditable under the treaty. Under the statute, the credit is authorized for all death taxes (national and local) imposed in the foreign country. Whether local taxes are the basis for a credit under a treaty depends upon the provisions of the particular treaty.

If a credit for death taxes paid in more than one foreign country is allowable, a separate computation of the credit must be made for each foreign country. The copies of Schedule P on which the additional computations are made should be attached to the copy of Schedule P provided in the return.

The total credit allowable in respect to any property, whether subjected to tax by one or more than one foreign country, is limited to the amount of the Federal estate tax attributable to the property. The anticipated amount of the credit may be computed on the return, but the credit cannot finally be allowed until the foreign tax has been paid and a Form 706-CE evidencing payment is filed. Section 2014(g) provides that for credits for foreign death taxes, each U.S. possession is deemed a foreign country.

Convert death taxes paid to the foreign country into U.S. dollars by using the rate of exchange in effect at the time each payment of foreign tax is made.

If a credit is claimed for any foreign death tax that is later recovered, see Regulations section 20.2016-1 for the notice required within 30 days.

Limitation Period

The credit for foreign death taxes is limited to those taxes that actually were paid and for which a credit was claimed within the later of the 4 years after the filing of the estate tax return, or before the date of expiration of any extension of time for payment of the Federal estate tax, or 60 days after a final decision of the Tax Court on a timely filed petition for a redetermination of a deficiency.

Credit Under the Statute

For the credit allowed by the statute, the question of whether particular property is situated in the foreign country imposing the tax is determined by the same principles that would apply in determining whether similar property of a nonresident not a U.S. citizen is situated within the United States for purposes of the Federal estate tax. See the instructions for Form 706-NA.

Computation of Credit Under the Statute

Item 1. Enter the amount of the estate, inheritance, legacy, and succession taxes paid to the foreign country and its possessions or political subdivisions, attributable to property that is (a) situated in that country, (b) subjected to these taxes, and (c) included in the gross estate. The amount entered at item 1 should not include any tax paid to the foreign country with respect to property not situated in that country and should not include any tax paid to the foreign country with respect to property not included in the gross estate. If only a part of the property subjected to foreign taxes is both situated in the foreign country and included in the gross estate, it will be necessary to determine the portion of the taxes attributable to that part of the property. Also attach the computation of the amount entered at item 1.

Item 2. Enter the value of the gross estate less the total of the deductions on items 20 and 21 of Part 5, Recapitulation.

Item 3. Enter the value of the property situated in the foreign country that is subjected to the foreign taxes and included in the gross estate, less those portions of the deductions taken on Schedules M and O that are attributable to the property.

Item 4. Subtract line 17 of Part 2, Tax Computation, Form 706 from line 16, Part 2, Form 706, and enter the balance at item 4 of Schedule P.

Credit Under Treaties

If you are reporting any items on this return based on the provisions of a death tax treaty, you may have to attach a statement to this return disclosing the return position that is treaty based. See Regulations section 301.6114-1 for details.

In general. If the provisions of a treaty apply to the estate of a U.S. citizen or resident, a credit is authorized for payment of the foreign death tax or taxes specified in the treaty. Treaties with death tax conventions are in effect with the following countries: Australia, Austria, Canada, Denmark, Finland, France, Germany, Greece, Ireland, Italy, Japan, Netherlands, Norway, Republic of South Africa, Sweden, Switzerland, and the United Kingdom.

A credit claimed under a treaty is in general computed on Schedule P in the same manner as the credit is computed under the statute with the following principal exceptions:

- The situs rules contained in the treaty apply in determining whether property was situated in a foreign country;

- The credit may be allowed only for payment of the death tax or taxes specified in the treaty (but see the instructions above for credit under the statute for death taxes paid to each political subdivision or possession of the treaty country that are not directly or indirectly creditable under the treaty);

- If specifically provided, the credit is proportionately shared for the tax applicable to property situated outside both countries, or that was deemed in some instances situated within both countries; and

- The amount entered at item 4 of Schedule P is the amount shown on line 16 of Part 2, Tax Computation, less the total of the amounts on lines 17 and 19 of the Tax Computation. (If a credit is claimed for tax on prior transfers, it will be necessary to complete Schedule Q before completing Schedule P.) For examples of computation of credits under the treaties, see the applicable regulations.

Computation of credit in cases where property is situated outside both countries or deemed situated within both countries. See the appropriate treaty for details.

Instructions for Schedule Q. Credit for Tax on Prior Transfers

General

You must complete Schedule Q and file it with the return if you claim a credit on line 19 of Part 2, Tax Computation.

The term "transferee" means the decedent for whose estate this return is filed. If the transferee received property from a transferor who died within 10 years before, or 2 years after, the transferee, a credit is allowable on this return for all or part of the Federal estate tax paid by the transferor's estate with respect to the transfer. There is no requirement that the property be identified in the estate of the transferee or that it exist on the date of the transferee's death. It is sufficient for the allowance of the credit that the transfer of the property was subjected to Federal estate tax in the estate of the transferor and that the specified period of time has not elapsed. A credit may be allowed with respect to property received as the result of the exercise or nonexercise of a power of appointment when the property is included in the gross estate of the donee of the power.

If the transferee was the transferor's surviving spouse, no credit is allowed for property received from the transferor to the extent that a marital deduction was allowed to the transferor's estate for the property. There is no credit for tax on prior transfers for Federal gift taxes paid in connection with the transfer of the property to the transferee.

If you are claiming a credit for tax on prior transfers on Form 706-NA, you should first complete and attach the Recapitulation from Form 706 before computing the credit on Schedule Q from Form 706.

Section 2056(d)(3) contains specific rules for allowing a credit for certain transfers to a spouse who was not a U.S. citizen where the property passed outright to the spouse, or to a "qualified domestic trust."

Property

The term "property" includes any interest (legal or equitable) of which the transferee received the beneficial ownership. The transferee is considered the beneficial owner of property over which the transferee received a general power of appointment. Property does not include interests to which the transferee received only a bare legal title, such as that of a trustee. Neither does it include an interest in property over which the transferee received a power of appointment that is not a general power of appointment. In addition to interests in which the transferee received the complete ownership, the credit may be allowed for annuities, life estates, terms for years, remainder interests (whether contingent or vested), and any other interest that is less than

FIGURE A.1 *Continued*

the complete ownership of the property, to the extent that the transferee became the beneficial owner of the interest.

Maximum Amount of the Credit

The maximum amount of the credit is the smaller of:

1. The amount of the estate tax of the transferor's estate attributable to the transferred property, or

2. The amount by which (a) an estate tax on the transferee's estate determined without the credit for tax on prior transfers, exceeds (b) an estate tax on the transferee's estate determined by excluding from the gross estate the net value of the transfer.

If credit for a particular foreign death tax may be taken under either the statute or a death duty convention, and on this return the credit actually is taken under the convention, then no credit for that foreign death tax may be taken into consideration in computing estate tax (a) or estate tax (b) above.

Percent Allowable

Where transferee predeceased the transferor. If not more than 2 years elapsed between the dates of death, the credit allowed is 100% of the maximum amount. If more than 2 years elapsed between the dates of death, no credit is allowed.

Where transferor predeceased the transferee. The percent of the maximum amount that is allowed as a credit depends on the number of years that elapsed between dates of death. It is determined using the following table:

Period of Time Exceeding	Not Exceeding	Percent Allowable
- - -	2 years	100
2 years	4 years	80
4 years	6 years	60
6 years	8 years	40
8 years	10 years	20
10 years	- - -	none

How To Compute the Credit

A Worksheet for Schedule Q is provided at the end of these instructions to allow you to compute the limits before completing Schedule Q. Transfer the appropriate amounts from the worksheet to Schedule Q as indicated on the schedule. You do not need to file the worksheet with your Form 706, but should keep it for your records.

Cases involving transfers from two or more transferors. Part I of the worksheet and Schedule Q enable you to compute the credit for as many as three transferors. The number of transferors is irrelevant to Part I of the worksheet. If you are computing the credit for more than three transferors, use more than one worksheet and Schedule Q, Part I, and combine the totals for the appropriate lines.

Section 2032A additional tax. If the transferor's estate elected special use valuation and the additional estate tax of section 2032A(c) was imposed at any time up to 2 years after the death of the decedent for whom you are filing this return, check the box on Schedule Q. On lines 1 and 9 of the worksheet, include the property subject to the additional estate tax at its FMV rather than its special use value. On line 10 of the worksheet, include the additional estate tax paid as a Federal estate tax paid.

How To Complete the Schedule Q Worksheet

Most of the information to complete Part I of the worksheet should be obtained from the transferor's Form 706.

Line 5. Enter on line 5 the applicable marital deduction claimed for the transferor's estate (from the transferor's Form 706).

Lines 10 - 18. Enter on these lines the appropriate taxes paid by the transferor's estate.

If the transferor's estate elected to pay the Federal estate tax in installments, enter on line 10 only the total of the installments that have actually been paid at the time you file this Form 706. See Rev. Rul. 83-15, 1983-1 C.B. 224, for more details. Do not include as estate tax any tax attributable to section 4980A, before its repeal by the Taxpayer Relief Act of 1997.

Line 21. Add lines 13, 15, 17, and 18 of Part 2, Tax Computation, of this Form 706 and subtract this total from line 10 of the Tax Computation. Enter the result on line 21 of the worksheet.

Line 26. If you computed the marital deduction on this Form 706 using the rules that were in effect before the Economic Recovery Tax Act of 1981 (as described in the instructions to line 14 of Part 4 of General Information), enter on line 26 the lesser of:

• The marital deduction you claimed on line 20 of Part 5 of the Recapitulation; or
• 50% of the "reduced adjusted gross estate."

If you computed the marital deduction using the unlimited marital deduction in effect for decedents dying after 1981, for purposes of determining the marital deduction for the reduced gross estate, see Rev. Rul. 90-2, 1990-1 C.B. 170. To determine the "reduced adjusted gross estate," subtract the amount on line 25 of the Schedule Q worksheet from the amount on line 24 of the worksheet. If community property is included in the amount on line 24 of the worksheet, compute the reduced adjusted gross estate using the rules of Regulations section 20.2056(c)-2 and Rev. Rul. 76-311, 1976-2 C.B. 261.

Instructions for Schedules R and R-1. Generation-Skipping Transfer Tax

Introduction and Overview

Schedule R is used to compute the generation-skipping transfer (GST) tax that is payable by the estate. Schedule R-1 (Form 706) is used to compute the GST tax that is payable by certain trusts that are includible in the gross estate.

The GST tax that is to be reported on Form 706 is imposed only on "direct skips occurring at death." Unlike the estate tax, which is imposed on the value of the entire taxable estate regardless of who receives it, the GST tax is imposed only on the value of interests in property, wherever located, that actually pass to certain transferees, who are referred to as "skip persons."

For purposes of Form 706, the property interests transferred must be includible in the gross estate before they are subject to the GST tax. Therefore, the first step in computing the GST tax liability is to determine the property interests includible in the gross estate by completing Schedules A through I of Form 706.

The second step is to determine who the skip persons are. To do this, assign each transferee to a generation and determine whether each transferee is a "natural person" or a "trust" for GST purposes.

The third step is to determine which skip persons are transferees of "interests in property." If the skip person is a natural person, anything transferred is an interest in property. If the skip person is a trust, make this determination using the rules under Interest in property below. These first three steps are described

in detail under the main heading, Determining Which Transfers Are Direct Skips.

The fourth step is to determine whether to enter the transfer on Schedule R or on Schedule R-1. See the rules under the main heading, Dividing Direct Skips Between Schedules R and R-1.

The fifth step is to complete Schedules R and R-1 using the How To Complete instructions on page 21, for each schedule.

Determining Which Transfers Are Direct Skips

Effective dates. The rules below apply only for the purpose of determining if a transfer is a direct skip that should be reported on Schedule R or R-1 of Form 706.

In general. The GST tax is effective for the estates of decedents dying after October 22, 1986.

Irrevocable trusts. The GST tax will not apply to any transfer under a trust that was irrevocable on September 25, 1985, but only to the extent that the transfer was not made out of corpus added to the trust after September 25, 1985. An addition to the corpus after that date will cause a proportionate part of future income and appreciation to be subject to the GST tax. For more information, see Regulations section 26.2601-1(b)(1)(ii).

Mental disability. If, on October 22, 1986, the decedent was under a mental disability to change the disposition of his or her property and did not regain the competence to dispose of property before death, the GST tax will not apply to any property included in the gross estate (other than property transferred on behalf of the decedent during life and after October 21, 1986). The GST tax will also not apply to any transfer under a trust to the extent that the trust consists of property included in the gross estate (other than property transferred on behalf of the decedent during life and after October 21, 1986).

The term "mental disability" means the decedent's mental incompetence to execute an instrument governing the disposition of his or her property, whether or not there has been an adjudication of incompetence and whether or not there has been an appointment of any other person charged with the care of the person or property of the transferor.

If the decedent had been adjudged mentally incompetent, a copy of the judgment or decree must be filed with this return.

If the decedent had not been adjudged mentally incompetent, the executor must file with the return a certification from a qualified physician stating that in his opinion the decedent had been mentally incompetent at all times on and after October 22, 1986, and that the decedent had not regained the competence to modify or revoke the terms of the trust or will prior to his death or a statement as to why no such certification may be obtained from a physician.

Direct skip. The GST tax reported on Form 706 and Schedule R-1 (Form 706) is imposed only on direct skips. For purposes of Form 706, a direct skip is a transfer that is:

1. Subject to the estate tax,
2. Of an interest in property, and
3. To a skip person.

All three requirements must be met before the transfer is subject to the GST tax. A transfer is subject to the estate tax if you are required to list it on any of Schedules A through I of Form 706. To determine if a transfer is of an interest in property and to a skip person, you must first determine if the transferee is a natural person or a trust as defined below.

FIGURE A.1 Continued

Trust. For purposes of the GST tax, a trust includes not only an explicit trust (as defined in Special rule for trusts other than explicit trusts below), but also any other arrangement (other than an estate) which, although not explicitly a trust, has substantially the same effect as a trust. For example, a trust includes life estates with remainders, terms for years, and insurance and annuity contracts.

Substantially separate and independent shares of different beneficiaries in a trust are treated as separate trusts.

Interest in property. If a transfer is made to a natural person, it is always considered a transfer of an interest in property for purposes of the GST tax.

If a transfer is made to a trust, a person will have an interest in the property transferred to the trust if that person either has a present right to receive income or corpus from the trust (such as an income interest for life) or is a permissible current recipient of income or corpus from the trust (e.g., may receive income or corpus at the discretion of the trustee).

Skip person. A transferee who is a natural person is a skip person if that transferee is assigned to a generation that is two or more generations below the generation assignment of the decedent. See **Determining the generation of a transferee**, below.

A transferee who is a trust is a skip person if all the interests in the property (as defined above) transferred to the trust are held by skip persons. Thus, whenever a non-skip person has an interest in a trust, the trust will not be a skip person even though a skip person also has an interest in the trust.

A trust will also be a skip person if there are no interests in the property transferred to the trust held by any person, and future distributions or terminations from the trust can be made only to skip persons.

Non-skip person. A non-skip person is any transferee who is not a skip person.

Determining the generation of a transferee. Generally, a generation is determined along family lines as follows:

1. Where the beneficiary is a lineal descendant of a grandparent of the decedent (e.g., the decedent's cousin, niece, nephew, etc.), the number of generations between the decedent and the beneficiary is determined by subtracting the number of generations between the grandparent and the decedent from the number of generations between the grandparent and the beneficiary.

2. Where the beneficiary is a lineal descendant of a grandparent of a spouse (or former spouse) of the decedent, the number of generations between the decedent and the beneficiary is determined by subtracting the number of generations between the grandparent and the spouse (or former spouse) from the number of generations between the grandparent and the beneficiary.

3. A person who at any time was married to a person described in 1 or 2 above is assigned to the generation of that person. A person who at any time was married to the decedent is assigned to the decedent's generation.

4. A relationship by adoption or half-blood is treated as a relationship by whole-blood.

5. A person who is not assigned to a generation according to 1, 2, 3, or 4 above is assigned to a generation based on his or her birth date, as follows:

a. A person who was born not more than 12$^1/_2$ years after the decedent is in the decedent's generation.

b. A person born more than 12$^1/_2$ years, but not more than 37$^1/_2$ years, after the decedent is in the first generation younger than the decedent.

c. A similar rule applies for a new generation every 25 years.

If more than one of the rules for assigning generations applies to a transferee, that transferee is generally assigned to the youngest of the generations that would apply.

If an estate, trust, partnership, corporation, or other entity (other than certain charitable organizations and trusts described in sections 511(a)(2) and 511(b)(2)) is a transferee, then each person who indirectly receives the property interests through the entity is treated as a transferee and is assigned to a generation as explained in the above rules. However, this look-through rule does not apply for the purpose of determining whether a transfer to a trust is a direct skip.

Generation assignment where intervening parent is dead. A special rule may apply in the case of the death of a parent of the transferee. For terminations, distributions, and transfers after December 31, 1997, the existing rule that applied to grandchildren of the decedent has been extended to apply to other lineal descendants.

If property is transferred to an individual who is a descendant of a parent of the transferor, and that individual's parent (who is a lineal descendant of the parent of the transferor) is dead at the time the transfer is subject to gift or estate tax, then for purposes of generation assignment, the individual is treated as if he or she is a member of the generation that is one generation below the lower of:

• the transferor's generation, or
• the generation assignment of the youngest living ancestor of the individual, who is also a descendant of the parent of the transferor.

The same rules apply to the generation assignment of any descendant of the individual.

This rule does not apply to a transfer to an individual who is not a lineal descendant of the transferor if the transferor has any living lineal descendants.

If any transfer of property to a trust would have been a direct skip except for this generation assignment rule, then the rule also applies to transfers from the trust attributable to such property.

Charitable organizations. Charitable organizations and trusts described in sections 511(a)(2) and 511(b)(2) are assigned to the decedent's generation. Transfers to such organizations are therefore not subject to the GST tax.

Charitable remainder trusts. Transfers to or in the form of charitable remainder annuity trusts, charitable remainder unitrusts, and pooled income funds are not considered made to skip persons and, therefore, are not direct skips even if all of the life beneficiaries are skip persons.

Estate tax value. Estate tax value is the value shown on Schedules A through I of this Form 706.

Examples. The rules above can be illustrated by the following examples:

Example 1. Under the will, the decedent's house is transferred to the decedent's daughter for her life with the remainder passing to her children. This transfer is made to a "trust" even though there is no explicit trust instrument. The interest in the property transferred (the present right to use the house) is transferred to a non-skip person (the decedent's daughter). Therefore, the trust is not a skip person because there is an interest in the transferred property that is held by a non-skip person. The transfer is not a direct skip.

Example 2. The will bequeaths $100,000 to the decedent's grandchild. This transfer is a direct skip that is not made in trust and should be shown on Schedule R.

Example 3. The will establishes a trust that is required to accumulate income for 10 years and then pay its income to the decedent's grandchildren for the rest of their lives and, upon their deaths, distribute the corpus to the decedent's great-grandchildren. Because the trust has no current beneficiaries, there are no present interests in the property transferred to the trust. All of the persons to whom the trust can make future distributions (including distributions upon the termination of interests in property held in trust) are skip persons (i.e., the decedent's grandchildren and great-grandchildren). Therefore, the trust itself is a skip person and you should show the transfer on Schedule R.

Example 4. The will establishes a trust that is to pay all of its income to the decedent's grandchildren for 10 years. At the end of 10 years, the corpus is to be distributed to the decedent's children. All of the interests in this trust are held by skip persons. Therefore, the trust is a skip person and you should show this transfer on Schedule R. You should show the estate tax value of all the property transferred to the trust even though the trust has some ultimate beneficiaries who are non-skip persons.

Dividing Direct Skips Between Schedules R and R-1

Report all generation-skipping transfers on Schedule R unless the rules below specifically provide that they are to be reported on Schedule R-1.

Under section 2603(a)(2), the GST tax on direct skips from a trust (as defined for GST tax purposes above) is to be paid by the trustee and not by the estate. Schedule R-1 serves as a notification from the executor to the trustee that a GST tax is due.

For a direct skip to be reportable on Schedule R-1, the trust must be includible in the decedent's gross estate.

If the decedent was the surviving spouse life beneficiary of a marital deduction power of appointment (or QTIP) trust created by the decedent's spouse, then transfers caused by reason of the decedent's death from that trust to skip persons are direct skips required to be reported on Schedule R-1.

If a direct skip is made "from a trust" under these rules, it is reportable on Schedule R-1 even if it is also made "to a trust" rather than to an individual.

Similarly, if property in a trust (as defined for GST tax purposes on page 19) is included in the decedent's gross estate under section 2035, 2036, 2037, 2038, 2039, 2041, or 2042 and such property is, by reason of the decedent's death, transferred to skip persons, the transfers are direct skips required to be reported on Schedule R-1.

Special rule for trusts other than explicit trusts. An explicit trust is a trust as defined in Regulations section 301.7701-4(a) as "an arrangement created by a will or by an inter vivos declaration whereby trustees take title to property for the purpose of protecting or conserving it for the beneficiaries under the ordinary rules applied in chancery or probate courts." Direct skips from explicit trusts are required to be reported on Schedule R-1 regardless of their size unless the executor is also a trustee (see page 21).

Direct skips from trusts that are trusts for GST tax purposes but are not explicit trusts are to be shown on Schedule R-1 only if the total of all tentative maximum direct skips from the

FIGURE A.1 *Continued*

entity is $250,000 or more. If this total is less than $250,000, the skips should be shown on Schedule R. For purposes of the $250,000 limit, "tentative maximum direct skips" is the amount you would enter on line 5 of Schedule R-1 if you were to file that schedule.

A liquidating trust (such as a bankruptcy trust) under Regulations section 301.7701-4(d) is not treated as an explicit trust for the purposes of this special rule.

If the proceeds of a life insurance policy are includible in the gross estate and are payable to a beneficiary who is a skip person, the transfer is a direct skip from a trust that is not an explicit trust. It should be reported on Schedule R and not on Schedule R-1 even if the total of all the tentative maximum direct skips from the company is $250,000 or more. Otherwise, it should be reported on Schedule R.

Similarly, if an annuity is includible on Schedule I and its survivor benefits are payable to a beneficiary who is a skip person, then the estate tax value of the annuity should be reported as a direct skip on Schedule R-1 if the total tentative maximum direct skips from the entity paying the annuity is $250,000 or more.

Executor as trustee. If any of the executors of the decedent's estate are trustees of the trust, then all direct skips with respect to that trust must be shown on Schedule R and not on Schedule R-1 even if they would otherwise have been required to be shown on Schedule R-1. This rule applies even if the trust has other trustees who are not executors of the decedent's estate.

How To Complete Schedules R and R-1

Valuation. Enter on Schedules R and R-1 the estate tax value of the property interests subject to the direct skips. If you elected alternate valuation (section 2032) and/or special use valuation (section 2032A), you must use the alternate and/or special use values on Schedules R and R-1.

How To Complete Schedule R

Part 1 — GST exemption reconciliation. Part 1, line 6 of both Parts 2 and 3, and line 4 of Schedule R-1 are used to allocate the decedent's GST exemption. This allocation is made by filing Form 706. Once made, the allocation is irrevocable. You are not required to allocate all of the decedent's GST exemption. However, the portion of the exemption that you do not allocate will be allocated by the IRS under the deemed allocation at death rules of section 2632(c).

The amount of the GST exemption is indexed to inflation for transfers made after 1998. For generation-skipping transfers made through 1998, the amount of the exemption is $1 million. For generation-skipping transfers made in 1999, the exemption is $1,010,000. This $10,000 increase can only be allocated to transfers made during or after 1999. Likewise, any future increases can only be allocated to transfers made during or after the year of the increase. The IRS will announce future exemption amounts in an annual revenue procedure.

Special QTIP election. In the case of property for which a marital deduction is allowed to the decedent's estate under section 2056(b)(7) (QTIP election), section 2652(a)(3) allows you to treat such property for purposes of the GST tax as if the election to be treated as qualified terminable interest property had not been made.

The 2652(a)(3) election must include the value of all property in the trust for which a QTIP election was allowed under section 2056(b)(7).

If a section 2652(a)(3) election is made, then the decedent will for GST tax purposes be treated as the transferor of all the property in the trust for which a marital deduction was allowed to the decedent's estate under section 2056(b)(7). In this case, the executor of the decedent's estate may allocate part or all of the decedent's GST exemption to the property.

You make the election simply by listing qualifying property on line 9 of Part 1.

Line 2. These allocations will have been made either on Forms 709 filed by the decedent or on Notices of Allocation made by the decedent for inter vivos transfers that were not direct skips but to which the decedent allocated the GST exemption. These allocations by the decedent are irrevocable.

Line 3. Make an entry on this line if you are filing Form(s) 709 for the decedent and wish to allocate any exemption.

Lines 4, 5, and 6. These lines represent your allocation of the GST exemption to direct skips made by reason of the decedent's death. Complete Parts 2 and 3 and Schedule R-1 before completing these lines.

Line 9. Line 9 is used to allocate the remaining unused GST exemption (from line 8) and to help you compute the trust's inclusion ratio. Line 9 is a Notice of Allocation for allocating the GST exemption to trusts as to which the decedent is the transferor and from which a generation-skipping transfer could occur after the decedent's death. If line 9 is not completed, the deemed allocation at death rules will apply to allocate the decedent's remaining unused GST exemption, first to property that is the subject of a direct skip occurring at the decedent's death, and then to trusts as to which the decedent is the transferor. If you wish to avoid the application of the deemed allocation rules, you should enter on line 9 every trust (except certain trusts entered on Schedule R-1, as described below) to which you wish to allocate any part of the decedent's GST exemption. Unless you enter a trust on line 9, the unused GST exemption will be allocated to it under the deemed allocation rules.

If a trust is entered on Schedule R-1, the amount you entered on line 4 of Schedule R-1 serves as a Notice of Allocation and you need not enter the trust on line 9 unless you wish to allocate more than the Schedule R-1, line 4 amount to the trust. However, you must enter the trust on line 9 if you wish to allocate any of the unused GST exemption amount to it. Such an additional allocation would not ordinarily be appropriate in the case of a trust entered on Schedule R-1 when the trust property passes outright (rather than to another trust) at the decedent's death. However, where section 2032A property is involved it may be appropriate to allocate additional exemption amounts to the property. See the instructions for line 10.

Note: To avoid application of the deemed allocation rules, Form 706 and Schedule R should be filed to allocate the exemption to trusts that may later have taxable terminations or distributions under section 2612 even if the form is not required to be filed to report estate or GST tax.

Line 9, column C. Enter the GST exemption included on lines 2 through 6 of Part 1 of Schedule R, and discussed above, that was allocated to the trust.

Line 9, column D. Allocate the amount on line 8 of Part I of Schedule R in line 9, column D. This amount may be allocated to transfers into trusts that are not otherwise reported on Form 706. For example, the line 8 amount may be allocated to an inter vivos trust established by the decedent during his or her lifetime and not included in the gross estate. This allocation is made by identifying the trust on line 9 and making an allocation to it using column D. If the trust is not included in the gross estate, value the trust as of the date of death. You should inform the trustee of each trust listed on line 9 of the total GST exemption you allocated to the trust. The trustee will need this information to compute the GST tax on future distributions and terminations.

Line 9, column E — trust's inclusion ratio. The trustee must know the trust's inclusion ratio to figure the trust's GST tax for future distributions and terminations. You are not required to inform the trustee of the inclusion ratio and may not have enough information to compute it. Therefore, you are not required to make an entry in column E. However, column E and the worksheet below are provided to assist you in computing the inclusion ratio for the trustee if you wish to do so.

You should inform the trustee of the amount of the GST exemption you allocated to the trust. Line 9, columns C and D may be used to compute this amount for each trust.

This worksheet will compute an accurate inclusion ratio only if the decedent was the only settlor of the trust. You should use a separate worksheet for each trust (or separate share of a trust that is treated as a separate trust).

WORKSHEET (Inclusion ratio for trust):

1	Total estate and gift tax value of all of the property interests that passed to the trust	___
2	Estate taxes, state death taxes, and other charges actually recovered from the trust	___
3	GST taxes imposed on direct skips to skip persons other than this trust and borne by the property transferred to this trust	___
4	GST taxes actually recovered from this trust (from Schedule R, Part 2, line 8 or Schedule R-1, line 6)	___
5	Add lines 2 - 4	___
6	Subtract line 5 from line 1	___
7	Add columns C and D of line 9	___
8	Divide line 7 by line 6	___
9	Trust's inclusion ratio. Subtract line 8 from 1.000	___

Line 10 — Special use allocation. For skip persons who receive an interest in section 2032A special use property, you may allocate more GST exemption than the direct skip amount to reduce the additional GST tax that would be due when the interest is later disposed of or qualified use ceases. See Schedule A-1 of this Form 706 for more details about this additional GST tax.

Enter on line 10 the total additional GST exemption you are allocating to all skip persons who received any interest in section 2032A property. Attach a special use allocation schedule listing each such skip person and the amount of GST exemption allocated to that person.

If you do not allocate the GST exemption, it will be automatically allocated under the deemed allocation at death rules. To the extent any amount is not so allocated it will be automatically allocated (under regulations to be published) to the earliest disposition or cessation that is subject to the GST tax. Under certain circumstances, post-death events may cause the decedent to be treated as a transferor for purposes of Chapter 13.

Line 10 may be used to set aside an exemption amount for such an event. You must attach a schedule listing each such event and the amount of exemption allocated to that event.

Parts 2 and 3. Use Part 2 to compute the GST tax on transfers in which the property interests transferred are to bear the GST tax on the transfers. Use Part 3 to report the GST tax on transfers in which the property interests

FIGURE A.1 *Continued*

transferred do not bear the GST tax on the transfers.

Section 2603(b) requires that unless the governing instrument provides otherwise, the GST tax is to be charged to the property constituting the transfer. Therefore, you will usually enter all of the direct skips on Part 2.

You may enter a transfer on Part 3 only if the will or trust instrument directs, by specific reference, that the GST tax is not to be paid from the transferred property interests.

Part 2 — Line 3. Enter zero on this line unless the will or trust instrument specifies that the GST taxes will be paid by property other than that constituting the transfer (as described above). Enter on line 3 the total of the GST taxes shown on Part 3 and Schedule(s) R-1 that are payable out of the property interests shown on Part 2, line 1.

Part 2 — Line 6. Do not enter more than the amount on line 5. Additional allocations may be made using Part 1.

Part 3 — Line 3. See the instructions to Part 2, line 3, above. Enter only the total of the GST taxes shown on Schedule(s) R-1 that are payable out of the property interests shown on Part 3, line 1.

Part 3 — Line 6. See the instructions to Part 2, line 6, above.

How To Complete Schedule R-1

Filing due date. Enter the due date of Schedule R, Form 706. You must send the copies of Schedule R-1 to the fiduciary by this date.

Line 4. Do not enter more than the amount on line 3. If you wish to allocate an additional GST exemption, you must use Schedule R, Part 1. Making an entry on line 4 constitutes a Notice of Allocation of the decedent's GST exemption to the trust.

Line 6. If the property interests entered on line 1 will not bear the GST tax, multiply line 6 by 55% (.55).

Signature. The executor(s) must sign Schedule R-1 in the same manner as Form 706. See **Signature and Verification** on page 2.

Filing Schedule R-1. Attach to Form 706 one copy of each Schedule R-1 that you prepare. Send two copies of each Schedule R-1 to the fiduciary.

Schedule T. Qualified Family-Owned Business Interest Deduction

Under section 2057, you may elect to deduct the value of certain family-owned business interests from the gross estate. You make the election by filing Schedule T, attaching all required statements, and deducting the value of the qualifying business interests on Part 5, Recapitulation, page 3, at item 22. You can only deduct the value of property that you have also reported on Schedule A, B, C, E, F, G, or H of Form 706.

The amount of the deduction cannot exceed the lesser of:

• The adjusted value of the qualified family-owned business interests (QFOBI) of the decedent otherwise includible in the gross estate, or

• $675,000.

Coordination with unified credit. The sum of the QFOBI deduction and the applicable exclusion amount cannot exceed $1.3 million. Thus, if the maximum QFOBI deduction of $675,000 is claimed, the applicable exclusion amount would be limited to $625,000, and the credit entered on line 11 of Part 2 - Tax Computation, would be $202,050.

If the amount of the QFOBI deduction is less than $675,000, increase the applicable exclusion amount by the difference between $675,000 and the amount of the QFOBI deduction (but not to exceed the maximum applicable exclusion amount in effect for the year of death).

For example, if the estate of a decedent dying in 1999 claimed a QFOBI deduction of $665,000, the applicable exclusion amount for the estate would be $635,000 (($675,000 − 665,000) + 625,000). But if the QFOBI deduction was $575,000, the applicable exclusion amount would be $650,000, the maximum for 1999.

General Requirements

Business interests may qualify for the exclusion if the following requirements are met:

• The decedent was a citizen or resident of the United States at the date of death.

• The business interests are includible in the gross estate.

• The interests must have passed to or been acquired by a qualified heir from the decedent.

• The adjusted value of the qualified family-owned business interests must exceed 50% of the adjusted gross estate (see below for a discussion of these terms).

• The interest must be in a trade or business that has its principal place of business in the United States.

• The business interest was owned by the decedent or a member of the decedent's family during 5 of the 8 years before the decedent's death.

• For 5 of the 8 years before the decedent's death, there was material participation by the decedent or a member of the decedent's family in the business to which the ownership interest relates.

Qualified Family-Owned Business Interest

In general. To qualify for the deduction, the business interest must be either an interest as a proprietor in a trade or business carried on as a proprietorship, or an interest in an entity carrying on a trade or business in which:

• At least 50% of the entity is owned by the decedent or members of the decedent's family;

• At least 70% of the entity is owned by members of two families, and at least 30% is owned by the decedent or members of the decedent's family; or

• At least 90% of the entity is owned by members of three families, and at least 30% is owned by the decedent or members of the decedent's family.

In all cases, ownership may be either direct or indirect.

Ownership rules. Ownership of the business interest may either be direct, or indirect through a corporation, partnership, or a trust. An interest owned, directly or indirectly, by or for such an entity is considered owned proportionately by or for the entity's shareholders, partners, or beneficiaries. A person is the beneficiary of a trust only if he or she has a present interest in the trust.

Corporations. Ownership of a corporation is determined by holding stock that has the appropriate percentage of the total combined voting power of all classes of stock entitled to vote and the appropriate percentage of the total value of shares of all classes of stock.

Partnerships. Ownership of a partnership is based on owning the appropriate percentage of the capital interest in the partnership.

Tiered entities. For the purpose of determining ownership of a business under section 2057, if the decedent, a member of the decedent's family, any qualified heir, or any member of the qualified heir's family owns an interest in a business, and by reason of that ownership the person is treated as owning an interest in any other business, the ownership interest in the other business is disregarded in determining the ownership interest in the first business. Likewise, you must apply the ownership rules separately in determining ownership of the other business.

Limitations

"Qualified family-owned business interests" shall not include the following:

• Any interest in a trade or business if its principal place of business is located outside the United States.

• Any interest in an entity if the stock or debt of the entity (or a controlled group of which the entity is a member) was readily tradable on an established securities market or secondary market at any time within 3 years of the date of the decedent's death.

• Any interest in a trade or business (excluding banks and domestic building and loan associations) if more than 35% of its adjusted ordinary gross income for the taxable year that includes the date of the decedent's death would qualify as personal holding company income (as defined in section 2057(e)(2)(C)) if such trade or business was a corporation.

• The portion of an interest in a trade or business that is attributable to:

1. Cash and/or marketable securities in excess of the reasonably expected day-to-day working capital needs, and

2. Any other assets (other than assets held in the active conduct of a bank or domestic building and loan) that produce or are held for the production of personal holding company income and most types of foreign personal holding company income. See section 2057(e)(2)(D) for more information.

Net cash lease. If the decedent leased property on a net cash basis to a member of the decedent's family, income from the lease is not considered personal holding company income for this purpose, and the property is not considered asset producing or held for the production of personal holding company income. However, if the income or property would have been personal holding company income or property if the decedent had engaged directly in the activities of the lessee, then this net cash lease rule does not apply.

Qualified Heir

A person is a qualified heir of property if he or she is a member of the decedent's family and acquired or received the interest from the decedent.

If a qualified heir disposes of any qualified family-owned business interest to any member of his or her family, that person will then be treated as the qualified heir with respect to that interest.

The term *member of the family* includes only:

• An ancestor (parent, grandparent, etc.) of the individual;

• The spouse of the individual;

• The lineal descendent (child, stepchild, grandchild, etc.) of the individual, the individual's spouse, or a parent of the individual; and

• The spouse, widow, or widower of any lineal descendent described above.

A legally adopted child of an individual is treated as a child of that individual by blood.

For the purpose of this deduction, qualified heir also includes any active employee of the trade or business to which the qualified

FIGURE A.1 *Continued*

family-owned business interest relates if the employee has been employed by the trade or business for a period of at least 10 years before the date of the decedent's death.

Interests Acquired From the Decedent

An interest in a business is considered to have been acquired from or to have passed from the decedent if one or more of the following apply:

• The interest is considered to have been acquired from or to have passed from the decedent under section 1014(b) (relating to basis of property acquired from a decedent).

• The interest is acquired by any person from the estate.

• The interest is acquired by any person from a trust, to the extent the property is includible in the gross estate.

Material Participation

To make the section 2057 election, either the decedent or a member of the decedent's family must have materially participated in the trade or business to which the ownership interest relates for at least 5 of the 8 years ending on the date of the decedent's death.

The existence of material participation is a factual determination, and the types of activities and financial risks that will support a finding of material participation will vary with the mode of ownership. No single factor is determinative of the presence of material participation, but physical work and participation in management decisions are the principal factors to be considered. Passively collecting rents, salaries, draws, dividends, or other income from the trade or business does not constitute material participation. Neither does merely advancing capital and reviewing business plans and financial reports each business year.

For more information on material participation, see page 7 of these instructions and Regulations section 20.2032A-3.

Specific Instructions

Line 4
If any qualified heir is not a U.S. citizen, the ownership interest he or she receives must pass, be acquired, or be held in a qualified trust. See section 2057(g) for details. If any qualified heir listed on line 4 is not a U.S. citizen, indicate along with their address "citizen of _____ " filling in the appropriate country.

Line 5
List on line 5 all qualified family-owned business interests included in the gross estate, even if they will not be included in the deduction because, for example, they pass to the surviving spouse and are deducted on Schedule M rather than Schedule T (see the instructions for line 15 below).

Line 7
Enter on line 7 the amount, if any, deductible from the gross estate as claims against the estate or indebtedness of the estate reported elsewhere on this Form 706. Do not include funeral or administrative expenses on this line.

Line 8a
Enter the amount of any indebtedness that is both:
• Included on line 7, and
• Indebtedness on a residence of the decedent that qualifies for the mortgage interest deduction under section 163(h)(3).

Line 8b
Enter the amount of any indebtedness:
• That is included on line 7, and

• The proceeds of which were used to pay educational or medical expenses of the decedent, the decedent's spouse, or the decedent's dependents.

Line 8c
Enter the amount of any other indebtedness included on line 7 but not on lines 8a or 8b, but DO NOT enter more than $10,000.

Line 11a
Enter on this line the amount of gifts, if any, that were:
• Included on line 4 of Part 2, page 1, Form 706;
• Of qualified family-owned business interests;
• From the decedent to members of the decedent's family other than the decedent's spouse; and
• Continuously held by such members of the decedent's family from the date of the gift to the date of the decedent's death.

Line 11b
Enter the amount, if any, of gifts that would have been included on line 11a except that they were excluded under the gift tax annual exclusion of section 2503(b).

Line 13a
Enter the amount from item 12, Part 5, Recapitulation.

Line 13e
Enter any amounts (other than qualified family-owned business interests and de minimis amounts) transferred from the decedent to the decedent's spouse (determined at the time of the transfer) and within 10 years of the date of the decedent's death. At the time this form went to print, the IRS had not issued guidelines on what constitutes a de minimis amount.

Line 13f
Enter the amount of any other gifts:
• That are not included on lines 13d or 13e;
• That were from the decedent;
• That were made within 3 years of the date of the decedent's death; and
• That were not both gifts to members of the decedent's family and excluded under the annual gift tax exclusion of section 2503(b).

Line 13h
Enter the amounts, if any, from lines 13d, 13e, or 13f, that are otherwise included in the gross estate (e.g., under section 2035).

Line 15
The interests listed on line 5 above are used to qualify the estate for the section 2057 deduction. You may choose, however, not to deduct on Schedule T all of the trade or business interests that are listed on line 5. For example, if a trade or business interest that is a qualified family-owned business interest passes to the surviving spouse and you choose to deduct it on Schedule M, you may not deduct on Schedule T the part of its value deducted on Schedule M. Or, you may simply choose not to include a particular trade or business interest in the section 2057 election.

Report on line 15 only the value of those trade or business interests listed on line 5 for which you are making the section 2057 election.

Also, you must reduce the amount of the Schedule T deduction by the amount of any Federal estate or GST tax and any state inheritance taxes paid out of, and any other deductions claimed with respect to, the interests that you elect to deduct on Schedule T.

Attach a schedule showing the following:
• Identify each trade or business interest from line 5 for which you are making the section 2057 election and the

amount being deducted.
• Specify the amount, if any, of the interests for which you are making the election that is deducted on Schedule M.
• List for each trade or business interest the type and amount of any taxes paid out of that interest.
• List for each trade or business interest the type and amount of any other deductions claimed with respect to that interest.

If there are no such reductions, enter the amount from line 10 on line 15.

Schedule U. Qualified Conservation Easement Exclusion

Under section 2031(c), you may elect to exclude a portion of the value of land that is subject to a qualified conservation easement. You make the election by filing Schedule U with all of the required information and excluding the applicable value of the land that is subject to the easement on Part 5, Recapitulation, page 3, at item 11. To elect the exclusion, you must include on Schedule A, B, E, F, G, or H, as appropriate, the decedent's interest in the land that is subject to the exclusion. You must make the election on a timely filed Form 706, including extensions.

For the estates of decedents dying in 1999, the exclusion is the lesser of:
• The applicable percentage of the value of land (after certain reductions) subject to a qualified conservation easement, or
• $200,000.
Once made, the election is irrevocable.

Note: See the Exclusion limitation table on page 24 for exclusion amounts after 1999.

General Requirements
Qualified Land
Land may qualify for the exclusion if all of the following requirements are met:
• The decedent or a member of the decedent's family must have owned the land for the 3-year period ending on the date of the decedent's death.
• No later than the date the election is made, a qualified conservation easement on the land has been made by the decedent, a member of the decedent's family, the executor of the decedent's estate, or the trustee of a trust that holds the land.
• The land is located:
1. In or within 25 miles of an area that, on the date of the decedent's death, is a metropolitan area, as defined by the Office of Management and Budget;
2. In or within 25 miles of an area that, on the date of the decedent's death, is a national park or wilderness area designated as part of the National Wilderness Preservation System (unless it has been determined that such land is not under significant development pressure); or
3. In or within 10 miles of an area that, on the date of the decedent's death, is an Urban National Forest, as designated by the Forest Service.

Member of Family
Members of the decedent's family include the decedent's spouse; ancestors; lineal descendants of the decedent, of the decedent's spouse, and of the parents of the decedent;

FIGURE A.1 *Continued*

and the spouse of any lineal descendant. A legally adopted child of an individual is considered a child of the individual by blood.

Indirect Ownership of Land
The qualified conservation easement exclusion applies if the land is owned indirectly through a partnership, corporation, or trust, if the decedent owned (directly or indirectly) at least 30% of the entity. For the rules on determining ownership of an entity, see the Schedule T instructions under the main heading, **Qualified Family-Owned Business Interest.**

Qualified Conservation Easement
A qualified conservation easement is one that would qualify as a qualified conservation contribution under section 170(h). It must be a contribution:
• Of a qualified real property interest;
• To a qualified organization; and
• Exclusively for conservation purposes.

Exclusion limitation. The conservation easement exclusion limitation is determined using the following table:

For the estates of decedents dying during:	The exclusion limitation is:
1999	$200,000
2000	300,000
2001	400,000
2002 or thereafter	500,000

Qualified real property interest. The term qualified real property interest means any of the following:
• The entire interest of the donor, other than a qualified mineral interest;
• A remainder interest; or
• A restriction granted in perpetuity on the use that may be made of the real property. The restriction must include a prohibition on more than a de minimis use for commercial recreational activity.

Qualified organization. Qualified organizations include:
• The United States, a possession of the United States, a state (or the District of Columbia), or a political subdivision of them, as long as the gift is for exclusively public purposes.
• A domestic entity that meets the general requirements for qualifying as a charity under section 170(c)(2) and that generally receives a substantial amount of its support from a government unit or from the general public.
• Any entity that qualifies under section 170(h)(3)(B).

Conservation purpose. The term conservation purpose means:
• The preservation of land areas for outdoor recreation by, or the education of, the public;
• The protection of a relatively natural habitat of fish, wildlife, or plants, or a similar ecosystem; or
• The preservation of open space (including farmland and forest land) where such preservation is for the scenic enjoyment of the general public, or pursuant to a clearly delineated Federal, state, or local conservation policy and will yield a significant public benefit.

Specific Instructions

Line 1
If the land is reported as one or more item numbers on a Form 706 schedule, simply list the schedule and item

numbers. If the land subject to the easement comprises only part of an item, however, list the schedule and item number and describe the part subject to the easement. See the instructions for Schedule A, Real Estate, in the Form 706 itself, for information on how to describe the land.

Line 4
Using the general rules for describing real estate, provide enough information so the IRS can value the easement. Give the date the easement was granted and by whom it was granted.

Line 5
Enter on this line the gross value at which the land was reported on the applicable asset schedule on this Form 706. Do not reduce the value by the amount of any mortgage outstanding. Report the estate tax value even if the easement was granted by the decedent (or someone other than the decedent) prior to the decedent's death.

Line 6
The amount on line 6 should be the date of death value of any qualifying conservation easements granted prior to the decedent's death, whether granted by the decedent or someone other than the decedent, for which the exclusion is being elected.

Line 8
You must reduce the land value by the value of any development rights retained by the donor in the conveyance of the easement. A development right is any right to use the land for any commercial purpose that is not subordinate to and directly supportive of the use of the land as a farm for farming purposes.

You do not have to make this reduction if everyone with an interest in the land (regardless of whether in possession) agrees to permanently extinguish the retained development right. The agreement must be filed with this return and must include the following information and terms:

1. A statement that the agreement is made pursuant to IRC section 2031(c)(5).

2. A list of all persons in being holding an interest in the land that is subject to the qualified conservation easement. Include each person's name, address, tax identifying number, relationship to the decedent, and a description of their interest.

3. The items of real property shown on the estate tax return that are subject to the qualified conservation easement (identified by schedule and item number).

4. A description of the retained development right that is to be extinguished.

5. A clear statement of consent that is binding on all parties under applicable local law:

a. To take whatever action is necessary to permanently extinguish the retained development rights listed in the agreement; and

b. To be personally liable for additional taxes under IRC section 2031(c)(5)(C) if this agreement is not implemented by the earlier of:
• The date that is 2 years after the date of the decedent's death, or
• The date of sale of the land subject to the qualified conservation easement.

6. A statement that in the event this agreement is not timely implemented, that they will report the additional tax on whatever return is required by the IRS and will file the return and pay the additional tax by the last day of the 6th month following the applicable date described above.

All parties to the agreement must sign the agreement.

For an example of an agreement containing some of the same terms, see Schedule A-1 (Form 706).

Line 11
Enter the total value of the qualified conservation easements on which the exclusion is based. This could include easements granted by the decedent or someone other than the decedent) prior to the decedent's death, easements granted by the decedent that take effect at death, easements granted by the executor after the decedent's death, or some combination of these.

Important: *Use the value of the easement as of the date of death, even if the easement was granted prior to the date of death.*

Explain how this value was determined and attach copies of any appraisals. Normally, the appropriate way to value a conservation easement is to determine the FMV of the land both before and after the granting of the easement, with the difference being the value of the easement.

You must reduce the reported value of the easement by the amount of any consideration received for the easement. If the date of death value of the easement is different from the value at the time the consideration was received, you must reduce the value of the easement by the same proportion that the consideration received bears to the value of the easement at the time it was received. For example, assume the value of the easement at the time it was granted was $100,000 and $10,000 was received in consideration for the easement. If the easement was worth $150,000 at the date of death, you must reduce the value of the easement by $15,000 ($10,000/$100,000 × $150,000) and report the value of the easement on line 11 as $135,000.

Line 16
If a charitable contribution deduction for this land has been taken on Schedule O, enter the amount of the deduction here. If the easement was granted after the decedent's death, a contribution deduction may be taken on Schedule O, if it otherwise qualifies, as long as no income tax deduction was or will be claimed for the contribution by any person or entity.

Line 17
You must reduce the value of the land by the amount of any acquisition indebtedness on the land at the date of the decedent's death. Acquisition indebtedness includes the unpaid amount of:
• Any indebtedness incurred by the donor in acquiring the property;
• Any indebtedness incurred before the acquisition if the indebtedness would not have been incurred but for the acquisition;
• Any indebtedness incurred after the acquisition if the indebtedness would not have been incurred but for the acquisition and the incurrence of the indebtedness was reasonably foreseeable at the time of the acquisition; and
• The extension, renewal, or refinancing of acquisition indebtedness.

Continuation Schedule
See instructions for Continuation Schedule on Form 706 itself.

FIGURE A.1 *Continued*

Worksheet for Schedule Q — Credit for Tax on Prior Transfers

Part I | Transferor's tax on prior transfers

Item	Transferor (From Schedule Q)			Total for all transfers (line 8 only)
	A	B	C	
1. Gross value of prior transfer to this transferee.				
2. Death taxes payable from prior transfer				
3. Encumbrances allocable to prior transfer ...				
4. Obligations allocable to prior transfer......				
5. Marital deduction applicable to line 1 above, as shown on transferor's Form 706				
6. TOTAL *(Add lines 2, 3, 4, and 5)*				
7. Net value of transfers *(Subtract line 6 from line 1)*				
8. Net value of transfers *(Add columns A, B, and C of line 7)*				
9. Transferor's taxable estate				
10. Federal estate tax paid				
11. State death taxes paid..................				
12. Foreign death taxes paid				
13. Other death taxes paid				
14. TOTAL taxes paid *(Add lines 10, 11, 12, and 13)* ..				
15. Value of transferor's estate *(Subtract line 14 from line 9)*				
16. Net Federal estate tax paid on transferor's estate				
17. Credit for gift tax paid on transferor's estate with respect to pre-1977 gifts (section 2012)				
18. Credit allowed transferor's estate for tax on prior transfers from prior transferor(s) who died within 10 years before death of decedent				
19. Tax on transferor's estate *(Add lines 16, 17, and 18)* .				
20. Transferor's tax on prior transfers ((Line 7 + line 15) × line 19 of respective estates). ...				

Part II | Transferee's tax on prior transfers

Item		Amount
21. Transferee's actual tax before allowance of credit for prior transfers *(see instructions)*	21	
22. Total gross estate of transferee *(from line 1 of the Tax Computation, page 1, Form 706)*	22	
23. Net value of all transfers *(from line 8 of this worksheet)*	23	
24. Transferee's reduced gross estate *(subtract line 23 from line 22)*	24	
25. Total debts and deductions (not including marital and charitable deductions) *(items 17, 18, and 19 of the Recapitulation, page 3, Form 706)*	25	
26. Marital and Qualified Family-Owned Business Interest deduction *(from item 20 and 22, Recapitulation, page 3, Form 706) (see instructions)*	26	
27. Charitable bequests *(from item 21, Recapitulation, page 3, Form 706)*	27	
28. Charitable deduction proportion ([line 23 + (line 22 − line 25)] × line 27)........	28	
29. Reduced charitable deduction *(subtract line 28 from line 27)*	29	
30. Transferee's deduction as adjusted *(add lines 25, 26, and 29)*..	30	
31. (a) Transferee's reduced taxable estate *(subtract line 30 from line 24)*..	31(a)	
(b) Adjusted taxable gifts	31(b)	
(c) Total reduced taxable estate *(add lines 31(a) and 31(b))*...	31(c)	
32. Tentative tax on reduced taxable estate...	32	
33. (a) Post-1976 gift taxes paid	33(a)	
(b) Unified credit (applicable credit amount)	33(b)	
(c) Section 2011 state death tax credit	33(c)	
(d) Section 2012 gift tax credit	33(d)	
(e) Section 2014 foreign death tax credit	33(e)	
(f) Total credits *(add lines 33(a) through 33(e))*...........................	33(f)	
34. Net tax on reduced taxable estate *(subtract line 33(f) from line 32)*	34	
35. Transferee's tax on prior transfers *(subtract line 34 from line 21)*	35	

FIGURE A.1 *Continued*

Index

FIGURE A.1 *Continued*

Form **709**	**United States Gift (and Generation-Skipping Transfer) Tax Return**	OMB No. 1545-0020
	(Section 6019 of the Internal Revenue Code) (For gifts made during calendar year 2000)	**2000**
Department of the Treasury Internal Revenue Service	▶ **See separate instructions.**	

Part 1 — General Information

1 Donor's first name and middle initial	2 Donor's last name	3 Donor's social security number

4 Address (number, street, and apartment number)	5 Legal residence (domicile) (county and state)

6 City, state, and ZIP code	7 Citizenship

		Yes	No
8	If the donor died during the year, check here ▶ ☐ and enter date of death _____ . _____ . _____		
9	If you received an extension of time to file this Form 709, check here ▶ ☐ and attach the Form 4868, 2688, 2350, or extension letter		
10	Enter the total number of separate donees listed on Schedule A — count each person only once. ▶		
11a	Have you (the donor) previously filed a Form 709 (or 709-A) for any other year? If the answer is "No," do not complete line 11b		
11b	If the answer to line 11a is "Yes," has your address changed since you last filed Form 709 (or 709-A)?		
12	Gifts by husband or wife to third parties. — Do you consent to have the gifts (including generation-skipping transfers) made by you and by your spouse to third parties during the calendar year considered as made one-half by each of you? (See instructions.) (If the answer is "Yes," the following information must be furnished and your spouse must sign the consent shown below. If the answer is "No," skip lines 13 - 18 and go to Schedule A.)		

13 Name of consenting spouse	14 SSN

		Yes	No
15	Were you married to one another during the entire calendar year? (see instructions)		
16	If the answer to 15 is "No," check whether ☐ married ☐ divorced or ☐ widowed, and give date (see instructions) ▶		
17	Will a gift tax return for this calendar year be filed by your spouse?		
18	**Consent of Spouse** — I consent to have the gifts (and generation-skipping transfers) made by me and by my spouse to third parties during the calendar year considered as made one-half by each of us. We are both aware of the joint and several liability for tax created by the execution of this consent.		

Consenting spouse's signature ▶   Date ▶

Part 2 — Tax Computation

1	Enter the amount from Schedule A, Part 3, line 15	1	
2	Enter the amount from Schedule B, line 3	2	
3	Total taxable gifts (add lines 1 and 2)	3	
4	Tax computed on amount on line 3 (see Table for Computing Tax in separate instructions)	4	
5	Tax computed on amount on line 2 (see Table for Computing Tax in separate instructions)	5	
6	Balance (subtract line 5 from line 4)	6	
7	Maximum unified credit (nonresident aliens, see instructions)	7	220,550.00
8	Enter the unified credit against tax allowable for all prior periods (from Sch. B, line 1, col. C)	8	
9	Balance (subtract line 8 from line 7)	9	
10	Enter 20% (.20) of the amount allowed as a specific exemption for gifts made after September 8, 1976, and before January 1, 1977 (see instructions)	10	
11	Balance (subtract line 10 from line 9)	11	
12	Unified credit (enter the smaller of line 6 or line 11)	12	
13	Credit for foreign gift taxes (see instructions)	13	
14	Total credits (add lines 12 and 13)	14	
15	Balance (subtract line 14 from line 6) (do not enter less than zero)	15	
16	Generation-skipping transfer taxes (from Schedule C, Part 3, col. H, Total)	16	
17	Total tax (add lines 15 and 16)	17	
18	Gift and generation-skipping transfer taxes prepaid with extension of time to file	18	
19	If line 18 is less than line 17, enter balance due (see instructions)	19	
20	If line 18 is greater than line 17, enter amount to be refunded	20	

Attach check or money order here.

Sign Here

Under penalties of perjury, I declare that I have examined this return, including any accompanying schedules and statements, and to the best of my knowledge and belief, it is true, correct, and complete. Declaration of preparer (other than donor) is based on all information of which preparer has any knowledge.

Signature of donor   Date

Paid Preparer's Use Only

Preparer's signature ▶	Date	Check if self-employed ▶ ☐
Firm's name (or yours if self-employed), address, and ZIP code ▶	Phone no. ▶	

ISA STF FED1435F.1   For Disclosure, Privacy Act, and Paperwork Reduction Act Notice, see page 11 of the separate instructions for this form.   Form **709** (2000)

FIGURE A.2 Form 709—United States Gift (and Generation-Skipping Transfer) Tax Return and Instructions

SCHEDULE A	Computation of Taxable Gifts (Including Transfers in Trust)

A   Does the value of any item listed on Schedule A reflect any valuation discount? If the answer is "Yes," see instructions .... Yes ☐ No☐

B   ☐ ◄ Check here if you elect under section 529(c)(2)(B) to treat any transfers made this year to a qualified state tuition program as made ratably over a 5-year period beginning this year. See instructions. Attach explanation.

Part 1 — Gifts Subject Only to Gift Tax. *Gifts less political organization, medical, and educational exclusions — see instructions*

A Item number	B • Donee's name and address • Relationship to donor (if any) • Description of gift • If the gift was made by means of a trust, enter trust's EIN and attach a description or copy of the trust instrument (see instructions) • If the gift was of securities, give CUSIP number	C Donor's adjusted basis of gift	D Date of gift	E Value at date of gift
1				

Total of Part 1 (add amounts from Part 1, column E) .... ►

Part 2 — Gifts That are Direct Skips and are Subject to Both Gift Tax and Generation-Skipping Transfer Tax. You must list the gifts in chronological order. *Gifts less political organization, medical, and educational exclusions — see instructions. (Also list here direct skips that are subject only to the GST tax at this time as the result of the termination of an "estate tax inclusion period." See instructions.)*

A Item number	B • Donee's name and address • Relationship to donor (if any) • Description of gift • If the gift was made by means of a trust, enter trust's EIN and attach a description or copy of the trust instrument (see instructions) • If the gift was of securities, give CUSIP number	C Donor's adjusted basis of gift	D Date of gift	E Value at date of gift
1				

Total of Part 2 (add amounts from Part 2, column E) .... ►

Part 3 — Taxable Gift Reconciliation

1	Total value of gifts of donor (add totals from column E of Parts 1 and 2)	**1**	
2	One-half of items _____ attributable to spouse (see instructions)	**2**	
3	Balance (subtract line 2 from line 1)	**3**	
4	Gifts of spouse to be included (from Schedule A, Part 3, line 2 of spouse's return — see instructions)	**4**	
	If any of the gifts included on this line are also subject to the generation-skipping transfer tax, check here ► ☐ and enter those gifts also on Schedule C, Part 1.		
5	Total gifts (add lines 3 and 4)	**5**	
6	Total annual exclusions for gifts listed on Schedule A (including line 4, above) (see instructions)	**6**	
7	Total included amount of gifts (subtract line 6 from line 5)	**7**	

Deductions (see instructions)

8	Gifts of interests to spouse for which a marital deduction will be claimed, based on items _____ of Schedule A	**8**			
9	Exclusions attributable to gifts on line 8	**9**			
10	Marital deduction — subtract line 9 from line 8	**10**			
11	Charitable deduction, based on items _____ less exclusions .	**11**			
12	Total deductions — add lines 10 and 11		**12**	
13	Subtract line 12 from line 7		**13**	
14	Generation-skipping transfer taxes payable with this Form 709 (from Schedule C, Part 3, col. H, Total)		**14**	
15	Taxable gifts (add lines 13 and 14). Enter here and on line 1 of the Tax Computation on page 1		**15**	

(If more space is needed, attach additional sheets of same size.)   Form **709** (2000)
STF FED1435F.2

FIGURE A.2 *Continued*

SCHEDULE A	Computation of Taxable Gifts *(continued)*

16 Terminable Interest (QTIP) Marital Deduction. (See instructions for line 8 of Schedule A.)

If a trust (or other property) meets the requirements of qualified terminable interest property under section 2523(f), and

  a. The trust (or other property) is listed on Schedule A, and

  b. The value of the trust (or other property) is entered in whole or in part as a deduction on line 8, Part 3 of Schedule A,

then the donor shall be deemed to have made an election to have such trust (or other property) treated as qualified terminable interest property under section 2523(f).

  If less than the entire value of the trust (or other property) that the donor has included in Part 1 of Schedule A is entered as a deduction on line 8, the donor shall be considered to have made an election only as to a fraction of the trust (or other property). The numerator of this fraction is equal to the amount of the trust (or other property) deducted on line 10 of Part 3, Schedule A. The denominator is equal to the total value of the trust (or other property) listed in Part 1 of Schedule A.

  If you make the QTIP election (see instructions for line 8 of Schedule A), the terminable interest property involved will be included in your spouse's gross estate upon his or her death (section 2044). If your spouse disposes (by gift or otherwise) of all or part of the qualifying life income interest, he or she will be considered to have made a transfer of the entire property that is subject to the gift tax (see Transfer of Certain Life Estates on page 3 of the instructions).

17 Election Out of QTIP Treatment of Annuities

  ☐ ◄ Check here if you elect under section 2523(f)(6) NOT to treat as qualified terminable interest property any joint and survivor annuities that are reported on Schedule A and would otherwise be treated as qualified terminable interest property under section 2523(f). (See instructions.) Enter the item numbers (from Schedule A) for the annuities for which you are making this election ►

SCHEDULE B	Gifts From Prior Periods

If you answered "Yes" on line 11a of page 1, Part 1, **see the instructions for completing Schedule B. If you answered "No," skip to the Tax Computation on page 1 (or Schedule C, if applicable).**

A Calendar year or calendar quarter (see instructions)	B Internal Revenue office where prior return was filed	C Amount of unified credit against gift tax for periods after December 31, 1976	D Amount of specific exemption for prior periods ending before January 1, 1977	E Amount of taxable gifts

1	Totals for prior periods (without adjustment for reduced specific exemption)	**1**			
2	Amount, if any, by which total specific exemption, line 1, column D, is more than $30,000		**2**	
3	Total amount of taxable gifts for prior periods (add amount, column E, line 1, and amount, if any, on line 2). (Enter here and on line 2 of the Tax Computation on page 1.)		**3**	

(If more space is needed, attach additional sheets of same size.)

Form **709** (2000)

STF FED1435F.3

FIGURE A.2 *Continued*

SCHEDULE C	Computation of Generation-Skipping Transfer Tax

Note: *Inter vivos direct skips that are completely excluded by the GST exemption must still be fully reported (including value and exemptions claimed) on Schedule C.*

Part 1 — Generation-Skipping Transfers

A Item No. (from Schedule A, Part 2, col. A)	B Value (from Schedule A, Part 2, col. E)	C Split Gifts (enter ½ of col. B) (see instructions)	D Subtract col. C from col. B	E Nontaxable portion of transfer	F Net Transfer (subtract col. E from col. D)
1					
2					
3					
4					
5					
6					

If you elected gift splitting and your spouse was required to file a separate Form 709 (see the instructions for "Split Gifts"), you must enter all of the gifts shown on Schedule A, Part 2, of your spouse's Form 709 here. In column C, enter the item number of each gift in the order it appears in column A of your spouse's Schedule A, Part 2. We have preprinted the prefix "S-" to distinguish your spouse's item numbers from your own when you complete column A of Schedule C, Part 3. In column D, for each gift, enter the amount reported in column C, Schedule C, Part 1, of your spouse's Form 709.	Split gifts from spouse's Form 709 (enter item number) S- S- S- S- S- S- S- S-	Value included from spouse's Form 709	Nontaxable portion of transfer	Net transfer (subtract col. E from col. D)

Part 2 — GST Exemption Reconciliation (Section 2631) and Section 2652(a)(3) Election

Check box ▶ ☐ if you are making a section 2652(a)(3) (special QTIP) election (see instructions)

Enter the item numbers (from Schedule A) of the gifts for which you are making this election ▶ _____

1	Maximum allowable exemption (see instructions)	**1**
2	Total exemption used for periods before filing this return	**2**
3	Exemption available for this return (subtract line 2 from line 1)	**3**
4	Exemption claimed on this return (from Part 3, col. C total, below)	**4**
5	Exemption allocated to transfers not shown on Part 3, below. You must attach a Notice of Allocation. (See instructions.)	**5**
6	Add lines 4 and 5	**6**
7	Exemption available for future transfers (subtract line 6 from line 3)	**7**

Part 3 — Tax Computation

A Item No. (from Schedule C, Part 1)	B Net transfer (from Schedule C, Part 1, col. F)	C GST Exemption Allocated	D Divide col. C by col. B	E Inclusion Ratio (subtract col. D from 1.000)	F Maximum Estate Tax Rate	G Applicable Rate (multiply col. E by col. F)	H Generation-Skipping Transfer Tax (multiply col. B by col. G)
1					55% (.55)		
2					55% (.55)		
3					55% (.55)		
4					55% (.55)		
5					55% (.55)		
6					55% (.55)		
					55% (.55)		
					55% (.55)		
					55% (.55)		
					55% (.55)		

Total exemption claimed. Enter here and on line 4, Part 2, above. May not exceed line 3, Part 2, above		Total generation-skipping transfer tax. Enter here, on line 14 of Schedule A, Part 3, and on line 16 of the Tax Computation on page 1	

(If more space is needed, attach additional sheets of same size.)   Form **709** (2000)

STF FED1435F.4

Figure A.2 *Continued*

2000

Instructions for Form 709

United States Gift (and Generation-Skipping Transfer) Tax Return

(For gifts made during calendar year 2000.)
For Disclosure, Privacy Act, and Paperwork Reduction Act Notice, see page 11 of the instructions.
Section references are to the Internal Revenue Code unless otherwise noted.

If you are filing this form solely to elect gift-splitting for gifts of not more than $20,000 per donee, you may be able to use Form 709-A, United States Short Form Gift Tax Return, instead of this form. See Who Must File on page 3 and When the Consenting Spouse Must Also File a Gift Tax Return beginning on page 5.

For Gifts Made			Use Revision of Form 709 Dated
After	and	Before	
— — — —		January 1, 1982	November 1981
December 31, 1981		January 1, 1987	January 1987
December 31, 1986		January 1, 1989	December 1988
December 31, 1988		January 1, 1990	December 1989
December 31, 1989		October 9, 1990	October 1990
October 8, 1990		January 1, 1992	November 1991
December 31, 1992		January 1, 1998	December 1996

Changes To Note

- You may have to mail this form to a different service center this year because the IRS has changed the filing location for several areas. See Where To File on page 4.
- For gifts made in 2000, the unified credit has increased to $220,550.
- For gifts made to spouses who are not U.S. citizens, the annual exclusion has increased to $103,000. See page 3.
- The generation-skipping transfer (GST) lifetime exemption has increased to $1,030,000. See page 10.

Photographs of Missing Children

The IRS is a proud partner with the National Center for Missing and Exploited Children. Photographs of missing children selected by the Center may appear in instructions on pages that would otherwise be blank. You can help bring these children home by looking at the photographs and calling 1-800-THE-LOST (1-800-843-5678) if you recognize a child.

General Instructions

Note: *If you meet all of the following requirements, you are not required to file Form 709:*

1. *You made no gifts during the year to your spouse;*

2. *You gave no more than $10,000 during the year to any one donee; and*

3. *All of the gifts you made were of present interests.*

For additional information, see Transfers Not Subject to the Gift Tax below and Who Must File on page 3.

Purpose of Form

Use Form 709 to report the following:

- Transfers subject to the Federal gift and certain generation-skipping transfer (GST) taxes and to figure the tax, if any, due on those transfers, and
- Allocation of the lifetime GST exemption to property transferred during the transferor's lifetime. (For more details, see the instructions for Part 2 — GST Exemption Reconciliation on page 10, and Regulations section 26.2632-1.)

All gift and GST taxes are computed and filed on a calendar year basis regardless of your income tax accounting period.

Transfers Subject to the Gift Tax

Generally, the Federal gift tax applies to any transfer by gift of real or personal property, whether tangible or intangible, that you made directly or indirectly, in trust, or by any other means to a donee.

The gift tax applies not only to the gratuitous transfer of any kind of property, but also to sales or exchanges, not made in the ordinary course of business, where money or money's worth is exchanged but the value of the money (or property) or money's worth received is less than the value of what is sold or exchanged. The gift tax is in addition to any other tax, such as Federal income tax, paid or due on the transfer.

The exercise or release of a general power of appointment may be a gift by the individual possessing the power. General powers of appointment are those in which the holders of the power can appoint the property subject to the power to themselves, their creditors, their estates, or the creditors of their estates. To qualify as a power of appointment, it must be created by someone other than the holder of the power.

The gift tax may also apply to the forgiveness of a debt, to interest-free or below market interest rate loans, to the assignment of the benefits of an insurance policy, to certain property settlements in divorce cases, and to the giving up of some amount of annuity in exchange for the creation of a survivor annuity.

Bonds that are exempt from Federal income taxes are not exempt from Federal gift taxes.

Code sections 2701 and 2702 provide rules for determining whether certain transfers to a family member of interests in corporations, partnerships, and trusts are gifts. The rules of section 2704 determine whether the lapse of any voting or liquidation right is a gift.

Transfers Not Subject to the Gift Tax

Three types of transfers are not subject to the gift tax. These are transfers to political organizations and payments that qualify for the educational and medical exclusions. These transfers are not "gifts" as that term is used on Form 709 and its instructions. You need not file a Form 709 to report these transfers and should not list them on Schedule A of Form 709 if you do file Form 709.

Political organizations. The gift tax does not apply to a transfer to a political organization (defined in section 527(e)(1)) for the use of the organization.

Educational exclusion. The gift tax does not apply to an amount you paid on behalf of an individual to a qualifying

FIGURE A.2 *Continued*

domestic or foreign educational organization as tuition for the education or training of the individual. A *qualifying educational organization* is one that normally maintains a regular faculty and curriculum and normally has a regularly enrolled body of pupils or students in attendance at the place where its educational activities are regularly carried on. See section 170(b)(1)(A)(ii) and its regulations.

The payment must be made directly to the qualifying educational organization and it must be for tuition. No educational exclusion is allowed for amounts paid for books, supplies, room and board, or other similar expenses that do not constitute direct tuition costs. To the extent that the payment to the educational institution was for something other than tuition, it is a gift to the individual for whose benefit it was made, and may be offset by the annual exclusion if it is otherwise available.

Contributions to a qualified state tuition program on behalf of a designated beneficiary do not qualify for the educational exclusion.

Medical exclusion. The gift tax does not apply to an amount you paid on behalf of an individual to a person or institution that provided medical care for the individual. The payment must be to the care provider. The medical care must meet the requirements of section 213(d) (definition of medical care for income tax deduction purposes). Medical care includes expenses incurred for the diagnosis, cure, mitigation, treatment, or prevention of disease, or for the purpose of affecting any structure or function of the body, or for transportation primarily for and essential to medical care. Medical care also includes amounts paid for medical insurance on behalf of any individual.

The medical exclusion does not apply to amounts paid for medical care that are reimbursed by the donee's insurance. If payment for a medical expense is reimbursed by the donee's insurance company, your payment for that expense, to the extent of the reimbursed amount, is not eligible for the medical exclusion and you have made a gift to the donee.

To the extent that the payment was for something other than medical care, it is a gift to the individual on whose behalf the payment was made and may be offset by the annual exclusion if it is otherwise available.

The medical and educational exclusions are allowed without regard to the relationship between you and the donee. For examples illustrating these exclusions, see Regulations section 25.2503-6.

Qualified disclaimers. A donee's refusal to accept a gift is called a disclaimer. If a person makes a qualified disclaimer with respect to any interest in property, the property will be treated as if it had never been transferred to that person. Accordingly, the disclaimant is not regarded as

making a gift to the person who receives the property because of the qualified disclaimer.

Requirements. To be a qualified disclaimer, a refusal to accept an interest in property must meet the following conditions:

1. The refusal must be in writing;

2. The refusal must be received by the donor, the legal representative of the donor, the holder of the legal title to the property to which the interest relates, or the person in possession of the property within 9 months after the later of (a) the day on which the transfer creating the interest is made or (b) the day on which the disclaimant reaches age 21;

3. The disclaimant must not have accepted the interest or any of its benefits;

4. As a result of the refusal, the interest must pass without any direction from the disclaimant to either (a) the spouse of the decedent or (b) a person other than the disclaimant; and

5. The refusal must be irrevocable and unqualified.

The 9-month period for making the disclaimer generally is determined separately for each taxable transfer. For gifts, the period begins on the date the transfer is a completed transfer for gift tax purposes. For a transfer by will, it begins on the date of the decedent's death.

Transfers Subject to the Generation-Skipping Transfer Tax

You must report on Form 709 the GST tax imposed on inter vivos direct skips. (See Regulations section 26.2662-1(b) for instructions on how to report other generation-skipping transfers.) An *inter vivos direct skip* is a transfer made during the donor's lifetime that is: (a) subject to the gift tax; (b) of an interest in property; and (c) made to a skip person. (See page 6.)

A transfer is *subject to the gift tax* if it is required to be reported on Schedule A of Form 709 under the rules contained in the gift tax portions of these instructions, including the split gift rules. Therefore, transfers that qualify for the medical or educational exclusions, transfers that are fully excluded under the annual exclusion, and most transfers made to your spouse are not subject to the GST tax.

Transfers subject to the GST tax are described in further detail in the instructions on page 6.

Important: *Certain transfers, particularly transfers to a trust, that are not subject to gift tax and are therefore not subject to the GST tax on Form 709 may be subject to the GST tax at a later date. This is true even if the transfer is less than the $10,000 annual exclusion. In this instance, you may want to apply a GST exemption amount to the transfer on this return or*

on a Notice of Allocation. For more information, see Part 2 — GST Exemption Reconciliation on page 10.

Transfers Subject to an "Estate Tax Inclusion Period"

If property that is transferred by gift in a GST direct skip would have been includible in the donor's estate if the donor had died immediately after the transfer (other than by reason of the donor having died within 3 years of making the gift), the direct skip will be treated as having been made at the end of the "estate tax inclusion period" (ETIP) rather than at the time it was actually made. For details, see section 2642(f).

Report the gift portion of such a transfer in Schedule A, Part 1, at the time of the actual transfer. Report the GST portion in Schedule A, Part 2, but only at the close of the ETIP. Use Form 709 only to report those transfers where the ETIP closed due to something other than the donor's death. If the ETIP closed as the result of the donor's death, report the transfer on Form 706.

If you are filing this Form 709 solely to report transfers subject to an ETIP, complete the form as you normally would with the following exceptions:

1. Write "ETIP" at the top of page 1;

2. Complete only lines 1 - 4, 6, 8, and 9 of Part 1, General Information;

3. Complete Schedule A, Part 2, as explained in the instructions for that schedule on page 8;

4. Complete Column B of Schedule C, Part 1, as explained in the instructions for that schedule on page 10;

5. Complete only lines 14 and 15 of Schedule A, Part 3. (Also list here direct skips that are subject only to the GST tax as the result of the termination of an "estate tax inclusion period." See instructions for Schedule C on page 10.)

Section 2701 Elections

The special valuation rules of section 2701 contain three elections that you must make with Form 709.

1. A transferor may elect to treat a qualified payment right he or she holds (and all other rights of the same class) as other than a qualified payment right.

2. A person may elect to treat a distribution right held by that person in a controlled entity as a qualified payment right.

3. An interest holder may elect to treat as a taxable event the payment of a qualified payment that occurs more than 4 years after its due date.

The elections described in 1 and 2 must be made on the Form 709 that is filed by the transferor to report the transfer that is

FIGURE A.2 *Continued*

being valued under section 2701. The elections are made by attaching a statement to Form 709. For information on what must be in the statement and for definitions and other details on the elections, see section 2701 and Regulations section 25.2701-2(c).

The election described in 3 may be made by attaching a statement to either a timely or a late filed Form 709 filed by the recipient of the qualified payment for the year the payment is received. If the election is made on a timely filed return, the taxable event is deemed to occur on the date the qualified payment is received. If it is made on a late filed return, the taxable event is deemed to occur on the first day of the month immediately preceding the month in which the return is filed. For information on what must be in the statement and for definitions and other details on this election, see section 2701 and Regulations section 25.2701-4(d).

All of the elections are revocable only with the consent of the IRS.

Who Must File

Only individuals are required to file gift tax returns. If a trust, estate, partnership, or corporation makes a gift, the individual beneficiaries, partners, or stockholders are considered donors and may be liable for the gift and GST taxes.

The donor is responsible for paying the gift tax. However, if the donor does not pay the tax, the person receiving the gift may have to pay the tax.

If a donor dies before filing a return, the donor's executor must file the return.

A married couple may not file a joint gift tax return. However, see Split Gifts — Gifts by Husband or Wife to Third Parties on page 4.

If a gift is of community property, it is considered made one-half by each spouse. For example, a gift of $100,000 of community property is considered a gift of $50,000 made by each spouse, and each spouse must file a gift tax return.

Likewise, each spouse must file a gift tax return if they have made a gift of property held by them as joint tenants or tenants by the entirety.

Citizens or Residents of the United States

If you are a citizen or resident of the United States, you must file a gift tax return (whether or not any tax is ultimately due) in the following situations:

Gifts to your spouse. Except as described below, you do not have to file a gift tax return to report gifts to your spouse regardless of the amount of these gifts and regardless of whether the gifts are present or future interests.

You must file a gift tax return if your spouse is not a U.S. citizen and the total gifts you made to your spouse during the year exceed $103,000, or if you made any gift of a terminable interest that does not meet the exception described in Life estate with power of appointment on page 9.

You must also file a gift tax return to make the QTIP (Qualified Terminable Interest Property) election described on page 9.

Gifts to donees other than your spouse. You must file a gift tax return if you gave gifts to any such donee that are not fully excluded under the $10,000 annual exclusion (as described below). Thus, you must file a gift tax return to report any gift of a future interest (regardless of amount) or to report gifts to any donee that total more than $10,000 for the year.

Gifts to charities. If the only gifts you made during the year are deductible as gifts to charities, you do not need to file a return as long as you transferred your entire interest in the property to qualifying charities. If you transferred only a partial interest, or transferred part of your interest to someone other than a charity, you must still file a return.

If you are required to file a return to report noncharitable gifts and you made gifts to charities, you must include all of your gifts to charities on the return.

Gift splitting. You must file a gift tax return to split gifts (regardless of their amount) with your spouse as described in the **Specific Instructions** for Part 1 on page 4.

The term *citizen of the United States* includes a person who, at the time of making the gift:

• Was domiciled in a possession of the United States;

• Was a U.S. citizen; and

• Became a U.S. citizen for a reason other than being a citizen of a U.S. possession or being born or residing in a possession.

Annual Exclusion

The first $10,000 of gifts of present interests to each donee during the calendar year is subtracted from total gifts in figuring the amount of taxable gifts. For a gift in trust, each beneficiary of the trust is treated as a separate donee for purposes of the annual exclusion.

All of the gifts made during the calendar year to a donee are fully excluded under the annual exclusion if they are all gifts of *present interests* and if they total $10,000 or less.

Note: *For gifts made to spouses who are not U.S. citizens, the annual exclusion has been increased to $103,000, provided the additional $93,000 gift would otherwise qualify for the gift tax marital deduction (as described in the line 8 instructions on page 9).*

A gift of a *future interest* cannot be excluded under the annual exclusion.

A gift is considered a *present interest* if the donee has all immediate rights to the use, possession, and enjoyment of the property and income from the property. A gift is considered a *future interest* if the donee's rights to the use, possession, and enjoyment of the property and income from the property will not begin until some future date. Future interests include reversions, remainders, and other similar interests or estates.

Note: *A contribution to a qualified state tuition plan on behalf of a designated beneficiary is considered a gift of a present interest.*

A gift to a minor is considered a present interest if all of the following conditions are met:

1. Both the property and its income may be expended by, or for the benefit of, the minor before the minor reaches age 21;

2. All remaining property and its income must pass to the minor on the minor's 21st birthday; and

3. If the minor dies before the age of 21, the property and its income will be payable either to the minor's estate or to whomever the minor may appoint under a general power of appointment.

The gift of a present interest to more than one donee as joint tenants qualifies for the annual exclusion for each donee.

Nonresident Aliens

Nonresident aliens are subject to gift and GST taxes for gifts of tangible property situated in the United States. Under certain circumstances, they are also subject to gift and GST taxes for gifts of intangible property. (See section 2501(a).)

If you are a nonresident alien who made a gift subject to gift tax, you must file a gift tax return if: (a) you gave any gifts of future interests; or (b) your gifts of present interests to *any donee* other than your spouse total more than $10,000; or (c) your outright gifts to your spouse who is not a U.S. citizen total more than $103,000.

When To File

Form 709 is an annual return.

Generally, you must file the 2000 Form 709 on or after January 1 but not later than April 16, 2001.

If the donor died during 2000, the executor must file the donor's 2000 Form 709 not later than the earlier of (a) the due date (with extensions) for filing the donor's estate tax return or (b) April 16, 2001. Under this rule, the 2000 Form 709 may be due before April 16, 2001, if the donor died before July 15, 2000. If the donor died after July 14, 2000, the due date (without extensions) is April 16, 2001. If

FIGURE A.2 *Continued*

no estate tax return is required to be filed, the due date for the 2000 Form 709 (without extensions) is April 16, 2001. For more details, see Regulations section 25.6075-1.

Extension of Time To File

There are two methods of extending the time to file the gift tax return. *Neither method extends the time to pay the gift or GST taxes.* If you want an extension of time to pay the gift or GST taxes, you must request that separately. (See Regulations section 25.6161-1.)

By letter. You can request an extension of time to file your gift tax return by writing to the service center for your area. You must explain the reasons for the delay. You MUST use a letter to request an extension of time to file your gift tax return unless you are also requesting an extension to file your income tax return.

By extending the time to file your income tax return. Any extension of time granted for filing your calendar year Federal income tax return will also extend the time to file any gift tax return. Income tax extensions are made by using Form 4868, 2688, or 2350, which have checkboxes for Form 709. See Form 4868 to get an automatic 4-month extension by phone using a credit card to pay part or all of the Federal income tax (but not gift or GST taxes) you expect to owe for 2000. You may only use one of these forms to extend the time for filing your gift tax return if you are also requesting an extension of time to file your income tax return.

Where To File

File Form 709 at the applicable IRS address listed below.

If you are located in	Use the following Internal Revenue Service Center address
New York *(New York City and counties of Nassau, Rockland, Suffolk, and Westchester)*	Holtsville, NY 00501
New York *(all other counties),* Connecticut, Maine, Massachusetts, New Hampshire, Rhode Island, Vermont	Andover, MA 05501
Florida, Georgia	Atlanta, GA 39901
Arkansas, Delaware, District of Columbia, Hawaii, Indiana, Iowa, Kentucky, Louisiana, Maryland, Michigan, Minnesota, Mississippi, Missouri, New Jersey, North Carolina, Ohio, Pennsylvania, South Carolina, Texas, West Virginia, Wisconsin	Cincinnati, OH 45999
Kansas, New Mexico, Oklahoma	Austin, TX 73301

Alaska, Arizona, California *(counties of Alpine, Amador, Butte, Calaveras, Colusa, Contra Costa, Del Norte, El Dorado, Glenn, Humboldt, Lake, Lassen, Marin, Mendocino, Modoc, Napa, Nevada, Placer, Plumas, Sacramento, San Joaquin, Shasta, Sierra, Siskiyou, Solano, Sonoma, Sutter, Tehama, Trinity, Yolo, and Yuba),* Colorado, Idaho, Montana, Nebraska, Nevada, North Dakota, Oregon, South Dakota, Utah, Washington, Wyoming	Ogden, UT 84201
California *(all other counties)*	Fresno, CA 93888
Illinois	Kansas City, MO 64999
Alabama, Tennessee	Memphis, TN 37501
Virginia	Philadelphia, PA 19255
American Samoa, Guam, the Virgin Islands, Puerto Rico, a foreign country, or have an APO or FPO address	Philadelphia, PA 19255

Adequate Disclosure

To begin the running of the statute of limitations regarding a gift, the gift must be adequately disclosed on Form 709 (or an attached statement) filed for the year of the gift.

In general, a gift will be considered adequately disclosed if the return or statement provides the following:

• A description of the transferred property and any consideration received by the donor,

• The identity of, and relationship between, the donor and each donee,

• If the property is transferred in trust, the trust's EIN and a brief description of the terms of the trust (or a copy of the trust instrument in lieu of the description), and

• Either a qualified appraisal or a detailed description of the method used to determine the fair market value of the gift.

See Regulations section 301.6501(c) - 1(e) and (f) for details, including what constitutes a qualified appraisal, the information required if no appraisal is provided, and the information required for transfers under sections 2701 and 2702.

Penalties

The law provides for penalties for both late filing of returns and late payment of tax unless you have reasonable cause. There are also penalties for valuation understatements that cause an underpayment of the tax, willful failure to file a return on time, and willful attempt to evade or defeat payment of tax.

The late filing penalty will not be imposed if the taxpayer can show that the failure to file a timely return is due to reasonable cause. Those filing late (after the due date, including extensions) should attach an explanation to the return to show reasonable cause.

A valuation understatement occurs when the reported value of property entered on Form 709 is 50% or less of the actual value of the property.

Joint Tenancy

If you buy property with your own funds and the title to such property is held by yourself and the donee as joint tenants with right of survivorship and if either you or the donee may give up those rights by severing your interest, you have made a gift to the donee in the amount of half the value of the property.

If you create a joint bank account for yourself and the donee (or a similar kind of ownership by which you can get back the entire fund without the donee's consent), you have made a gift to the donee when the donee draws on the account for his or her own benefit. The amount of the gift is the amount that the donee took out without any obligation to repay you. If you buy a U.S. savings bond registered as payable to yourself or the donee, there is a gift to the donee when he or she cashes the bond without any obligation to account to you.

Transfer of Certain Life Estates

If you received a qualifying terminable interest (see page 9) from your spouse for which a marital deduction was elected on your spouse's estate or gift tax return, you will be subject to the gift (and GST, if applicable) tax if you dispose of all or part of your life income interest (by gift, sale, or otherwise).

The entire value of the property involved less (a) the amount you received on the disposition and (b) the amount (if any) of the life income interest you retained after the transfer will be treated as a taxable gift. That portion of the property's value that is attributable to the remainder interest is a gift of a future interest for which no annual exclusion is allowed. To the extent you made a gift of the life income interest, you may claim an annual exclusion, treating the person to whom you transferred the interest as the donee for purposes of computing the annual exclusion.

Specific Instructions

Part 1 — General Information

Split Gifts — Gifts by Husband or Wife to Third Parties

A married couple may not file a joint gift tax return.

FIGURE A.2 *Continued*

However, if after reading the instructions below, you and your spouse agree to split your gifts, you should file both of your individual gift tax returns together (i.e., in the same envelope) to avoid correspondence from the IRS.

If you and your spouse agree, all gifts (including gifts of property held with your spouse as joint tenants or tenants by the entirety) either of you make to third parties during the calendar year will be considered as made one-half by each of you if:

• You and your spouse were married to one another at the time of the gift;

• If divorced or widowed after the gift, you did not remarry during the rest of the calendar year;

• Neither of you was a nonresident alien at the time of the gift; and

• You did not give your spouse a general power of appointment over the property interest transferred.

If you transferred property partly to your spouse and partly to third parties, you can only split the gifts if the interest transferred to the third parties is ascertainable at the time of the gift.

If you meet these requirements and want your gifts to be considered made one-half by you and one-half by your spouse, check the "Yes" box on line 12, page 1; complete lines 13 through 17; and have your spouse sign the consent on line 18. If you are not married or do not wish to split gifts, skip to Schedule A.

Line 15. If you were married to one another for the entire calendar year, check the "Yes" box and skip to line 17. If you were married for only part of the year, check the "No" box and go to line 16.

Line 16. Check the box that explains the change in your marital status during the year and give the date you were married, divorced, or widowed.

Consent of Spouse

To have your gifts (and generation-skipping transfers) considered as made one-half by each of you, your spouse must sign the consent. The consent may generally be signed at any time after the end of the calendar year. However, there are two exceptions:

1. The consent may not be signed after April 15 following the end of the year in which the gift was made. (But, if neither you nor your spouse has filed a gift tax return for the year on or before that date, the consent must be made on the first gift tax return for the year filed by either of you.)

2. The consent may not be signed after a notice of deficiency for the gift or GST tax for the year has been sent to either you or your spouse.

The executor for a deceased spouse or the guardian for a legally incompetent spouse may sign the consent.

The consent is effective for the entire calendar year; therefore, all gifts made by both you and your spouse to third parties during the calendar year (while you were married) must be split.

If the consent is effective, the liability for the entire gift and GST taxes of each spouse is joint and several.

When the Consenting Spouse Must Also File a Gift Tax Return

If the spouses elect gift splitting (described under Split Gifts on page 4), then both the donor spouse and the consenting spouse must each file separate gift tax returns unless all the requirements of either Exception 1 or 2 below are met.

Exception 1. During the calendar year:

• Only one spouse made any gifts;

• The total value of these gifts to each third-party donee does not exceed $20,000; and

• All of the gifts were of present interests.

Exception 2. During the calendar year:

• Only one spouse (the donor spouse) made gifts of more than $10,000 but not more than $20,000 to any third-party donee;

• The only gifts made by the other spouse (the consenting spouse) were gifts of not more than $10,000 to third-party donees other than those to whom the donor spouse made gifts; and

• All of the gifts by both spouses were of present interests.

If either Exception 1 or 2 is met, only the donor spouse must file a return and the consenting spouse signifies consent on that return. This return may be made on Form 709-A, United States Short Form Gift Tax Return. This form is much easier to complete than Form 709, and you should consider filing it whenever either of the above exceptions is met and the gifts consist entirely of present interests in tangible personal property, cash, U.S. Savings Bonds, or stocks and bonds listed on a stock exchange.

Specific instructions for Part 2 — Tax Computation are continued on page 11. Because you must complete Schedules A, B, and C to fill out Part 2, you will find instructions for these schedules below.

Schedule A — Computation of Taxable Gifts

Do not enter on Schedule A any gift or part of a gift that qualifies for the political organization, educational, or medical exclusions. In the instructions below, "gifts" means gifts (or parts of

gifts) that do not qualify for the political organization, educational, or medical exclusions.

Valuation Discounts

If the value of any gift you report in either Part 1 or Part 2 of Schedule A reflects a discount for lack of marketability, a minority interest, a fractional interest in real estate, blockage, market absorption, or for any other reason, answer "Yes" to the question at the top of Schedule A. Also, attach an explanation giving the factual basis for the claimed discounts and the amount of the discounts taken.

Qualified State Tuition Programs

If your total 2000 contributions to a qualified state tuition plan on behalf of any individual beneficiary exceed $10,000, then for purposes of the annual exclusion you may elect under section 529(c)(2)(B) to treat up to $50,000 of your total contributions as having been made ratably over a 5-year period beginning in 2000.

You must report in 2000 the entire amount of the contribution in excess of $50,000.

You make the election by checking the box on line B at the top of Schedule A. The election must be made for the calendar year in which the contribution is made. Also attach an explanation that includes the following:

• The total amount contributed per individual beneficiary;

• The amount for which the election is being made;

• The name of the individual for whom the contribution was made.

If you make this election, report only ⅕ (20%) of your total contributions (up to $50,000) on the 2000 Form 709. You must then report an additional 20% of the total in each of the succeeding 4 years. If you are electing gift splitting for the contributions, apply the gift-splitting rules before applying these rules. In this case, both spouses must make the section 529(c)(2)(B) election on their respective returns.

Note: *Contributions to qualified state tuition plans do not qualify for the educational exclusion.*

How To Complete Schedule A

After you determine which gifts you made are subject to the gift tax and therefore should be listed on Schedule A, you must divide these gifts between those subject only to the gift tax (gifts made to nonskip persons — see page 6) and those subject to both the gift and GST taxes (gifts made to skip persons — see page 6). Gifts made to nonskip persons are entered in Part 1. Gifts made to skip persons are entered in Part 2.

If you need more space, attach a separate sheet using the same format as Schedule A.

STF FED1435I.5

FIGURE A.2 *Continued*

Gifts to Donees Other Than Your Spouse

You must always enter all gifts of *future interests* that you made during the calendar year regardless of their value.

If you do not elect gift splitting. If the total gifts of *present interests* to any donee are more than $10,000 in the calendar year, then you must enter *all such gifts* that you made during the year to or on behalf of that donee, including those gifts that will be excluded under the annual exclusion. If the total is $10,000 or less, you need not enter on Schedule A any gifts (except gifts of future interests) that you made to that donee.

If you elect gift splitting. Enter on Schedule A the entire value of any gift you made during the calendar year while you were married, even if the gift's value will be less than $10,000 after it is split on line 2 of Part 3.

Gifts to Your Spouse

You do not need to enter any of your gifts to your spouse on Schedule A unless you gave a gift of a terminable interest to your spouse, you gave a gift of a future interest to your spouse as described below, or your spouse was not a citizen of the United States at the time of the gift.

Terminable interest. Terminable interests are defined in the instructions to line 8. If all the terminable interests you gave to your spouse qualify as life estates with power of appointment (defined on page 9) you do not need to enter any of them on Schedule A.

However, if you gave your spouse any terminable interest that does not qualify as a life estate with power of appointment, you must report on Schedule A all gifts of terminable interests you made to your spouse during the year.

You should not report any gifts you made to your spouse who is a U.S. citizen that are not terminable interests (except as described under Future Interest below), whether or not they can be deducted.

Charitable remainder trusts. If you make a gift to a charitable remainder trust and your spouse is the only noncharitable beneficiary (other than yourself), the interest you gave to your spouse is not considered a terminable interest and, therefore, should not be shown on Schedule A. For definitions and rules concerning these trusts, see section 2056(b)(8)(B) and Regulations section 20.2055-2.

Future Interest. Generally, you should not report gifts of future interests to your spouse unless the future interest is also a terminable interest that is required to be reported as described above. However, if you gave a gift of a future interest to your spouse and you are required to report the gift on Form 709 because you gave the present interest to a donee other than your spouse, then you should enter the entire gift, including the future interest given to your spouse, on Schedule A. You should use the rules under Gifts Subject to Both Gift and GST Taxes, below, to determine whether to enter the gift on Schedule A, Part 1 or Part 2.

Non-U.S. citizen spouse donee. If your spouse is not a U.S. citizen and you gave him or her a gift of a future interest, you must report on Schedule A all gifts to your spouse for the year. If all gifts to your spouse were present interests, do not report on Schedule A any gifts to your spouse if the total of such gifts for the year does not exceed $103,000 and all gifts in excess of $10,000 would qualify for a marital deduction if your spouse were a U.S. citizen (see the instructions for Schedule A, Part 3, line 8, on page 9). If the gifts exceed $103,000, you must report all of the gifts even though some may be excluded.

Gifts Subject to Both Gift and GST Taxes

Direct Skip

The GST tax you must report on Form 709 is that imposed only on inter vivos direct skips. An "inter vivos direct skip" is a gift that (a) is subject to the gift tax, (b) is an interest in property, and (c) is made to a skip person. All three requirements must be met before the gift is subject to the GST tax.

A gift is "subject to the gift tax" if you are required to list it on Schedule A of Form 709 (as described above). However, if you make a nontaxable gift (which is a direct skip) to a trust for the benefit of an individual, this transfer is also subject to the GST tax unless:

1. During the lifetime of the beneficiary, no corpus or income may be distributed to anyone other than the beneficiary; and

2. If the beneficiary dies before the termination of the trust, the assets of the trust will be included in the gross estate of the beneficiary.

Note: *If the property transferred in the direct skip would have been includible in the donor's estate if the donor had died immediately after the transfer, see Transfers Subject to an "Estate Tax Inclusion Period" on page 2.*

To determine if a gift "is of an interest in property" and "is made to a skip person," you must first determine if the donee is a "natural person" or a "trust" as defined below.

Trust

For purposes of the GST tax, trust includes not only an explicit trust, but also any other arrangement (other than an estate) that although not explicitly a trust, has substantially the same effect as a trust. For example, trust includes life estates with remainders, terms for years, and insurance and annuity contracts. A transfer of property that is conditional on the occurrence of an event is a transfer in trust.

Interest in Property

If a gift is made to a "natural person," it is always considered a gift of an interest in property for purposes of the GST tax.

If a gift is made to a trust, a natural person will have an interest in the property transferred to the trust if that person either has a present right to receive income or corpus from the trust (such as an income interest for life) or is a permissible current recipient of income or corpus from the trust (e.g., possesses a general power of appointment).

Skip Person

A donee who is a natural person is a skip person if that donee is assigned to a generation that is two or more generations below the generation assignment of the donor. See Determining the Generation of a Donee below.

A donee that is a trust is a skip person if all the interests in the property transferred to the trust (as defined above) are held by skip persons.

A trust will also be a skip person if there are no interests in the property transferred to the trust held by any person, and future distributions or terminations from the trust can be made only to skip persons.

NonSkip Person

A nonskip person is any donee who is not a skip person.

Determining the Generation of a Donee

Generally, a generation is determined along family lines as follows:

1. If the donee is a lineal descendant of a grandparent of the donor (e.g., the donor's cousin, niece, nephew, etc.), the number of generations between the donor and the descendant (donee) is determined by subtracting the number of generations between the grandparent and the donor from the number of generations between the grandparent and the descendant (donee).

2. If the donee is a lineal descendant of a grandparent of a spouse (or former spouse) of the donor, the number of generations between the donor and the descendant (donee) is determined by subtracting the number of generations between the grandparent and the spouse (or former spouse) from the number of generations between the grandparent and the descendant (donee).

FIGURE A.2 *Continued*

3. A person who at any time was married to a person described in 1 or 2 above is assigned to the generation of that person. A person who at any time was married to the donor is assigned to the donor's generation.

4. A relationship by adoption or half-blood is treated as a relationship by whole-blood.

5. A person who is not assigned to a generation according to 1, 2, 3, or 4 above is assigned to a generation based on his or her birth date as follows:

a. A person who was born not more than 12½ years after the donor is in the donor's generation.

b. A person born more than 12½ years, but not more than 37½ years, after the donor is in the first generation younger than the donor.

c. Similar rules apply for a new generation every 25 years.

If more than one of the rules for assigning generations applies to a donee, that donee is generally assigned to the youngest of the generations that would apply.

If an estate or trust, partnership, corporation, or other entity (other than certain charitable organizations and trusts described in sections 511(a)(2) and 511(b)(2) and governmental entities) is a donee, then each person who indirectly receives the gift through the entity is treated as a donee and is assigned to a generation as explained in the above rules.

Charitable organizations and trusts described in sections 511(a)(2) and 511(b)(2) and governmental entities are assigned to the donor's generation. Transfers to such organizations are therefore not subject to the GST tax. These gifts should always be listed in Part 1 of Schedule A.

Charitable Remainder Trusts

Gifts in the form of charitable remainder annuity trusts, charitable remainder unitrusts, and pooled income funds are not transfers to skip persons and therefore are not direct skips. You should always list these gifts in Part 1 of Schedule A even if all of the life beneficiaries are skip persons.

Generation Assignment Where Intervening Parent Is Dead

If you made a gift to your grandchild and at the time you made the gift, the grandchild's parent (who is your or your spouse's or your former spouse's child) is dead, then for purposes of generation assignment, your grandchild is considered to be your child rather than your grandchild. Your grandchild's children will be treated as your grandchildren rather than your great-grandchildren.

This rule is also applied to your lineal descendants below the level of grandchild. For example, if your grandchild is dead, your great-grandchildren who are lineal descendants of the dead grandchild are considered your grandchildren for purposes of the GST tax.

This special rule may also apply in other cases of the death of a parent of the transferee. Beginning with gifts made in 1998, the existing rule that applies to grandchildren of the decedent has been extended to apply to other lineal descendants.

If property is transferred to an individual who is a descendant of a parent of the transferor and that individual's parent (who is a lineal descendant of the parent of the transferor) is dead at the time the transfer is subject to gift or estate tax, then for purposes of generation assignment, the individual is treated as if he or she is a member of the generation that is one generation below the lower of:

• the transferor's generation or

• the generation assignment of the youngest living ancestor of the individual who is also a descendant of the parent of the transferor.

The same rules apply to the generation assignment of any descendant of the individual.

This rule does not apply to a transfer to an individual who is not a lineal descendant of the transferor if the transferor has any living lineal descendants.

If any transfer of property to a trust would have been a direct skip except for this generation assignment rule, then the rule also applies to transfers from the trust attributable to such property.

Examples

The generation-skipping transfer rules can be illustrated by the following examples:

Example 1. You give your house to your daughter for her life with the remainder then passing to her children. This gift is made to a "trust" even though there is no explicit trust instrument. The interest in the property transferred (the present right to use the house) is transferred to a nonskip person (your daughter). Therefore, the trust is not a skip person because there is an interest in the transferred property that is held by a nonskip person. The gift is not a direct skip and you should list it in Part 1 of Schedule A. (However, on the death of the daughter, a termination of her interest in the trust will occur that may be subject to the generation-skipping transfer tax. See the instructions for line 5, Part 2, Schedule C (on page 10) for a discussion of how to allocate GST exemption to such a trust.)

Example 2. You give $100,000 to your grandchild. This gift is a direct skip that is not made in trust. You should list it in Part 2 of Schedule A.

Example 3. You establish a trust that is required to accumulate income for 10 years and then pay its income to your grandchildren for their lives and upon their deaths distribute the corpus to their children. Because the trust has no current beneficiaries, there are no present interests in the property transferred to the trust. All of the persons to whom the trust can make future distributions (including distributions upon the termination of interests in property held in trust) are skip persons (i.e., your grandchildren and great-grandchildren). Therefore, the trust itself is a skip person and you should list the gift in Part 2 of Schedule A.

Example 4. You establish a trust that pays all of its income to your grandchildren for 10 years. At the end of 10 years, the corpus is to be distributed to your children. Since for this purpose interests in trusts are defined only as present interests, all of the interests in this trust are held by skip persons (the children's interests are future interests). Therefore, the trust is a skip person and you should list the entire amount you transferred to the trust in Part 2 of Schedule A even though some of the trust's ultimate beneficiaries are nonskip persons.

Part 1 — Gifts Subject Only to Gift Tax

List gifts subject only to the gift tax in Part 1. Generally, all of the gifts you made to your spouse (that are required to be listed, as described earlier), to your children, and to charitable organizations are not subject to the GST tax and should, therefore, be listed only in Part 1.

Group the gifts in four categories: gifts made to your spouse; gifts made to third parties that are to be split with your spouse; charitable gifts (if you are not splitting gifts with your spouse); and other gifts. If a transfer results in gifts to two or more individuals (such as a life estate to one with remainder to the other), list the gift to each separately.

Number and describe all gifts (including charitable, public, and similar gifts) in the columns provided in Schedule A. Describe each gift in enough detail so that the property can be easily identified, as explained below.

For real estate provide:

• A legal description of each parcel;

• The street number, name, and area if the property is located in a city; and

• A short statement of any improvements made to the property.

For bonds, give:

• The number of bonds transferred;

STF FED1435L7

FIGURE A.2 *Continued*

- The principal amount of each bond;
- Name of obligor;
- Date of maturity;
- Rate of interest;
- Date or dates when interest is payable;
- Series number if there is more than one issue;
- Exchanges where listed or, if unlisted, give the location of the principal business office of the corporation; and
- CUSIP number. The CUSIP number is a nine-digit number assigned by the American Banking Association to traded securities.

For stocks:

- Give number of shares;
- State whether common or preferred;
- If preferred, give the issue, par value, quotation at which returned, and exact name of corporation;
- If unlisted on a principal exchange, give location of principal business office of corporation, state in which incorporated, and date of incorporation;
- If listed, give principal exchange; and
- CUSIP number. The CUSIP number is a nine-digit number assigned by the American Banking Association to traded securities.

For interests in property based on the length of a person's life, give the date of birth of the person.

For life insurance policies, give the name of the insurer and the policy number.

Clearly identify in the description column which gifts create the opening of an estate tax inclusion period (ETIP) as described under **Transfers Subject to an "Estate Tax Inclusion Period"** on page 2. Describe the interest that is creating the ETIP. You may not allocate the GST exemption to these transfers until the close of the ETIP. See the instructions for Schedule C on page 10.

Donor's Adjusted Basis of Gifts

Show the basis you would use for income tax purposes if the gift were sold or exchanged. Generally, this means cost plus improvements, less applicable depreciation, amortization, and depletion.

For more information on adjusted basis, see Pub. 551, Basis of Assets.

Date and Value of Gift

The value of a gift is the fair market value of the property on the date the gift is made. The fair market value is the price at which the property would change hands between a willing buyer and a willing seller, when neither is forced to buy or to sell, and when both have reasonable knowledge of all relevant facts. Fair market value may not be determined by a forced sale price, nor by the sale price of the item in a market other than that in

which the item is most commonly sold to the public. The location of the item must be taken into account wherever appropriate.

The fair market value of a stock or bond (whether listed or unlisted) is the mean between the highest and lowest selling prices quoted on the valuation date. If only the closing selling prices are available, then the fair market value is the mean between the quoted closing selling price on the valuation date and on the trading day before the valuation date. To figure the fair market value if there were no sales on the valuation date, see the instructions for Schedule B of Form 706.

Stock of close corporations or inactive stock must be valued on the basis of net worth, earnings, earning and dividend capacity, and other relevant factors.

Generally, the best indication of the value of real property is the price paid for the property in an arm's-length transaction on or before the valuation date. If there has been no such transaction, use the comparable sales method. In comparing similar properties, consider differences in the date of the sale, and the size, condition, and location of the properties, and make all appropriate adjustments.

The value of all annuities, life estates, terms for years, remainders, or reversions is generally the present value on the date of the gift.

Sections 2701 and 2702 provide special valuation rules to determine the amount of the gift when a donor transfers an equity interest in a corporation or partnership (section 2701) or makes a gift in trust (section 2702). The rules only apply if, immediately after the transfer, the donor (or an applicable family member) holds an applicable retained interest in the corporation or partnership, or retains an interest in the trust. For details, see sections 2701 and 2702, and their regulations.

Supplemental Documents

To support the value of your gifts, you must provide information showing how it was determined.

For stock of close corporations or inactive stock, attach balance sheets, particularly the one nearest the date of the gift, and statements of net earnings or operating results and dividends paid for each of the 5 preceding years.

For each life insurance policy, attach Form 712, Life Insurance Statement.

Note for single premium or paid-up policies: *In certain situations, for example, where the surrender value of the policy exceeds its replacement cost, the true economic value of the policy will be greater than the amount shown on line 59 of Form 712. In these situations, report the full economic value of the policy on Schedule A. See Rev. Rul. 78-137, 1978-1 C.B. 280 for details.*

If the gift was made by means of a trust, attach a certified or verified copy of the trust instrument to the return on which you report your first transfer to the trust. However, to report subsequent transfers to the trust, you may attach a brief description of the terms of the trust or a copy of the trust instrument.

Also attach any appraisal used to determine the value of real estate or other property.

If you do not attach this information, you must include in Schedule A full information to explain how the value was determined.

Part 2 — Gifts That are Direct Skips and are Subject to Both Gift Tax and Generation-Skipping Transfer Tax

List in Part 2 only those gifts that are subject to both the gift and GST taxes. You must list the **gifts in Part 2 in the chronological order that you made them.** Number, describe, and value the gifts as described in the instructions for Part 1 on page 7.

If you made a gift in trust, list the entire gift as one line entry in Part 2. Enter the entire value of the property transferred to the trust even if the trust has nonskip person future beneficiaries.

How to report GST transfers after the close of an ETIP. If you are reporting a generation-skipping transfer that was subject to an "estate tax inclusion period" (ETIP) (provided the ETIP closed as a result of something other than the death of the transferor — see Form 706), and you are also reporting gifts made during the year, complete Schedule A as you normally would with the following changes:

Report the transfer subject to an ETIP on Schedule A, Part 2.

1. Column B. In addition to the information already requested, describe the interest that is closing the ETIP; explain what caused the interest to terminate; and list the year the gift portion of the transfer was reported and its item number on Schedule A of the Form 709 that was originally filed to report the gift portion of the ETIP transfer.

2. Column D. Give the date the ETIP closed rather than the date of the initial gift.

3. Column E. Enter "N/A" in Column E.

The value is entered only in Column B, Part 1, Schedule C. See the instructions for Schedule C.

Part 3 — Taxable Gift Reconciliation

If you have made no gifts yourself and are filing this return only to report gifts made by your spouse but which are being split with you, skip lines 1 - 3 and enter your share of the split gifts on line 4.

FIGURE A.2 *Continued*

Line 2. If you are not splitting gifts with your spouse, skip this line and enter the amount from line 1 on line 3. If you are splitting gifts with your spouse, show half of the gifts you made to third parties on line 2. On the dotted line indicate which numbered items from Parts 1 and 2 of Schedule A you treated this way. Generally, if you elect to split your gifts, you must split ALL gifts made by you and your spouse to third-party donees. The only exception is if you gave your spouse a general power of appointment over a gift you made.

Line 4. If you are not splitting gifts, skip this line and go to line 5. If you gave all of the gifts, and your spouse is only filing to show his or her half of those gifts, you need not enter any gifts on line 4 of your return or include your spouse's half anywhere else on your return. Your spouse should enter the amount from Schedule A, line 2, of your return on Schedule A, line 4, of his or her return.

If both you and your spouse make gifts for which a return is required, the amount each of you shows on Schedule A, line 2, of his or her return must be shown on Schedule A, line 4, of the other's return.

Line 6. Enter the total annual exclusions you are claiming for the gifts listed on Schedule A (including gifts listed on line 4). See **Annual Exclusion** on page 3. If you split a gift with your spouse, the annual exclusion you claim against that gift may not be more than your half of the gift.

Deductions

Line 8. Enter on line 8 all of the gifts to your spouse that you listed on Schedule A and for which you are claiming a marital deduction. Do not enter any gift that you did not include on Schedule A. On the dotted line on line 8, indicate which numbered items from Schedule A are gifts to your spouse for which you are claiming the marital deduction.

Do not enter on line 8 any gifts to your spouse who was not a U.S. citizen at the time of the gift.

You may deduct all gifts of nonterminable interests made during this time that you entered on Schedule A regardless of amount, and certain gifts of terminable interests as outlined below.

Terminable Interests. Generally, you cannot take the marital deduction if the gift to your spouse is a terminable interest. In most instances, a terminable interest is nondeductible if someone other than the donee spouse will have an interest in the property following the termination of the donee spouse's interest. Some examples of terminable interests are:

- A life estate;
- An estate for a specified number of years; or
- Any other property interest that after a period of time will terminate or fail.

If you transfer an interest to your spouse as sole joint tenant with yourself or as a tenant by the entirety, the interest is not considered a terminable interest just because the tenancy may be severed.

Life estate with power of appointment. You may deduct, without an election, a gift of a terminable interest if all four requirements below are met:

1. Your spouse is entitled for life to all of the income from the entire interest;

2. The income is paid yearly or more often;

3. Your spouse has the unlimited power, while he or she is alive or by will, to appoint the entire interest in all circumstances; and

4. No part of the entire interest is subject to another person's power of appointment (except to appoint it to your spouse).

If either the right to income or the power of appointment given to your spouse pertains only to a specific portion of a property interest, the marital deduction is allowed only to the extent that the rights of your spouse meet all 4 of the above conditions. For example, if your spouse is to receive all of the income from the entire interest, but only has a power to appoint one-half of the entire interest, then only one-half qualifies for the marital deduction.

A partial interest in property is treated as a specific portion of an entire interest only if the rights of your spouse to the income and to the power constitute a fractional or percentile share of the entire property interest. This means that the interest or share will reflect any increase or decrease in the value of the entire property interest. If the spouse is entitled to receive a specified sum of income annually, the capital amount that would produce such a sum will be considered the specific portion from which the spouse is entitled to receive the income.

Election to deduct qualified terminable interest property (QTIP). You may elect to deduct a gift of a terminable interest if it meets requirements 1, 2, and 4 above, even though it does not meet requirement 3.

You make this election simply by listing the qualified terminable interest property on Schedule A and deducting its value on line 8, Part 3, Schedule A. There is no longer a box to check to make the election. You are presumed to have made the election for all qualified property that you both list and deduct on Schedule A. You may not make the election on a late filed Form 709.

Line 9. Enter the amount of the annual exclusions that were claimed for the gifts you listed on line 8.

Line 11. You may deduct from the total gifts made during the calendar year all gifts you gave to or for the use of:

- The United States, a state or political subdivision of a state or the District of Columbia, for exclusively public purposes;

- Any corporation, trust, community chest, fund, or foundation organized and operated only for religious, charitable, scientific, literary, or educational purposes, or to prevent cruelty to children or animals, or to foster national or international amateur sports competition (if none of its activities involve providing athletic equipment (unless it is a qualified amateur sports organization)), as long as no part of the earnings benefits any one person, no substantial propaganda is produced, and no lobbying or campaigning for any candidate for public office is done;

- A fraternal society, order, or association operating under a lodge system, if the transferred property is to be used only for religious, charitable, scientific, literary, or educational purposes, including the encouragement of art and the prevention of cruelty to children or animals;

- Any war veterans' organization organized in the United States (or any of its possessions), or any of its auxiliary departments or local chapters or posts, as long as no part of any of the earnings benefits any one person.

On line 11, show your total charitable, public, or similar gifts (minus annual exclusions allowed). On the dotted line, indicate which numbered items from the top of Schedule A (or line 4) are charitable gifts.

Line 14. If you will pay GST tax with this return on any direct skips reported on this return, the amount of that GST tax is also considered a gift and must be added to your other gifts reported on this return.

If you entered gifts on Part 2, or if you and your spouse elected gift splitting and your spouse made gifts subject to the GST tax that you are required to show on your Form 709, complete Schedule C, and enter on line 14 the total of Schedule C, Part 3, column H. Otherwise, enter zero on line 14.

Line 17. Section 2523(f)(6) creates an automatic QTIP election for gifts of joint and survivor annuities where the spouses are the only possible recipients of the annuity prior to the death of the last surviving spouse.

The donor spouse can elect out of QTIP treatment, however, by checking the box on line 17 and entering the item number from Schedule A for the annuities for which you are making the election. Any annuities entered on line 17 cannot also be entered on line 8 of Schedule A, Part 3. Any such annuities that are not listed on line 17 must be entered on line 8 of Part 3, Schedule A. If there is more

FIGURE A.2 *Continued*

than one such joint and survivor annuity, you are not required to make the election for all of them. Once made, the election is irrevocable.

Schedule B — Gifts From Prior Periods

If you did not file gift tax returns for previous periods, check the "No" box on line 11a of Part 1, page 1, and skip to the Tax Computation on page 1. (However, be sure to complete Schedule C, if applicable.) If you filed gift tax returns for previous periods, check the "Yes" box on line 11a and complete Schedule B by listing the years or quarters in chronological order as described below. If you need more space, attach a separate sheet using the same format as Schedule B.

If you filed returns for gifts made before 1971 or after 1981, show the calendar years in column A. If you filed returns for gifts made after 1970 and before 1982, show the calendar quarters.

In column B, identify the Internal Revenue Service office where you filed the returns. If you have changed your name, be sure to list any other names under which the returns were filed. If there was any other variation in the names under which you filed, such as the use of full given names instead of initials, please explain.

In column E, show the correct amount (the amount finally determined) of the taxable gifts for each earlier period.

See Regulations section 25.2504-2 for rules regarding the final determination of the value of a gift.

Schedule C — Computation of Generation-Skipping Transfer Tax

Part 1 — Generation-Skipping Transfers

You must enter in Part 1 all of the gifts you listed in Part 2 of Schedule A in that order and using those same values.

Column B. Transfers subject to an ETIP. If you are reporting a generation-skipping transfer that occurred because of the close of an "estate tax inclusion period" (ETIP), complete column B for such transfer as follows:

1. Provided the GST exemption is being allocated on a timely filed gift tax return, enter the value as of the close of the ETIP.

2. If the exemption is being allocated after the due date (including extensions) for the gift tax return on which the transfer should be reported, enter the value as of the time the exemption allocation was made.

Column C. If you elected gift splitting, enter half the value of each gift entered in column B. If you did not elect gift splitting, enter zero in column C.

Column E. You are allowed to claim the gift tax annual exclusion currently allowable with respect to your reported direct skips (other than certain direct skips to trusts — see Note below), using the rules and limits discussed earlier for the gift tax annual exclusion. However, you must allocate the exclusion on a gift-by-gift basis for GST computation purposes. You must allocate the exclusion to each gift to the maximum allowable amount and in chronological order, beginning with the earliest gift that qualifies for the exclusion. Be sure that you do not claim a total exclusion of more than $10,000 per donee.

Note: *You may not claim any annual exclusion for a direct skip made to a trust unless the trust meets the requirements discussed under Direct Skip on page 6.*

Part 2 — GST Exemption Reconciliation

Line 1. Every donor is allowed a lifetime GST exemption. The amount of the exemption is indexed for inflation and is published annually by the IRS in a revenue procedure. For transfers made through 1998, the GST exemption is $1 million. For transfers made in 2000, the exemption is $1,030,000. For transfers made in 1999, the exemption is $1,010,000.

The $20,000 increase in 2000 from 1999 can only be allocated to transfers made during or after calendar year 2000. The $10,000 increase in 1999 can only be allocated to transfers made during or after calendar year 1999.

Example. A donor had made $1.5 million in GST transfers through 1998 and had allocated all $1 million of the exemption to those transfers. In 2000, the donor makes a $5,000 taxable generation-skipping transfer. The donor can allocate $5,000 of exemption to the 2000 transfer but cannot allocate $5,000 of the unused exemption to pre-1999 transfers or $20,000 of the unused exemption to pre-2000 transfers.

You should keep a record of your transfers and exemption allocations to make sure that any future increases are allocated correctly.

Enter on line 1 of Part 2 the maximum GST exemption you are allowed. This will not necessarily be the highest indexed amount if you have made no GST transfer during the year of the increase. For example, if your last GST transfer was in 1998, your maximum GST exemption would be $1,000,000, not $1,030,000.

The donor can apply this exemption to inter vivos transfers (i.e., transfers made during the donor's life) on Form 709. The executor can apply the exemption on Form 706 to transfers taking effect at death. An allocation is irrevocable.

In the case of inter vivos direct skips, a portion of the donor's unused exemption is automatically allocated to the transferred property unless the donor elects otherwise. To elect out of the automatic application of exemption, you must file Form 709 and attach a statement to it clearly describing the transaction and the extent to which the automatic allocation is not to apply. Reporting a direct skip on a timely filed Form 709 and paying the GST tax on the transfer will qualify as such a statement.

Special QTIP election. If you have elected QTIP treatment for any gifts in trust listed on Schedule A, Part 1, then you may make an election on Schedule C to treat the entire trust as non-QTIP for purposes of the GST tax. The election must be made for the entire trust that contains the particular gift involved on this return. Be sure to identify by item number the specific gift for which you are making this special QTIP election.

Line 5. You may wish to allocate your exemption to transfers made in trust that are not direct skips. For example, if you transferred property to a trust that has your children as its present beneficiaries and your grandchildren and great-grandchildren as future beneficiaries, the transfer was not a direct skip because the present interests in the trust are held by nonskip persons. However, future terminations and distributions made from this trust would be subject to the GST tax.

You may elect to reduce the trust's inclusion ratio by allocating part or all of your exemption to the transfer. Because this transfer would be entered on Schedule A, Part 1, it will not be shown on Schedule C.

In other cases you may wish to allocate your exemption to a trust that is not involved in a transfer listed on Schedule A or C. For example, if your only gift for the year was $10,000 transferred to a trust that had your children as present beneficiaries and your grandchildren as future beneficiaries, you would not be required to file Form 709 for the year. However, future distributions from the trust or the termination of the trust may result in GST tax being due. In this case, you may want to allocate GST exemption to the transfer at the time of the transfer.

To allocate your exemption to such transfers, attach a statement to this Form 709 and entitle it "Notice of Allocation." You may file one Notice of Allocation and consolidate on it all of your Schedule A, Part 1, transfers, plus all transfers not appearing on Form 709, to which you wish to allocate your exemption. The notice must contain the following for each trust:

FIGURE A.2 *Continued*

- Clearly identify the trust, including the trust's EIN, if known;
- The item number(s) from column A, Schedule A, Part 1, of the gifts to that trust (if applicable);
- The values shown in column E, Schedule A, Part 1, for the gifts (adjusted to account for split gifts, if any, reported on Schedule A, Part 3, line 2) (or, if the allocation is late, the value of the trust assets at the time of the allocation);
- The amount of your GST exemption allocated to each gift (or a statement that you are allocating exemption by means of a formula such as "an amount necessary to produce an inclusion ratio of zero"); and
- The inclusion ratio of the trust after the allocation.

Total the exemption allocations and enter this total on line 5.

Note: *Where the property involved in such a transfer is subject to an estate tax inclusion period because it would be includible in the donor's estate if the donor died immediately after the transfer (other than by reason of the donor having died within 3 years of making the gift), you cannot allocate the GST exemption at the time of the transfer but must wait until the end of the estate tax inclusion period. For details, see* Transfers Subject to an "Estate Tax Inclusion Period" *on page 2, and section 2642(f).*

Part 3 — Tax Computation

You must enter in Part 3 every gift you listed in Part 1 of Schedule C.

Column C. You are not required to allocate your available exemption. You may allocate some, all, or none of your available exemption, as you wish, among the gifts listed in Part 3 of Schedule C. However, the total exemption claimed in column C may not exceed the amount you entered on line 3 of Part 2 of Schedule C.

You may enter an amount in column C that is greater than the amount you entered in column B.

Column D. Carry your computation to three decimal places (e.g., "1.000").

Part 2 — Tax Computation (Page 1 of Form)

Line 7. If you are a citizen or resident of the United States, you must take any available unified credit against gift tax. Nonresident aliens may not claim the unified credit. If you are a nonresident alien, delete the $220,550 entry and write in zero on line 11.

Line 10. Enter 20% of the amount allowed as a specific exemption for gifts made after September 8, 1976, and before January 1, 1977. (These amounts will be among those listed in column D of Schedule B, for gifts made in the third and fourth quarters of 1976.)

Line 13. Gift tax conventions are in effect with Australia, Austria, Denmark, France, Germany, Japan, Sweden, and the United Kingdom. If you are claiming a credit for payment of foreign gift tax, figure the credit on an attached sheet and attach evidence that the foreign taxes were paid. See the applicable convention for details of computing the credit.

Line 19. Make your check or money order payable to "United States Treasury" and write the donor's social security number on it. You may not use an overpayment on Form 1040 to offset the gift and GST taxes owed on Form 709.

Signature. As a donor, you must sign the return. If you pay another person, firm, or corporation to prepare your return, that person must also sign the return as preparer unless he or she is your regular full-time employee.

Disclosure, Privacy Act, and Paperwork Reduction Act Notice. We ask for the information on this form to carry out the Internal Revenue laws of the United States. We need the information to figure and collect the right amount of tax. Form 709 is used to report (1) transfers subject to the Federal gift and certain generation-skipping transfer (GST) taxes and to figure the tax, if any, due on those transfers, and (2) allocation of the lifetime GST exemption to property transferred during the transferor's lifetime.

Our legal right to ask for the information requested on this form is sections 6001, 6011, and 6019, and their regulations. You are required

to provide the information requested on this form. Section 6109 requires that you provide your social security number; this is so we know who you are, and can process your Form 709.

Generally, tax returns and return information are confidential, as stated in section 6103. However, section 6103 allows or requires the Internal Revenue Service to disclose or give such information shown on your Form 709 to the Department of Justice to enforce the tax laws, both civil and criminal, and to cities, states, the District of Columbia, U.S. commonwealths or possessions, and certain foreign governments for use in administering their tax laws.

We may disclose the information on your Form 709 to the Department of the Treasury and contractors for tax administration purposes; and to other persons as necessary to obtain information which we cannot get in any other way for purposes of determining the amount of or to collect the tax you owe. We may disclose the information on your Form 709 to the Comptroller General to review the Internal Revenue Service. We may also disclose the information on your Form 709 to Committees of Congress; Federal, state and local child support agencies; and to other Federal agencies for the purpose of determining entitlement for benefits or the eligibility for, and the repayment of, loans.

If you are required to but do not file a Form 709, or do not provide the information requested on the form, or provide fraudulent information, you may be charged penalties and be subject to criminal prosecution.

Table for Computing Tax

Column A	Column B	Column C	Column D
Taxable amount over —	Taxable amount not over —	Tax on amount in Column A	Rate of tax on excess over amount in Column A
– – –	$10,000	– – –	18%
$10,000	20,000	$1,800	20%
20,000	40,000	3,800	22%
40,000	60,000	8,200	24%
60,000	80,000	13,000	26%
80,000	100,000	18,200	28%
100,000	150,000	23,800	30%
150,000	250,000	38,800	32%
250,000	500,000	70,800	34%
500,000	750,000	155,800	37%
750,000	1,000,000	248,300	39%
1,000,000	1,250,000	345,800	41%
1,250,000	1,500,000	448,300	43%
1,500,000	2,000,000	555,800	45%
2,000,000	2,500,000	780,800	49%
2,500,000	3,000,000	1,025,800	53%
3,000,000	10,000,000	1,290,800	55%
10,000,000	17,184,000	5,140,800	60%
17,184,000	– – –	9,451,200	55%

STF FED1435L11

FIGURE A.2 *Continued*

375

You are not required to provide the information requested on a form that is subject to the Paperwork Reduction Act unless the form displays a valid OMB control number. Books or records relating to a form or its instructions must be retained as long as their contents may become material in the administration of any Internal Revenue law.

The time needed to complete and file this form will vary depending on individual circumstances. The estimated average time is:

Recordkeeping .... 40 min.
Learning about the law or
the form .... 1 hr., 5 min.
Preparing the form .... 1 hr., 54 min.
Copying, assembling, and
sending the form to the IRS .... 1 hr., 3 min.

If you have comments concerning the accuracy of these time estimates or suggestions for making this form simpler, we would be happy to hear from you. You can write to the Tax Forms Committee, Western Area Distribution Center, Rancho Cordova, CA 95743-0001. Do not send the tax form to this office. Instead, see Where To File on page 4.

Page 12

STF FED1435L12

FIGURE A.2 *Continued*

376

APPENDIX

B

Tax Rates

Individuals, Estates, and Trusts

(Tax Years Beginning in 2001)

Col. 1 Taxable Income $	Separate Return Tax on Col. 1 $	Separate Return Rate on Excess %	Joint Return Tax on Col. 1 $	Joint Return Rate on Excess %	Single Return Tax on Col. 1 $	Single Return Rate on Excess %	Head of Household Tax on Col. 1 $	Head of Household Rate on Excess %	Trusts and Estates Tax on Col. 1 $	Trusts and Estates Rate on Excess %
0	0	10	0	10	0	10	0	10	0	15
1,800	180	10	180	10	180	10	180	10	270	27.5
4,250	425	10	425	10	425	10	425	10	944	30.5
6,000	600	10	600	10	600	15	600	10	1,488	30.5
6,500	650	10	650	10	675	15	650	10	1,630	35.5
8,900	890	10	890	10	1,035	15	890	10	2,482	39.1
10,000	1,000	10	1,000	10	1,200	15	1,000	15	2,912	39.1
12,000	1,200	15	1,200	15	1,500	15	1,300	15	3,694	39.1
22,600	3,390	27.5	2,790	15	3,090	15	2,890	15	7,839	39.1
27,050	4,614	27.5	3,458	15	4,058	27.5	3,558	15	9,578	39.1
36,250	7,144	27.5	4,838	15	6,588	27.5	5,438	27.5	13,176	39.1
45,200	9,605	27.5	6,780	27.5	9,049	27.5	7,899	27.5	16,675	39.1
54,625	12,197	30.5	9,372	27.5	11,641	27.5	10,491	27.5	20,360	39.1
65,550	15,529	30.5	12,376	27.5	14,645	30.5	13,495	27.5	24,632	39.1
83,250	20,928	35.5	17,244	27.5	20,044	30.5	18,363	27.5	31,553	39.1
93,650	24,620	35.5	20,104	27.5	23,216	30.5	21,223	30.5	35,619	39.1
109,250	30,158	35.5	24,394	30.5	27,974	30.5	25,981	30.5	41,719	39.1
136,750	39,921	35.5	32,782	30.5	36,361	35.5	34,369	30.5	52,472	39.1
148,675	44,153	39.1	36,419	30.5	40,594	35.5	38,006	30.5	57,135	39.1
151,650	45,316	39.1	37,326	30.5	41,650	35.5	38,913	35.5	58,298	39.1
166,500	51,122	39.1	41,855	35.5	46,922	35.5	44,185	35.5	64,104	39.1
297,350	102,284	39.1	88,307	39.1	93,374	39.1	90,636	39.1	115,266	39.1

Individuals, Estates, and Trusts

(Tax Years Beginning in 2002 and 2003)

Col. 1 Taxable Income $	Separate Return Tax on Col. 1 $	Separate Return Rate on Excess %	Joint Return Tax on Col. 1 $	Joint Return Rate on Excess %	Single Return Tax on Col. 1 $	Single Return Rate on Excess %	Head of Household Tax on Col. 1 $	Head of Household Rate on Excess %	Trusts and Estates Tax on Col. 1 $	Trusts and Estates Rate on Excess %
0	0	10	0	10	0	10	0	10	0	15
1,800	180	10	180	10	180	10	180	10	270	27
4,250	425	10	425	10	425	10	425	10	932	30
6,000	600	10	600	10	600	15	600	10	1,457	30
6,500	650	10	650	10	675	15	650	10	1,607	35
8,900	890	10	890	10	1,035	15	890	10	2,097	38.6
10,000	1,000	10	1,000	10	1,200	15	1,000	15	2,522	38.6
12,000	1,200	15	1,200	15	1,500	15	1,300	15	2,908	38.6
22,600	3,390	27	2,790	15	3,090	15	2,890	15	7,000	38.6
27,050	4,592	27	3,458	15	4,058	27	3,558	15	8,718	38.6
36,250	7,076	27	4,838	15	6,542	27	5,438	27	12,269	38.6
45,200	9,493	27	6,780	27	8,959	27	7,855	27	15,724	38.6
54,625	12,038	30	9,325	27	11,504	27	10,400	27	19,362	38.6
65,550	15,316	30	12,275	27	14,454	30	13,350	27	23,579	38.6
83,250	20,626	35	17,055	27	19,764	30	18,129	27	30,411	38.6
93,650	24,266	35	19,863	27	22,884	30	20,937	30	34,425	38.6
109,250	29,726	35	24,075	30	27,564	30	25,617	30	40,447	38.6
136,750	39,351	35	32,325	30	35,814	35	33,867	30	51,062	38.6
148,675	43,525	38.6	35,903	30	39,988	35	37,445	30	55,665	38.6
151,650	44,673	38.6	36,796	30	41,029	35	38,388	35	56,813	38.6
166,500	50,405	38.6	41,251	35	46,227	35	43,536	35	62,545	38.6
297,350	100,913	38.6	87,049	38.6	92,025	38.6	94,044	38.6	113,053	38.6

Individuals, Estates, and Trusts

(Tax Years Beginning in 2004 and 2005)

Col. 1 Taxable Income $	Separate Return Tax on Col. 1 $	Separate Return Rate on Excess %	Joint Return Tax on Col. 1 $	Joint Return Rate on Excess %	Single Return Tax on Col. 1 $	Single Return Rate on Excess %	Head of Household Tax on Col. 1 $	Head of Household Rate on Excess %	Trusts and Estates Tax on Col. 1 $	Trusts and Estates Rate on Excess %
0	0	10	0	10	0	10	0	10	0	15
1,800	180	10	180	10	180	10	180	10	270	26
4,250	425	10	425	10	425	10	425	10	907	29
6,000	600	10	600	10	600	15	600	10	1,415	29
6,500	650	10	650	10	675	15	650	10	1,585	34
8,900	890	10	890	10	1,035	15	890	10	2,061	37.6
10,000	1,000	10	1,000	10	1,200	15	1,000	15	2,475	37.6
12,000	1,200	15	1,200	15	1,500	15	1,300	15	2,851	37.6
22,600	3,390	26	2,790	15	3,090	15	2,890	15	6,837	37.6
27,050	4,547	26	3,458	15	4,058	26	3,558	15	8,510	37.6
36,250	6,939	26	4,838	15	6,450	26	5,438	26	11,969	37.6
45,200	9,266	26	6,780	26	8,777	26	7,765	26	15,334	37.6
54,625	11,717	29	9,231	26	11,228	26	10,216	26	18,928	37.6
65,550	14,885	29	12,072	26	14,069	29	13,057	26	22,986	37.6
83,250	20,018	34	16,674	26	19,202	29	17,659	26	29,641	37.6
93,650	23,554	34	19,378	26	22,218	29	20,363	29	33,551	37.6
109,250	28,858	34	23,434	29	26,742	29	24,887	29	39,417	37.6
136,750	38,208	34	31,409	29	34,717	34	32,862	29	49,753	37.6
148,675	42,263	37.6	34,867	29	38,772	34	36,320	29	54,241	37.6
151,650	43,382	37.6	35,730	29	39,784	34	37,183	34	55,360	37.6
166,500	48,966	37.6	40,037	34	44,833	34	42,232	34	60,944	37.6
297,350	98,166	37.6	84,526	37.6	89,322	37.6	89,721	37.6	110,154	37.6

Individuals, Estates, and Trusts

(Tax Years Beginning in 2006)

Col. 1 Taxable Income $	Separate Return Tax on Col. 1 $	Separate Return Rate on Excess %	Joint Return Tax on Col. 1 $	Joint Return Rate on Excess %	Single Return Tax on Col. 1 $	Single Return Rate on Excess %	Head of Household Tax on Col. 1 $	Head of Household Rate on Excess %	Trusts and Estates Tax on Col. 1 $	Trusts and Estates Rate on Excess %
0	0	10	0	10	0	10	0	10	0	15
1,800	180	10	180	10	180	10	180	10	270	25
4,250	425	10	425	10	425	10	425	10	883	28
6,000	600	10	600	10	600	15	600	10	1,373	28
6,500	650	10	650	10	675	15	650	10	1,513	33
8,900	890	10	890	10	1,035	15	890	10	1,975	35
10,000	1,000	10	1,000	10	1,200	15	1,000	15	2,360	35
12,000	1,200	15	1,200	15	1,500	15	1,300	15	2,710	35
22,600	3,390	25	2,790	15	3,090	25	2,890	15	6,420	35
27,050	4,503	25	3,458	15	4,058	25	3,558	15	7,978	35
36,250	6,803	25	4,838	25	6,358	25	5,438	25	11,198	35
45,200	9,041	28	6,780	25	8,596	25	7,676	25	14,331	35
54,625	11,397	28	9,136	25	10,952	28	10,032	25	17,630	35
65,550	14,456	33	11,867	25	13,683	28	12,763	25	21,454	35
83,250	19,412	33	16,292	25	18,639	28	17,188	25	27,649	35
93,650	22,844	33	18,892	28	21,551	28	19,788	28	31,289	35
109,250	27,992	33	22,792	28	25,919	28	24,156	28	36,749	35
136,750	37,067	33	30,492	28	33,619	33	31,856	28	46,374	35
148,675	41,241	35	33,831	28	37,554	33	35,195	28	50,548	35
151,650	42,282	35	34,664	28	38,536	33	36,028	33	51,586	35
166,500	47,480	35	38,822	33	43,437	33	40,929	33	56,787	35
297,350	93,278	35	82,003	35	86,618	35	84,110	35	102,585	35

Index

Printed in the United States
202051BV00003B/73-267/A